D1625484

WHITFIELD HISTORY AND GENEALOGY OF TENNESSEE

BY
VALLIE JO WHITFIELD

WHITFIELD BOOKS

FOR AMERICAN FAMILIES .

Copyright © , VALLIE JO FOX WHITFIELD , 1979

All Rights Reserved

Library of Congress
Catalog Card Number 79 - 64403

First edition , 1964
ISBN 0-930920-00-7

Second edition , 1979
ISBN   0-930920-12-0   Hard Bound

WHITFIELD BOOKS
Whitfield Court
1841 Pleasant Hill Road
Pleasant Hill, California 94523

Printed in the United States of America.

CONTENTS

V

ILLUSTRATIONS

James Dee Whitfield and Oda Whitfield

Christa Whitfield

Joseph Edward Fox and Valley Schiefer Fox

Robert Edward Whitfield and Vallie Jo Fox
Whitfield   . Elizabeth Schiefer

Ralph Whitfield and Mildred Whitfield

James Dee Whitfield and Oda Whitfield

Rozelle Whitfield Daniel and Billie R. Daniel

Mary Hester Whitfield

Raymond Whitfield and Frances Whitfield

Lillie May Whitfield Phillips

John Regan Whitfield

Clara Whitfield   . Phillip Whitfield

Henry Edward Whitfield

Sandra Whitfield . James David Whitfield

Brenda Whitfield . Jack Wilson Whitfield

Janice Whitfield . Elizabeth Heiner Fox

Claude Chilton, Jack Meredith, Glen De Priest,
  Brodie Dreden, Thomas J. Whitfield, Don
  Manning

Thomas Cleveland Whitfield

Whitfield House   . Cliffe House

Rita Ann Whitfield   . Belle Whitfield & Family

Joanne Vallie Whitfield

Jeffrey Whitfield, Linda Whitfield, Richard
  Whitfield

James Dee, Delia, Cleveland, Clara, Henry
  Edward Whitfield

Roger Lee Bundy , Jason Bundy, Natasha Bundy,
  Justin, Christa Whitfield Bundy

Martha Jane Nicks Whitfield and Robert Whitfield

Ruby Hensley Hopkins and Hicks Hopkins

Vivien Gale and Ralph Whitfield

WHITFIELD

NUMBER SYSTEM

One can continue through the descendants of this system with the use of the numbers. WT VI is Whitfield, Thomas of Generation Six ; and (53) Thomas Jefferson Whitfield are taken as examples. Number (53) first appears as a child. The numerical number 53 in the long family group distinguishes him from all other persons, and this number appears elsewhere. The numbers lets the reader follow the family line of descent.

The person can be followed forward with 53 Thomas Whitfield and his listing of children . A son in the list of children is (85) Thomas Jefferson Whitfield , and under his name as head of a family we can locate his children and the line carries forward.

Fourth and fifth generations are a listing of names thought to be of this generation from an immigrant parent . Sixth generation to the tenth generation is an accurate order. The letter G is an initial for generation.

It is a tremendous task by one person to develop fully several family genealogies and histories completely and print them. So for this book the first Whitfields of the State of Tennessee have been researched, studied and laid down in print. If the material is not clear and conflict of statements occur it is because of the length of time it has taken and the method of collecting data; so the last appearing statement regarding a history of a person should be taken as the accurate material.

*   *   *

This book was first printed in 1964 and the same order has been followed in this second book edition in 1979. The Whitfield families of Tennessee are from several roots for family trees but this book edition gives the first ancestors for these several roots, and the material has the few first immigrants from North Carolina and Virginia to Tennessee. The several family roots narrow in Tennessee early history to a few first heads of families , and going back to Colonial Virginia to even the first immigrants to the America , and a gleam of the location in southern England .

Read and gleam herein whatever joy and benefit you find.

HONOR THE LORD, SERVE THEIR COUNTRY AND PASS THE NAME UNSULLIED.

PART I

The Calendar of Virginia States Papers.   **VIRGINIA**
8 C 228 Williamsburg,Virginia , June 29 , 1776.

Nansemond Co., Va. - "Same to Mr. William Whitfield for F15. 82 1/2 for the prison fees and sundries furnished prisoners condemned to Nansemond jail ." (5 C 632)

Norfolk Co., Va. - The bond of William Wilson, Jr. July 16th , 1792. He was appointed Clerk of the County Court of Norfolk by the Justices of the said Court. Signed and sealed , in presence of Willis Whitfield.

Princess Anne Co., Va. - A Louisa Whitfield and William Whitfield 1776 in Princess Anne County, Va from The Lower Norfolk County, Va. Antiquary by Edward James . Vol. 1, 2, 3.

Virginia Cousins by G. Brown Goode has listing Elizabeth Whitfield who is of Cary family , third generation genealogy , Virginia.

From Virginia Magazine of History and Biography , volume 29 , 1921. Thomas Whitfield , A.B. Styled "of the eastern shore." 1798. Student at College House , the property of William and Mary College.

From Virginia Magazine of History and Biography . vol. 15, p. 193. "Virginia militia in the Revolution , June 9 , 1777, William Whitfield , for Dietting, committing and releasing Des'ters. p. accot, 15 . 15- "

From Virginia Magazine of History and Biography . vol . 5 - 1897-1898. Abstracts of Virginia Land Patents :   John Chandler was member of the House of Burgesses from Elizabeth City, Virginia in November 1645, and November 1647 , and a justice of that County in 1652.   John Chandler, 1, 000 acres in Elizabeth City County, Virginia, bounded on the west by Harris Creek , and extending easterly towards Point Comfort Creek , and lying on a bay, being on the inside of the broken islands. Do .. 950 for the transport -ation of nineteen persons. By west, July 6, 1636 . Names include one William Whitfield . Elizabeth City County , Virginia , 1636.

All of the names in these records are compiled as biographies in the book Virginia History and Whitfield Biographies   by Vallie Whitfield.

From the book Early Virginia Immigrants   1623 - 1666. Gilbert Whitfield , 1637 , by Daniel Gookins, New Norfolk County, Virginia. William Whitfield , 1636 by John Chandler , Elizabeth City County, Va. Richard Whitefield , 1635 by Thomas Warren , Charles City County, Virginia.

Lists of Emigrants To America 1600-1700 by John C. Hotten . p. 415. List of Tickets granted out of the Secretaries Office of Barbados , for the departure from this island , beginning January 1678 , ending the December following.

Matthew Whitfield , May 2, 1679 , in the ketch "Prosperous" for Virginia. David Fogy , Commander.
Page 355 . Roger Whitfield , Commander of the ship "Lixboa Merchant " for New York . Oct. 2, 1679 . Another trip on Sept. 19, 1679.
Gilbert Whitfield had come in the ship "Flying Hart" , 1621 , and lived at Bass's Choice , Virginia , Feb. 16, 1623.
Page 119 - August 1635 . "These underwritten names are to be transported to Virginia , imbarqued in the "Globe" of London, Jeremy Blackman , Master, have been examined by the Minister of Gravesend, of their conformitie , and have taken the oaths of alleg ance and Supremacie."
John Whitfield , aged 20 , in this list.

Other Whitfields came before 1700 , such as William Whitfield, Thomas Whitfield, John Whitfield.
The many Whitfields began to come about 1760. We have not found the immigration records of some of them.

VIRGINIA

In Virginia Magazine of History and Genealogy , vol .29 , pp. 259-260. Letter of Robert Michie of William and Mary College , to David Watson of Louisa County, Virginia , Dec. 21, 1797 . In this letter he mentions a Whitfield. A footnote states that this was Thomas Whitfield , A.B. styled, of Eastern Shore studying law.

In The Edward Pleasants Valentine Papers. 4 vols.
Samuel Whitfield is mentioned as one of the appraisers of the estate of Peter Ballard, deceased, Oct. 13, 1748 . Isle of Wight County, Virginia . Vol. I, p. 146.

Richard Exum was a witness to a deed from Mathew Whitfield and Priscilla his wife, of Nansemond County, Virginia, to John Lawrence of Newport Parish , Isle of Wight County, for 520 acres, part of a patent in Newport Parish , which was granted to Mr. John Lawrence now deceased , (father of the aforesaid Priscilla), June 5 , 1678 and by will of said John Lawrence was devised to his daughter Elizabeth , deceased, who devised it to her sister the said Priscilla by Will, Feb. 9 , 1708. p. 463 , Book 2 , p. 116.

Copeland Whitfield, Jr , was a witness to the will of John Jordan of Isle of Wight County, Virginia , Feb. 15, 1790 . Vol. II, p. 673.

Thomas Whitfield was one of the appraisers of the estate of Johanna Scott , Sept. 17 , 1756 . Vol. III, p. 1528.

Thomas Whitfield and John Barland, and Benjamin Harrison were appraisers of the estate of James Tooke Scott, Isle of Wight County, Virginia , Nov. 3, 1763. p. 1529.

<u>VIRGINIA</u>   - State of the United States.

Williamsburg County, Virginia . Records of Wills.
"Copeland Whitefield, Jr. was witness to Will of John Godwin, Isle of Wight ,
December 22, 1789 - Jan. 7 , 1790."

From book <u>Darden Family History</u> compiled by Newton J. Darden , 1953.
In an order book of Isle of Wight County, Virginia , Elisha Darden filed   a
petition versus Miles Whitfield for debt on March 4 ,.1773 , and again   on
July 1, 1773 . Sometime   after 1782 he left Nansemond County, Virginia.

<u>Spotsylvania County, Virginia , 1721-1800. Deed Book F 1761-1766.</u>
May 16, 1758 . John Gawith, Mariner, Master of the ship JOHNSON , belong-
 ing to Liverpool in Great Britain, power of attorney to Robert Jackson of
Fredksby, Virginia.   Merchant witness , John Whitfield , and other names
on Dec. 5 , 1758.   and
July 11, 1763 , Dickey Swan Edwards of Northumberland County, Virginia to
Robert Jackson of Fredsg, Merchant. F25 curr. Lot 54 in town of Fredksbg.
Witness John Whitfield , and others on Oct . 3 , 1763.

From book <u>Seventeenth Century : Isle of Wight County, Virginia</u> by John
Bennett Boddie. Chicago Law Printing Co. , Chicago. Published 1938.
Eliz Whitfield married John Smith (p. 495) . Eliz Whitfield Smith children
shown in North Carolina G. R.   Vol 2, p. 159.
                    and
Colonel Thomas Godwin , born 1705-1749, had a wife and six children . A child,
Mary Holloday Godwin married Henry Whitfield and had a number of children,
and among them (1) Robert Whitfield , member of the Confederate Congress,
and member of Virginia State Senate. (2) Fannie N. Whitfield married June
24 th , Dr. Crawford Finney . She died Dec. 20, 1841 and he married her
sister Margaret A. Whitfield (3) on Dec. 31, 1842 and she died on Sept. 24 ,
1852 . (4) John Whitfield , a son, lives in Enfield , North Carolina.

    At a Court held, and Company, May 4 , 1775 Harrison Whitfield , Lieuten-
 ant of the Militia of this County,   severally took the Oaths to King and Company. (p. 185).
A record of Revolution service , Harrison Whitfield appointed a Lieutenant at
a Court held, and Company , May 1, 1777. (p. 186)
In Isle of Wight County , <u>Deed Book 1704 - 1715 of Nansemond County, Va.</u>
Priscilla M. and Matthew Whitfield sold John Lawrence a parcel of land, in
exchange for 5,000 lbs. of Tobacco. (p. 494)

<u>Seventeenth Century , Isle of Wight County, Virginia</u> by John Bennett Boddie.
Priscilla ... married Matthew Whitfield , Feb. 9 , 1708 .
Matthew received grant of land in Nansemond County, Virginia in 1682 for
transporting thirteen people.

    "Ordered that Harrison Whitfield be appointed a Lieutenant to the Company formerly commanded by Thomas Day." Harrison Whitfield was loyal to the King of England and Lt. in his colonial army.

Jan. 16, 1781, Matthew Whitfield, shoemaker, age 27 of Isle of Wight ... Mathew Whitfield name on return of the prisoners taken in arms on parole, Portsmouth, 12 th, April 1781.

William Whitfield paid his debt to Richard Calloway with his cattle 30 th, Nov. 1681. From Will and Deed Book I, 1662-1682, p. 591.
William Whitfield appoints Hugh Campbell attorney in two actions appealed from Isle of Wight, 20 th day August 1692. p. 616.

A William Whitfield was an ancestor of Nathan Bryan Whitfield, who moved to Marengo County, Alabama, purchased land from General Gaines, and built the famous "Gainswood," a country home.

From book - Wills and Administrations of Isle of Wight County, Virginia, 1647-1800 ", Book III.
In this record book of Wills and administration of estates appears these names of Whitfield :
Abraham Whitfield
Coupland (Copeland) Whitfield
Africa Whitfield
Frances Whitfield
George Whitfield
Harrison Whitfield
Haynes Whitfield
Hester Whitfield
Ivey Whitfield
Jeminma Whitfield
John Whitfield
Joshua Whitfield
Macon Whitfield

Mary Whitfield
Mathew Whitfield
Miles Whitfield
Milla Whitfield
Milley Whitfield
Permelia Whitfield
Polly Driver
Samuel Whitfield
Thomas Whitfield
Thomas Whitfield
Thomas Whitfield
William Whitfield
Wilson Whitfield

The Will of Miller Nichalos appraised by Thomas Whitfield, April 1, 1762. Will Book 7, p. 142.

Will appraised June 7, 1765 of James T. Scoott, by Thomas Whitfield.

Thomas Whitfield witness to Will, Nov. 4, 1762. p. 18

Will of William Harrison appraised by Thomas Whitfield April 7, 1763. p21.

Will of Ingram Jenning appraised by Thomas Whitfield, May 5, 1763. p .22
Estate appraised by Thomas Whitfield of John Gibbs, Sept. 16, 1769.
Will appraised by Harrison Whitfield, May 1, 1777.

Wills and Administrations of Elizabeth City County, Virginia, 1610-1800.

> Ann Whitfield   , p. 139 , 250.
> Elizabeth Whitfield , p. 250.
> Hannah Whitfield , p. 111
> John Whitfield , p. 94 , 104 , 196 , 250.
> Joseph Whitfield , p. 249.
> Mary Whitfield , p. 250.
> Mary Ann Whitfield , p. 233, 249.
> Robert Whitfield , p. 233.
> Thomas Whitfield , p. 250.
> William Whitfield , p. 249.
> Abraham Whitfield , p. 249.
> Hannah Whitfield was a witness March 15 , 1718 , to James
>   Brown's Will. Book 1715-1721, p. 156.

Family :

Thomas Whitfield and wife Ann, and son , John of 16 years., son Thomas , daughter Mary , daughter Elizabeth .   Dated July 26 , 1694. Recorded Nov. 26, 1694.   Administration of his estate granted to Ann Whitfield - Book 1689-1699 , page 156, Elizabeth City , Virginia.

Family :   Will -   Eliz. Whitfield of the town of Hampton , Virginia had son Abraham Whitfield, son William Whitfield , son Joseph Whitfield , daughter Mary Anne Whitfield , dated Feb. 2, 1727 . Recorded May 16, 1728.

P. Taylor , p. 233. "In case of my death my land transferred from Woff and wife to me to Robert Whitfield , son of Mary Ann Whitfield , with reversion to the said Mary Ann Whitfield." Book 1763-1771 , p. 45.   Elizabeth City, Va.

George Whitefield , New Light minister came from New England 1754 and visited Louisa County, Virginia.

Cumberland Parish , Lunenburg County, Virginia, 1746-1816.

Susie C. Cameron, daughter of William E. Cameron born Nov. 29 , 1842 . He was 1876 elected mayor of Petersburgh , Virginia and served continuously until he was elected for the Governorship of Virginia 1881 and took office Jan. 1, 1882 . His first child, Susie Cameron married Byran C. Whitfield of Florida and had children : Evelyn Cameron Whitfield   and Lou Egerton Whitfield.

VIRGINIA - COLONIAL ABSTRACTS

York County, Virginia , 1648 - 1739 .

Martha Whitfield, daughter of Sarah Whitfield , born July 28, 1729.

Family :
John Whitfield, born February 28 , 1702, was son of John and Sarah Whitfield.
Mary Whitfield was born November 4, 1705 , daughter of John and Sarah Whitfield.

Lancaster County, Virginia . Record Book No. 2 , 1654.

William Whitfield was witness to power of attorney for tobacco due . Recorded Dec. 13, 1663.
Herbert Whitfield was witness to 100 acres on Chessemans Creek , Oct. 26 , 1657.

Nansemond County, Virginia , 1743-1793 . Vestry Book of Upper Parish.

John Whitfield and Miles Whitfield present at processioning of Virginia land, Oct. 25, 1763.
"We the subscribers appointed in the said order have Process all the said bounds of land contained in the said order ... Line between Robert Whitfield and David Meade , Miles Whitfield present ... Line between widow Vaughan and Widow Sanders, John Whitfield present.
Eine Whitfield , present at land processioning. "
and another
John Whitfield , at a Vestry held for the Upper Parish of Nansemond County, August 31, 1747.
Line between Sanders and Thomas Whitfield and John Whitfield and Issac Fleming .... and line between Thomas Whitfield and John Hedgpeth . (pages 32, 69, 112, 136, 165, 136 , 63, 70 , 208)
John Whitfield had several lines taken between him and Henry Holand. (112 , 136)
John Whitfield and Charles Vaughan process all the bounds of land according to law. (p. 208)
Sol Whitfield present at land processioning . (p. 263)
William Whitfield , sexton of Suffolk church , Feb. 1772 , and in vestry book several times for repairs in the Church, for Sunday work, for burying, etc.

KENTUCKY

Robert A. Whitfield , born 1831 and died Nov. 11, 1856 . He was born in Grayson County, Kentucky . Son of Martin and Rebecca Whitfield.

Theodore Whitfield, wrote a graduate school thesis : "On Inquiry as to the Consciousness of the Soul After Death " in 1902 in Kentucky.

Nellie H. Whitfield , wrote a graduate school thesis : on "Study of the Culture, Histology and Development of Certain Species of Narcissi " in 1904 in Kentucky.

NORTH CAROLINA

Marriage and Death notices in Raleigh Register and North Carolina Gazette newspapers 1826-1845 , compiled by Carrie Broughton.

1826 .   George W. Whitfield to Catharine Hart , Feb. 29 , 1828.
Johnson County, North Carolina.
1829 .   Emanuel Whitfield to Jane Jerkins , Sept . 1829 , Washington County, North Carolina.
Winifred Whitfield to Richard Croom, April 9 , 1829, of Lenoir Co., North Carolina.
1830.   Mrs. Elizabeth Whitfield of Johnson County to William Fort of Wake County, Dec. 20, 1830 .
1831 .   Kezia Whitfield of Lenoir County to Henry Moore of Chatham County , North Carolina , July , 1831.
Lewis Whitfield of Lenoir County to Mary Ann Glasgow , Oct. 1831 .
1834.   Eliza Whitfield to Hester Moore , Nov. 5, 1834 of Granville Co.
Gaius Whitfield of Alabama to Mary Ann B. Whitfield , July 15 , 1834, Lenoir County.
1841.   William A. Whitfield to Charity Hellen Jones Dec . 1, 1841, Wake County.
Marriage 1842 , John H. Whitfield of Duplin County to Nancy S. Clifton, Jan. 1842 Sampson County.
Mary Whitfield to H. B. Clifton of Sampson County , April 1842 of Duplin County.
Marriage 1843 , Emanuel Whitfield to Mary Phillips of Washington County, North Carolina . August,1843.

DEATH RECORDS

Julia Bryan Whitfield of Wayne County, North Carolina , Aug. 2, 1833.
Mrs. J.O. Whitfield of Wayne County, Nov. 22, 1833 and Tipton County, Georgia.
Mary Whitfield , Oct. 19 , 1835 of Raleigh .
Elizabeth Whitfield on Sept. 21, 1844 .
Allen Whitfield on Sept. 17 , 1845 of Wayne County, North Carolina.

WILLS OF NORTH CAROLINA   1690 - 1760

Original and recorded Wills.
Thomas Johnston of Onslow Co. , No. Carolina . Will dated August 13, 1751 mentions daughters , Sarah Powell, also Ann Whitfield. (p. 189)
Elisah Whitfield was witness to Will of Jonathan Ryding.
Court session in May 1754 in Bertie County. (p. 323)

William Whitfield was witness to Will of Richard Green , Sept 13 , 1742 in Chowan County . (p 149)

William Whitfield was witness to Will of John Jones , Jan. 12, 1759 (194)

These Wills in book Abstracts of North Carolina Wills 1690-1760 by J. Bryan Grimes . Published 1910.

The Wills of 1768 to 1800 are found in Abstracts of North Carolina Wills 1768 to 1800 by Fred Old. Published 1954.

In 1781 , Thomas Whitfield , Israel Whitfield and Hardy Whitfield in Nash County, North Carolina.

In 1761, Will of William Whitfield who had children Martha, William, Jesse, John, Winnie and Stephen Whitfield in Tyrrell County, North Carolina.

April 1795 , Will of William Whitfield by wife ; Needham Whitfield , Lewis Whitfield , William Whitfield and Bryan Whitfield were the sons , and Elizabeth Campbell, Charity Smith , and Rachel Bryan were the daughters of Wayne County, North Carolina.

NORTH CAROLINA MARRIAGE RECORDS
by William M. Clemens.

Martha Whitfield (a widow) and Issac Glisson, June 1762 in Tyrrell Co., North Carolina.

William Whitfield married Rachel Bryan , November 6 , 1741 of Bertie County, North Carolina.

1790 CENSUS OF NORTH CAROLINA
Halifax District , Martin County , North Carolina.

William Whitfield had one boy over 16 years , and one girl.

John Whitfield had one boy under 16 years and one boy over 16 years , and three girls under 16 years , and living with wife.

The Census list : Thomas Whitfield , Sol Whitfield , Willis Whitfield , Mathew Whitfield, William Whitfield , Ruben Whitfield , Benjamin Whitfield , William Whitfield , Benjamin Whitfield, and Nancy Whitfield.

In Granville Co., No. C. of Hillsborough district lived John Whitfield . In the same district lived William Whitfield with son John Whitfield.

In Newbern District , Dobbs County, North Carolina , John Whitfield had one boy under 16 years and three girls, two free adults and ten slaves.

Virginia Tax Payers 1782-1787 . In Goochland County, Virginia , William Whitfield had one poll and one slave for 1782.

Will of Constantine Whitfield , dated 1797 , Craven County, North Carolina. Two daughters Elizabeth Whitfield Herring and Barbara Tooley. Executors was son James Whitfield and friend George Lane. This Will in file case at D. A. R. Library , Washington , D. C.

The Reverend James P. Whitfield , pastor of St. Brigid's Roman Catholic Church of Memphis, Tennessee was born in New York City, June 12, 1884, a son of William and Mary (Wynn) Whitfield , both of Irish descent .
From the book Tennessee the Volunteer State ,1769-1923 by S. J. Clarke Publishing Co. , Chicago.

Edwin Bates Whitfield was born in Clarksville, Tennessee, Jan. 24, 1856 , a son of John Pashley Yardley Whitfield, and Martha Bates Whitfield. Edwin Bates married in January 1877, Miss Alice Emma Roth , daughter of G. A. Roth and had four children who were Daisy Whitfield , Rose Whitfield , Louisa Whitfield and Lillian Whitfield (p.1353) . John Pashley Yardley Whitfield was born Sept 29 , 1827 in Philadelphia, Penn., son of William and Rachel (Yardley) Whitfield , both descendants of English families. He was educated in Philadelphia and went to Brownsville, Pennsylvania where he served an apprenticeship in a foundry. About 1850 he went to Nashville, Tennessee where he worked at the Nashville Manufacture Company . (p.429) .
Picturesque Clarksville, Tennessee by W. P. Titus , 1887.

TENNESSEE - State of United States

From book Tennessee Cousin by Worth S. Ray.
"William Whitfield paid a debt owing to Richard Callaway in November of 1681 with a bunch of cattle. James Bennett, John Kae and Joseph Bridger, Jr. of Isle of Wight were witnesses to the transfer."

Tennessee Cousin by Worth S. Ray.
"John Whitfield orginated in England in 1561, a Virginia ancestor whose name appears in Yorkshire, Northumberland , and other English counties."

Tennessee Land Grants. John Whitfield held 20, 000 acres of land in 1839 in Coffee County, Tennessee.

Notes in vertical file at Tennessee Archives :
Dr. T. A. Whitfield , son of J. S. and Mattie Pettus Whitfield was born 1887 in Veto, Alabama. Graduated, Old University of Nashville with a medical degree in 1908 . Physician practice in Nashville, Tennessee. He married Hattie Campbell in 1907 and had children : 1. Captain Joseph T. Whitfield 2. Robert S. Whitfield , who was a medical student in 1945 . T. A. Whitfield died at Nashville, Tennessee and buried in Veto, Alabama on April 9 , 1945 . He had a brother Ben S. Whitfield, and sister Mrs . Ben F. Williams living in 1945.

Hickman County, Tennessee.   In May 26 , 1847, Volunteers of regiments to the Mexican War numbered 2,800 men.   30,000 answered the call of the governor before war was won.   One of the first volunteers was John Wilkins Whitfield.

From book Tennessee Genealogical Records , edited by Edythe Rucker Whitley. Vol I to X . Years 1779-1850 records. Vol. 3 , pages 3,4,5,6. Records of Middle District of Tennessee :
        "In 1776 John Dickerson sold to John Boddie of Granville County, North Carolina, planter, land on Cedar Creek granted in 1760 ," "600 acres to Richard Bridges, from Bridges to Wimingham, from Wimingham to John Dickerson and from John Dickerson to John Boddie. This Deed proved May Court 1776." Deed Book L on page 35.

October 6 , 1777 , John Boddie sold to John Whitfield,both of Granville County, this tract of land on cedar creek containing 600 acres of land. Deed Book L on page 240. This record here is a North Carolina record , and tells John Boddie moved to Edgefield district in South Carolina .(p378)

     People   in the above locale sold to Middle Tennessee settlers. Some of the residents of Williamson County, Tennessee in 1830 came from Mecklenburg County, North Carolina.   (Vol. 5 , index of Vol. 6 compiled by Edythe Rucker Whitley , 2710 Belmont Blvd. , Nashville, Tennessee.)

████████████████████████████████

THE WHITFIELD STORY OF ENGLAND AND THE UNITED STATES.

Witefeld - Whytfeld - Whitfield of England.
=================================

     If merit be worthy of note or selfless devotion deserves remembrance , we should gratefully appraise the Whitfield Story of England as being the work of Emma Morehead Whitfield and others. We record it because it is also the beginning story for the families of Tennessee who came from Virginia and North Carolina.

     Many English houses saw the beginning of their rise to fame and importance co-incident with the settlement upon England's soil of William the Conqueror and his Norman legions.

     William the Conqueror did not find England a country of barbarians. Though sparsely populated, the country was divided into districts and areas, each often being many miles of the country . The headship of an ancient house was a district which in turn gave allegiance to its overlords, the pre-Norman kings of England. These houses held the councils of the districts and the churches.

Scotland was still independent and frequently at war with England. However, the highest families of both sides of the border were united in marriage. David I , king of Scotland married Maud , (Matilda), heiress of the Earl of Northumberland , England , and by this marriage a large part of England proper became the inheritance of the kings of Scotland. This franchise to English land contained the lands of Whitfield (Witefeld) of some 12,157 acres or nearly twenty square miles.

By the marriage of Maud , a large part of England proper being the northern half of Bernicia, became the inheritance of the kings of Scotland. Included in this portion of Bernicia was the ancient franchise of Tindale, the western part of the present county of Northumberland . This franchise contained the parish of Whitfield of nearly twenty square miles.

Of the marriage of David I and Maud was born Henry , Earl of Northumberland. David was King of Scotland from 1124-1153 . He in turn married the Countess Ada of whom were born the Scottish kings Malcolm IV and William the Lion. Countess Ada gave to her chaplain, Robert , the lands of "Witefeld."

So begins the Whitfield story —

Not long after the grant to Robert the chaplain, Countess Ada jointly with a son Robert granted the lands of Whitfield to the Prior and Convent of Hexham. Later the land was given as " a Grant of the Manor of Whitfield from the Prior and Convent of Hexham to Matthew, son of Robert , the chaplain of the Countess Ada. "

Robert the chaplain becoming the lord of Whitfield had less need of his living associated with his ecclesiastical functions, and he gave his living means to his nephew Robert between the years 1154 and 1194. The chaplain was permitted to have a coat of arms. This consisted of a shield , argent, upon which was a bend plain between two cotises , engrailed sable. A crest was added in the form of a pallisado , or radiated, crown, silver, out of which sprang a stag's head, gold.

The immediate descendants of the chaplain Robert Whitfield are difficult to trace since two branches of the family lived in the presence one of the other. The senior line claimed descent from the owners of the manor of Whitfield . The other branch was descended from the holders of the living of the church at Whitfield.

Matthew de Whitfield resided at the Prior and Convent of Hexham 1280 ca.

Beatrix de Quitfeld , Robert Whitefeld and Johanne de Whitefeld , lived there in 12 th and 13 th century . Then Richard Whitfield married Isabel de Vipont and the house became allied with the descendants of the Saxon Earls of Mercia and the important families of de Buslie, de Espec, and many others.

From this time onward for several generations , the house of Whitfield grew in importance . It was thought that the house of Whitfield in 1434 was at the height of its power and influence. Decline was , however , not a rapid one , and the condition of the family does not appear to have much altered until 1607. Conflict over legal ownership of land occurred, and expensive and prolonged legal proceedings crippled the family revenues, and the lands and estate became impoverished about 1695 . Although the Whitfield family still retained a legitimate claim to the properties of the ancient family.

The village of Whitfield is situated on the north side of the river west Allen eleven miles west-southwest from Hexham where the famous Whitfield Hall was erected.

The parent line of Whitfield of Whitfield Hall was divided into three branches about the year 1600. The senior branch remained at Whitfield. The second branch settled in Durham, England , and the third at Wadhurst, County Sussex.

* The Whitfield Story of England and the compiled English Pedigree ; and also Whitfields in West Indies is found in book , Whitfield , Bryan, Smith and Related Families , by Emma M. Whitfield.

========================

Council House of Bristol, England had two volumes bearing the inscription Servants To Foreign Plantations, 1654-1679 , and records the Whitfields who sailed to West Indies.

It is from the English records that we know about the immigrants to Virginia in the sixteenth and seventeenth century. In the seventeenth century there were many Whitfield families living in Virginia. The Whitfield line in which this study is chiefly concerned with begins with tide-water coast land of Virginia where the first grandfather landed from England or West Indies. It includes the first three generations of the William Whitfield and Elizabeth Goodman Whitfield lines since the descendants lived in nearby districts in Tennessee. We know the link of the North Carolina families to those kinship in Tennessee.

Somewhere among those leaving England for the Indies or the Virginia colony must be found the links to establish the relationship between the lines in America and England. There were Whitfields as an individual who came from Kent, England, and Gloucester and Devon and other places in England.

There were a number of immigrants from England to the tide - water Virginia colony between 1610 and 1750 years. The Virginia colonial records on Whitfields are found in the book, Virginia History and Whitfield Biographies, published in 1976. And there are many links of Virginia ancestors to be found who have descendants in other States of the United States.

This genealogical history is connected to those ancestors of England and Virginia. Thomas Whitfield was born about 1735 , and he died 1794 in Sussex County, Virginia. Thomas Whitfield was married to Winifer who was called Winney. They lived in Albemarle Parish with their children : Mary , William, Elizabeth , Francis , Martha Patty, Wilkins , Betty , Nancy , Harrison , Jack. On the death of the father Thomas Whitfield in 1794 the children stayed a few years in Virginia and left there for Tennessee in 1808 , and the young families all stayed together going to Williamson County.

The lineage line starts with Wilkins Whitfield and his wife, Polly Mary Sturdivant Whitfield and their children , and this book has mostly the descendants of this father and mother for the Tennessee generations. The brothers of Wilkins Whitfield leave descendants who records appear here . Also a few records of other Tennesseeans . It includes the short lineage of Charles Whitfield who had the des - cendants to move to Missouri.

---

* The Whitfield story of England is the work of Ralph C. V. Whitfield of Middlesex, England. Mr Whitfield was, 1931, the head of the senior Northumberland Line in England.

The Whitfield Story of England and the compiled English Pedigree; and the Whitfields in West Indies is found in the book Whitfield, Bryan, Smith and Related Families by Emma M. Whitfield.

COLONIAL VIRGINIA

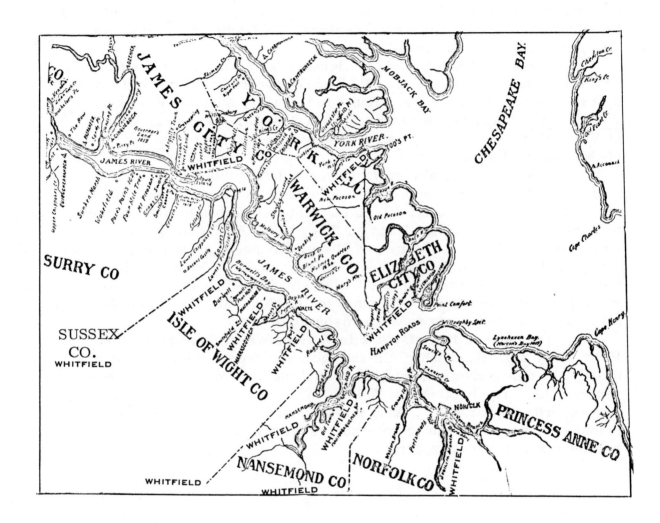

Whitfield Families lived in these Counties in the
Virginia Colony.   Settlements and later Counties.
1621 to 1700 , the 17 th Century.
1700 to 1800 , the 18 th Century.

whitfield immigrants to virginia

The lower counties of Virginia were the homes of the early immigrants. Sir Thomas Gates was the interim Governor of Virginia , Feb. 28 , 1610 . He was a veteran soldier of the King of England , and like Sir Thomas Dale served in the Netherlands before training the companies in Virginia. Sir Gates placed Captain John Smith in charge of the outpost at Point Comfort, Virginia. The purposes of the founders of Virginia may clearly be inferred in the Virginia Company's charter and in the instructions prepared for the first settlers.

On May 13, 1607 , they chose as the place for their settlement a peninsula, now Jamestown Island , on the north side of the James River. After coming on shore at Jamestown the colonists proceeded to work in accordance with instructions brought with them. From time to time Indians made friendly visits to the settlement. A week after their arrival at Jamestown, Captain Newport with twenty-one men, including John Smith, George Percy, and Gabriel Archer, went up to the falls of the James River. Soon after at Jamestown the first Indians attacked them.

Captain Newport and Smith decided to return to England and George Percy , son of the Earl of Northumberland, was put in Captain John Smith's place. It was the Northumberland land of England that was the home of the Whitfields. We wonder about the Whitfields that came to America and leave no records of this early time. Colonial records give references to Whitfields who went to Barbados, West Indies . These ships brought the supplies to the first colony fort. Then George Percy wrote from bitter experience , "There were never Englishmen left in a forreigne countrey in such miscerie as we were in this new discovered Virginia." Out of the 490 settlers whom Smith had left in Virginia only about 60 survived that winter.

So Fort Algernon and Point Comfort shifted activity to Jamestown. Sir Gates and his Councilors tried in vain to find a way to save the colony, but, the ships with immigrants kept coming and the settlers stayed and some survived. The Whitfields have worked and carved this country into the mold it now has been made from, and they continue to live on the land and have passed it to many generations.

Sir Thomas Dale took over the government from George Percy , and laid out a town named Henrico.

Daniel Gookin's ship patent was recorded 1620, and he brought to Virginia , Gilbert Whitfield in the "Flying Harte" and others. In February on the sixth , 1623, he was living at Bass's Choice Point . In November

1628 , he was a guard at the Court of James City, Virginia.

William Whitfield came as a headright of John Chandler and settled at Point Comfort , Elizabeth City County, Virginia. Chandler's patent is dated 1636.

It was on Saturday, Dec. 20, 1606, that 144 colonists in three small ships set sail from London to Virginia in Susan Constant , 100 tons, Godspeed , 40 tons and the Discovery , 20 tons. The first two ships returned to England but the Discovery stayed at the port of the colony.

John Whitfield came over in the Globe of London in 1635. He was twenty years old.

Richard Whitfield came about 1635 as a headright of Thomas Warren and moved to Lower Norfolk County later. Ruth Whitfield was another person brought to colony at same time.

Mathew Whitfield departure to the colony was August 5, 1664, according to the Tolzey Books of England.

Tobias Whitfield is listed in the crew of the Fellowship. In 1666 , James, Duke of York , issued a pass to permit this ship to sail for Virginia without hindrance from any of the crown officers.

"William Whitfield bound to William Smith for four years in Virginia in the ship Triall." This entry in the Tolsey Books.

Matthew Whitfield , May 2, 1679 , in the ketch "Prosperous" for Virginia. David Fogy, Commander.

Roger Whitfield , Commander of the ship "Lixboa Merchant " for New York , Oct. 2, 1679.

The first born generations we know about are William Whitfield , Mathew Whitfield, John Whitfield , Thomas Whitfield , Elizabeth Whitfield and Sarah Whitfield who are born from these immigrants. This first early Virginia generation would include some from West Indies since ships often brought supplies from there.

When William Whitfield arrived in Virginia there were nine colonists of the name William Smith there. The suffering of disease and the Indian massacres killed so many of the first settlers that these late sixteenth century produce the accurate first generations of Whitfield head of families in America. The families are at the West Indies , Virginia and New York ports among the very first families ; and the first Whitfields are in the ships connected with Sir George Percy who became deputy governor of Virginia. These records are among the destroyed. Elizabeth Whitfield seem to have survived or came as several immigrants because there are many genealogies of colonists who married a Elizabeth Whitfield . In 1616 six settlements in the colony with few people surviving but settlers at Henrico (Farrar's Island) ,

Bermuca Hundred, West and Shirley Hundred, Jamestown , Kecoughton which was later Elizabeth City, Virginia, and Dale's Gift (Cape Charles across Chesapeake Bay).

There came during 1619 eleven ships with 1, 216 persons. Of this number 666 were for the private plantations and remainder for the Company's land under Charter. Many of these persons immigrant records are not available. Savage attacks on the colonists out of total of 4, 270 people brought over. Elizabeth Whitfield and Sarah Whitfield were the sturdy women who set many examples for the few women that came. It was Robert Bennett who came over and planted the Fort colony at Warrosqueoc, now Burwell's Bay, Isle of Wight County, Virginia, and his planters on joint plantation had campaign later against neighboring Indians. William and Matthew Whitfield of this colony change land in 1681 and 1684.

In 1636 the county south of river James was formed into a new county, Upper and Lower Norfolk. Upper Norfolk took the Indian name Nansemond in 1646. In 1691 Lower Norfolk county was made into two Counties, Norfolk and Princess Ann. Warrasqueoc was the name of the Indians living on Isle of Wight County when the English came. The name was changed when it became Christopher Lawne's plantation. In 1652 part became Surry County. Our line of Whitfields seem to survive the Indians and the Tennessee history indicates that they knew well the way of the Indians, respected their treaties, warned the new white settlers against wrong to Indians, and they seem to have freedom among the tribes of the Indians, and moved westward among early Indians and acted as agents for colonists. These were the servants who furnished the sure supply of labor essential for turning a wilderness into farms and plantations. For each person brought over the master received 50 acres.

The colonists were not safe from the Indian attacks,and three forts were built north of the James River. In 1645, Fort Henry at the falls of the Appomattox for the defense of the people of the south side of the James river with Abraham Wood in command.

These Virginian Whitfields did not carry a pedigree naming system from one generation to another but often named their children from the leaders of their country. In 1650 Captain Abraham Wood, Edward Bland, Sackford Brewster, and Elias Pennant took a trail to Meherrin River and visited friendly Indians, then the explorers came to falls of the Roanoke where the Dan and Stauntaon rivers join to make that river , the present site of Clarksville, Virginia. The second party of James Needham and Gabriel Arthur left Fort Henry to explore southwestern divide April 10,

1673 using Occaneechee trading path.

The Indian calamities were so pitiful that Nathaniel Bacon Rebellion occurred in the colony. After 1675 the Indians were pushed back from the Tidewater area, and negroes began to be used as the labor force to help the farmers. *

In 1667 the great London fire happened and many left England. When the Virginia Board of Trade and Plantation was set up 1692, Virginia had a population of 70, 000. There were several Whitfields who were heads of families. Maryland had a population of 20, 000, Carolina had 5, 000. New York had 20, 000 and Massachusetts had 48, 000 people.

The State house of Virginia was burned at Jamestown , October 1698. Continued ownership of the land was secured on three conditions : (1) That the land be seated or planted in three years. (2) If on the frontier, the owner keep four able-bodied , well-armed men upon it , (this was one of the reasons for taking slaves to the west country) , (3) that an annual rent of two shilling for every fifty acres , the quitrent , be paid the King. However, few owners made any attempt to keep armed men on frontier land or to pay the quitrent but they needed able-bodied men to clear the trees and plant the crops. The rent roll gives the size of many small land holders in Virginia at the time of 1704. The plantation was several farms of small size under a royal personage jurisdiction but each farmer was a grantee . The Whitfields do not appear on these early records and probably because they had been here for a long time, and they do not appear among the North Carolina Regulators records that have survived. It is through family tradition and records that the most is known about them in the western part of the country in 1750. The Vestry books tell something about the families.

The Smiths in their genealogy have constantly and persistently claimed that their immigrant ancestor settled in Isle of Wight , and that the Smiths and Whitfields at an early date intermarried, and emigrated to North Carolina and Tennessee. We see this in the first 1788 records of Tennessee concerning Smith, Whitfield and Campbell.

The Thomas Whitfield families of Elizabeth City County, Virginia crosses the isthmus later and goes south and southwest , and north . The grandchildren are located in Nash County, Virginia. Several expeditions had gone to the Valley of Virginia by 1725 . In 1676 an English fort stood away from the main stream of the Charles River at the Fall line and a trail led over Occaneechea Path to the southern Piedmont region of North Carolina, and a trail led over the route of Batts and Fallam to Gap of Peter's Mtn. in the Blue Ridge Mountains in western Virginia. We are concerned with

these families on trails for the first Virginians of this line appear to
be in this area about 1749 . The frontier   people have not been recorded
in many incidents.   The first land record is with John Whitfield who
sold to John Boyd of the Bacon's Quarter's plantation . Then in 1788
some of the family is well established at Clinch Mountain on Bull Run
River at Whitfield et al's camp. It is the crowding at Bennett's plantation that we see the families moving south and southwest.

Matthew Whitfield surveyed the 700 acres of land for the orphans
of Walter Bruce in Nansemond County. When boys and girls were old
enough they moved with families to new frontiers and able-bodied people
were always needed in setting up a camp. Many of the family parties
that went to the first camps in Tennessee took with them able bodied
boys of other families. In 1752 the vestry of Suffolk Parish in Nansemond County allowed Hester Whitfield 400 pounds of tobacco for the
keep of a child of one Matthew Whitfield . In 1758 the children   of
Thomas Whitfield and his son Matthew left with William Goodwin , and
Esther was placed with George Whitfield. Esther Whitfield   probably
went to Tennessee for Thomas, John, Esther appear in Davidson County
records of a D. A. R.   chapter in 1794 . Esther married in 1799.

The descendants of William Whitfield and his wife , Elizabeth
Goodman Whitfield are known. It is very early at Isle of Wight and
Nansemond Counties we see the two families linked , and through
Captain William Whitfield,born in 1715. We see the link again from those
who migrated early to Christian County, Kentucky who are the grand -
children of William Whitfield III , born June 1, 1743. The connecting
link by intermarriage would have to be an early tie.

The records of Virginia have   been gone over throughly by
me and I have seen no indexed analytical record survey by the State of
Virginia if one does exist. It is my opinion that many of this early
history is out of the land of Isle of Wight and a river and Indian trail.
We must be content with the records we have here and the Tennessee
story , that is in the first edition print of the book manuscript , and
editions to follow.

John and Sarah Whitfield lived in Elizabeth City, Virginia and
had son , John Whitfield , born Feb. 28, 1702 , and daughter Mary
Whitfield , born Nov. 4 , 1705.

Another Sarah Whitfield had a daughter , born July 28 , 1729 ,
and named Martha.

William Whitfield gave a parcel of land lying and being in the town Hampton to his eldest son, Abraham Whitfield, May 20 , 1735.

Another William Whitfield had lived there earlier and had an attorney, Hugh Campbell , Aug. 20 , 1694, to conduct a case in Isle of Wight.

Thomas Whitfield had lived there and had children : John, Thomas, Mary and Elizabeth.

These Virginians appear to have a line of families for thirteen generations. If the first Whitfield had survived the Indians he would have a line of families about fifteen families. We can ascertain factually about eleven generations but believe it to be the thirteen line family ; or an immigrant of this same crop of people . I have recorded here what is known, or historical proof.

William Godwin lived on southern branch of Nansemond River in August, 1726 . He treated people with an abundance of primitive hospitality. "Mr Godwin (Goodwin) was so kind he shorten travelers journey by setting them over the river March 1726 ." The country of Nansemond was a swamp and the ground broken by sloughs. Trees that grew near it looked very reverend, with the long moss hanging dangling from their branches . Both cattle and horse eat this moss greedily in winter when the other provisions is scarce, though it is apt to scour them at first . *

People could live with less labor in North Carolina and the Valley of Virginia, by the great felicity of the climate, the easiness of raising provisions and the slothfulness of the frontier acceptance of the people . Indian corn was of so great increase that little would subsist a very large family with bread , and meat could be gotten easily by the help of the low grounds and the great variety of most that grows on the high land. North Carolina was made out of the Virginia colony in 1729 and the boundary line drawn. About 1750 the people spread quickly to the south and southwest of the Tidewater area, although the trail was usually south . They also could grow flax and cotton.

It was at the Guilford Courthouse in North Carolina that the first tension of colonists developed against the British about 1761. Then the Boston Tea Party occurred. The colonists and British battled in 1775 in Boston . In 1776 the Continental Congress began but soon was against the taxation and British acts imposed on the people. The fighting continued from 1775 until 1781 when the British accepted the final defeat. These years the colonists remained in their homestead location. Tax returns began in 1782 in Isle of Wight . The first United States colonial census was taken in 1790. In these ten years and very soon after the Revolution the migration began with large numbers to the west and they poured through the Cumberland Gap. The Whitfields on Kentucky and Tennessee first tax return. The first census of Kentucky and Tennessee was destroyed in the War of 1812.

*From book - "William Byrd of Virginia " by Wright and Tinling.

Our story must begin in the middle valley of Virginia near Dan River about 1749 , and in North Carolina we do not know the location until 1779 when Needham , James, Bryant and William Whitfield are out of Salisbury road from Rowan and have land deeds in Anson region of the present Montgomery County, North Carolina.

In 1768 the Watauga Valley had a settlement in Tennessee. Second settlement on the north side of the Holston below the junction of its Virginia forks. Third, farther east on north of Holston was Shelby settlement of Maryland. Fourth settlement Nolichicky Valley. These Tennessee camps set up for the Regulators and Piedmonters to easily move westward. It was after the Revolutionary War that the Tennessee settlement grew into towns. People could take the Clinch Mountain trail or the farther north take the Kentucky trail to the fork and go to Christian County, Kentucky to reach middle Tennessee.

The records are somewhat fragmentary for this period before the Revolutionary War and after this war the Tennessee migration gives a better picture of the early Virginians and North Carolinans with this name who head families.

ISLE OF WIGHT, VIRGINIA

Matthew Whitfield and his wife Prisilla deeded certain property to her brother John Lawrence. The deed was acknowledged by the drawers Feb. 9 , 1709.

Matthew Whitfield with others joined themselves according to the order of the vestry to mark out as "processioners" the real properties of their neighborhood , 1723. (From the Newport Vestry book.)

A bill of sale , March 24 , 1745 , from Samuel Whitfield to Jordon Thomas.

An inventory of the estate of William Whitfield was taken June 12, 1750.
Benjamin Whitfield received a deed from William Hollowell and wife, June 6 , 1751.

Thomas and his wife Mary H. Whitfield were engaged June 1751 , in settling the division of property left by her father William Harrison.

In a list of the company commanded by Capt. Robert Mc Kenzie , July 13 , 1756 , is the name of James Whitfield . He is described as 21 years of age, five feet , six and one-half inches tall. Shoemaker.

John Whitfield appears in the same list. He was a year younger than James, but was the same height and was engaged in the same profession.

Robert Whitfield possessed 230 acres of land in Isle of Wight County. Jan. 12 , 1765 , he deeded property to Rebecca Vaughan.

John Whitfield was witness to the birth of John Chapman , February 29 , 1763.

On August 12, 1772 , Benjamin Whitfield and wife, Mary , sold a plantation on Kingsale Swamp to Henry Vaughan for 100 pounds. They received a deed from him.

Harrison Whitfield appeared before the May court, 1775 , to take an oath to " his Majesty's person and government . "

It is from 1750 to 1780 that the English ships come frequently to the ports of the colony , and specially to Chesapeake Bay , New York , and New England Bay. When the Revolution War started many ships came but all did not return to England.

In 1782 the people of Isle of Wight began to file tax returns on personal property , and we found these records which may be seen in the Archives , Richmond , Virginia :

1782 William Whitfield and Abraham Whitfield.

1783 Samuel , his son George , John, Copeland, Miles , and William Whitfield.

1784 Samuel, George, William, Abraham, John, John Jr., Copeland, Copeland Jr., and Milley Whitfield.

1785 William, Wilson , Copeland, Copeland Jr., Abraham , and Milly Whitfield.

1786 Samuel, Copeland, Copeland Jr., John , John Jr., and Wilson Whitfield.

1787 John, Milley, Samuel, Wilson, Copeland , and Copeland Whitfield Jr.

1788 John, John Jr., Samuel, Wilson , Copeland , and Copeland Whitfield Jr.

1789 Wilson, Copeland, Copeland Jr., Mildred , John, and Fanney Whitfield.

1790 Milley, Copeland , Copeland Jr., John, Fanney, and Priscilla Whitfield.

1791 Wilson, Copeland Jr., John, and Milley Whitfield .

1792 Wilson , Copeland Sr., John, and Fanny Whitfield.

1793 Wilson , Thomas, Copeland Sr., John, and Fanney Whitfield.

1794 Copeland Jr. , Wilson, John, and Fanny Whitfield.

1795 Copeland, Wilson, Hardy, Fanny, and John Whitfield.

1796 Thomas, Jacob , Wilson, Hardy, Copeland, Macon , Fanney , and the estate of John Whitfield.

1797 Fanney, Mary , Hardy, Wilson , Copeland, Macon, and Thomas Whitfield.

1798 Wilkinson, Copeland , Mason, Hardy , and Thomas Whitfield.

1799 Rachelle and Copeland Whitfield.

In the Revolutionary War we found that   many Whitfields fought for freedom. Still living when the tax return was made was James, Jesse , John, John, Needham, Needham, Needham, Reuben, Wilson , Will B., several William Whitfields and others.

The following appear in the Virginia First Census , as heads of families in Isle of Wight , Virginia in 1782 : Abraham, Catey, Copeland, Frances , John , Mary , Matthew , John, Molley, Samuel , Thomas , William , and Wilson Whitfield.

There were fewer heads of families recorded for 1790 than for 1782 . Those in 1790 were : Abraham, Copeland, John, Samuel, Thomas , and William Whitfield.

This showed a trend away from old towns to new lands. In the new counties many of the people were not taken on the census because the entry takers counted and obtained in dwellings the names . The back farms were too far away and hard to locate , so the count was taken by dwellings known.

The 1790 United States Census was supposed to represent for each of the states concerned a complete list of the heads of families in the United States at the time of the adoption of the Constitution.

Kentucky, Tennessee Census and other population returns to the State Department at Washington , D. C. were destroyed when the British burned the capital at Washington during the War of 1812.

The other names on the Virginia Census as heads of families by the name of Whitfield:

Africa Whitfield

Frances Whitfield

Ivey Whitfield

Ivy Whitfield

Mary Whitfield

Matt Whitfield

John Wrenn Whitfield

Molly Whitfield

Sol Whitfield

Thomas Whitfield (Sussex Co.)

William Whitfield

John Whitfield

Samuel Whitfield

VIRGINIA

County and Church records of Virginia from 1783 to 1871 can be found in book Whitfield, Bryan, Smith and Related Families . Virginia State Archives, Virginia Papers.

The early years are recorded here because in these records are the ancestors or kinship of the Virginians and North Carolinans that moved to Tennessee, and a few that moved to Kentucky.

In 1798 Wilkinson, Copeland, Macon, Hardy, and Thomas Whitfield paid a personal tax in the Isle of Wight , Virginia.

John Whitfield made a deed to Wilkinson Whitfield and another to William Whitfield during 1795.

Wilkinson Whitfield was a principal in eight deeds beginning Sept. 18, 1816.

Reuben Whitfield was a neighbor to the lands of Atkins Whitfield located in "King Sale Swamp."

Polly Whitfield married Mills Manning,Dec. 20, 1827.

In Norfolk County, George Whitfield married Elizabeth Kinley , Nov. 10, 1789 . In the same County , Willis Whitfield was a witness to the will of John Boush, July 24, 1790.

There are several lawyers in Virginia with the name of Thomas Whitfield.

Solomon Whitfield is listed in the Revolutionary War Pension Roll under Nansemond County, Virginia . (Report of the Secretary of War, Pension Rolls, II , p. 175 .)

The Will of William Whitfield , Tyrrell County, North Carolina , 1761, included references to Martha , William, Jesse, John, Winnie, and Stephen Whitfield.

Some of the citations on Jesse (Jepe) refer to the Jesse Whitfield who had land grant after Revolutionary War to eastern Tennessee for 640 acres, July 15, 1793.

1781 Wills of Thomas Whitfield, Israel Whitfield, and Hardy Whitfield, in Nash County, North Carolina.

1792 Wills of Mary Whitfield and Elisha Whitfield in Nash County, North Carolina.

1796 Wills of Isaac Whitfield and Solomon Whitfield in Nash County, North Carolina.

Dec. 24, 1835 , John Webb Keeling married Mary Whitfield, daughter of Joshua and Martha Whitfield.

Early History of Tennessee

Captain William Bean in 1769 came from Pittsylvania County, Virginia to help with the beginning of the Watauga Settlement in Tennessee. In 1770 James Robertson came from North Carolina. Much of the land settled on the Holston south of the Virginia fall line was free of the Cherokee Indian title by a treaty, but it was not the case of the Wataugans.

A History of the Pioneer Families of Missouri has been compiled by William Smith Bryan and Rose Rose in 1876. This book does not record Whitfield name. The first Whitfields appear to have penetrated Missouri about 1848.

Before the close of the Revolutionary War, October 7, 1780, 440 East Tennesseans, under Colonel John Sevier and Isaac Shelby, gave Great Britain a sample of frontier fights by assisting in the defeat of Ferguson at King's Mountain. In this engagement the Americans loss in dead or wounded 88, the British lost 505 killed and wounded, and 600 captured. Zelphie Whitfield was a four year old girl in Eastern Tennessee and her father was of that region. She lived to tell many stories about the British and died at 76 years of age in Davidson County, Tennessee.

James Robertson (1783) was Davidson County's first representative in North Carolina. This year, Rev. Jeremiah Lambert came to the Holston Circuit and was the first Methodist to preach in Tennessee. The following year a town was established at the Bluffs on the Cumberland by the North Carolina Legislature, the old name of Nashborough giving way later to Nashville. A century and a half later Vallie Jo Fox (Whitfield) lived on the bluff in an apartment over a merchant's shop, and visited the preserved fort Nashborough often for it was only three city blocks away.

In 1789 the North Carolina Legislature passed the Act ceding to the United States territory embracing the present State of Tennessee. In the following year a deed was made, and on April 2, 1790, the territory was accepted by Act of Congress. In 1787, Needham Whitfield and all on September 20th received the land warrant and deed on the north side of Tennessee River near Green County. In 1788, the company and Needham Whitfield purchased several sections of land in a large flat lying between Clinch Mountain near Bull Run River. William Whitfield, Joseph Greene and Company in 1787 and 1788 purchased land adjoining the land of Needham Whitfield. Soon with their many camps resembling an Indian village spread out along the Bull Run it was to become one of the first settlements in Tennessee. The travelers from the east found cabins along the Holston, in the Gap and through the Clinch Mountain. There the Whitfields and friends lived with their descendants in Hawkins and Greene and Knox Counties. Many of these families of Whitfield with growing boys left the Clinch Mountain and went to Christian County in Kentucky and to Montgomery County in Tennessee.

Some of them settled in Sumner where they soon built a fort.

This land was part of North Carolina and when the territory was accepted by Congress, Needham Whitfield, Needham Whitfield, and William Whitfield et al had already several thousand acres of land that had been purchased at ten pounds per hundred acres. The territory was divided into two districts - Washington and Miro. The Washington District embraced the eastern part of Tennessee. The Miro District changed to Mero District and embraced the Cumberland settlement or the Old Tennessee County which is today Sumner, Robertson, Montgomery, Davidson Counties of Tennessee. William Blount was appointed Governor of this Territory, called "the Territory South of the Ohio River," and in Tennessee in 1790 it was the southern most part of the Ohio River territory.

The Cumberland and Tennessee River area was called MERO in all the old records, but the name was given in honor of Don Estevan Miro, the Spanish Governor of New Orleans, who had control of the Mississippi River. James Robertson was appointed Brigadier General of this district by President George Washington. A few months later he was with Edwin Hickman, in what is now Hickman County, being present at the time of the Indians attack upon the party near the present site of Centerville. It did not take long to spread the Cumberland Settlement boundary to the south of Hickman. Continental soldiers and Revolutionary soldiers who had been promised land warrants in the War wanted their pay so they helped to develop the new country and prove that freedom was theirs.

June 26, 1792, Zeigler's Station in Sumner County, Tennessee was captured and burned by Creek Indians. On September 30, 1792, an attack took place on Buchanan's Station four miles south of Nashville. The Indians were 700 strong, but were defeated by the fort's fifteen gallant defenders. When the Indian attack quieten down the scouts in the Station passed the word more supplies were needed from the eastern Washington District. They must have called on the Clinch Mountain people to help for soon afterwards families with large number of boys and men from this area and the North Carolina Military reservation at Granville move to the Cumberland settlement.

The Continental and Revolution men of North Carolina land warrants were ready and granted in 1793. Many of the Whitfield families were recipients of these Tennessee land warrants. July 29, 1793, Lewis Whitfield received land on the north side of Tennessee River, in eastern District. Jesse (Jepe) Whitfield received 640 acres on July 15, 1793. In the same year, 1793, Bryan, and Bryan Whitfield received land warrants to land in Tennessee in the Mero District. These were warrants given soldiers of the North Carolina Continental Line in lieu of pay, and while many of these land warrants were sold in North Carolina by the soldiers or their heirs to those who settled in the western territory,there was one , Bryan Whitfield, who with land owners of North Carolina hired G. Rutherford to locate their grants.   Bryan Whitfield was granted three thousand,one hundred and seventy-four acres of land on May 20 , 1793. He left Anson region of the backwoods of North Carolina and moved north through the Cumberland Gap and settled in Montgomery County, Tennessee. It was his kinship, heirs, and clan that settled his land on Stones River on both sides of the River , and later on Duck River.   Bryan Whitfield settled and developed with others four square miles of land in still an Indian country. The people from North Carolina   and Virginia settled far in the west near the Indians burial mounds in Franklin town of William- son County, Tennessee.

In 1676 , the Virginia London Secretary of State was Joseph William- son. In 1680 , the Virginia Secretary of State was Nicholas Spencer . These secretaries left descendants whom we know are farmers that along with Whitfield of Virginia settled the southern Mero District near Hickman County.

On June 1, 1796 , Tennessee was admitted into the Union. Previous to this on January 11 th, a Constitutional Convention convened at Knox- ville, and, upon the suggestion credited to Andrew Jackson, a delegate from Davidson County, who was formerly a resident of the same North Carolina location as Bryan Whitfield , named the State "Tennessee". On November 12 th he was commissioned as the first Representative in Congress from the new State.

We must now record the pioneers to Tennessee with the name WHITFIELD , for by 1796 they have settled in the west that is now a new State of the Colonial States of the Union.   These pioneers are picked from the official records of the State of Tennessee preserved at the Tennessee State Library and Archives, and are found in the collected records on Whitfield Families of Tennessee , compiled in this book , taken from other sources, such as records in Washington , D. C.

        Zelphie Whitfield - Watauga   (1776)
        William Whitfield - Clinch Mountain (1780)
        William Whitfield- Clinch   Mountain (1788)
        William Whitfield - Clinch Mountain (1787)
        Needham Whitfield - Clinch Mountain (1788)
        Needham Whitfield - Clinch Mountain (1788)
        Elizabeth Whitfield - Clinch Mountain
        Sarah Whitfield - Clinch Mountain
        Elizabeth Whitfield - Campbell - Gap of Cumerland
        Others at Whitfield 's Camp on Bull Run River   (1790)
        Jesse Whitfield - East Tennessee (1793)

Lewis Whitfield - East Tennessee   (1793)
Needham Whitfield - Hawkins County, Tennessee (1788)
Bryan Whitfield - Hawkins County, Tennessee (1788)

PIONEERS TO TENNESSEE

George Whitfield - Washington Co., Tennessee (1790) (Suffix Co. Va.).
Bryan(t) Whitfield - Montgomery Co., Tennessee (1793)
 and Children :   (Stones River land deeds.)
 William, James, Mary Jane, Bryan, Margaret , Duncan,
 Catherine , Ann Maria.
Needham Whitfield (1776-1858) and children : George N., Sarah C.,
 Miriam R., Needham B. , Montgomery County, Tennessee (1793).
Lewis Whitfield and children : Needham, Lewis , Robert , Sarah,
Elizabeth , George , Joseph W., Bryan, Susan, Catherine ,
Montgomery County, Tennessee (1793).
William Whitfield - Montgomery County, Tennessee (before 1800).
William S. Whitfield - Montgomery County, Tennessee.
Sumner County Tennessee in 1794 ,   John Whitfield. William Whit-
field .   Willis Whitfield and children : Ansil, Wright , Christian,
Sally , Temperance, Rhody , Thomas Y., Arthur A., Willis , Eli ,
Elizabeth E., Alfred Whitfield.   (Nash County , North Carolina)

Thomas Whitfield - Davidson County, Tennessee   (1794) .
Esther Whitfield - Davidson County, Tennessee   (1794) .
John Whitfield - Davidson County, Tennessee   (1794) .
John W. Whitfield - Davidson County , Tenn   (1830) .

William Whitfield and Mary Beck children : William, Needham,
Joseph, Lewis , Hester , John , Harriet , Mary , Lucy, Bryan .
Christian County, Kentucky , and Steward County, Tennessee. (1800)

Wilkins Whitfield - Williamson County, Tennessee (1808).
Mary Whitfield - Williamson County, Tennessee (1808) .
Harrison Whitfield - Williamson County, Tennessee (1808) .
John Whitfield - Williamson County, Tennessee (1808) , and his son
 John Whitfield.
Rebecca Whitfield - Williamson County, Tennessee (1815) .
Martha Ann Whitfield - Williamson County, Tennessee (1812) .
Eliza Whitfield - Williamson County, Tennessee.
William Whitfield and children : James, John L., Sally . Lawrence
 County, Tennessee (1808) .
Whitfield women who were wives to these pioneer men , and the sisters,
and the names of the unknown.
These are the TENNESSEE PIONEERS of Whitfield families , compiled
by Vallie Jo Fox Whitfield, wife of Robert Edward Whitfield.

Hickman County of Tennessee

It was after the first settling at Sumner County Fort and the Montgomery County land that the Whitfields of this lineal took their roots at Franklin , Tennessee,in Williamson County after passing through Davidson County. They were one of the first families in Williamson County and after they had lived there for twenty years they moved first to Rutherford, and about 1825 to Hickman County. It was in Rutherford , Coffee , Cannon and Wilson that some of the descendants of Harrison , John , and Willis Whitfield established their roots in Tennessee. Coffee County was owned by John Whitfield , and he purchased the County by getting the land deed of twenty thousand acres in 1839. The land was released in parcels of four allotments of five thousand acres each on May 8 th and 9 th in 1839.

Wilkins Whitfield 's descendants went to Hickman County with George W. Whitfield buying a farm there near Vernon. In 1830 William George Clagett with his wife, Theodosia Whitfield Clagett moved to Hickman near Centerville and helped in the mercantile business.

While more of the family lived to the east of Franklin , Tennessee as the years passed we are concerned with the family whose genealogy is complete , and developed the Whitfield Town on Beaver Dam of the Duck River .For this background we have recorded here a brief history on Hickman County, Tennessee,which is situated on the western side of the Highland Rim of Middle Tennessee. The surface of the county is much broken , being composed of high , rolling ridges and deep ravines, pointing generally toward the numerous streams. The plateau lands of the northern section of the County form the watershed between the Cumberland and Tennessee Rivers. As they approach Duck River these plateau lands sink , but appear again on the south side of that stream.

In the valleys of the Duck and Piney Rivers the soil is rich and productive. The streams of the County are Duck River and its numerous tributaries : Piney River at the head of the stream is south of Davidson County and the first land grant there was made to Bryan Whitfield in 1793. The first white men to set foot there were the surveyors under Edmund Hickman , who came in 1785 to survey a tract of land on Piney River. Adam Wilson was the first settler on Piney River. He had come from east Tennessee , cleared the cane away and the undergrowth in 1806 , and raised the first crop in the County. During the winter of 1806 other settlers located near him and were William Curl and Reuben Copeland from east Tennessee whose people earlier lived in Virginia. Samuel Walker , John Lowe , John Ward and Eli Hornbeck from South Carolina. A year afterward,Ship Landing, on Duck River was settled by Josiah Ship,

John Huddleston and Joseph Mc Connell. Between 1807 and 1810 several settlements were made. *

The other creek tributaries of the Duck River which flows from the Tennessee River were Sugar , Beaver Dam, Swan, Lick, Leatherwood, Cane, Taylor , Mill , Wade and Bird Branch. Duck River is navigable for small steamboats at certain seasons, and boats have ascended as far as Centerville.

The whites soon discovered the mineral springs and the rich iron ores. The crops that grew the best were corn, wheat , tobacco , oats, peanuts , and all the grasses, and the timbers of white and red oak , gum, hickory , poplar, maple , beech, walnut, dogwood and mulberry . Potter's clay was used by the Indians at Beaver Dam Creek.

Hickman made another trip and lost his life , 1791 , at the hands of the Camp Indians, who attacked the surveying party near the mouth of Defeated Creek, on Duck River.

During the years 1801-1802 the Natchez Road, which touches this County on the east, was opened by United States soldiers, under command of Captain Robert Butler and Lieutenant Edward P. Gains.In the latter part of the first year the soldiers at Gordon Ferry on Duck River, there established a trading house. In 1805 the land title of the Chickasaw Indians was taken, and in 1812 Captain Gordon settled there. He employed Thomas H. Benton as a Clerk in his store at Gordon Ferry in 1807 and 1808. Thomas studied law at odd times and at nights. Thomas H. Benton later became the Missouri Senator , who served in the United States Senate for thirty-six years. Samuel Oliphant and Rosin L. Bishop located at Gordon's Ferry in 1806 and 1807.

Hickman County at first included several counties. The act authorizing the establishment of Hickman County appointed David Love, Joel Walker, John S. Prim and Joseph Lynn as commissioners to run the boundary lines of the County and select a County seat site.

The magistrates met at the house of William Joslin, on Piney River, two miles north of Vernon , Monday , April 1808 and organized the County Court by electing William Wilson as chairman ; Millington Easley , clerk; William Phillips, sheriff ; John Easley, Sr., trustee ; Bart G. Stewart, register ; James Lynn, ranger, and Alex Gray , coroner.

The commissioners appointed by the General Assembly met in 1809

* History of Hickman County, Tennessee , page 790

and selected county site of lands of James Wilson and Joseph Lynn , on a high bluff on the east bank of Piney River , and layed off the town Vernon , in honor of George Washington's home in Virginia.

While Hickman was being developed, Wilkins Whitfield was busy organizing his plantation in Franklin , Tennessee ; and Polly Mary was busy giving birth and caring for their cabin house.

The settlers crushed the corn in mortar bowls and travelled to mill in Dickson County but in 1808 the first mill was erected on Mill Creek by William Hale , an East Tennessean. Andrew Carrothers erected a horse-power mill on Sugar Creek. In 1828 Edward Corender erected a mill on Lick Creek. William Briggs erected a water-power mill for corn on Swan Creek in 1830.

The settlers after hearing of the purchase of the Chickasaw claim on the south side of Duck River in 1818 settled rapidly the northern part of County. An election was held and Centerville was selected as the County seat after John C. Mc Lemore and Charles Stewart donated sixty-one acres of land to the County. In 1823 the courts and records were moved to Centerville from the log court house on the bluff and the Vernon courthouse was torn down, and with the same logs another courthouse erected in Centerville. In 1825 a brick court house was erected and enlarged in 1849. It was here at this house that John Wilkins Whitfield practiced his first law , and many of the mercantile business people collected debts from the citizens through action of the court - house. During the years 1830 , 1832 , 1833 the Supreme Court of Tennessee met at Centerville. This building was burned by Federal soldiers during the Civil War, and in 1867 a new building was built. When the Chancery Court held its first session in Centerville on the 6 th of September 1852 , Chancellor John S. Brien was presiding, and John Wilkins Whitfield was clerk and master. The list of the many distinguished judges and court personnel can be located in The History of Tennessee of Hickman County.

Hickman County is bounded on the north by Dickson County, east by Williamson and Maury, south by Lewis , and west by Perry and Humphreys but these counties were not formed until the Congressional districts were well established. The middle counties were represented in the war of 1812 by individual volunteers, such as Ansil Whitfield. Such was the case of the Florida War 1836 . For the war with Mexico in 1846, Hickman County of Tennessee furnished her full quota.

Thomas Jefferson Whitfield was Brigadier General of the Davidson County 17 th Brigade at Nashville. Many of the Whitfield boys learned early the importance of the scout and rangers. Since travellers took the Natchez Road to the Mississippi the local people often acted as guards through their Chickasaw land. Under the younger Whitfield brother , John Wilkins Whitfield , the Volunteers were organized and set out under his command May,1846. President Polk was now the commander of militias and a neighbor at Columbia, Tennessee.

The Centerville Town was formed in 1823. The Whitfield town on Beaver Dam to the west of Centerville about 1830 , and was a busy happy farming town.

Hickman County of Tennessee responded to the call of Governor Harris for State troops in 1861, the people were enthusiastic for the Confederacy. The first Company organized in the County was com - manded by Captain T.P. Bateman, and went out in May 1861 , the 11 th Reg. Inf. Captain Levi Mc Collum's Co. - joined 42 nd Reg. Infantry
Captain Josiah H. Hubbard - joined 42nd Reg. Inf.
Captain J.J. Williams Co. - joined 24th Reg. Inf.
Captain S.J. George 's Co. - joined 48 th Reg. Inf.
Captain William Beal's Co . - joined 24 th Reg. Inf.
Captain J.P. Morrison's Co. - joined 48 th Reg. Inf.
R.M. Whitson Co. of Cavalry - joined 9 th Battalion
George Mayberry Co. of Cavalry - joined 9 th Battalion
Captain F.S. Easley Co., of Cavalry - joined 10 th Tenn. Cav.

Throughout all the engagements of their respective regiments the Hickman County companies participated , losing many men , but acquitting themselves nobly each time they went into battle. This County was overrun by raiding parties sent out by the Federals, and while many Federal troops passed through the County, destroying much valuable property and confiscating arms, stock, and such , no regular encamp- ments were made in the County ; nor did any engagements occur in the County during the war, and preyed unmercifully upon the farmers , stealing horses, cattle and provisions of all kinds, and committing many depredations.

When Thomas Jefferson Whitfield died he was living in Perry County, Tennessee where he is buried . Most of his children moved to new farm land at Bakersville, Tennessee in Humphreys County.

When George W. Whitfield , which is probably George Washington Whitfield died, he was living in Dallas County, Texas.

Last record of James Monroe Whitfield is in Hickman County, but he moved to Texas. He has family in Benton and Henry Counties.

John W. Whitfield left a daughter in Hickman County. After his second marriage his family settled in Texas, and his descendants were located in Medina County, Texas.

The descendants of these men are living near the Tennessee River Counties in the middle of the nineteenth century, and their children into the twentieth century.

When Tennessee became a State in 1796, the Cumberland County of North Carolina was divided into Montgomery and Robertson Counties, Montgomery County including the territory now embraced in Hickman County north of Duck River. In 1803 Steward,County, bounded on the North by the northern boundary of the State and on the south by the southern boundary, was established. It was bounded on the west by the Tennessee River, while its eastern boundary was a north and south line running thirteen miles west of Clarksville. Steward County, as then established as Stewart included all of the present Counties of Houston, Humphreys, Perry, and Wayne west of this line and all of Hardin County east of this line and all of Hardin County east of the Tennessee River. It is this land and this linked trail across counties now existing that we found the Whitfields from Virginia as early pioneers who left few records.

The seaports along the Atlantic Ocean were entrance depots for the ancestors that came to America. The first Whitfields, their children, and grandchildren,spent their lives for almost a hundred years in the country east of the Cumberland Mountains. It was the scouts and Revolutionary soldiers on expeditions that helped to develop the new west. Before they brought wives and children,the men went first to build cabins for their families. Each man would make a "deadening" by girdling the trees to make them die. Then he planted a crop of corn, so that there would be bread when the family came. The Whitfields like to spend their time fishing and exploring water streams. Belongings were loaded on horses and the adventurers walked the trails. This family always walked and even behind the wagon when they had one to carry along.

The families which moved together from the eastern settlements to the backwoods and river basins were neighbors and kin folks, for nearly everybody was kin to everybody else and marrying cousins was an acceptable thing. Since the Whitfields have married relatives they are linked as generation cousins by an earlier ancestor. Several sets of brothers have married a set of sisters, or at death, the remaining spouse has married a relative. Nature made Tennessee a farming state and this became the chief occupation of many of the families; although in the nineteenth century many are in medicine, ministry, allied industries, and some in the service of the government.

These people are in the Cumberland settlement when the County lines are established. Therefore that portion of Hickman County which embraced Dickson County north of Duck River was not permanently settled until after the treaties made by the United States in 1805 and 1806, and that portion of Hickman County south of Duck River was permamently settled after the final treaty of 1818.

Bear Creek took its name when William Shipp killed two bears and wounded a third near the Creek on the south side of the river. Near Shipp's Bend is the northeast corner of a large survey, or entry of land in the name of William J. Council, which contained about 12,000 acres, and was made about 1812. This entry includes the fertile lands near the Huddleston Bridge, on the south side of the river. The entry includes the bend just below, named "Council's Bend," from the man who first obtained a legal claim to it. "Council's Bend contains about 1,000 acres of good farming lands, and a portion was once occupied by George Whitfield, a brother of General Thomas Jeff. Whitfield, General John W. Whitfield, and J. Monroe Whitfield. Whitfield sold to Abraham Dansly."

Then they occuppied land south of Duck River and children move north along Duck River east of Buffalo River to Bakerville town in Humphreys County.

All of the descendants still inhabit the land in the region their fore-fathers settled in Tennessee over one hundred and fifty years ago. The counties near Davidson have retained the Whitfield citizens a long time. On occasions a Whitfield has left the location and has made a name that rebounds to Tennessee; for the sprig that is broken off from the tree is still a piece of that tree. They have gone to the four corners of the State and far from its boundaries. The tidal flow of human beings that left the Atlantic Ocean coast and moved to Tennessee to stay has a few sprigs that left the inland and in another generation and another time of history in the beginning of that tidal flow of human beings from middle Atlantic States to the Pacific Ocean Coast were a few Whitfield families. Robert Edward Whitfield moved from Waverly, Tennessee after marrying Vallie Jo Fox and with some of the same spirit as his forefathers moved to California the day of the wedding, March 26, 1943 to find new opportunity for a job awaited in Oakland, California. They came as a young man and wife leaving Nashville, Tennessee on the Louisville and Nashville Railroad to Chicago, then they took a Southern Pacific train across the western states on the Union Pacific trail. Here they lived to become one of the first Whitfields to inhabit the California land in 1943. It was the time of the second World War and many soldiers and kinship moved to the region. A few Whitfields from the southwest who were settled in San Francisco and Oakland region were kinship of soldiers who were sent to war service duty in the Pacific region of islands owned by the United States. They came mostly from the Oklahoma State and nearby States of Oklahoma. When Robert and Vallie Jo Whitfield moved to Berkeley, California of Alameda County there were about eight families living in Northern California who were named Whitfield.

Another half dozen Whitfield persons have records in California from 1900 to 1935 , that is , in the region of Northern California . Only a few of this southern family came to California before 1935. The World War travels and openings on new land have brought many to California . The towns of San Francisco and Oakland were large cities but Oakland had a population smaller than Nashville when Robert Whitfield and Vallie Jo Whitfield stepped off the Southern Pacific train at the Oakland mole on April 1, 1943 . They had spent four days and three nights travelling on the overland coach and sleeper railroad car to California. They left the railroad depot and walked to the end stop of a streetcar and inquired of the conductor "Where is a good place to stay ? " They boarded the train and said , "We have just left the University of Tennessee in Knoxville , Tennessee. Do you have a University here ? " The conductor said , "You want to go to Berkeley and gave a transfer ticket and instructions." They found their way to Berkeley and settled in a hotel room a block from Bancroft Avenue near Sather Gate.

A week went by and Robert Whitfield took his first chemical job with Shell Development Company in Emeryville, California, and Vallie Jo located an apartment on Piedmont Avenue near the campus. It was here they settled and after the War returned to college attending Harvard University in Cambridge , Massachusetts. The settlers roots were made in California. Vallie Jo Fox had visited California with her parents, Joseph Edward Fox and Valley Schiefer Fox in July 1939 for travel and the Golden Gate Exposition in the west. She had encouraged young Robert Edward Whitfield to take the job offered him in California when they were engaged before marriage.

California was a young undeveloped State far west in the Union. The movie industry had done much to publicize California as a land for development. The State was mostly a coast line development with farms ranchos in the valley beyond the coastal hills of the Pacific Ocean.

---

* Life of Vallie Jo Whitfield , published 1969 , Whitfield Books.

41

Population in parts of eastern Virginia dwindled after 1800 as planters moved south and west in search of richer farmland. This migration was increased after Eli Whitney invented the cotton gin in 1793, stimulating the demand of British mills for the fibre and luring former tobacco planters to seek new cotton land. Unfortunately for Virginia, the boom in agriculture created by cotton in the 1820s and '30s increased the need for slaves and prevented the crystallization of sentiment to free and repatriate Virginia's Negroes, which Jefferson had proposed to the General Assembly in 1776.

Virginia's population west of the Blue Ridge increased greatly, but the entrenched power of eastern planters continued to control the state Since adoption of the Virginia Constitution in 1776.

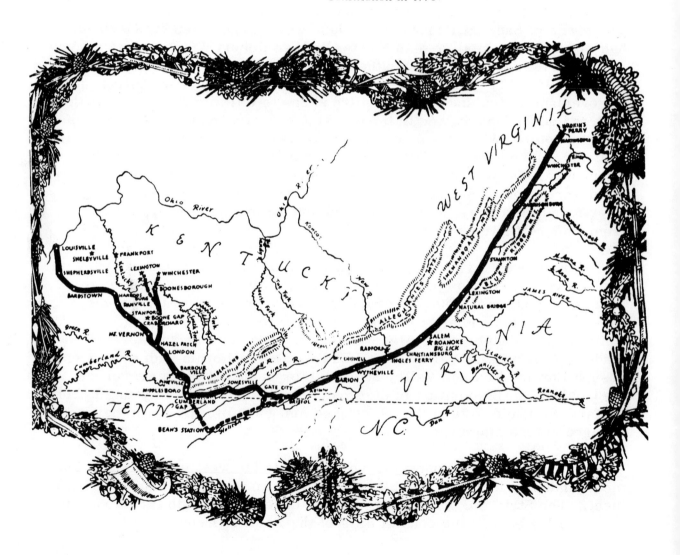

PART II

GENEALOGY

Virginians   named Whitfield , and Families beginning in Virginia.

Richard Whitfield 1635 in Charles City County, Virginia.
John Whitfield 1635 in ship "Globe of London" to Virginia.
William Whitfield 1636 in Elizabeth City, Virginia.
Gilbert Whitfield 1637 in New Norfolk County, Virginia.
Tobias Whitfield 1666 in ship "Fellowship" to Virginia.
William Whitfield 1666 "Triall " ship to Virginia.
Mathew Whitfield , wife Priscilla from Newport Parish of Isle of Wight.
County was 1678 in Nansemond County, Virginia. 1709 in Isle of Wight Co.
Roger Whitfield in 1679 went to New York, and is not a Virginian.
Matthew Whitfield 1679 in "Prosperous " ship to Virginia.
William Whitfield , 1681 , farmer in Isle of Wight County, Virginia.
Samuel Whitfield 1745 in Isle of Wight County, Virginia.
William Whitfield , died 1749 in Isle of Wight Co., Virginia.
John Whitfield 1758 in "Johnson " ship to Virginia.
Elizabeth Whitfield of Hampton , Virginia died 1727 ; and her children:
>   1. Abraham Whitfield
>   2. William Whitfield
>   3. Joseph Whitfield
>   4. Mary Anne Whitfield

Henry Whitfield, wife Mary Holloday Godwin Whitfield 1760 in Isle
   of Wight County, Virginia and children :
>   1. Robert Whitfield , born and died in Virginia.
>   A member of Confederate Congress , and
>   Virginia State Senate.
>   2. Fannie Whitfield (Finney) , died Dec. 20, 1841 .
>   3. Margaret A. Whitfield (Finney) , died Sept 24, 1852.
>   4. John Whitfield, born in Virginia, and died in
>   Enfield , North Carolina.

William Whitfield 1776 in Nansemond County, Virginia.
Louisa and William Whitfield 1776 in Princess Anne County, Virginia.

Seventeenth Century in Elizabeth City County, Virginia.

Ann Whitfield
Elizabeth Whitfield
Elizabeth Whitfield
Hannah Whitfield , 1718
Hannah Whitfield
John Whitfield
John Whitfield
Joseph Whitfield
Mary Whitfield
Mary Ann Whitfield who had son,
Robert Whitfield living in 1770.

Mary Whitfield
Robert Whitfield
Thomas Whitfield
Thomas Whitfield
William Whitfield
Abraham Whitfield

Seventeenth Century in Isle of Wight County, Virginia.

Abraham Whitfield	Permelia Whitfield
Copeland Whitfield	Thomas Whitfield
Frances Whitfield	Thomas Whitfield
George Whitfield	Wilson Whitfield
Haynes Whitfield	Samuel Whitfield
Hester Whitfield	William Harrison Whitfield , 1763
John Whitfield	Robert Whitfield , 1765
Jemima Whitfield	John Whitfield , 1763
Joshua Whitfield	Thomas Whitfield , wife Mary
Macon Whitfield	H. Whitfield , 1751.
Milla Whitfield	Thomas Whitfield , 1762
Milley Whitfield	Copeland Whitfield , 1790
Matthew Whitfield 1754	Thomas Whitfield , 1756
and died 1781	Willis Whitfield 1792 , in
	Norfolk County, Va.

William Whitfield , born 1751 January . Enlisted 1778 in Revolution service in Goochland County, Virginia . Pension grant Nov. 25, 1829 when living in Saint Clare County, Alabama. He had twelve children , all married in 1829 , one child died before 1829. This family was a Whitefield family.

Hester Whitfield living 1752 in Nansemond County, Virginia and adopted child, Matthew Whitfield.

Thomas Whitfield , died 1758 ca. , Nansemond County , Virginia. Children : 1. Matthew Whitfield , cared for by Hester Whitfield.

(41) 2. Esther Whitfield

George Whitfield living 1758 in Nansemond County, Virginia.

Descendants of Samuel Whitfield 1714-58   Generations
Family groups   Virginia, 1, 2, 3, 4.

Samuel Whitfield (WS I) , born 1714 , whose father was perhaps Matthew Whitfield of Nansemond County, Virginia, although not sure. Samuel died 1758 .   Wife, Elizabeth Whitfield. Children:

1. Mathias Whitfield	2. George Whitfield
3. Margaret Whitfield	4. Jemima Whitfield
5. Elizabeth Whitfield	

And Mathias Whitfield or George Whitfield had a son , Samuel Whitfield , and he had a son , Samuel Whitfield who married Frances Norsworthy, daughter of Tristram Norsworthy . He died 1799. The children : Samuel Whitfield (WS4) and Henry Whitfield .   And the descendant , Samuel Whitfield married Mary Drew , and had Mary Frances Whitfield who married Dr . James Southall.

Henry Whitfield (1758-1823) married Mary Holladay Godwin in

1809 . Resided Ragged Island, Isle of Wight County, Virginia . Children:

1. John Godwin Whitfield
2. Samuel Whitfield (1812-1833)
   of Smithfield , Virginia.
3. Robert Henry Whitfield
4. Frances Whitfield who married
   Dr. Finny of Chuckatuck, Va.
   After her death Dr. Finny married
   sister, Margaret.

5. Mary Holladay Whitfield
   married Rev. Mc Wigan.
6. Margaret Whitfield
7. Sarah Whitfield

John Godwin Whitfield 1800 - 1879. He moved from Smithfield , Virginia to North Carolina . He married Miss Cofield and had children: Samuel G. W. , Fanny Whitfield (1836-1927) who married Charles Diddrick, "Bettie" (or Bobbie) W. (1842-1929).

Robert Henry Whitfield 1814- 1868 . Lawyer of Smithfield and Isle of Wight County, Virginia. He married Rebecca Ann Peebles. He was nominated for Congress in 1851. Ten years later he was a member of the Virginia Secession Convention . A member of the Confederate Congress. Children : Henry E. Whitfield, Leucretia H. Whitfield , Samuel Whitfield , Robert P. Whitfield , John P. Whitfield, Susan Whitfield , Janet Whitfield.

GENERATIONS I II III IV

Descendants of Thomas Whitfield –1694 & Ann .

(1) THOMAS WHITFIELD lived in Elizabeth City County, Virginia in the seventeenth century.   We are not sure Thomas Whitfield was an immigrant for we have no record of entry for a Thomas Whitfield . He was the native son of an early Virginian. He died and left a Will recorded November 26, 1694 in Elizabeth County, Va. He was married to Ann and they had children :

> (2)   1. John Whitfield
> (3)   2. Thomas Whitfield
> (4)   3. Mary Whitfield
> (5)   4. Elizabeth Whitfield

WT 2   (Thomas)

(2) JOHN WHITFIELD and THOMAS WHITFIELD had children , and Thomas Whitfield had a son of the same name.

WT 3   (Thomas , Thomas)

(3) THOMAS WHITFIELD , the grandson was born in Virginia 1721 and died 1781 in Nash County , North Carolina . He was an ardent patriot and served in the Revolutionary armies. In 1740 he married in Virginia and he and his wife had thirteen children .

(7) 1. Thomas Whitfield
(8) 2. Reuben Whitfield
(6) 3. Solomon Whitfield
(WT 4) (7) 4. John Whitfield
(11) 5. William Whitfield
(9) 6. Benjamin Whitfield
(10) 7. Elisha Whitfield
(11) 8. Zurah Whitfield
(12) 9. Hardy Whitfield
(13) 10. Mary Whitfield
(14) 11. Sarah Whitfield
(15) 12. Mildred Whitfield
(16) 13. Elizabeth Whitfield

(WT 4) THOMAS WHITFIELD

(Thomas, Thomas, Thomas)

Thomas Whitfield married 1740 to girl named Mary (1725-1792). He was of Josias Crump (1734-1812) marriage kinship who was staff officer and commissioner of specific supplies. Josias Crump born New Kent County, Virginia and died in Northampton County , North Carolina.

Thomas and Mary Whitfield had children.

(8) (WT 4) REUBEN WHITFIELD

(Thomas, Thomas, Thomas)

He was born about 1745 in Nansemond County, Virginia, and died at Nash County, North Carolina. He married in Virginia.

(20) 1. Ivey Whitfield
(21) 2. Reuben Whitfield
(22) 3. William Whitfield
    4. Miles Whitfield , and died 1782 in Isle of
       Wight County, Virginia.
    Others.

(6) (WT 4) SOLOMON WHITFIELD

(Thomas, Thomas, Thomas)

He lived in Nansemond County, Virginia. His children were probably the Solomon Whitfield descendants.

(23) (WT 5)   1. Solomon Whitfield

(7) (WT 4) JOHN WHITFIELD

(Thomas, Thomas, Thomas)

There are many of this name , and it is very hard to record the correct lineal.

(24) 1. John Whitfield

(WT 4) WILLIAM WHITFIELD

(Thomas, Thomas, Thomas)

William Whitfield was born in 1759 . He married,1779,to Elizabeth.

He was a soldier from Martin County, North Carolina in the Revolution.

He and Elizabeth Whitfield had children , and they appear in the northeast of North Carolina. He is of Joshua Jones (1756 ,born ,Halifax,North Carolina - died 1820) marriage kinship who was sheriff, canteen maker and artificer in wood. Joshua Jones married 1778 to Amaryllis _____ (1759-1820).

(25) 1. William Whitfield.

(WT 4) BENJAMIN WHITFIELD

(Thomas, Thomas, Thomas)

On August 12, 1772 Benjamin Whitfield and wife , Mary sold a plantation on Kingsale Swamp , Isle of Wight County, Virginia . We believe this Benjamin Whitfield a resident of Nash County, North Carolina area.

(10) (WT 4) ELISHA WHITFIELD

(Thomas, Thomas, Thomas)

He is a man living in Nash County, North Carolina area at the time.

(11) (WT 4) ZURAH WHITFIELD

(Thomas , Thomas, Thomas)

The son of Thomas Whitfield who was born 1721 and died 1781 in Nash County, North Carolina. He has a name like those connected with pedigree lines of England and John Whitfield.

(12) (WT 4) HARDY WHITFIELD

(Thomas. Thomas, Thomas)   In 1798, there are Hardy Whitfields in   Isle of Wight County, Virginia, in Tyrell County, and Nash County, North Carolina (27). In 1781 a Hardy Whitfield left a Will in Nash County, North Carolina.

(13) (WT 4) MARY WHITFIELD   (Thomas, Thomas, Thomas)
(14) (WT 4) SARAH WHITFIELD
(15) (WT 4) MILDRED WHITFIELD
(16) (WT 4) ELIZABETH WHITFIELD

(WT 4) REUBEN WHITFIELD

He lived in Isle of Wight County, Virginia , 1814.

Generation 5 and 6.

WT 5   REUBEN WHITFIELD
        (Ivey , Reuben, Thomas, Thomas, Thomas)
    Nansemond County, Virginia.

W 5   WILLIAM WHITFIELD
        William Whitfield , b. 1780
WT 5   (William , Thomas, Thomas, Thomas)
    1. ____   Whitfield married Mr. Powers, and they had
    two daughters.
        1. Ida T. Powers married Mr. Wilkins.

    2.   William Thomas Whitfield. He was b. 1819; d. 1909.

W 5 JOHN WHITFIELD

W 5 THOMAS WHITFIELD

WT 5 WILLIAM WHITFIELD
        (William, Thomas, Thomas, Thomas)
   He married,1809,to Temperance Jones (1783-1854). They were of
the kinship line of Charles Crump who died 1817 ; grandfather Josias
Crump married Mary Cook, died 1820.
    (17)   1. James Wesley Whitfield.

WT 6 WILLIAM THOMAS WHITFIELD
        (William, Thomas, Thomas, Thomas)
   William Thomas Whitfield (1811-1909) married,1841, Mrs. Mary
Jane Crump Squiggins , of Roanoke Rapids, North Carolina. They
lived in Beaufort, North Carolina , and later in Weldon, North
Carolina .   Children :
    1. Alice Whitfield ; married _____ Timberlake.
    2. Eugenia Whitfield ; married _____ Anderson.
    3. Charles Thomas Whitfield.
(Lieutenant Henry Timberlake with Virginia troops at Fort
Robinson; he took voyage in the fall of 1761 down the Holston and the
Tennessee River to the Overhill towns, and his was the beginning of
many voyages to come from the direction of Virginia.)

    ELIZABETH WHITFIELD married Miles Cary in Virginia .
Miles Cary lived 1703; and the third generation of Cary line.

WT   MILES WHITFIELD
             (Reuben , Thomas, Thomas, Thomas)
   Miles Whitfield was born in Virginia before 1740, and died
November 14, 1782 , Isle of Wight County, Virginia. He was living

there in 1773 , and then at Nansemond County, Virginia. The last date on a record for him was 1782.

Family Group: G 4   (John)

John Whitfield b. 1743 and d. January 2, 1832 in Granville County, North Carolina. He was a Revolution soldier, served three tours of duty in all of nine months.

He married in 1774 to Molly Grimsley. She died Nov. 15, 1839. John and Molly had nine children ; and survived by five of the children who were over 58 years in 1846.

1. Polly Whitfield
2. Sally Whitfield
3. Mary Whitfield   married John Vestal , and was
    living in 1846.
4. Martha Whitfield married James Hester and
    living in 1846.
5. William Whitfield living in 1846.
6. Elizabeth Whitfield
7. Nancy Whitfield
8. John W. Whitfield b. July 4, 1780.
    He filed pension claim # R 11396 on his father's
    Revolution service.
9. George Whitfield.

Descendants of William Whitfield & Elizabeth Goodman Whitfield

WILLIAM WHITFIELD   (WW 1)   G 1 North Carolina

He was born in England 1688 ca., and died 1770 when killed by Indians traveling to Lenoir County, North Carolina.

William Whitfield married Elizabeth Goodman (1697-1773) of Gates County, North Carolina in 1713. They had ten children :

1. William Whitfield
2. Matthew Whitfield
3. Luke Whitfield
4. Mary Whitfield
5. Patience Whitfield
6. Margaret Whitfield married Solomon Barfield,
    of Duplin County, North Carolina, and then married
                    Winkfield.
7. Elizabeth Whitfield
8. Sarah Whitfield
9. Charity Whitfield
10. Constantine Whitfield

---

*This North Carolina Genealogy has been published in the book : Whitfield, Bryan, Smith and Related Families.   Only those of this line who moved to Tennessee are in this book here.

(WW 2)   North Carolina Genealogy
WILLIAM WHITFIELD   (William)
     William Whitfield was born in Virginia of Nansemond County ,
May 20 , 1715, and died March 31, 1795, in North Carolina. He married
on Nov. 6, 1741, Rachel Bryan, and after her death married Frauzan
_____. They moved on that portion to become Lenoir County, North
Carolina . There they built Rockford house, then they moved to White
Hall, on the south bank of the Neuse River in Wayne County, No. C.
The wife, Rachel Bryan Whitfield was born June 10 , 1723 and died in
November 1780.
     William Whitfield was a member of the Governor's Council in 1779,
captain of a company of North Carolina Militia, and was at the battle of
Guilford Court House, North Carolina. He was in the Revolution War
service and lived in Wayne County, No. C. William and Rachel had
children: (WW 3)
        1. William Whitfield , b. June 1, 1743 , and married
              Hester Williams.
        2. Elizabeth Whitfield , b. 1745 ca. at White Hall, d. 1800 in
              Cumberland Settlement of North Carolina in Old Tennessee
              County. She married Alexander Smith and was living in
              Knox County, Tennessee , and then married Sir Farqu-
              hard Campbell. She had children.
        3. Sarah Whitfield
        4. Bryan Whitfield , b. Feb. 9, 1754 , and married Nancy Bryan.
        5. Charity Whitfield
        6. Needham Whitfield , b. 1758, and married Lucy Hatch.
        7. Rachel Whitfield
        8. Mary Whitfield
        9. Lewis Whitfield , b. 1766 , and married Charlotte Bryan.

Will of William Whitfield , Wayne County, North Carolina, Sept. 20,
1794. Recorded , April Court 1795.
     "To wife - Fruzen Whitfield , use of plantation and negroes ;
To four sons : William, Bryan, Needham, Lewis Whitfield ;
To three daughters , Elizabeth Campbell, Charity Smith, Rachel
Bryan ; To heirs of deceased daughters , Sarah Green and Mary
Bryan.   Executors : Sons, Needham and Lewis Whitfield.
Witnesses: Buckner Killebrew , William Herring , and William
Wilkins. "
(From - "Mississippi Genealogical Records Committee, N.S.D.A.R.
 1950 ." Typed and bound volume. Washington, D. C.)
                    Virginia and Tennessee Record
     In Knox County, Tennessee Superior Court in 1796 , Samuel Smith,
administered the estate of John Smith.

(WW 3)
WILLIAM WHITFIELD

North Carolina and Tennessee
(William, William)

William Whitfield III, b. June 1, 1743 at Rockford, at the home
of his parents who later moved across the Neuse River to White Hall,
modern Seven Springs, North Carolina.

William Whitfield married (1) in 1763 Hester Williams, (2) Mrs
Sarah (Oliver) Hurst, (3) in 1792 Hephzibah Hatch , (4) in 1795 Sarah
Bryan Hatch.

William Whitfield was the father of twenty-nine children , twenty-
one of whom reached maturity. He managed thirty-six slaves as early
as 1790. He was a prosperous good-spirited citizen.

He served in the Revolution War and in Battle of Moore's Creek
Bridge, Feb. 27, 1776 . In 1778 he was justice of peace for Dobbs
County, No. C. In 1779 the Governor was requested to furnish William
Whitfield, "Commissary to the State Regiment, with a Warrant, on
the Treasury for two thousand five hundred pounds."

In 1787 William Whitfield and his son William together with Joseph
Green were appointed "Directors and Trustees" for designing and
building the town of "Wanesboro." William had several other public
trusts. Did his son William Whitfield and Joseph Green help build
the Whitfield village in Clinch Mountain of Tennessee ? We think that
this family had the pioneer land grants. William's children who became orphans because of the death of their mothers moved to Tennessee with other orphans of Whitfield kinship in Virginia and North
Carolina.

Captain William Whitfield died in 1817 and is buried at the homestead in Wayne County near the Neuse River. He had forty descendants and relatives in the Revolutionary War.

William married Hester Williams and they had children :
1. William Whitfield 1764-1825
2. Mary Whitfield , born June 14, 1765 , and married
   Buckner Killebrew.
3. Bryan Whitfield , born 1766 ca and died 1825 in Tenn.
   He became orphan of the heirs of Coleburn Totevine
   receiving land grants in Tennessee. His brothers:
   William, Needham and Lewis Whitfield was in Tennessee with him. He married Anne Neville about 1797
   and Catherine Bailey about 1798. Children.
4. Joseph Whitfield , d. 1835.
5. Needham Whitfield, b. 1776 in North Carolina , and died
   1858 in Tennessee. He married 1798.
6. Lewis Whitfield
7. Elizabeth Whitfield
8. Rachel Whitfield
9. Sarah Whitfield , and (1) married Thomas Collier ;
   and (2) married Edward St. George.

North Carolina and Tennessee

JOHN SMITH .   Family group:
  1. Jane Smith married to Thomas Phelps
  2. Pheruba Smith married to John Hinton
  3. Anne Smith married to Needham Bryan
  4. Samuel Smith
  5. Elizabeth Smith married to William Bryan
  6. John Smith
  7. Alexander Smith , deceased, his wife, Elizabeth
     Whitfield Smith married later Farquhard (Farguard) Campbell.
     Alexander Smith died before 1796 and had for his Will the
     Executors, David Smith, Bryan Whitfield, and his wife ,
     Elizabeth Whitfield.

(WW)

NEEDHAM WHITFIELD (1758-1812) White Hall, Wayne County, North
Carolina. He received a thousand acres of land as a warrant for Re-
volutionary service in Eastern Tennessee in 1788. Some of his kin-
ship move to Montgomery County, Tennessee and purchased land there.
He married four times, (1) married Lucy Louisa Hatch , then (2)
Elizabeth Hatch , then (3) Sarah Watkins, and (4)   Mrs. Penelope Lane
Bush. He had many children. He is in generation three of North
Carolina Genealogy.

JESSE WHITFIELD
    In 1793 he received land in eastern Tennessee.

BRYAN WHITFIELD
    In 1793 he received land in eastern Tennessee, and settled his
land with children on the North side of Cumberland River, Tennessee
Country. He had son, Bryan Whitfield.

NEEDHAM WHITFIELD
    In 1787 and 1788 with William Whitfield and all, a company of
people settled land in Greene County , Tennessee.

WILLIAM WHITFIELD
    In 1787 and 1788 he and Needham Whitfield had families, and Whit-
field camp in Clinch Mountain on Clinch River and Bull Run River.
    We do not have a record of Whitfields who lived there in camp of
Clinch Mountain , 1790. It appears that William, Bryan and Lewis
moved from this Clinch Mountain kinship in camps, and cabins, to
Montgomery County, Tennessee. We have a record of their children.
Bryan Whitfield and Lewis Whitfield also received a land warrant for
land in eastern Tennessee in 1793. Lewis Whitfield received his land
grant in the eastern district on the north side of Tennessee River.
Bryan Whitfield received his land grant in Tennessee County on the

north side of Cumberland River.

This gives an idea how the North Carolinians settled land in Greene County, Hawkins and Montgomery Counties of Tennessee.

North Carolina Genealogy

(W W) WILLIAM WHITFIELD

(William, William, William)

William Whitfield (1764- d. Aug. 8, 1825). He was born in Wayne County, North Carolina. He married in Duplin County in 1785 , Mary Beck. He then moved to Christian County, Kentucky and later to Steward County, Tennessee where he died. Mary Whitfield , the wife , was living in Effingham County, Illinois in 1844. Tradition says they had thirteen children , but we know of ten.

1. William Whitfield
2. Needham Whitfield
3. Joseph Whitfield
4. Lewis Whitfield
5. Hester Whitfield . She married Charles Whitfield, son of William Whitfield III.
6. John Beck Whitfield
7. Harriet Whitfield
8. Mary Whitfield
9. Lucy Whitfield , died unmarried at the home of her brother Bryan Whitfield in Nauvoo, Illinois.
10. Bryan Whitfield

Some of these were children in North Carolina and Steward County, Tennessee which is adjacent land of Christian County, Kentucky, and Illinois.

North Carolina Genealogy

(W W) BRYAN WHITFIELD

(William, William , William)

Bryan Whitfield was born in North Carolina and moved to Montgomery County, Tennessee in 1793. He married Anne Neville about 1797 , and Catherine Bailey about 1798 . Bryan died 1825.

Children :
1. William Whitfield
2. James Whitfield
3. Mary Jane Whitfield . She married Charles Minor
4. Bryan Whitfield
5. Margaret Whitfield . She married _____ Harrington.
6. Duncan Whitfield . He married Lettie Scott.
    This family moved from Tennessee to Mississippi.
7. Catherine E. Whitfield . She married John F. Williams.
8. Ann Maria Whitfield
9. Rachel Whitfield married _____ Herring.

Tennessee

Some of these children crossed the Tennessee and visited on the west side of the River. Some of the early Henry County, Tennessee records may be of this family and their uncles. They were friends of the Killebrew families in Montgomery County, Tennessee. The children make a Tennessee family tree since Bryan Whitfield was a pioneer to Tennessee. *
.... And the same Bryan Whitfield ....

North Carolina and Tennessee
(W W) BRYAN WHITFIELD
(William, William , William)

Bryan wrote his name with an ending letter and then crossed it with an x and the name appears to be Bryant. He was born Bryan Whitfield in North Carolina about 1766, the son of William Whitfield III (1743-1817) and Hester Williams of Seven Springs , North Carolina near the Neuse River.

When he was a youth he became an orphan. After the death of his mother, Hester W. Whitfield he was an orphan heir of North Carolina residents. His uncles settled in western North Carolina off Salisbury road in Ansom region. Bryan Whitfield migrated to Tennessee in 1793 when 3, 174 acres of Tennessee land was granted to him. His brothers had migrated to Clinch Mountain in 1788. In the Company of Whitfield orphans , young boys, others from North Carolina and Virginia , Bryan Whitfield settled at Clinch Mountain and then in Christian , Kentucky and Montgomery County, Tennessee.

North Carolina warrants on land were issued soldiers of North Carolina Continental Line in lieu of pay , and many of these were sold or given in North Carolina by the soldiers or their heirs to those planning to settle in the western territory of North Carolina which is now Tennessee.

Bryan Whitfield was a responsible and prosperous person in frontier Cumberland region of Mero district in Tennessee. He married Anne Neville about 1797, and Catherine Bailey about 1798. She was a granddaughter of Daniel Williamson from Maryland. Bryan and Catherine Whitfield had eight children.

Bryan Whitfield was one of the commissioners of orphanage in Montgomery and Davidson Counties, and in Henry County, Tennessee. He appeared several times at the Davidson County, Tennessee Court and the Montgomery County Court. He witnessed many duties of the middle Tennessee government between 1793 and 1820. He helped the

---

* These pioneers from North Carolina to Tennessee have a genealogy found in the book Whitfield, Bryan, Smith and Related Families. pages 85 , 86 , 87.

overseers on the wilderness Port Royal Road and the Clarksville to
Russelville, Kentucky Road.

Bryan Whitfield was truly a Tennessee Pioneer. He cleared the wilderness roads, the Tennessee land to farm , fought the Indians , managed his
cabin plantation , and cared for many slaves.

Bryan Whitfield wrote his Will April 1822. He died 1825. On motion
ordered by the Court of Montgomery County, Tennessee, it was ordered at
Court that Charles Minor and William B. Whitfield be furnished with Letters
of Administration on the Estate of Bryan Whitfield , deceased with the Will
annexed , and the said Charles Minor and William B. Whitfield enter into
Bond and Security to satisfy the Court and qualify agreeable to law. Court
session July 1825 , the Will recorded...

"In the name of God Amen. I Bryan Whitfield of the County of Montgomery
and State of Tennessee being well of body and sound of mind but having in remem-
berance the uncertainty of human life , do make and ordain this my last Will and
Testament revoking all others viz I give unto my son William B. Whitfield a negro
boy Ennis , and all my lands on the north side of Spring Creek except the bluff
immediately on the Creek, which I reserve for the benefit of the mill, and one
bed an furniture. I give and bequeath unto my son James B. Whitfield two
negroes Simon and Emily . A horse saddle and bridle one bed an furniture
and fifty Dollars to finish his education. I give and bequeath unto my son Bryan
Whitfield a negro boy Allen, a horse saddle and bridle and a bed and furniture,
and a note on William Killebrew for forty two dollars to educate her — I give
and bequeath unto my daughter Margaret Ann Whitfield three negroes Iuch,
Grace and Buck a horse saddle and bridle, bed and furniture and two hundred
dollars from my personal estate to educate her. I further Will and bequeath
all my land on the south side of Spring Creek together with the Bluff on the
North side of the Creek to my three sons James, Bryan and Duncan to be equally
divided be tween them. It is further my wish that of either of my sons William
B. Whitfield , James B. Whitfield , Bryan Whitfield and Duncan Whitfield should
die without issue that the survivors survivor shall inherit the land of him or
them so dying without issue — and further if either of my daughters Mary Jane
Minor , Catharine Whitfield or Margaret Ann Whitfield shall die without issue,
that the property conveyed to them by this Will and its increase shall be equally
divided among the survivors or survivor of my daughters above mentioned or
Mary Jane Minor , Catharine Whitfield and Margaret Ann Whitfield. I hereby
ratify and confirm all that I have heretofore given to my daughter Rachel Herring.
And wish that after all my j ust debts are paid that the balance of the many
equally divided among my children William , James , Bryan, Duncan , Rachel,
Mary Jane, Catharine and Margaret Ann. Given under my hand and seal this
eighth day of April 1822.

Jas H. Bryan   Bryan Whitfield
Reuben Rofs
O.S. Walton
Chas. Bailey   Rendered at July   Term 1825

Land Grants to Bryan(t) Whitfield : 1793 year . Grant number 1765, 1778 , 1879 , 1909 , 1911 in Book E # 5 on pages 179 , 185, 235 , 249 , 250 . Grant number 487 , 1502 , 2201 , 2202 in Book B - 2 on pages 51 , etc. These grants of land in Sumner , Davidson, Williamson, Wilson , Rutherford Counties of Tennessee. In Book Q , pages 160 , 164 , 165 , 167 in Montgomery County, Tennessee, Bryan Whitfield's public records are borne as Bryant Whitfield . He was given the name Bryan Whitfield but most of his records are in the name of Bryant Whitfield. Records: Tennessee State Archives analytical index to Montgomery County, Tennessee Court Minutes 1813-1815 Vol. 5 Bryant Whitfield was at Clinch Mountain , Tennessee , and North Carolina.

Land Deed of Bryan Whitfield . State of North Carolina No. 1909. Know ye, that we have granted unto Bryant Whitfield orphan (opigna) of the Heirs of Coleburn Totevine a non Commission officer in the Continental line of said State one thousand acres of land in our bounty of Sumner. On the waters of Stones River, between the East and West fork nearly on a North East distance from the Black Fox's Camp, beginning about a quarter of a mile below the Spring near a small Creek at a Black Oak and White Oak, then West four hundred and fifty two poles to a White Oak , then South three hundred and seventy six poles to a stake, thence East four hundred and fifty two poles to a stake, thence north to the beginning. To hold to the said Bryan Whitfield his heirs and orphans for ever. Dated 20 th day , May 1793.

J. Glasgon Suntany   Ruth Dobbs Spaight
Warrant No. 1096 Wm. Nash
No chain carriers -

Bryan(t) Whitfield , May 20 , 1793 , land grants to Tennessee pioneer Indian land was the assignee in North Carolina of John Johnston , William Frost, Coleburn Totevina, Eran Bass, Aaron Nueson, John Smith , Hughey Stephenson . The Montgomery area purchases were made by himself.

" Andrew Jackson was often a visitor to the home which Moses Ridley, a Revolutionary soldier, built on the main stem of Stone's River at the northwest corner of the county 2, 800 acres of land granted to Ridley was hunting ground of Indians. " *

---

* A History of Rutherford County by Carlton C. Sims.

RELATED GENEALOGY

FOURTH GENERATION
Virginia and Tennessee

(9) SOLOMON WHITFIELD

He was born 1762 , Nansemond County, Virginia and died there Sept. 10, 1836. Enlisted 1780 in Revolution service. Pension S18281 , grant May 13, 1832.

(29) WILLIS WHITFIELD , wife NANCY WHITFIELD

They were of Raleigh County, North Carolina. He had a military service certificate , probably of Revolution service. R 11395.

(30) WILLIS WHITFIELD, wife RHODA WHITFIELD

He was born Nash County, North Carolina , 1760. He married Rhoda who died Sept. 3, 1826 in Cannon County, Tennessee. He was a private Revolution soldier in the Company of Captain Carter , com - manded by Col. Source in North Carolina line for seventeen months. They received a pension. He was in Rutherford County, Tennessee , August 1832. They had children : Four boys and two girls, from seven to twenty five years in 1820. Willis and Rhoda were over 45 years in 1820.

Family group.

(31) WILLIS WHITFIELD , wife RHODA ALLEN WHITFIELD

He was born in Virginia or North Carolina ; and died Sept. 3 , 1836 in Tennessee at Sumner County, or Rutherford County. He mar- ried Rhody , daughter of Arthur and Elizabeth Allen , November 1, 1788 . He served in the Revolution service. Rhody Whitfield was born Dec. 1, 1767. They moved to Sumner County in 1792. After Willis Whit- field died his widow was living in Cannon County , Tennessee in January 1840.   They had twelve children :

(32) 1. Ansil Whitfield , b. Aug. 25, 1780 in Virginia or North Carolina.

(33) 2. Wright Whitfield , b. March 20 , 1791 in Va. or No. C.

3. Christian Whitfield , b. Nov. 1, 1793 in Christian County, Kentucky , or Sumner County, Tennessee.

4. Sally Whitfield , b. May 5, 1795 in Tennessee.

5. Temperance Whitfield , b. Feb. 26 , 1797 in Tennessee.

6. Rhody Whitfield , b. Dec. 27 , 1798 in Tennessee.

(34) 7. Thomas Y. Whitfield, b. Feb. 5, 1801 in Tennessee.

8. Arthur Allen Whitfield , b. Jan. 30, 1803 in Tennessee.

(35) 9. Willis Whitfield , b. Jan. 30, 1805 in Tennessee.

(36) 10. Eli Whitfield , b. July 2, 1807.

11. Elizabeth Eason Whitfield , b. Feb. 26, 1810 in Tennessee.

(37) 12. Alfred Whitfield , b. Jan. 19, 1812

The descendants of these children are found in the middle Counties of Tennessee: Williamson, Davidson, Rutherford , Wilson, Cannon, Coffee, Maury , and Hickman Counties of Tennessee , and elsewhere.

(13) ELISAH WHITFIELD

He was in May Court session 1754 in Bertie County, North Carolina. Son of Elisah Whitfield.

(38) JAMES WHITFIELD

He was   living 1797 in Sumner County, Tennessee , and was an adult then. He may be the son of Bryan Whitfield or one of the brothers. The name appears on a Sumner County record.

(28) BRYAN WHITFIELD , and wife, ELIZABETH WHITFIELD

Bryan Whitfield and wife Elizabeth Whitfield lived in 1796 in Hamilton district of Knox County, Tennessee. He was a relative of Elizabeth Whitfield , wife of Alexander Smith , and later wife of Sir Farquhard Campbell.

KENTUCKY RECORDS

Catharine Whitfield married Thomas Ogilvie Nov. 3, 1775 , and resided in Kentucky.

Thomas Ogilvie was a British soldier in the Revolution War , and fought in western North Carolina.

Elizabeth Whitfield married Giles Cooper Sept. 12, 1765 and resided in Kentucky.

Bryant Whitfield was born Feb. 17 , 1793 , and died Dec. 6, 1863 in Kentucky. Wife, Seanea Whitfield is buried beside him in Kentucky . She was born Nov. 17, 1802, and died Nov. 14, 1884.

TENNESSEE RECORDS

(39) THOMAS WHITFIELD lived in Davidson County, Tennessee in 1794.

(40) JOHN WHITFIELD lived in Davidson County, Tennessee in 1794.

(41) ESTHER WHITFIELD lived in Davidson County, Tennessee in 1794.

These names appear on an old D. A. R. chapter record on Tennessee located in the University of California Library in the Document Department.

We believe an ANSEL WHITFIELD also lived in Davidson County, Tennessee at this time.

We can make a case over ESTHER WHITFIELD. She is a Virginian. In 1752 the vestry of Suffolk Parish in Nansemond County took care of orphans. In 1758 Thomas Whitfield died and Matthew Whitfield and Esther Whitfield were orphans. Matthew Whitfield was left with William Goodwin and Esther was placed with George Whitfield . 350 pounds were allowed for each of the children in 1759 and 1760, but no allowance for Esther.

A GEORGE WHITFIELD was a pioneer to Greene County from Suffolk, Virginia. Esther was a pioneer to Cumberland Settlement then of North Carolina. The same Esther Whitfield married , or her daughter married John Fletcher , November 5, 1799 in Davidson County, Tennessee.

NORTH CAROLINA -TENNESSEE

(WW) LEWIS WHITFIELD

(William, William, William)

Lewis Whitfield left North Carolina in 1793 and settled land grant along with brothers Needham Whitfield , and Bryan Whitfield in Tennessee. He married Elizabeth Wimberly, daughter of Joseph or John Wimberly and then later married Sarah Diggs, a widow.

G 4

Children of Lewis Whitfield and Elizabeth Whitfield:
1. Needham Whitfield ; md. Sallie Bourne.
2. Lewis Whitfield ; md. Ann Williams, a cousin.
3. Robert Whitfield
4. Sarah Whitfield
5. Elizabeth Whitfield ; md. (1) Ila Metcalf , (2) Thomas Trigg.
   Six children by her first husband.
6. George Whitfield
7. Joseph W. Whitfield ; b. Aug. 23, 1806 ; md. Mrs. Miriam Richardson Whitfield Fort. Second marriage.
8. Bryan Whitfield
9. Susan Whitfield ; md. Joseph Fort.
10. Catherine Whitfield ; md. James Buckner Osborne.
    Their children moved to Texas.

Lewis Whitfield's grandson, William Whitfield (1785-1810) married 1808, Elizabeth Wimberly, daughter of George Wimberly III and Pheraba Hinton. After his death the widow married William Fort and moved to Auburn , eight miles south of Raleigh , North Carolina. They had kinship to settle at Montgomery County, Tennessee.

THOMAS WHITFIELD of Suffolk, Virginia in 1790 was the attorney for GEORGE WHITFIELD of Washington County, Tennessee , then western North Carolina. G 5

_____ Whitfield came from North Carolina and settled Hickman County, Tennessee at Lick Creek. He came to Tennessee about the time Methodist preacher _____ Williamson came from Baltimore , Maryland, who had a daughter Minerva Williamson and other children. The preacher Williamson married Polly Graves who came from Baltimore, Maryland 1799. Grandfather Whitfield settled at Williamson County, Tennessee , and moved to Hickman County, Tennessee .

G 6

FELIX GRUNDY WHITFIELD
He was born about 1815 on Lick Creek, Hickman County, Tennessee and died there. He was a farmer. Felix G. married daughter of Preacher Williamson and Polly Graves Williamson of Williamson County, Tennessee. Felix Whitfield and Minerva Williamson married January 3, 1837 in Williamson County, Tennessee. They had three sons and girl . Felix Grundy Whitfield is on 1840 Hickman County, Tennessee Census. Wife was the same age. Children:
(112) 1. Thomas Harrison Whitfield
(113) 2. Felix Whitfield , between 10 to 15 years.
     3. Smith Whitfield , under 5 years.
     4. Girl - Whitfield , under 5 years.

SARAH WHITFIELD 1747- 1780. She married May 19, 1768 to Colonel JOSEPH GREEN of Wayne County, North Carolina. She had seven children. Two of the sons married Misses Martha Jeffries and Elizabeth Jeffries of Franklin, Tennessee about 1800.

Sarah Whitfield was the daughter of William Whitfield II; and the great aunt to Bryan Whitfield . *

FIFTH GENERATION

G5

TENNESSEE

(42) REBECCA WHITFIELD

Rebecca Whitfield , born in Virginia. She was the daughter of Harrison Whitfield who came to Tennessee in 1808. She married Lewis Allen Oct. 11, 1823 in Williamson County, Tennessee. Some of the children of their marriage moved to Texas.

(43) ELIZA WHITFIELD, born in Virginia or Tennessee. She married Oct. 25, 1825 Robert C. Owen.

(44) MARTHA ANN WHITFIELD CHARTER

She was born 1812 in Williamson County, Tennessee, the daughter of Wilkins Whitfield and Polly Mary Whitfield. She married Robert Charter June 7, 1827 of Williamson County, Tennessee. They had five daughters. First daughter , born about 1828 named Catharine Whitfield who married young in Tennessee . They were the owners of a Franklin , Tennessee mercantile business. Robert Charter was a well known person and trained many boys in the mercantile business. He died 1847 in Franklin, Tennessee.

(45) WILLIAM WHITFIELD

William Whitfield came to Tennessee and settled in Sumner County, Tennessee in 1794 . He was in the company of Willis and Rhoda Whitfield of Sumner County, Tennessee. He had a few children . He purchased his own land deed.

(48) WILLIAM WHITFIELD

He was born 1780 in Virginia or North Carolina. He may be the same William Whitfield living 1794 in Sumner County, Tennessee, but perhaps there are two William Whitfields. He and his wife of age forty five years were living in Williamson County, Tennessee with their seven children .

1. Boy , 20 to 30 years of age.	
2. Boy, 5 to 10 years.	
3. Boy, 5 to 10 years.	Names of the girls:
4. Boy, under 5 years.	Rebecca
5. Girl, 5 to 10 years.	Mary
6. Girl , 10 to 15 years.	Lucy
7. Girl , 15 to 20 years.	Nancy

* Whitfield, Bryan, Smith and Related Families , page 70 .

(46) JOHN WHITFIELD   G 5

   John Whitfield was born in Virginia , about 1770 , and moved to Tennessee with his family. He died before 1820 in Williamson County , Tennessee. His wife was fifty years of age in 1820, and was living with her son, John Whitfield who was about twenty-five years of age , and unmarried , at Williamson County. After her death the son, John ,moved to a location southeast of Stones River. The descendants were named John Whitfields , who lived in Rutherford, Cannon , and Coffee Counties in Tennessee.

(Thomas)

(50) HARRISON WHITFIELD, and wife , POLLY MARY SLEDGE WHIT-
  FIELD.

   He was born 1783 ca. in Sussex County, Virginia , the son of Thomas and Winifer Whitfield. He came with his mother, brothers , and sisters to Franklin Town in Williamson County, Tennessee in 1808. Harrison Whitfield married Polly Sledge and their marriage bond was dated August 18, 1804 , Albemarle Parish , Sussex County, Virginia. Harrison and Polly Whitfield had ten children:

 1. Thomas Whitfield

(42)2. Rebecca Whitfield

 3. Boy , born between 1810-1820 , Williamson County, Tennessee.

 4. Boy , born 1810-1820 ; died young.

 5. Boy, born between 1825 - 1830 , Williamson County, Tennessee.

 6. Boy, born between 1825-1830 , Williamson County, Tennessee.

 7. Girl , died young.

(50) 8. Nancy Whitfield , born 1811 and died 1885 . She married
   J. Winstead , and lived in Williamson County, Tennessee.

 9. Girl , born 1814 ca.

 10. Girl , born 1826 ca.

Harrison Whitfield died 1864 in Franklin, Tennessee.

   Harrison Whitfield had an older woman living in the house , according to the Census record, and it may have been his aunt Francis Whitfield. His mother , Winifer lived with him after her husband's death. Winifer Whitfield lived in the home of the brother , Wilkins Whitfield, at Franklin, Tennessee , and died there on July 9, 1838.

   Harrison Whitfield   had a plantation , and a land grant of fifty acres in Davidson County, Tennessee in January 30 , 1834. On the Census record he had five slaves , and eight children in Williamson County. The sons were named Thomas, John, Felix , Harrison . Harrison Whitfield , Sr. died in 1864 at Williamson County, Tennessee.

   The descendants appear in Williamson and Hickman Counties of Tennessee : and the son Harrison Whitfield moved to Lincoln County , Texas in 1870 with his family.

   In 1808 a few houses marked the towns of Franklin and Columbia, and Nashville, Tennessee consisted of a few scattered log houses.

G 5

(51) WILKINS WHITFIELD , wife Polly Mary Sturdivant Whitfield.
(Thomas , ___, ___, ___) Virginia (1561 John)

Wilkins Whitfield was born 1781 ca in Albemarle Parish of Sussex County, Virginia, the son of Thomas Whitfield (d. 1794) and Winifer Whitfield.

Wilkins Whitfield grew up on farm land in Sussex County, Virginia, and had brothers William, Harrison, Jack (John) , and sisters Mary, Elizabeth , Francis , Martha Patty, Betty , and Nancy.

In 1801 Wilkins Whitfield married Polly Mary Sturdivant. The marriage bond of the Minister's Return is dated 23 December 1801 , Sussex County, Virginia. Surety was Harrison Whitfield. Albemarle Parish.

In 1808 they moved to Franklin town, Williamson County, Tennessee with other Whitfield families of his kinship. He settled on the land grant of Bryan Whitfield in Franklin , or that of purchase . He has record in open Court 1816 and 1827 with estate inventory accounts. He attended open court in Franklin , Tennessee. At the inventory account of Samuel Mc Cutchen, deceased, in "Court session July 1816 , Wilkins Whitfield bought one colt $ 5.12 1/2 , Jas. Shaw's note W. Whitfield $5.12 1/2 , Jesse Porter , Colt for $ 10.12 1/2 , note J. Porter , sec."

In the inventory account 1817 of Elizah Hunter account of sales in open court session October 1817. Wilkins Whitfield bought four briddles for $ 3.56 1/4. *

Franklin, Tennessee had Indians living there when the settlers came from Virginia and was part of Davidson County until Williamson County was formed. Wilkins Whitfield had communication with the Council or travellers of State that passed through Franklin for he named his children after the new Presidents of the United States. In April 1819 when President James Monroe came to Nashville for a brief visit and stayed with Andrew Jackson , the new baby of Mary Whitfield was named from him.

In open Court , 1827 , Wilkins Whitfield received article - one cross out saw $ 3.56 1/2 . Part of the residue of the property belonging to the estate of Joseph German, Seur., deceased , October 9 , 1827. **

He is on the 1820 Census of Williamson County , Tennessee with eight children and thirteen slaves.

Wilkins Whitfield and Polly Mary knew the families of Franklin, and his brothers and sisters and their married families lived there in Williamson County, Tennessee.

A few of Wilkins Whitfield's children remained in Williamson County when they married but most of them moved to Hickman County where they bought farms near Council Bend creating the town of Hickman County near Centerville called Whitfield Town. The children assisted in the mercantile business there.

Wilkins and Polly Mary had children : The children were seven boys and four girls.

⊛ Corrections and change from the first edition of this book.

G 5

children G 6

1.   Henry Whitfield , b. 1802 ca, Sussex County, Virginia ,

2.   George Whitfield , b. March 12 , 1806 in Sussex Co., Virginia,
        and died August 12, 1894 in Dallas County, Texas near Garland
        town. His family and children moved to Texas.
3. William Whitfield , lived in Tennessee.
4. Harrison Whitfield , born in Tennessee.
5. Thomas Jefferson Whitfield , born Feb. 10 , 1810 in Williamson Co.,
        Tennessee , and died January 10, 1873 in Perry County, Tennessee.
6. Martha Ann Whitfield, born 1812 in Williamson Co., Tennessee,
        and died 1847 in Franklin, Tennessee. Married Robert Charter.
7. Theodosia Whitfield , born 1816 in Williamson County, Tennessee,
        and died Oct. 1, 1839 in Hickman County, Tennessee.
8. Sarah Whitfield , born 1817 in Williamson County, Tennessee, and
        moved to Hickman County, Tennessee, and lived to old age as
        Sarah Nichols.
9. John Wilkins Whitfield , born 1818 in Williamson County, Tennessee,
        and died October 27 , 1879 near Halletsville in Lavoca County, Texas.
10. James Monroe Whitfield , born 1819 in Williamson County, Tennessee
        and he lived in the county, and moved to Texas with his family.
11. Virginia C. Whitfield , born 1821 ca, youngest child . She married
        Daniel Cliffe on November 15 , 1842 in Williamson County, Tenn.

The descendants of his children are in Tennessee and Texas. The
sons moved to Texas because they "came into possession of thousands
of acres of land in Texas." They " sold the land for small sum of money
for in those days land was looked upon as blame nothing." John Wilkins
Whitfield and Dr Daniel Mc Phail, the husband of sister Sarah , and
others of the family fought in the Mexican War not far from Texas.
        His son, George Washington Whitfield says he died at age sixty
(1841 year). Robert A. Hill was the executor for a Wilkins Whitfield
in 1852. The wife, Polly Mary Sturdivant Whitfield lived to be eighty
years old.
        Robert Hill was in court at the 1852 session versus William Spence.
"It is ordered by the Court in this cause by the consent of the parties that
each party leave to take deposition generally upon giving to the adverse
party the notice required by the rules in Chancery and that the plaintiff
take depositions of Leroy G. W. Napier this day in the law office of
Thomas Bateman in Centerville and that this order be notice to the
defendant." Recorded in the Hickman County, Tennessee Court Minutes
1844-1855.

* Williamson County, Tennessee. Wills and Inventories, Vol B ,
    1811-1818, p 348   and ** Williamson County, Tennessee Records
    of Wills 1825-1830. Part II, p. 282.

Western Weekly Review , Franklin, Tennessee , dated 13 July 1838 printed this Death Notice : "On Monday 9th at the residence of Wilkins Whitfield, Esq. Mrs Whitfield , a upwards of 100 years. She lived long, respected, loved and esteemed by all who knew her and died in good old age, mourned, regretted by a large circle of relatives and friends. "

The only person that would be this age would have to be Winifer Whitfield, the Mother of Harrison and Wilkins Whitfield.

WILKINS WHITFIELD , wife ELIZABETH RIDLEY WHITFIELD.

He was born in Tennessee, the son of a brother to Wilkins Whitfield 1781 ca- d. 1851 , or a son of one of their children. Wilkins and Elizabeth Ridley married Sept. 3 , 1846 in Williamson County, Tennessee. The marriage was solemnized by Robert Davis. William H. Hill was bondsman.

****

John Whitfield 1561 of England is regarded as the pedigree ancestor of Tennesseans. This is a tradition that has been printed and is now a legend. The pedigree names in seventeenth century were John, Hugh , Henry, and Thomas but many names are the American short names that originated in the back woods and hill regions such as Briant, Needham and Ansel , and the initialed name.

The tradition has been passed from the first Thomas Jefferson Whitfield to those living that the first grandfather was WILL WHITFIELD. Does this family legend refer to the first man from England to Virginia in the seventeenth century , or does it give the name of a Virginian grandfather whose descendants were Tennessee pioneers to settle in Williamson County, Tennessee, and after others of the name Whitfield had settled at Montgomery County and Sumner County, Tennessee ?

These traditional sayings are important for a slip from a genealogical tree when transplanted to a new soil resembles the parent tree as surely as does a cutting from any of Nature's forest.

****

G 5

(58) JOHN WHITFIELD   (John   )

John Whitfield was born about 1782 in Virginia . His ancestors came from England to North Carolina then over to Pulaski, Tennessee to Hickman County, Tennessee. John Whitfield appears on the 1820 Census of Giles County, Tennessee. He has a descendant living in Paris, Tennessee in 1960 , John Whitfield who is writing this genealogy of the Giles County early pioneer.

John Whitfield and his wife were about the same age , and had seven children , born in Giles County, Tennessee , and North Carolina.

This John Whitfield was a later immigrant period   , and he had a son named John Whitfield (WJ 6) , and he had a son named John Whitfield (WJ 7) , and he had child John Whitfield (WJ 8) who had a son named John Whitfield who is a medical chiropractor , 1960, in Paris, Tenn.

In 1805 in Steward County lived the following in Tennessee :
                    Daniel Whitfield
                    William Whitfield
                     Charles Whitfield et al
                    Jessie Whitfield
                    C. Whitfield , Ann Whitfield , Mary
                       Whitfield , Willis Whitfield.
(Stewart County, Deed Book 1804-1806 , Tennessee , compiled
by W. P. A. Historical Records Survey).

G 6 ca.

WILLIS WHITFIELD

He married Nancy Rayford , Oct. 31, 1846 in Guilford County,
North Carolina.

(59) MATHEW WHITFIELD   G5

(_____)

He was born in Virginia or North Carolina. He and his wife ,
Levina Whitfield lived in Rutherford County, Tennessee with their
children born in Tennessee. Mathew Whitfield was born about 1772
and died leaving a Will in 1827 . Children:

1. Mathew Whitfield , born about 1814 . He married Fanny R.
   Monahan, July 30, 1834 in Rutherford County, Tennessee.
2. Benjamin Whitfield was born about 1805 . He married
   Elizabeth Herrod , July 5, 1827 in Rutherford County,
   Tennessee.
3. William Whitfield was between 10 and 26 years of age
   in 1820.
4. Mary Whitfield
5. Girl

Will of Mathew Whitfield : "In the name of God Amen - I, Mathew
Whitfield of the County of Rutherford and State of Tennessee being of
perfect sound mind and memory - Blessed be God, do this sixth day
of September in the year of our Lord one thousand eight hundred and
twenty three make and publish this my last will and testament in manner   following : That is first, I give and bequeath to my wife Levina
the whole of my estate both real and personal of every discription
for her use entirely during her natural life or widowhood and at her
marriage or death , then my will and pleasure is that all my personal
estate be sold at public sale by my executors and the amount arising
from said sale to be equally divided between my children namely ,
Benjamin , Mary and Mathew and all my real estate or landed property at that time, I allow to my daughter Mary and lastly I do hereby appoint and ordain my wife Levina and my son William Whitfield
executors of this my last Will and Testament and I do hereby revoke

all other wills and testaments by me made and establish this and no other to be my last Will and Testament. In testimony whereof I have hereunto set my hand and seal the day and year first above written - Signed and sealed in presents of,

      H. Robinson, Jurat   his mark

      Jane Robinson   Mathew X

      Levina Robinson, Jurat   Whitfield

                              (Seal)   *

Levina Robinson Whitfield had a land deed to 168 acres in Rutherford County, Tennessee on June 19, 1837. The children lived in Rutherford County, Tennessee and the descendants are there.

(60) JOHN WHITFIELD   (_____)

      John Whitfield was born about 1770 in Virginia or North Carolina. We favor these births to be in Virginia. John and his wife were living 1820 in Rutherford County, Tennessee. His earlier kinship is in Williamson County, Tennessee, and the descendants are in the Stones River areas. The 1820 Cenus of Rutherford County, Tennessee gives this information:

        1. Boy - under 10 yrs.   A son named, John .

        2. Boy- under 10 yrs.

        3. Boy- 10 to 16 yrs.

        4. Girl - under 10 yrs.

        5. Girl - under 10 yrs.

        6. Girl - 10 to 16 yrs.

        7. Girl - 10 to 16 yrs.

The father , John Whitfield was in Court in 1823.

(61) THOMAS WHITFIELD   G5 or 6

      Thomas G. Whitfield married Melinda Guiley, Dec. 31, 1825 in Rutherford County, Tennessee , and they had children.

(32) ANSIL WHITFIELD   G 5

          (Willis, grandfather in Sumner and Rutherford County, Tennessee)

      Ansil Whitfield was born August 25, 1780 in Virginia or North Carolina. She was the daughter of Willis and Rhody Whitfield. She married a William Whitfield . They appeared in Rutherford Co., Tennessee Court in 1817. They had children :

      Son, ANSEL WHITFIELD

Ansil is a boy's name but it is used for girl in Whitfield family.

*Rutherford County, Tennessee , Wills, Settlements , Inventories , Vol 7 - 1827-1830 , p 294 of the State of Tennessee Library analytical index, and the 1820 Rutherford County, Tennessee Census.

ANSEL WHITFIELD   (_____)

Ansel Whitfield was a pioneer to Tennessee. He was probably in the company of Willis Whitfield and William Whitfield who migrated to Sumner County from eastern district of Tennessee and Virginia. He was a Volunteer of Tennessee in the War of 1812. He paid a poll tax that year from Rutherford County, Tennessee. He may have married in 1815. A son, Ansel Whitfield, who may have been the father to one of the following also named Ansel Whitfield.

(62) ANSEL WHITFIELD

He lived in Rutherford County, Tennessee. He had a daughter Milberry Whitfield and represented her in Court April 19, 1825 when she versus Willis Whitfield. An Ansel Whitfield married Janey Tisdale March 8, 1815 in Wilson County, Tennessee and resided there. He had Will of his father-in-law Ed Tisdale 1816 in Court in Wislon County, Tennessee. It is unknown if these are one person or two persons with the name. The father of Milberry Whitfield of 1825 ; and the following of a like name appear as two persons.

(63) ANSEL WHITFIELD

Father migrated to Tennessee. He married Fanny Tisdale March 8, 1815 in Dickson County, Tennessee.

LAVINA WHITFIELD

Had 168 acres in Rutherford County, Tennessee on May 27, 1846. Kinship of Levina Whitfield.

(64) HENRY W. WHITFIELD

Henry W. Whitfield purchased a land deed Feb. 18, 1825 in Madison County, Tennessee. We do not know his family but he appears to be the first in Madison County of Tennessee.

Land Deeds

CARTER B. WHITFIELD had land deed 1830 in White County, Tennessee. He married and has descendants in White County. There was an early JOHN WHITFIELD in the County. John Whitfield had land deed 1829 in White County, Tennessee.
JOHN WHITFIELD had land deed 1828 in White County, Tenn.
THOMAS WHITFIELD had land deed 1828 in White Co., Tenn.
The kinship from this County in area of San Antonio, Texas in the 19 th and 20th century.

*Tennessee Land Deeds. Copies of the Court minutes of Rutherford and Wilson County, Tennessee found in Historical Notes written by Vallie Jo Fox Whitfield.

(65) THOMAS I. WHITFIELD   G 5
      He was born in Virginia or North Carolina about 1780. He and his
wife over forty-five years in 1830 was living in Hickman County, Tenn.
with their children. He may have come to Tennessee with his father.
      1. Boy - 20 to 30 yrs.
      2. Boy - 20 to 30 yrs.   Son named, Thomas.
      3. Boy - 20 to 30 yrs.
      4. Girl - 15 to 20 yrs.
      One slave.
He was a relative and friend of George W. Whitfield on Duck River in
Whitfield Town. Thomas I. and George appear in Hickman Court together,
and were cousins of Virginian grandfather.

(66) WILLIS WHITFIELD   G 6
      He married Alemeada Rhodes . Son of a person in Rutherford
County, Tennessee. He married July 27 , 1825 in Rutherford Co. , Tenn.

(34) THOMAS Y. WHITFIELD   (Willis)
      Thomas Yough Whitfield was born Feb. 5, 1801 in Tennessee in
Sumner or Rutherford County . He married and had children and the
descendants in the Rutherford County.

(36) ELI WHITFIELD   (Willis)
      Eli was the tenth child of Willis and Rhody Whitfield. She was
born July 2, 1807 in Tennessee. Resided Rutherford County, Tennessee
1835 and descendants there in this location. Eli married Martin Clark.

(37) ALFRED WHITFIELD   (Willis)
      Alfred Whitfield was the youngest child of Willis and Rhody
Whitfield of Rutherford County , b. Jan. 19, 1812. He resided Rutherford
County, Tennessee, and was living in 1835.

(67) WILLIAM WHITFIELD
      He died 1834 in Lawrence County, Tennessee then the country
of the Chickasaw Indians above Mississippi. He had a large sale of his
estate in Lawrence County in Tennessee , August 1834 , and sold both
cattle and merchandise of household. He was a farmer among the first
settlers in Lawrence County which was then Hickman County.
Children :   (68) 1. James Whitfield
         (69) 2. John L. Whitfield
            3. Sally Whitfield
The family resided in Lawrence County, Tennessee.

COURT MINUTES AND ORPHANS
      In the Henry County, Tennessee Court Minutes for 1836-1849 are
a list of the Whitfield children that were orphans. Their fathers were
from North Carolina and from Virginia . They are cared for by John,
Needham, William and Lewis Whitfield of Henry County, Tennessee.
There was another orphanage in Montgomery County, Tennessee , and
some of the same people help the children in Henry County, which was
across the Tennessee River.
* Henry County Court Minutes 1836-1849, Tennessee.
 * Eli Whitfield , a correction .

(70) JAMES WHITFIELD , died before 1848. His children :
      1. Briant Whitfield   (A Briant Whitfield had 1811 land
      2. Lucy Whitfield   deed in Steward County, Tenn.)
      3. Sarah Whitfield

After James Whitfield's death the Court of Henry County, Tenn.
appointed Lewis Whitfield of the same county the guardian for the children in 1848 , and Isaac Wimberly, John Whitfield , and Needham Whitfield secured the Bond.

(71) WILLIAM WHITFIELD

      He lived in Henry County, Tennessee , and died about 1842. He
had child, Elizabeth Whitfield and she had a guardian, John Walker of
Henry County, Tennessee.

     The Whitfield orphans in Henry County, Tennessee between 1836
and 1849 were the following children:
    Elizah Whitfield . Hannah Whitfield , James Whitfield ,John Whitfield,
    Elizabeth Whitfield, Lewis Whitfield , Needham Whitfield , Sally
    Whitfield , William Whitfield.

(33) WRIGHT WHITFIELD   (Willis)

      He was born March 20,1791 . First son of Willis and Rhody Whit-
field of Sumner County, Tennessee. He was born in Virginia or North
Carolina. He lived near Wilkins Whitfield in Franklin, Tennessee in
Williamson County , 1820. He may have died after this date for he does
not appear on Census , or he lived on Wilkins Whitfield plantation and
was probably unmarried.

(72) AARON WHITFIELD

      Aaron Whitfield was born in Tennessee or Virginia. He was
a soldier in the Mexican War. He died Jan. 14, 1848 in service at Mexico
City, Mexico . Parents in the Hickman County location.

(50) HARRISON WHITFIELD   (Harrison, Thomas) G 6

      He appears on 1840 Williamson County, Tennessee Census with
wife and children. He was living 1851 in Hickman County, Tennessee.
Harrison Whitfield moved from Williamson County, Tennessee in 1870
to Lincoln County, Texas. He was the son of Harrison Whitfield and
grandson of Thomas Whitfield and Winifer Whitfield of Sussex County,
Virginia. He had brothers named John and Felix , and sisters named
Rebecca Whitfield and Nancy Whitfield. Harrison Whitfield born 1783
and died 1864 was the father of this son Harrison Whitfield of Texas.
He moved from Lincoln County, Texas to Cook County, Texas and has
records there. Harrison Whitfield married Sophronia Conn about 1845
in Williamson County, Tennessee, and later the family with children
moved to Texas.

(49) THOMAS J. WHITFIELD

      His parents were born in Tennessee, and he was born 1845
in Tennessee. He married Marthy ____ who was born 1855 in Tenn.,
and her parents born in Tennessee. He was a farmer in Humphreys

County, Tennessee near Bakerville , civil district number one.

Children: 1. Lafayette Whitfield , b. 1867

                2. Millie Whitfield , b. 1872

                3. James D. Whitfield , 1877. He appears in Court

                     Minutes.

(1880 Census of Humphreys County, Tennessee)

(73) JOHN WHITFIELD

      His father was born in Tennessee and living with him in 1840 in Hickman County, Tennessee. The father between 70 and 80 years. Wife of John Whitfield   was   born between 1810 and 1820. Children :   1. Boy - under 5 years

                    2. Boy - under 5 years

                    3. Girl - born about 1829

(1840 Census of Hickman County, Tennessee)

(74) WILLIAM WHITFIELD .

      On the 1840 Census of Hickman County, Tennessee , William Whitfield was under 40 years, his wife was under 30 years.

        1. Boy - under 5 years

        2. Girl - under 5 years

        3. Girl - under 10 years

        4. Girl - under 5 years

SIXTH GENERATION

(52) GEORGE W. WHITFIELD   (Wilkins, Thomas, ____)

      George W. Whitfield was born in Sussex County, Virginia, February 12, 1806 , son of Wilkins and Polly Mary. His father moved to Williamson County, Tennessee at Franklin in 1808. In 1836 he married Louisa King by whom he had three children : Daniel, Virginia , and Sarah. Louisa King Whitfield died at the age of twenty-five in 1848. George married then Sarah Bond;and had children born in Texas who were John, Thomas, Dundenah, Belle , Walter C and daughter Davis.

      George W. Whitfield and family went to Texas in December5, 1849. He first located in Harrison County, Texas and stayed four years. Then a year in Limestone County, and then moved to Dallas County , Texas and purchased 160 acres of land , located a mile northwest of Garland town. He increased his land estate to 900 acres. In 1892 he was eighty-five years of age and living in Garland.

      A Biography of George W. Whitfield appears at the back of this book.

      In 1849 in Hickman County, Tennessee lived the following of his kinship : (75) I.S. Whitfield , (76) I. W. Whitfield , (77) Felix I. Whitfield , Mary Whitfield, (78) William Whitfield , (79) Thomas B. Whitfield , Sarah Whitfield.

GEORGE WHITFIELD married Wareena Spence Oct. 24, 1843 in Davidson County, Tennessee.

(56) JOHN WILKINS WHITFIELD   (Wilkins , Thomas , _____)

     John Wilkins Whitfield was born March 11, 1818 in Franklin , Tennessee of Williamson County. The son of Wilkins and Polly Mary from Sussex County, Virginia. He married Catharine Dansby April 13, 1839. They had one daughter. After Catharine died in 1846 he married Sarah B. Dibrell, a daughter of General George Dibrell. She was born Dec. 11, 1827 in White County, Tennessee. They married in Davidson County, Tennessee on May 28 , 1853.

     John W. Whitfield served in the Mexican War , and in 1852 he was Clerk and Master of Hickman County Chancery Court. In 1853 he moved to Independence, Missouri in 1853 to serve as Indian agent to the Pottawatomies Indians at Westport, Missouri , and to the Arkansas Indians in 1855 and 1856.

     John W. Whitfield served in the Tennessess State Assembly from Sixth Congressional District of Hickman County , and to the twenty - ninth Assembly of the State of Tennessee from Seventh District.

     In 1858 John Whitfield was the Registrar at Dolphin , Kansas. In 1861 and during the Civil War he served in the Army. He moved to Texas and pursued farming near Hallettsville after the Civil War. John Whitfield died Oct. 27, 1879 in Lavoca County, Texas.

     A Biography of John Wilkins Whitfield appears at the back of this book.

     John and Sarah had a son named Anthony Whitfield who resided in Texas.

     It is John Wilkins Whitfield , and others of courage like him that have made the pages of history texts.

JOHN ANTHONY WHITFIELD   (John W. , Wilkins, Thomas, ____)

     John Anthony was born 1855 and died 1909 in Texas, the son of John and Sarah Whitfield. He married Helena Briscoe Whitfield and they had four children all of Texas.
1. George Dibrell 2. Sadie Whitfield   3. Ruth Whitfield 4 Mamie Whitfield who married W. D. Moore.

SARAH B. DIBRELL WHITFIELD

     She was born Dec. 11, 1827 in White County, Tennessee, the daughter of General George Dibrell who moved to Tennessee. She married John Wilkins Whitfield on May 28 , 1853 and lived in Tennessee, Missouri, Kansas, and Texas at Lavoca County, and then moved to Medina County, Texas in 1890 . She died April 26, 1918 and was cared for by her sister , Lucinda Herd.

(53) THOMAS JEFFERSON WHITFIELD
              (Wilkins, Thomas, _____)

Thomas Jefferson Whitfield was born February 10, 1810 on his parents' plantation in Williamson County, Tennessee. He died Jan. 10, 1873 near Whitfield Town in Perry County, Tennessee. He married

Eliza Nolan , January 24, 1829 in Williamson County, and had two
children : Henry and Martha. He married second wife , Sallie L . Dillahunty in Davidson County, Tennessee in January 27, 1835 , and they had
seven children . These children were all born in Hickman County, Tenn.

(80) 1. Henry W. Whitfield , b. July 30, 1830 ; d. Jan. 6, 1905 ,
       Bakersville, Tennessee.
(81) 2. Martha Eliza Whitfield , b. November 15, 1832.
(82) 3. Silas D. Whitfield, b. May 25, 1836 ; died in Illinois
(83) 4. Jack Whitfield, b. February 5, 1839.
(84) 5. George Monroe Whitfield , b. October 25, 1841.
(85) 6. Thomas Jefferson Whitfield , b. February 25, 1845; d. July 22,
       1908 Benton County, Tennessee.
(86) 7. Sarah Virginia Whitfield, b. February 26 , 1849.
(87) 8. Mary Delilah Whitfield , b. February 24, 1851.
(88) 9. Josephine Whitfield , b. March 20, 1854 ; died 1919.

Thomas J. and Eliza Nolan were natives of Williamson County,
Tennessee and lived there until Eliza died. Then Thomas and Sarah
Whitfield purchased farm in Hickman County near Whitfield Town,but
after the boundary lines of Perry and Hickman Counties were drawn
he was residing in Perry County, Tennessee. He lived near Council
Bend close to Duck River on rich and fertile farm land . Thomas J.
Whitfield was elected Colonel and then Brigadier-General of Davidson
County Militia in 1845 , 97th and 98th Regiment. He helped to organize
the Hickman County and local volunteers to the Mexican War. He
received a warrant to thousand of acres of Texas land,but sold it for
small sum of money, for in those days land was looked upon as blame
nothing.

Thomas Jefferson was named from the President of the United
States, and from his grandfather Thomas Whitfield of Sussex County,
Virginia. He appears in Hickman County Court minutes several times,
and traded at the merchants store of his kinfolks. He served in the Civil
War and was wounded and taken prisoner. He felt grievances because
peace was not a permanent thing. He was a farmer and a well known
guard. He appears as General Jeff Whitfield in some of the Tennessee
books.

This book is the genealogy of his family and descendants ; and
the other first pioneers to Tennessee from Virginia and those from
North Carolina.

(90) THOMAS R. WHITFIELD b. Middle Tennessee ; d. Carrollton,
    Missouri.

1849 appears to be the early date that Whitfield families of
this genealogy left Tennessee and moved to Missouri. Thomas R. left
Tennessee in 1849 and moved to Pike County in Missouri. He enlisted
in the Civil War in Pike County and discharged 1865. He had a land

deed there , but moved to Carrollton, Missouri where he purchased land and resided.

Thomas R. Whitfield married Mrs.Elizabeth Morgan Stalting, daughter of James (John) Morgan of Carroll County, Missouri. She was the widow of Frederick Stalting and had daughter, Mattie Stalting. Thomas R. and Elizabeth married at Carrollton town , Missouri , and the children were born there.

(91) 1. Charles Rush Whitfield
2. John William Whitfield. Unmarried.
John W. Whitfield was a Spanish American War soldier.
3. Ada Whitfield , died in 1920s.

JOHN T. WHITFIELD

Resided in Missouri and Kansas. He was in the company of Senator John Wilkins Whitfield with other cousins from Tennessee. John T. Whitfield was Major of 27th Confederate Trans-Mississippi Regiment under Colonel John Wilkins Whitfield.

JOHN WHITFIELD   (John,_____)

John Whitfield in May 1839 purchased twenty thousand acres of land in Coffee County, Tennessee. He made the first deed May 8th for 5,000 acres. Grant number 6847 of the orginial first grants. Then on May 9th he purchased three deeds of 5,000 acres each that were grants numbers 6840, 6849 and 6850. This is the first Whitfield record that we have in Coffee County, Tennessee. John Whitfield may have purchased this land with another John Whitfield. He was born in Tennessee of Virginia ancestors.

(There are many John Whitfield names of Virginia and Tenn . genealogy but they have not been compiled into family groups for genealogical lines.)

(55) SARAH WHITFIELD   (Wilkins, Thomas, _____)

Sarah Whitfield was b. 1817 the daughter of Wilkins and Polly Mary Whitfield from Sussex County, Virginia . She married Daniel Mc Phail , October 11, 1831 in Williamson County, Tennessee where they resided, before moving to Hickman County. Doctor Daniel Mc Phail was a physician in the third district of Hickman County, Tenn. When the volunteers of Tennessee were organized for the Mexican War he became the medical surgeon of Company A. First Tennessee Regiment under Captain John W. Whitfield , his brother-in-law. The Regiment left June 17 from Tennessee for Brazos Santiago, an island about nine miles from the mouth of the Rio Grande River. At Camp Brazos Santiago, Mexico, Dr Daniel McPhail became sick with dysentery and was nursed by Dr Starnes, his assistant and Joseph Weens and George Martin of Tennessee. Dr. McPhail died July 12, 1846 and was buried on the following day with military honors on the island. Dr. William D. Dorris succeeded him as Regiment doctor and kept a diary of the Company, and the Mexican War.

Sarah Whitfield McPhail had children in Tennessee. In 1849 she married James Nichols and moved to Hickman County, Tennessee.

(54) THEODOSIA WHITFIELD   (Wilkins, Thomas , _____)

Theodosia Whitfield married William George Clagett July 21, 1835 at Williamson County, Tennessee. She was born 1 April 1816. They lived in Franklin, Tennessee and moved 1830 to Centerville , Tenn. of Hickman County. The husband was in the mercantile business. She died Oct. 1, 1839 and left no children. Her husband later married Elizabeth O. Hornbeak on Feb. 10, 1842. She was married to William G. Clagett.

(50) NANCY A. WHITFIELD   (Harrison, Thomas, _____)

Nancy A. Whitfield was the daughter of Harrison and Polly Whitfield, and the granddaughter of Thomas and Winifer Whitfield from Virginia. Nancy A. Whitfield married March 8, 1827 , John M. Winstead in Williamson County, Tennessee. She was the daughter of Harrison Whitfield (1783-1864) at Franklin of Williamson County, Tenn. Nancy was born August 5, 1811 and died Feb. 7 , 1885. Her husband John M. Winstead was born March 9 , 1807 in Williamson County. They had twelve children , all born in Tennessee.

(57) JAMES MONROE WHITFIELD   (Wilkins, Thomas , _____)

The youngest child of Wilkins and Polly Mary Whitfield from Sussex County, Virginia who lived at Franklin, Tennessee. He was named after the President of the United States, as were his other brothers , when born in 1819, on the plantation in Williamson County, Tennessee. He was married on January 3- 1845 in Maury County, Tennessee to Mary Dansby Oliphant, daughter of Tabitha and Samuel Oliphant . They had eight children : three of the children were born in Tennessee and moved to Texas as small children. He had kinship with Frances B. Starr (Mrs. William T. Starr), Dallas 18, Texas. She was living in 1965.

JAMES MONROE WHITFIELD

James M. married Rebecca A. Newson , May 16, 1845, and they owned land at Council Bend on Duck River, Whitfield Town, in Hickman County, Tenn. in 1847. He was a farmer and appears in

John Whitfield- Coffee County, land deeds of Tennessee. State Archives. Sarah Whitfield McPhail Nichols- Hickman County History by Spence. Theodosia Whitfield Clagett - History of Tennessee by Goodspeed.

Hickman County Court Minutes but does not have records after the
Civil War. James M. and Rebecca had a few children. Descendants
in Hickman County and Henry County, Tennessee.

THEODOCID WHITFIELD

She married John J. Clow Dec. 11, 1833 in Williamson County,
Tennessee. She was the daughter of William or Harrison Whitfield of
the County.

VIRGINIA C. WHITFIELD   (Wilkins , Thomas, _____)

Daughter of Wilkins Whitfield and Polly Mary Sturdivant Whitfield. She was the youngest girl and married Dr. Daniel Mc Phail's
nephew , Dr. Daniel B. Ciffe, November 15, 1842 at Franklin, Tenn.
They lived at Franklin and had children. Dr. Cliffe practiced medicine
there.

LUCY WHITFIELD

She married Smith Criddle Sept. 4, 1832 in Williamson County,
Tennessee. She may have been a daughter of Thomas Whitfield.

(WW IV) BRYANT WHITFIELD   (_____, William of No. Carolina)

He was the grandson of William and Mary Beck Whitfield of
Steward County, Tennessee. He was born 1811 and living with his grandmother in 1844 in Effingham County, Illinois.

HENRY W. WHITFIELD   (Henry, Wilkins , Thomas, _____)

Henry W. Whitfield was living in 1965 in Austin County, Texas and
was the son of Henry W. Whitfield , the oldest son of Wilkins Whitfield
and Martha Loftin Whitfield of Tennessee. He was married to Susanna
De Moss Oliphant in Maury County, Tennessee on June 13 , 1850. They
had children in Texas.

SEVENTH GENERATION

(80) HENRY W. WHITFIELD   (Thomas, Wilkins, Thomas, ___)

Henry W. Whitfield was born July 30, 1830 in Hickman County
and died January 6, 1906 at Bakerville , Tennessee of Humphreys
County. He married Nancy C. Porch 1851 . They had two children,
Annie and John D. Whitfield. Dr. Henry Whitfield has a sketch in the
book History of Tennessee by Goodspeed , published in 1886.

"Dr Henry Whitfield, a successful practicing physician of
Bakerville, Tennessee was born July 30, 1830 in Hickman County,
Tennessee, and is the son of Thomas J. and Eliza Nolan Whitfield,
natives of Williamson County. The father , a well known farmer,
was elected colonel of the militia of Davidson County, and afterward
elected brigadier -general. At the time of his death, which occurred
in 1873 , he was living in Perry County. Our subject was reared on a
farm and received the rudiments of his education in the common
schools, but in 1848 he entered the Memphis Medical College , but
being in adverse circumstances was compelled to walk the entire

distance from this county to Memphis. In 1849 he returned to Humphreys County and practiced medicine until 1856, then attended one term in the Nashville Medical University, where he graduated and received his diploma March 1857. After this he returned home and followed his profession in the vicinity of Bakerville, Tennessee of Humphreys County, and has at present a large and increasing practice. He has a fine farm of 100 acres and is surrounded by all the comforts of life. In 1851 he wedded Miss Nancy C. Porch, and to this union were born two : Annie and John D. Mr.Whitfield is a Democrat in politics and he and family are members of the Christian Church." Children:

> (96) 1. Annie Whitfield . She married William Hedge
> of Tennessee , and had child , JOHN HEDGE ,
> who married Lela Fowlkes and had children:
> (1) Ruby Hedge (2) Carrie Hedge (3) John Hedge
> (97) 2. John Dee Whitfield , born December 29, 1857

Abstract of the Will of Dr Henry W. Whitfield (1830-1906. Dated Jan. 25, 1904. Half of the estate to daughter, Ann Hedge Whitfield and half to children of dec. son, John Whitfield . Annie W., Fannie W., Betsy W., Dillie W., Belle W., John Whitfield. Dr.Henry W. Whitfield divided tract of land giving subdivision parcels to each grandchild ; and to Annie H. Whitfield 350 acres of a farm at Bakerville, Tennessee in Humphreys County. Will is handwritten on County courthouse book on several pages.

> Dillie was Nancy Delilah Whitfield.

(81) MARTHA ELIZA WHITFIELD

> She was born Nov. 15, 1832 and died in Tennessee. She married
> J. D. Murray , who was born May 2, 1829 . They had children and
> both of them lived to old age. He was a farmer.

(84) GEORGE MONROE WHITFIELD

> (Thomas J., Wilkins, Thomas, ___)

George Monroe Whitfield , born October 25, 1841 and died May 1, 1863. Unmarried. Civil War Confederate Soldier. Hickman Co., Tenn.

(82) SILAS D. WHITFIELD

> (Thomas J., Wilkins, Thomas, ___)

Silas D. Whitfield was born May 25, 1836 in Hickman County, Tenn. He married Eliza Richardson August 31 , Humphreys County, Tennessee , and then moved to Quincy, Illinois. The family became associated with Morman Mineral Company in Illinois and became wealthy people. Children:

> 1. Jefferson Whitfield (Jeff. W.)
> 2. James Whitfield
> 3. William Whitfield (Will W.)
> 4. Robert Whitfield (Bob W.)
> 5. John Whitfield
> 6. Kit Whitfield

(83) JACK H. WHITFIELD
(Thomas J. , Wilkins, Thomas, _____)
Jack H. Whitfield , born Feb. 5, 1839 in Hickman County, Tennessee and died 1901. He was a Civil War soldier and Captain in the
service.

(85) THOMAS JEFFERSON WHITFIELD
and M. L. CUNMINGHAM and MARTHA JANE NICKS.
(Thomas J. , Wilkins, Thomas, _____)
He was born Feb. 25, 1845 , son of Thomas J. and Sallie Dillahunty
Whitfield ; and died July 22, 1908. He was born in Hickman County, or
Perry County which the town had been split off and named; and died in
Benton County, Tennessee. The family resided in Benton County, Tenn.
on Tennessee River land at Pavatts Landing. He married first wife ,
M. L. Cunmingham April 4, 1866. They had children : Jefferson L.,
Salle and Lillie May Whitfield. He was a farmer and fisherman. He
married second wife, Martha Jane Nicks , April 1875 of Benton County,
Tennessee.
M. L. Cunmingham Whitfield was born 1847 ; and died March 1,
1874 in Benton County, Tennessee. The Cunmingham family is written
in the "compedium of genealogy. "
Martha Jane Nicks Whitfield was born Sept. 28, 1855; and died
April 16, 1930 in Benton County, Tennessee. She was the daughter of
JAMES H. NICKS and ANN CUMMINS. She was sister to Sam Nicks
and John Nicks who moved to Texas.
Thomas Jefferson Whitfield's children: All born in Tennessee.
(98) 1. Jefferson Lafayette Whitfield , b. Jan. 28, 1867, Hickman Co. , Tenn.
(99) 2. Salle Whitfield, b. Nov. 28, 1868.
(100)3. Lillie May Whitfield , b. Aug. 13, 1871.
(101) 4. James Dee Whitfield , b. Feb. 10, 1877 and died 1954, Humphreys Co.
(102) 5. John Regan Whitfield, Oct. 18, 1880.
(103) 6. Thomas Cleveland Whitfield, b. Nov. 8, 1884.
(104) 7. Henry Edward Whitfield , May 1, 1888 born in Benton County, Tenn.
(105) 8. Delie Ann Whitfield, Dec 2, 1891 born in Decatur County, Tenn.
(106) 9. Clara May Whitfield , b. June 10, 1894 born in Decatur County, Tenn.
Thomas Jefferson Whitfield was a farmer and fisherman , and so
were his sons who did farming. He was conscripted in the Civil War near
the close of the war, and served in the army of the Confederate under
General Nathan Bedford Forest. He helped to swim horses across the
Tennessee River at Pavatts Landing and close by. They had a Battle
at Johnsonville, Tennessee and sunk boats and one went down at Pavatts
Landing.
Thomas J. is buried in Benton County, Tennessee. The home
place and farm was taken over by the Tennessee Valley Authority for
the Tennessee River improvement and project, and the family moved
to Carroll County.

(86) SARAH VIRGINIA WHITFIELD   (Thomas)
      Sarah was born Feb. 26, 1849 in Hickman County, Tennessee.
She married JAMES H. MULLINICKS.   Children:
      1. Sarah Mullinicks. She married Leon Bennett.
      2. Josie Wilkins Mullinicks . She married Dr J. N. Smith.
      3. Annie Mullinicks.
      4. Chass Whitfield Land Mullinicks.

(87) MARY DELILAH WHITFIELD   (Thomas)
      Mary Delilah, b. Feb. 24, 1851 in Tennessee. She married
Robert Horner. Children:
1. Anna Horner who married Jim Frank Daniel.
   They had child : Betty Lee Daniel.
2. Jefferson Horner. Unmarried. A school teacher.
3. Foster Horner married Betty Lancaster.
4. Robert Horner married Elizabeth Rains and they had children:
   (1) Dillie Horner (2) Mattie Horner (3) John Horner who married
    Susan Simpson.
5. _____ Horner.

(88) JOSEPHINE WHITFIELD   (Thomas)
      She was born March 20, 1854 in Hickman County changed
to Perry County, Tennessee ; and died 1919 in Tennessee. She married
JOHN D. MULLINICKS.   Children:
      1. John D. Mullinicks, b. Oct. 21, 1873 and married Cora
         Carroll and had children : (1) William Carroll Mullinicks,
         born 1906 . (2) Lura V. Mullinicks , born 1911.
      2. Robert Lee Mullinicks, b. Dec 8, 1876, married Victoria
         Porch and had children : (1) William Robert Mullinicks
         (2) George Evans Mullinicks who had children: (1) Lou Ann
         Mullinicks (2) Vicky Mullinicks
      3. Lola Mullinicks, May 6 , 1878 she was born. She married
         Lem Council and had child: (1) Raymond Lee Council , b.
         1905 and died 1956.
      4. Mary Virginia Mullinicks, b. Nov. 8, 1884 , and married
         first to Rex Smith, and then married second to Melvin
         Le Duke , and married third to R. H. Crockett. Mary had
         children: (1) William Rex Smith, b. May 7, 1908, and d.
         1918. (2) John Melvin Le Duke, b. March 18, 1912.
         (3) Delmus Le Duke , b. Oct. 22, 1913.
      Mary Virginia was a Waverly, Tennessee teacher of
      Robert E. Whitfield who was born August 11, 1921.

(113) SMITH C. WHITFIELD   (Felix , Harrison, Thomas)
      He was born in Hickman County, Tennessee . He resided in
Nashville, Tennessee of Davidson County where he died. He was born
after brother Thomas Harrison Whitfield , and was living in 1922. He
was a Civil War soldier.

(88) Descendants of Josephine Whitfield.   Jennie Mullinicks had three boys and one boy. She had Sallie D. Mullinicks and Wilkins Mullinicks.

(87) Descendants of May Delilah Whitfield. Delia Horner had three boys and one girl. (1) Robert Horner (Bob) (2) John D. Horner (3) Jennie Horner (4) Lola Horner

(91) CHARLES RUSH WHITFIELD   (Thomas R.)

The son of Thomas R. Whitfield and Elizabeth. He was born in Carrollton Town, Missouri. He resided in Missouri. Charles and wife had child : (127) BESSIE WHITFIELD , b. in Missouri and resided in the State of Iowa in 1964.

Steward County and Henry County, Tennessee Land Deeds

BRIANT WHITFIELD had land deed 1811 in Steward County, Tenn. He was from North Carolina or Virginia . He had descendants in Steward and Henry County, Tennessee. He had 640 acres of land on north waters of Tennessee River.

HAM WHITFIELD had a land deed 1811 in Steward County, Tenn. He was from Virginia. He had a 100 acres of land on Piney Fork of Red River.

(WW3) BRYANT WHITFIELD had a land deed 1811 in Steward County, Tenn. He was from Virginia or North Carolina. He had descendants in Steward and Henry County, Tennessee. He also had some kinship in Montgomery County, Tennessee. He also had a land deed in Henry County, Tennessee after 1822.

We know these men appear in Steward and Henry Counties of Tennessee Court Minutes and Land Deeds. They are Virginians and of the same kinship. There were orphans in Henry County, Tennessee Court Minutes for 1836-1849. They appear to be with the North Carolina Whitfield men but also stand alone across the river from them.

Henry County, Tennessee Land Deeds

William Whitfield land deed Oct. 1847.
Lewis Whitfield land deed Oct. 18, 1847
William Whitfield land deed Nov. 10, 1849

In Jackson County, Tennessee , William Whitfield had a land deed August 1849.

Henry County, Tennessee - 1850 Census

JOHN WHITFIELD , and wife ELIZABETH WHITFIELD.

John was 32 years old and born in Tennessee, his wife, Elizabeth was 33 years and born in North Carolina. Children :
1. Mary Whitfield, b. 1840 in Tenn.
2. William Whitfield, b. 1841 in Tenn.
3. James Whitfield, b. 1842 in Tenn.
4. Martha Whitfield, b. 1846 in Tenn.
5. Needham Whitfield , b. 1848 in Tenn.
5. Elizabeth Whitfield, b. 1849 in Tenn.

The family resided in Henry County, Tennessee.

Cynthia Whitfield, b. 1826 in Tennessee. In 1850 living in Henry Co.
Lewis Whitfield, 33 years old, born in Tennessee and living 1850
in Henry County, Tennessee. His wife, Rebecca was born 1818 in
Kentucky. They had two children in 1850. (1) James Whitfield, b. 1834
in Tennessee (2) Eliza Whitfield, b. 1837.
Needham Whitfield, born 1821 in Tennessee. He was a farmer in 1850
in Henry County, Tennessee.
Araminta Whitfield, b. 1830 in Tennessee. Living 1850 in Henry Co.
William Whitfield, b. 1830 in Tennessee. Living 1850 in Henry Co.
Sarah Whitfield, b. 1830 in Tennessee. Living in Henry County, 1850.
Martha Ann Whitfield, b. 1840 in Tennessee. Resided in Henry Co.

(107) WILLIAM WHITFIELD, HENRY WHITFIELD, JOHN WHITFIELD
lived 1856 in Cheatham County, Tennessee. In 1856 William and Henry
Whitfield were appointed overseer of road Hannah Ford from junction
end of Tennessee Pike road to top of Hurricane Hill from Charlotte,
Tennessee to Nashville, Tennessee. In 1858 William, Henry, and
John Whitfield were the overseer of the Hannah Ford Road in Cheatham County, Tennessee.   G 7
(108) WILLIS E. WHITFIELD   (Willis, Willis)
        Willis E. Whitfield paid a tax in 1849 in Rutherford Co., Tenn.
WILLIAM WHITFIELD paid a Tax 1834 in Henry County, Tennessee.

(150) ANDREW ALFORD WHITFIELD
        (Family descendant from #37 Willis Whitfield)
He was born Oct. 13, 1829 and died May 7, 1859 in Rutherford Co.,
Tennessee. He married Emeline Eleanor Lyon. She was born Oct. 24,
1834 in Tennessee and died March 2, 1920. They married August 31,
1851 and resided in Rutherford County, Tennessee, near the boundary
line of Cannon County.   Children:
(151) 1. Andrew Willis Whitfield 1852 - 1934.
        2. Elizabeth Whitfield, b. 1855 - d. 1930.
(152) 3. Nathan James Thomas Whitfield 1856-1939.
(153) 4. Alfred Johnson Whitfield 1859-1942

(109) THOMAS W. WHITFIELD
        Thomas W. Whitfield was born Feb. 1827 in Tennessee at
Davison Co. or Williamson County. He married Sarah M. Berry,
daughter of John and Annie Berry of Cheatham County, Tennessee.
John Berry died Oct 8, 1856 and Annie Berry died Sept. 1876, a
member of Christian Church. Thomas and Sarah were married March
4, 1855. Thomas assisted father in farming. In Davidson County, Tenn.
Dr. Thomas W. Whitfield practiced medicine in Davidson County and
moved to Henry County to work, after fifteen years at Henry County
he moved to Williamson County, Tenn. He died July 13, 1879 at

HILL SIDE HOME. A mason and member of Christian Church Dr. Whitfield and Sarah had eight children.

1. John H. Whitfield   (110) 5. Jimmie D. Whitfield
2. Mattie H. Whitfield   6. Thomas W. Whitfield
3. Anna E. Whitfield   7. William B. Whitfield
4. Julia Whitfield   8. Clifton B. Whitfield

HENRY W. WHITFIELD   (Henry , Henry, Thomas)

Henry Whitfield was born 1802 in Sussex County, Virginia , the son of Wilkins Whitfield and Polly Mary Sturdivant Whitfield. He went to Franklin, Tennessee in 1808. Henry Whitfield married Martha Ann Loftin Oct. 22, 1823. The family appears on the 1830 Census of Williamson County, Tennessee. A record reports Henry predeceased his father.   He would have died in Tennessee.

His son, HENRY W. WHITFIELD married to Susanna De Moss Oliphant in Maury County, Tennessee on June 13 - 1850. This family moved to Austin, Texas and was living there in 1891. They had children.

HENRY W. WHITFIELD was the son of Henry W. Whitfield and was living in 1965 in Austin County, Texas , and had a family. His ancestral fathers were Henry W. Whitfield, Henry W. Whitfield , and Thomas Whitfield (d. 1794 Va.).

THOMAS WHITFIELD 1735ca- 1794.   Virginia to Tennessee.

Thomas Whitfield , born 1735 ca. , and died 1794 in Sussex County, Virginia. Thomas Whitfield married Winifer before 1760, and she was called "Winney." They lived in Albermarle Parish, Sussex County , Va. and was there from 1760 to 1808 years. Winifer Whitfield and her children migrated to Middle Tennessee to Williamson County.

Winifer Whitfield was born 1740 ca. , and the Tennessee Western Weekly Review at Franklin printed her death notice , death date was July 9 , 1838 at the home of her son , Wilkins Whitfield. She gave birth to ten children : 1. Mary b.1760. Married Laburn Hobbs in 17781
2. William , b. 1762. He married Elizabeth Tomlinson 1782. 3. Elizabeth who married Benjamin Sturdivant in 1783. 4. Francis , b.1765 .
5. Martha Patty, b. 1767. She married William Hobbs in 1789. 6.Wilkins Whitfield , b. 1770 ca. He married Polly Sturdivant in 1801. 7. Betty called Betsy, b. 1774. She married Benjamin Sturdivant in 1793.
8. Nancy , b. 1774. She married William Knight in 1799. 9. Harrison b. 1778 ca. He married Polly Sledge 1804. 10. Jack "John", b. 1780.

All the births were in Sussex County, Virginia. Winifer Whitfield died on July 9 , 1838 in Franklin, Tennessee. This family of hers mostly migrated together in 1808 to Williamson County, Tennessee.

At Franklin , Tennessee the children all had families, and they were a prominent family . The grandsons were also pioneers to Tennessee to build the County and State of Tennessee. This book has their records.

Pennsylvanian -   No kinship to Hickman County people.
    William and Rachel Yardley Whitfield of Pennsylvania had son,
John Pashley Yardley Whitfield in Philadelphia, and they moved to
Tennessee in 1850.   Children:
1. Edwin Bates Whitfield , b. Jan. 24, 1856, Clarksville, Tennessee.
    He married Alice Emma Roth and had children:
    1. Daisy Whitfield   3. Louisa Whitfield
    2. Rose Whitfield   4. Lillian Whitfield

Floridian -   No kinship to Hickman County people.
BRYAN C. WHITFIELD of Florida, wife Susie Cameron, daughter of
Virginia State governor. She was born about 1867 in Lunenburg Co.,
Virginia or nearby. She and Bryan C. Whitfield moved to Florida.
Children: 1. Evelyn Cameron Whitfield   2. Lou Egerton Whitfield

(111) SILUS D. H. WHITFIELD   G 7
        He was born 1840 in Tennessee. Ancestors from Virginia.
Parents from Hickman County. He married Eliz J. Whitfield in
Humphreys County, Tennessee. Silus D. Whitfield was a grocery
store merchant in Bakerville , Tennessee. Eliza J. Whitfield father
was born Tennessee but the mother in Virginia. John and Eliza had
children: 1. Jeff M. Whitfield , b. 1876. He worked in grocery store
at Bakerville , Tennessee. 2. John D. Whitfield 3. Robert E. H.
Whitfield 4. William E. W. Whitfield.   All children born in Tennessee
near Bakerville , Tennessee or in the town. *
        The Bakerville , Tennessee families moved from Whitfield Town
to this location. The fathers at Whitfield town sold land to others who
settled there and the new town grew in the direction of Bakerville in
Humphreys County for these relatives. Farming, merchant stores,
and medicine seem to be the career pursued by these people.
WT 7 JAMES WESLEY WHITFIELD (17)   G 7
              (William, William, Thomas, Thomas, Thomas)
    Captain James Wesley Whitfield , b. Jan. 1, 1822- d. Aug. 26,
1904. Children: 1. Virginia C. Whitfield , married G. T. Wade of
Wilmington, North Carolina , and resided Charlotte, North Carolina.
2. daughter ____ Whitfield married J. M. Morrow of Albermarle,
North Carolina. 3. Elizabeth Whitfield 4. W. Lee Whitfield
5. John Whitfield 6. Mary Whitfield   7. G. M. Whitfield
8. W. T. Whitfield 9. ____ Whitfield.   These children were living
1928 in Maxton, North Carolina.

Silus Whitfield - 1880 Census , Humphreys County, Tennessee.

(112) THOMAS HARRISON WHITFIELD   (Felix)

He was born 1838 and died July 6, 1921 in Hickman County ,
Tennessee and was buried at Clovercroft, Tennessee in Williamson
County. " Gentleman with the stamp of the Old South , elegant, courte-
ous, beloved and respected by all." Mt. Hope Cemetery. In 1865 he
married Nancy Ann Stephens. She died 1907. Children survived their
father. 1. John T. Whitfield   2. Mrs Eugene Rice 3. Ben F.
Whitfield 4. Mrs Richard Herbert   5. Others

Thomas and Nancy Whitfield resided in Hickman and Williamson County, Tennessee. Methodist. Democrat. He attended subscription
county school before farming.

Civil War Record : In May 1861 when the Civl War broke over
the South, Thomas Harrison Whitfield volunteered and enlisted Company
H, Tenth Tennessee Confederate Infantry.

First battle at Fishing Creek. He went from Fishing Creek to
Shiloh battlefield , during the battle the enemy retreated to their Gun
boats. He was discharged and sent home. He was compelled to take
the Oath or go to prison and enlisted again and joined the old command
twentieth Tennessee regiment at Murfressboro - Hoover Gap- Chickamauga and Missionary Ridge at Chicamauga. He was captured at the
battle of Missionary Ridge in November 1863, when he was carried to
Rock Island prison, where he was held until hostilities were over.

His regiment which included boys from Williamson County,
Tennessee fought in the battle of Franklin , commanded by Colonel
Will Shy , who fell near there.

Comrades included Nathan Morris, Joe Carl, William Roberson,
John Miller, Isaac Wright of Lynnhurst , Tennessee, Joseph Smith ,
Jesse Short and others.

Thomas H. Whitfield was released March 26, 1865. He came
home anyway he could get convey, and besides walking with all others,
walking was usual hardship at that time.

(114) JAMES H. WHITFIELD

He was born in Tennessee. Kinship of the Whitfields in Baker-
ville, Tennessee. He married Delia Whitfield, whose sister was Annie
Whitfield. They lived in Benton County, Tennessee for a long time.
They had children:

1. Mary Whitfield, b. 1872 in Tennessee. She lived to be
   eighty-nine years of age. She knew all of the genealogy
   of her family line, and many old folks tales. She took
   a visit to Anaheim, California in her old age. She died
   1961.
2. Gus Whitfield , b. Tennessee. Resided in Benton County.
3. Foster Whitfield , b. Tennessee, and resided in Benton Co.
The descendants live near Centerville, Tennessee.

(116) FRANK WHITFIELD G 7

He was born 1839 of parents born in Tennessee. Physican and practiced medicine in Humphreys County, Tennessee 1880. He was married to Margaret who was born 1850 in Tennessee. They had two children in 1880 with them. They are kinship to family of Whitfield Town location in Hickman County, Tennessee.

1. Bettie Whitfield, b. 1873 in Tennessee.
2. Beckie Whitfield, b. 1875 in Tennessee.

Many of the people that the early Whitfields were associated with came from Prince Edward County, Virginia. It is thought by the Author, Vallie Jo Whitfield, that the Whitfield ancestors resided in the middle area of Virginia in the region of Lunenburg and Prince Edward and Mecklenburg Counties of Virginia, but later study and research work for the published book Virginia History and Whitfield Biographies, confirmed that these families of Whitfield were from Isle of Wight County, Virginia and Nansemond County, Virginia, and a very few from other Virginia counties. The families when they moved from Virginia, and the other families when they moved from North Carolina were in the company of negroes or black people . Both Bryan Whitfield of North Carolina, and Wilkins Whitfield of Sussex County, Virginia and others migrated with negroes in their expeditions to Tennessee.

JOHN COFFEE was born in Prince Edward County, Virginia June 2, 1772, and moved to Davidson County, Tennessee in 1798. During the War of 1812 and the Creek War he served with distinction being colonel and brigadier-general of Tennessee Volunteers. He took part in battles at Pensacola and New Orleans. He was appointed surveyor of public lands in March 1817. He died July 1834 in Alabama.

It was John Whitfield who was afterwards granted twenty thousand acres of land in Coffee County, Tennessee.

G 8

(105) DELIE ANN WHITFIELD   (Thomas J., Thomas, Wilkins, Thomas)

Delie Ann Whitfield married Jim Sikes. She was born in 1891 on 2nd of December, Decatur County, Tennessee. After she married she lived in Benton County, Tennessee and had one child. She moved to McKenize, Tennessee and resided there in 1962 and was living in 1977. The child - MATTIE SIKES, b. Aug. 10, 1917 in Hickman County, Tenn. Resided in Florida and 1962 in Carroll County, Tennessee. She married CHESTER VERNER on Oct. 17, 1945 and had three children :

    1. James Ray Verner, b. May 15, 1947.
    2. Mattie Verner, b. Sept. 4, 1948.
    3. Charles Verner, b. Aug. 13, 1949.

(97) JOHN DEE WHITFIELD (Henry , Thomas, Wilkins, Thomas)
John Dee Whitfield was born Dec. 29, 1857 in Humphreys County
at Bakerville , Tennessee. He died before 1904. John married Mollie
Fowkles , Dec. 18, 1878. They had six children.

The book, History of Tennessee published 1886 has a sketch of
John D. Whitfield , son of Dr Henry W. Whitfield of Bakerville , Tenn.
"John D. Whitfield, a farmer of the Twelfth District of Humphreys
County was born December 29, 1857, in this county, and is the son of
Henry W. and Nancy Porch Whitfield. Our subject was reared on the
farm and secured a fair education in the country schools. After reaching the age of twenty-one years he started to make a livelihood for himself on life's rough journey. At first he undertook clerking in his father's
store but soon gave that up and went to farming on a portion of his father's
land, and has been quite successful, having control of 250 acres of well
improved land in the Twelfth District. December 18, 1878 he married
Miss Mollie B. Fowlkes, and the fruits of this union were an interesting
family of children: Annie, Fannie, Belle, Bessie, Nancy D., and John
Whitfield. Mr Whitfield is a stanch Democrat and a moral upright man.
He and wife are consistent members of the Christian Church and have
the esteem of all who know them. "

John D. Whitfield died a young man. His father, Henry W. Whit-
field, the Bakerville town doctor helped raise all of the children. One
of the girls moved to New York when she grew up, but the other children
lived at Bakerville , Tennessee, and resided in Humphreys County,
Tennessee as their children do now. The earlier location of grandfather
Wilkins Whitfield in Williamson County pointed to Whitfield Town in
Hickman and Perry County then north again to Bakerville and then to
Waverly and all over the Humphreys County area.

John Dee Whitfield and Mollie Fowlkes Whitfield had children:
1. Annie Whitfield , b. 1880; d. about 1938.
2. Fannie Whitfield , b. 1882 ; d. 1958 . She married Bert C. Lytton.
3. Belle Whitfield , b. 1884 ; d. 1941 . She married Doss B. Daniel.
(121) 4. Bessie Whitfield , b. 1887 ; d. 1948.
(122) 5. Nancy Delilah Whitfield, b. 1890 . She married William B. Nolan.
(123) 6. John Hedge Whitfield , b. 1893 and d. 1923.

(98) JEFFERSON LAFAYETTE WHITFIELD
(Thomas, Thomas, Wilkins, Thomas)
Jefferson Lafayette was known to his friends as Fate or Jeff
Whitfield. He was born Jan. 28, 1867 in Tennessee and died June 21, 1937
in Missouri. He was born in Benton County, Tennessee on Tennessee
River land at Pavatts Landing five miles away at Eagle Creek, where
he resided until he moved to Steele, Missouri in 1916. He married the

first wife and marriage lasted a short time, and no children. Jefferson Lafayette Whitfield married the second time to LOU ELLEN NATLOCK in 1888 in Tennessee. She was born in the southland and died 1938 in August month at Steele, Missouri. To this marriage was born seventeen children. Four sets of twins. Eight children died young, and the living children went with him to Missouri but some of them returned to Tennessee to live. He was a farmer and fisherman. The living children are recorded here.

(124) 1. Thomas Wesley Whitfield, b. 1889 ; d. 1942.
    2. Cleather Jennie Whitfield married ____ Ward. Cleather J. Ward and family lived at Steele, Missouri in 1960. They had six children.
    3. James Whitfield. He married, and he and his wife raised three girls. He was a farmer.

(125) 4. Carlie Whitfield, d. 1925
    5. Neal Whitfield
    6. Ollie Whitfield. A twin of Ola Whitfield.
    7. Ola Whitfield. She is a twin of Ollie Whitfield. She married and had two children.
    8. Veatric Whitfield. She married Claude Thorton and he died before 1962. They had four Thorton children and lived in Memphis, Tennessee.
    9. Annie Whitfield. She married Tommy Henlsy. They live in Memphis, Tennessee in 1962.

(99) SALLE WHITFIELD (Thomas, Thomas, Wilkins, Thomas)
    She was born November 28, 1868 in Tennessee. A married person.

(100) LILLIE MAY WHITFIELD
    (Thomas, Thomas, Wilkins, Thomas)

Lillie May Whitfield married Mat Phillips and had eleven children : seven boys, three girls residing in Humphreys County, Tennessee. Lillie May Whitfield Phillips was born August 13, 1871 in Tennessee. All of her children were born in Humphreys County.

1. Cletus Phillips
2. Thomas Phillips
3. Clarence Phillips
4. Dennis Phillips
5. Melvin Phillips
6. Marshal Phillips
7. Billie (William) Phillips
8. Stella Phillips
9. Ora Phillips
10. Mary Ellen Phillips
11. Infant died.

(102) JOHN REGAN WHITFIELD (Thomas, Thomas, Wilkins, Thomas)
    John Regan Whitfield was called Jack Whitfield. He was born May 1, 1880 near Bakerville, Tennessee and died from a tooth infection in 1901. Unmarried. He was a farmer and fisherman.

G 8

(104) HENRY EDWARD WHITFIELD

(Thomas, Thomas, Wilkins , Thomas)

Henry was the son of Thomas Jefferson Whitfield and Martha Jane Nicks. He was born May 1, 1888 in Benton County, Tennessee. He resided at Eagle Creek, Tennessee in 1962 in Benton County. He was a farmer and fisherman. Unmarried. Duck River and Tennessee River has been a fishing place for Henry Edward Whitfield. He died December 29 , 1972 at Mc Kenzie , Tennessee in Benton County.

(106) CLARA MAY WHITFIELD

(Thomas   , Thomas, Wilkins, Thomas)

Clara May Whitfield was born June 10, 1894 in Decatur County, Tennessee. Unmarried. She lived with her parents, and sister and brothers , at Benton County and Humphreys County. She was living in the old home place near the Tennessee River when the Tennessee Valley Authority took the house and farm in the River Control project in Benton County. She lived with sister, Delie Whitfield Sikes in 1962 to April 9 , 1978 at Carroll County at Mc Kenize, Tennessee. She is the family member who owns the Whitfield Bible which records this family lineage beginning in 1883. The third member of this household was Edward Whitfield , the brother. She is buried beside her mother, 4-9-1978.

CHARLES THOMAS WHITFIELD

(William, William, Thomas , Thomas, Thomas)

Charles Thomas Whitfield married Adelaide Barham Lifsey.

1. Frances Mary Whitfield, died Jan 23, 1929 .   (Children)
2. _____ Whitfield married H. G. Goodman, Petersburg, Va.
3. _____ Whitfield married W. H. Bryant, Richmond , Va.
4. J. T. Whitfield , Atlanta , Georgia.
5. J.J. Whitfield of Detroit , Michigan.
6. W. E. Whitfield of Richmond , Virginia.
7. W. L. Whitfield of Richmond, Virginia.

G 8

(103) THOMAS CLEVELAND WHITFIELD

(Thomas, Thomas J., Wilkins, Thomas)

Thomas was born November 8 , 1884 in Humphreys County, Tennessee. He was living in 1964. He married Bessie Lee Primm on December 17, 1905 in Benton County, Tennessee. His parents moved from Humphreys County to Benton County, Tennessee when he was in early childhood . Thomas was a farmer in Benton County, Tennessee. They had   children : Maybelle Whitfield who married Frank C. Manning , and Beulah Anne Whitfield. He was the son of Thomas Jefferson Whitfield.   He died 19 65 .

MAYBELLE WHITFIELD

(Thomas C., Thomas J., Wilkins, Thomas)

Maybelle Whitfield was born September 30 , 1906 at Coxburg , Tennessee in Benton County. She married Frank Cleveland

Manning, December 9, 1930. He resided in Concord, New Hampshire.
They had two boys : 1. Frank Cleveland Manning, b. December 9 , 1933,
and died October 4 , 1955 in Texas in a test flight over Texas. U.S. Air
Force Jet fighter pilot. Unmarried.
2. Donald Manning ,b. October 2, 1935 at Concord, New Hampshire.
He resided with his parents in Mc Kenize, Tennessee in 1962. He married
in Tennessee.

BEULAH ANNE WHITFIELD

She was born October 12, 1908 in Benton County, Tennessee. She
married Herbert Tippett 1927 who resided in Camden, Tennessee. They
had one child named Annette Tippett, born 1945 in Milan , Tennessee
of Gibson County. She was a college student in 1962 residing in Camden,
Tennessee.

(126) THOMAS JEFFERSON WHITFIELD , born 1910 in Tennessee.

(127) BESSIE WHITFIELD
(Charles, Thomas)
Bessie Whitfield of Missouri and Iowa married Errol L. Gailey.
They resided 1964 in Storm Lake, Iowa. They had children :
1. Mary Whitfield Gailey who married _____ Williams, and resided
in Fort Dodge, Iowa.
2. John Whitfield Gailey . Attorney in Fort Dodge, Iowa in 1964 .
3. Margaret Whitfield Gailey married _____ Mick. Resided in Ames,
Iowa.
4. James Whitfield Gailey. 1964 student graduate at the University of
Iowa , Iowa City, Iowa.

(101) JAMES DEE WHITFIELD
(Thomas J. , Thomas J. , Wilkins, Thomas)
James Dee Whitfield was born February 10, 1877 in Bakerville ,
Tennessee of Humphreys County. He died in Paris , Tennessee on
September 19, 1954. He married first wife, Mary Hester Mc Keel Sept-
ember 1, 1899. She was the daughter of William Hyman Mc Keel and
Louisa Deaubra Harder of Maury County, Tennessee. She was the grand-
daughter of James Mc Keel and Darcas Walker of Tennessee and North
Carolina , whose ancestry was from Ireland and England.
James Dee Whitfield married second wife, Mrs Oda I. De Priest
H. Daniel on April 17, 1926 in Bakerville . Tennessee.
James D. and Mary Hester Whitfield purchased the land deed to
Rockdale Farm in 1919 and resided there where the four children were
born in Humphreys County at Waverly town. Mary Hester Whitfield was
a school teacher and then a housewife. They resided in Benton and
Humphreys Counties. The history is written in the records of Tennessee
on Whitfield.
MARY HESTER MC KEEL was born March 10, 1878 and died.

May 15, 1924 in Waverly, Tennessee of Humphreys County. After her death Mrs Oda Whitfield came to care for the children and reside at Rockdale Farm. Oda Whitfield was the maternal influence on the Whitfield children and a beloved grandmother.

James D. Whitfield is buried in Mc Keel Cemetery in Humphreys County, Tennessee. He was owner of Rockdale Farm. He managed the farm Cannery using his own crops to perserve. In 1917 he helped to organize the Humphreys County National Farm Loan Association. He was secretary and treasurer of that organization until 1936. There were children in the home of James Dee and Mary Hester Whitfield. One foster child, a girl; and three boys of their own and a daughter.

ANNIE CARR was taken as a foster child for adoption from the Tennessee Orphans Home, but finances did not permit her adoption. She married when a youth to Albert Baker and resided in Camden, Tennessee. Annie Carr Baker was a beloved daughter of James D. and Mary Hester. She was born about 1910 and died March 20, 1962. She had five children who resided in Tennessee and St Louis, Missouri.

The children born to James Dee Whitfield and Mary Hester Mc Keel Whitfield were four:

    (128)   1. James Raymond Whitfield, born 1915.
    (129)   2. Ralph Wilson Whitfield, born 1918.
    (130)   3. Hester Rozelle Whitfield, born 1916.
    (131)   4. Robert Edward Whitfield, born 1921.

These children were born at Waverly, Tennessee in Humphreys County.

(132) ODA IDELLA DE PRIEST HENSLEY DANIEL WHITFIELD G 8

Oda Idella De Priest was born May 8, 1888 in Lobelville, Tennessee in Perry County. She was the daughter of Olin Legrande De Priest and his wife, Mozella Cotton De Priest. She resided in Waverly, Tennessee at Rockdale Farm in 1963. Oda I. De Priest married first husband Bert Hensley of Lobelville, Tennessee. One child was born of this marriage named Ruby Hensley on June 13, 1910. She married Hicks Hopkins and they had two daughters:

    1. Judy Hopkins. She was born in Nashville, Tennessee. She married and had two boys.
    2. Joan Hopkins. She married in 1962 and has children.

The Hopkins family have lived in Nashville, Tennessee and in Florida.

Oda I. De Priest Hensley after the death of her first husband married Bob Daniel, physician of Lobelville, Tennessee. One child was born of this marriage named Martha Frances Daniel on May 18, 1920 in Lobelville, Tennessee. Dr Daniel was a young man when he died in Perry County, Tennessee.

Oda I. De Priest H. Daniel then married James Dee Whitfield 1926 in Bakerville, Tennessee.

Oda had two girls and they moved to Waverly, Tennessee and joined the household of James Dee Whitfield who had four children. She was step-mother to James Raymond Whitfield, Ralph Wilson Whitfield , Hester Rozelle Whitfield and Robert Edward Whitfield. She lived one third of her life on Rockdale Farm in Waverly, Tennessee. After the death of James Dee Whitfield she remained at Rockdale Farm with Rozelle Whitfield Daniel and her husband , Billie Daniel who purchased the farm.   She has lived happily with her children and fourteen grand - children, the Hopkins and Whitfields.

The daughter , Martha Frances Daniel married James Raymond Whitfield and lived at Rockdale Farm . They had five children . They settled at Denver, Tennessee in a house they had built . In the golden days of the last years of her life Oda Whitfield lived with her daughter and died August 18 , 1971 , age 83, at Denver, Tennessee.

G 7 & G 8

(151) ANDREW WILLIS WHITFIELD
           (Andrew , ____ , Willis)
He was born Dec. 30, 1852 and died May 19, 1934 . He married three times. Andrew and first wife had six children. Andrew and second wife had six children . All of Rutherford County, Tennessee.

ELIZABETH WHITFIELD
           (Andrew , _____ , Willis)
She was born Feb. 4 , 1855 and died July 12, 1930. No children.

(152) NATHAN JAMES THOMAS WHITFIELD
           (Andrew, _____ , Willis)
He was born Nov. 19, 1856 and died Jan. 18, 1939 . Nathan J. Thomas Whitfield had three girls. One daughter living in 1963.

(153) ALFRED JOHNSON WHITFIELD
           (Andrew , _____ , Willis)
Alfred Whitfield was born Jan. 10, 1859 in Rutherford County, Tennessee and died March 13, 1942 in Cannon County, Tennessee. He married two times. Alfred and first wife had four children . Alfred Whitfield and second wife had seven children . These children are living in Cannon County and Rutherford County, Tennessee. They had child - JESSE BLACKBURN WHITFIELD (154) .

(148) BENJAMIN WHITEFIELD
           Benjamin Whitefield and wife , Mary living July 1907 in Rutherford County, Tennessee. He received a pension on his Mexican War service.

(97) JOHN D. WHITFIELD   (John)
      He married Mollie Faulks , Dec. 18, 1878 , Humphreys County,
      Tennessee.
(149) J. M. WHITFIELD married Annie Porch , Dec. 2, 1891 ,
      Humphreys County, Tennessee.
    J. L. WHITFIELD married M. A. Christopher , Dec. 17, 1884 ,
   Humphreys County, Tennessee.
    S. J. WHITFIELD married Alice Huffines , Sept. 13, 1890 in
   Sumner County, Tennessee where they resided.
    RUSHIE WHITFIELD married Ella Douglas May 19 , 1901 in Sumner
   County, Tennessee where they reside.

NINTH GENERATION

(126) THOMAS JEFFERSON WHITFIELD
          (Thomas C. , Thomas J. , Thomas J. , Wilkins, Thomas)
     Thomas was born February 8, 1910 in Benton County, Tennessee.
He married Earlene Dobson in 1928 . They resided on Eagle Creek ,
Tennessee in Benton County.   Children:
        1. Anna Sue Whitfield , born 1929 . She married
           Bennett Curtis 1945 in Tennessee. They resided
           in Benton County, Tennessee.

(125) CARLIE WHITFIELD
          (Jefferson L. , Thomas J. Thomas J. , Wilkins, Thomas)
     Carlie Whitfield died 1925 of typhoid fever. He married Erie
Baker , and had two sons.
        1. Hurshel Whitfield . He lived at Pepley, Tennessee in
           1962 , and has a service station for automobiles.
        2. Harley Whitfield , died in 1930.

(154) JESSE BLACKBURN WHITFIELD
          (Alfred, Andrew,_____, Willis)
     Jesse married Grace _____ August 31, 1929. She was a school
teacher . Resided 1963 in Readyville, Tennessee. Jesse has a farm
and grocery store.

(124) THOMAS WESLEY WHITFIELD
          (Thomas L. , Thomas J. Thomas J. , Wilkins, Thomas)
     Thomas Wesley Whitfield was born August 2, 1889 in Tennessee
and died June 18 , 1942 in Steele, Missouri. He married Leza Belle
Hatley, daughter of Jim and Belle Hatley of Eagle Creek, Tennessee

on December 1, 1907. Thomas W. and Leza B. Whitfield had eight children :

(133) 1. Gladys Irene Whitfield, born Aug. 24, 1908 . She married M. William Leslie Hatley.

(134) 2. Nomah Chrestine Whitfield , born 1910.

(135) 3. James Lafayette Whitfield , born 1912.

(136) 4. Thomas C.R. Whitfield , born 1915.

5. Elseelene Whitfield. Died April 25, 1918 at Coater, Missouri.

6. Samuel Whitfield , born December 6 , 1920 in Missouri . He married Montana Crawford in August 1941.   Child : 1. Davie Kay Whitfield, born November 29, 1943 . She married James Carey on June 6, 1961. He is a R. F. D. Rural Mail Carrier at Steele, Missouri.

(137) 7. Wilson Durwood Whitfield , born 1923.

(138) 8. Dauthitt Glendall Whitfield , born 1928.

(118) ANNIE WHITFIELD

(John , Henry , Thomas , Wilkins , Thomas)

Annie Whitfield was married to John Bowman. She was born 1880 in Tennessee. They had children :

1. Maybelle Bowman who died 1946.

2. Anne Whitfield Bowman. She was born in Tennessee . She lived in Boston , Massachusetts in 1963 . She worked at D. C. Heath and Company, publishers in Boston. Afterwards she retired and moved back to Humphreys County, Tenn.

(119) FANNIE WHITFIELD

(John, Henry, Thomas , Wilkins, Thomas)

Fannie Whitfield married Bert C. Lytton on July 14, 1906 in Humphreys County, Tennessee . They had child , John Lytton , born in Tennessee.

(120) BELLE WHITFIELD

(John, Henry, Thomas, Wilkins, Thomas)

Belle Whitfield married Doss B. Daniel . The marriage license issued Nov. 7, 1904. Belle and Doss had children.

1. Virginia Daniel , born 1907 and later married W. R. Chapman who had child : William Whitfield Chapman.

Belle was born 1884 and died 1941 in Tennessee.

(121) BESSIE WHITFIELD

(John, Henry, Thomas, Wilkins, Thomas)

Bessie Whitfield married Wilson Larkin about Nov. 7, 1904 . She was born 1887 and died 1948 in Tennessee. They moved to Dyersburg , Tennessee after marrying and they had five children . All the children reside in Dyersburg, Tennessee in 1963 and this has been their location. The five Larkin children :

1. Elise Larkin, b. 1907 and d. Nov. 14, 1963 in Dyersburg, Tennessee.
   She married William Walker of Nashville, Tenn. who was a retired
   captain of U.S. Army. William Walker d. 1961 and was buried in
   Nashville.
2. George Wilson Larkin who married Lillie May Jackson. No children.
3. Evelyn Larkin who married Damon Moore of Dyersburg, Tennessee.
   They had one child: Betty Moore who resides in Dyersburg, Tenn.
4. Sam Whitfield Larkin . He married Judy Smith and they had children:
   (1) Sam Whitfield Larkin, Jr. (2) Jeffery Larkin . The son Sam
   Larkin is a manager of a Gas Company in Dyersburg, Tennessee, 1963.
5. John Franklin Larkin . John was born Nov. 2 8 , 1923 in Tennessee
   and living at Dyersburg in 1963. He was living in Waverly, Tenn.
   in 1950. He married Elaine Walker of Dyersburg, Tennessee.
   They had three children:
   1. Linda Larkin . A student sophomore at University of
      Tennessee in 1963.
   2. Brenda Larkin
   3. John Franklin Larkin, Jr.

(122) NANCY DELILAH WHITFIELD
           (John, Henry , Thomas , Wilkins, Thomas)
       She was born 1890 in Tennessee . She married William B.
Nolan and they had children : (1) William B. Nolan, b. 1916 who
married Margaret.   They had children : (1) Nancy Nolan, b. 1947 .
(2) William B. Nolan, b. 1951.

(123) JOHN HEDGE WHITFIELD
           (John, Henry, Thomas, Wilkins, Thomas)
       John H. Whitfield was born 1893 and d. 1923 in Tennessee. He
married Arbie Teas in Feb. 13, 1915. They had two children . The
father died when the children were young and they were cared for by
their mother and grandfather Dr. J.J. Teas , physician of Waverly,
Tennessee in Humphreys County.
       (147) 1. John Hedge Whitfield , born 1916.
              2. Mary Anne Whitfield . She was born 1918 in Humphreys
                 County, Tennessee. She married Harry Beasley. They
                 reside in Waverly, Tennessee. Child : John William
                 Beasley, born 1943 . John was a student at the Univer-
                 sity of Tennessee in 1963.

(128) JAMES RAYMOND WHITFIELD
           (James D., Thomas J., Thomas J., Wilkins, Thomas)
       James Raymond Whitfield was the son of James Dee Whitfield
(1877-1954) and Mary Hester Mc Keel Whitfield of Humphreys County,
Tennessee where he was born March 9 , 1915 in Waverly. He was

living 1979 in Denver having moved there about 1963 where they built a
house in Denver, Tennessee. Occupation was electrician. He had a hobby
of fishing and varied activities. James Raymond Whitfield married the
daugher of Oda I. De Priest Whitfield , Martha Frances Daniel about
1936 in Steele, Missouri. She was born May 18 , 1920 in Perry County,
Tennessee. J. Raymond and M. Frances Whitfield have always lived
in Tennessee. They had two boys and three girls.

(139) 1. Jack Wilson Whitfield , born 1938 in Tennessee.
(140) 2. Phillip Wayne Whitfield , born March 8 , 1948 in Tenn.
       3. Janice Kay Whitfield , born October 26 , 1949 in Tenn.
       4. Brenda Gail Whitfield , born April 7, 1951 in Tenn.
       5. Sandra Faye Whitfield , born December 4, 1956 in Tenn.

(130) HESTER ROZELLE WHITFIELD
       (James D. , Thomas J. , Thomas J. , Wilkins, Thomas)

She was the daughter of James Dee and Mary Hester Whitfield
of Humphreys County, Tennessee. She was born December 4, 1916 in
Waverly, Tennessee. Hester Rozelle Whitfield married Billie Randolph Daniel of Lobelville, Tennessee in Perry County, Tennessee
on December 8, 1934.

BILLIE RANDOLPH DANIEL was the son of William Andrew
and Nellie J. Daniel who was born September 11, 1910 at Daniel Landing of Lobelville, Tennessee in Perry County. When he married he
and his wife continued to live in the large house of the parents at
Lobelville and did farming on the Daniel farm. When James Dee Whitfield sold his farm , the son-in-law and daughter purchased the place
at Waverly , Tennessee and the name was changed from Rockdale
Farm to Billie Daniel's Farm . Thus the Whitfield House stayed in
the family for another generation with Rozelle Whitfield Daniel.

William Andrew Daniel , the father, and Oda I. Whitfield ,
the step-mother resided with Billie and Rozelle Daniel in Waverly.
William lived to be 96 years old dieing in Waverly, Tenn. After his
death Rozelle Whitfield Daniel studied nursing and was a nurse, and
served at the local Waverly, Tennessee hospital for ten years and
more. No children of this marriage but children visit there on the
farm. Billie and Rozelle Daniel are the uncle and aunt that many of
the Daniel and Whitfield children and their families often visit on
the farm.

In 1979 , Rozelle Whitfield works at the local Waverly Hospital.
Billie who worked for ten years at the Boot factory was back on the
farm full time farming in 1977 and enjoying retirement.

RALPH WILSON WHITFIELD
(129)

(James D. , Thomas J. , Thomas J. , Wilkins, Thomas)

Ralph W. Whitfield was born on December 25 , 1918 in Waverly ,
Tennessee. He married Mildred Lucile Daniel in Dougherty County ,
Albany, Georgia on October 6 , 1942 . The daughter of Nelson Amiles
Daniel (died in 1977) and Nancy May Johnson Daniel of Humphreys
County, Tennessee. Mildred Daniel Whitfield was born January 12 ,
1921 in Hurricane Mills, Tennessee.

Ralph W. Whitfield enlisted in the Air Force on September 19,
1942 , Volunteer, Hq. Sq. 67 th Air Base Group , 556 School Sq. Admin.
Clerk, Supply Sergeant , Airplane Mechanic, Flight Chief and Aircraft
Observer (Flight Engineer B 29).

Ralph and Mildred with children resided in Henry County, Tennessee at Paris in 1962 where they purchased a house. The family lived
on Reynoldsburg Road in Paris, Tennessee. Ralph was a Carburetor
Technician by occupation. He was employed by a Paris Manufacturing
Company.

Ralph W. Whitfield was the son of James Dee Whitfield and Mary
Hester Whitfield of Humphreys County, Tennessee. He married Mildred
Daniel in Dougherty County, Albany, Georgia on October 6 , 1942. They
had three children, Ralph Wilson Whitfield, Jr. , Richard Lewis Whit -
field , and a daughter , Rita Ann Whitfield. The children all attended the
local Paris, Tennessee schools, and the University of Tennessee in the
town of Knoxville.

Ralph W. Whitfield said: "I enlisted in the Air Force as
a Tennessee Volunteer on September 19, 1942 . I was
with Headquarters : Squadron, 67 Air Base Group , 556
School Squadron. My duties while in the service were ,
Administration Clerk, Supply Sergeant, Airplane Mech-
anic, Flight Chief and Aircraft Observer (Flight Engi-
neer B 29). My highest rank was Technical Sergeant .
I was stationed in the training commands and helped train
air crews. The stations were Maxwell Field , Alabama;
Craig Field , Selma , Ala. ; Turner Field , Albany ,
Georgia; Air Force Detch., Philadelphia , Pa.; AAFB se,
Sebring , Florida ; AAF Base Amirillo, Texas ; Boeing
Aircraft Detch.; Seattle, Washington ; Lowry Field ,
Denver, Colorado; Maxwell Field , Montgomery , Alabama;
Roswell AAF Base , Roswell, New Mexico, I served in
sequence at the bases listed in order. " After the World
War II, he returned to Tennessee and farmed for a short
while at Puryear , Tennessee. He also said, "We have

never bought anything on credit since our marriage excepting our house, not even to one dimes worth of groceries or clothes. I have not missed a single month of having income since I was 21 years old. " He was a typical one hundred percent American Citizen . He was accidently killed by electricity in Paris, Tennessee on October 3 , 1964 , and is buried there.

(131) ROBERT EDWARD WHITFIELD
(James D. , Thomas J. , Thomas J. , Wilkins, Thomas)

Robert was the son of James Dee Whitfield and Mary Hester Mc Keel Whitfield of Humphreys County, Tennessee. Robert was called Bob Whitfield. He was raised by James Dee Whitfield and Oda I. De Priest Whitfield. Robert was born August 11, 1921 in Waverly , Tennessee at the home place. He resided there attending the local Waverly schools, and in 1940 attended the University of Tennessee at Knoxville. Robert Whitfield married Vallie Jo Fox on March 26, 1943   at Nashville, Tennessee. They moved to Alameda County, California   on April 1, 1943 for Robert E. Whitfield was employed by Shell Development Company . They settled for three years in Berkeley , and later in 1951 at Contra Costa County, California . They resided at Pleasant Hill town near Walnut Creek. Robert Edward Whitfield is a research Chemist by occupation.
Robert and Vallie had four children :

(143)   1. Christa Marie Whitfield, born December 30 , 1945 in Berkeley, California of Alameda County. She married Roger Lee Bundy.
(144)   2. Robert Edward Whitfield , born November 21, 1948 in Boston, Massachusetts in Suffolk County. He died October 14 , 1971 in Ghana, Africa.
(145)   3. James David Whitfield , born March 14 , 1955 in Berkeley , California of Alameda County.
(146)   4. Joanne Vallie Whitfield , born March 14, 1955 in Berkeley , California of Alameda County.

Robert E. Whitfield began employment on August 1, 1958 with the United States Department of Agriculture , and was employed in Albany , California with the Western Regional Laboratory in 1979. He has a biography printed he rein this book.
Robert and Vallie Whitfield moved to Berkeley , California in April 1943 and stayed there for three years. He moved to Cambridge, Massachusetts for advanced schooling at Harvard University. In 1951 Whitfield Family moved to Walnut Creek of Pleasant Hill and the land location was incorporated as Pleasant Hill town in 1962. Whitfield has always lived on Pleasant Hill Road at the same location in California of Contra Costa County.

VALLIE JO FOX WHITFIELD

Vallie Jo was born March 18, 1922 at Nasvhille, Tennessee . The daughter of Joseph Edward Fox and Valley   Schiefer Fox of Nashville. The granddaughter of Joseph T. Fox and Elizabeth Heiner Fox ; and the granddaughter of Joseph Schiefer and Elizabeth Schiefer. Ancestors at Germany.   The genealogy is printed under Fox Family and Schiefer Family. The genealogical line is Schiefer of Kentucky and Fox (Fuchs) of Kentucky and Tennessee.

She married Robert E. Whitfield called Bob Whitfield on March 26, 1943 at Nashville, Tennessee. She was raised in Nashville, Tenn. Attended the local schools , and Belmont College and the University of Tennessee. She moved to California in April 1943. She moved to Cambridge, Massachusetts in 1946. She moved to New Brunswick, New Jersey in 1949 . She moved to Pleasant Hill of Walnut Creek , California in 1951 and continued to live at Pleasant Hill , California in 1979, the Whitfield Home.

Vallie Jo Fox Whitfield has public biographical records and has a biography : Life of Vallie Jo Whitfield .

Robert and Vallie had four children : 1. Christa Marie Whitfield, b. Dec. 30 , 1945 . 2. Robert Edward Whitfield , b. Nov. 21, 1948 and died October 14, 1971. 3. James David Whitfield , b. Feb. 21, 1953 . 4. Joanne Vallie Whitfield , b. March 14, 1955.

TENTH GENERATION	G 10

(133) GLADYS IRENE WHITFIELD

Daughter of Thomas Wesley Whitfield and Leza Belle Whitfield of Eagle Creek, Tennessee and Steele, Missouri . She was born August 24, 1908 on Eagle Creek, Tennessee. Gladys lived 1963 in Holladay , Tennessee. She married William Leslie Hatley on August 6, 1937. Children : 1. William Leslie Hatley, Jr. , born March 25, 1938 in Tennessee. He married June Schmitt of Wyandatte, Michigan on April 13, 1959. They had children :
(1) Salley Ann Hatley, born Nov. 13, 1959 in Tenn.
(2) Pamela Louise Hatley , born June 6, 1961 in Tenn.
2. Gladys Noami Hatley , born December 27 , 1939 in Tenn. She married Michael Mc Cormack II on Dec. 5, 1958 . They had children : (1) George Michael Mc Cormack III who was born December 9, 1959 in Tenn. (2) Noami Lynne Mc Cormack, born February 7, 1962 in Tennessee.
3. Ketha Lynne Hatley , born November 1, 1941 in Tenn. Attended Bethel College , Mc Kenzie , Tennessee. He received his B. S. degree from school in June 1963.
4. Thomas Whitfield Hatley , born December 21, 1943 Tenn. Unmarried in 1963 at Halladay, Tennessee.

(134) N. CHRESTINE WHITFIELD was born October 10, 1910 in Tenn. She married Emmette Eugene Yates of Repley, Mississippi in January 1931 . She resided in Memphis, Tennessee in 1962, 169 N. Belvedered Street.   Children :
   1. Jere Eugene Yates , born April 1941. Married Caroline _____
      on June 8 , 1962.
   2. Judy Yates , born May 1944 . They all reside in Memphis,
      Tennessee.

(135) JAMES LAFAYETTE WHITFIELD
     (Thomas, Thomas L., Thomas J., Thomas J., Wilkins, Thomas)
   He was born 1912. He married Estelle Hamilton on January 25,
1934. Children :
   1. Sandra Lynne Whitfield , born February 22, 1936 . She married
      Jimmy Jones.
   2. James Wesley Whitfield of Hayte , Missouri . He married
      Brenda Mc_____. They had children:
     (1) Terry Lynne Whitfield
     (2) Tracy Whitfield
     (3) Kimberly Whitfield
   3. Janie Sue Whitfield
   4. Dwane Whitfield . They all live in Missouri.

(136) THOMAS C. RYE WHITFIELD
    (Thomas W., Thomas L., Thomas J., Thomas J., Wilkins, Thomas)
    Thomas C. was born May 23, 1915 in Tennessee. He married
Kathlene Fisk , September 1935 of Steele, Missouri . They had children:
   1. Thomas Clark Whitfield , born in Tennessee.
   2. Jefferson David Whitfield , born in Tennessee.
 Thomas C. Rye Whitfield moved to Steele, Missouri when he was a year old from Eagle Creek, Tennessee where he was born. He moved to Nashville, Tennessee in 1944 . Thomas attended Harding Christian College, Searcy, Arkansas. He is a minister of Central Church of Christ. Teacher at David Lipscomb College in Nashville, Tennessee. He resided in Nashville, Tennessee in 1979.

(137) WILSON DURWOOD WHITFIELD
    He was born October 24, 1923 in Missouri. The son of Thomas Wesley Whitfield . He married Betty Ruth Fromes on August 7, 1943. Children: 1. Gary Whitfield, born October 18, 1944 in Missouri.
       2. Gwen Whitfield , born August,in Missouri.
     He has a store at Steele, Missouri, auto parts.

(138) DAUTHITT GLENDALL WHITFIELD
    He was born January 19, 1928 in Missouri. He married Laura Moore , June 1947 .

MILDRED DANIEL WHITFIELD

Mildred Lucile Daniel was born January 12, 1921 in Hurricane Mills, Tennessee , the daughter of Nelson Amiles Daniel and Nancy May Johnson Daniel. She married Ralph Wilson Whitfield on October 6, 1942 in Albany, Georgia. Ralph was stationed in Army there . Ralph and Mildred had three children : 1. Ralph Wilson Whitfield, born Sept. 16, 1943. 2. Richard Lewis Whitfield , born Feb. 4, 1946. 3. Rita Ann Whitfield , born July 30 , 1951.

Ralph died in 1964 and Mildred went to work in Paris, Tenn. She married second husband, L. G. Richie on November 30 , 1975 in Nashville, Tennessee. Mildred Daniel Whitfield Richie lived in the home place at Paris, Tennessee.

(143) CHRISTA MARIE WHITFIELD

(Robert E., James D., Thomas J., Thomas J., Wilkins, Thomas)

Christa was born December 30 , 1945 in Berkeley, California in Alameda County. She resided with her parents Robert Edward and Vallie Jo Whitfield . She had brothers Robert Edward and James David and sister Joanne Vallie Whitfield. Christa Marie Whitfield graduated from the Pleasant Hill High School 1963 . Diablo Valley College 1965. University of California at Berkeley 1967 .

Christa married Roger Lee Bundy on November 18 , 1967 in Pleasant Hill, California of Contra Costa County. Roger Bundy was born April 14, 1941 in San Francisco, California .

The son of Robert C. Bundy and Glayds Welch Bundy. Roger served in the United States Army . He graduated from Diablo Valley College and the University of California in 1967. He graduated from Law School and was an attorney in 1977. Roger Bundy was from Antioch , California. Roger and Christa Bundy had children :

1. JASON EDWARD BUNDY was born July 15, 1970 , Oakland, Calif.
2. NATASHA MARIE BUNDY was born August 18 , 1972, Oakland, Calif.
3. JUSTIN ALEXANDER BUNDY was born September 6 , 1975 in Oakland, California.

The Bundy family lived on Taft Street in Oakland, California in 1970 and was living there in 1977. Christa Whitfield Bundy was a school teacher in elementary schools in Oakland.

(144) ROBERT EDWARD WHITFIELD

(Bob Whitfield , Jr.)

(Robert E., James D., Thomas J., Thomas J., Wilkins, Thomas)

Robert was born November 21, 1948 , the son of Robert Edward Whitfield and Vallie Jo Fox Whitfield . He was born at Boston , Massachusetts of Suffolk County. Robert was called Bob Whitfield, Jr. He resided in Pleasant Hill, California of Contra Costa County for twenty one years. Bob Whitfield, junior attended Pleasant Hill Schools. Graduated from Pleasant Hill High School in June 1966. Summer of 1968 he attended Anthony Business School. He attended Diablo Valley College and graduated from the University of California at Davis in Child Development work, June 17, 1970. He enrolled in the Peace Corps program of the United States Department of State, March 1970, and on July 1, 1970 left for Ghana in West Africa. Bob Whitfield was serving at Nalerigu Training College as a teacher in Gambaga, Ghana. He was in the northern part of Ghana in West Africa at Nalerigu. On October 10, 1971, Sunday afternoon he was struck by sky lightning and electricity during a rain storm. He died October 14, 1971 at Accra, Ghana. Unmarried. He returned by airplane and was interred at Oakmont Cemetery in Pleasant Hill, California, at Lafayette.

JAMES DAVID WHITFIELD (145)   G 10
(Robert E., James D., Thomas J., Thomas J., Wilkins, Thomas)
James David called David Whitfield. He was born February 21, 1953 in Berkeley, California, Alameda County. He was the son of Robert and Vallie Whitfield. Brother of Christa, Robert, Jr. and Joanne Whitfield. James David lived in Pleasant Hill for all his youth and some twenty two years. He attended the Pleasant Hill schools. Graduate of the Pleasant Hill High School in June 1971. He attended Diablo Valley College. He has travelled around world, and visited in several places such as Asia and Australia. He has worked with the Trans World Airlines and visited in London, England and Israel, 1977. Unmarried in 1978.

JOANNE VALLIE WHITFIELD (146)
(Robert E., James D., Thomas J., Thomas J., Wilkins, Thomas)
Joanne was born March 14, 1955 in Berkeley, California of Alameda County. The daughter of Robert E. and Vallie Jo Fox Whitfield. The granddaughter of James Dee Whitfield and Hester Mc Keel Whitfield; and Joseph Edward Fox and Valley Schiefer Fox Westkamper. The grandparents of Tennessee. She lived all her youth in Pleasant Hill and some nineteen years. She attended Pleasant Hill High School and graduated in June 1973. She graduated from Diablo Valley College June 1975. A graduate of San Francisco State College, December 30, 1976. Major study in Art and Creative Writing. Unmarried in 1979 and living in San Francisco, California. An artist and writer.

(141) RALPH WILSON WHITFIELD
(Ralph, James D., Thomas J., Thomas J., Wilkins, Thomas)
Ralph was born September 16, 1943 in Dougherty County at Albany, Georgia. He resided in Paris, Tennessee and attended local school. He was the son of Ralph Wilson Whitfield and Mildred Daniel Whitfield from Humphreys County, Tennessee. He attended the University of Tennessee at Knoxville, and graduated 1966, B.A. degree.

Ralph W. Whitfield II married Vivien Gale Brewer on June 11, 1966 at Crossville, Tennessee. Vivian was the daughter of Elmo Mitchell Brewer. Ralph and Vivian were both graduates of the University of Tennessee at Knoxville. After their marriage they lived a short time in Pennsylvania where the first daughter was born and named Emily Whitfield. The second daughter, Tracie Robyn Whitfield was born on January 30, 1977. Ralph Wilson Whitfield 's occupation was in the chemical industry. In 1977 he moved to middle Tennessee, then to Nashville, and in 1978 to Brentwood, Tennessee.

(142) RICHARD LEWIS WHITFIELD
(Ralph W., James D., Thomas J., Thomas J., Wilkins, Thomas)

Richard was born 1946, the son of Ralph W. and Mildred Daniel Whitfield of Paris, Tennessee. Richard Whitfield graduated from Grove High School in Paris, and from the University of Tennessee at Knox - ville on June 10, 1969. He married Linda Gale Pendergrass on Decem- ber 23, 1967 in Chattanooga, Tennessee. Linda was the daughter of the Ben Frank Pendergrass. Richard and Linda were both graduates of the University of Tennessee at Knoxville. Richard and Linda are the parents of two sons in 1977 who were born in middle Tennessee. The sons are Jeffrey Whitfield, and Nathan Whitfield. Richard Whitfield was employed in the transportation work and in the postoffice in Tennessee.

RITA ANN WHITFIELD
(Ralph W., James D., Thomas J., Thomas J., Wilkins, Thomas)

Rita Ann was born the youngest child of Ralph W. and Mildred Daniel Whitfield. She was the sister to brothers Ralph Wilson Whitfield and Richard Lewis Whitfield. Rita Ann Whitfield was graduated from Grove High School in Paris, Tennessee on May 13, 1969. She attended the Univer- sity of Tennessee at Knoxville, and graduated with a degree. Unmarried in 1978. Rita Whitfield was employed as a Director of Publications in the Governor's office at the Tennessee State Capitol, and she did television broadcasting reports. In 1979 she resided in Nashville, Tennessee.

(147) JOHN HEDGE WHITFIELD
(John H., John D., Henry W., Thomas J., Wilkins, Thomas)

John Hedge Whitfield is in the ninth generation list but this lineage is believed to be longer ago. John was the son of John Hedge Whitfield and Arbie Teas Whitfield of Waverly, Tennessee. He was born on October 17, 1916 at Waverly, Tennessee. He married first, Bertha Powers of

Humphreys County, Tennessee.

John H. Whitfield served in the Army. August 1942 , Armed Forces of the United States , 566 Squadron , 389 Bomb Group , 8 th Air Force , and stationed for two years in Norwich, England. Dis - charge honorable from service , September 1945.

John Hedge Whitfield married Margaret Louise Rice , the daughter of Alfred Walker and Amanda Johnson Rice of Humphreys County, Tennessee, April 28 , 1946 in Corinth, Missippi . He is a Cashier at the Citizens Bank of Waverly , Tennessee.

John and Margaret have children :
1. James Alfred Whitfield , d. infancy.
2. Donna Elaine Whitfield , born October 16 , 1952 in Davidson County, Tennessee. She resided in Waverly.
3. Margaret Anne Whitfield , born August 17 , 1954 in Davidson County, Tennessee. She resided in Waverly.
4. John Hedge Whitfield , born December 12, 1959 in Humphreys County, Tennessee. He resided in Waverly.

(139) JACK WILSON WHITFIELD
(James R. , James D. , Thomas J. , Thomas J. , Wilkins,
Thomas)

Jack was born on August 3, 1938 in Waverly, Tennessee. He lived there in Waverly on the Whitfield Farm until 1944 when he moved with his father and grandfather to Henry , Tennessee, and then moved with the families to Puryear, Tennessee in 1949 ; and in 1954 to the Denver, Tennessee area where the father Raymond Whitfield lived , and Jack Wilson Whitfield resided there in 1978.

Jack Wilson Whitfield married Lynda Rae Diensberger on July 31, 1966 in Clarksville, Tennessee. Lynda was born in Michigan and raised there. Jack and Lynda resided at Denver, Tennessee and had children.

1. Marc Wilson Whitfield , born April 15, 1967.
2. Mellisa Ann Whitfield , born April 15, 1967.
Mellisa and Marc were twins and born in Hillsdale, Michigan.
3. Michael Lee Whitfield , born April 15, 1968 in Waverly, Tennessee.

Jack W. Whitfield and Lynda Diensberger Whitfield had divorce. Lynda moved to her hometown and resides in Michigan with the three children , Marc Whitfield , Mellisa Ann Whitfield , Michael Whitfield. Lynda married second husband.

Jack W. Whitfield married second wife Mrs Sandra Mc Carson Lane on December 1,1977 in Humphreys County, Tennessee. Sandra was from Mc Ewen, Tennessee. Sandra has two children by former marriage.

(140) PHILLIP WAYNE WHITFIELD
   (James R., James D., Thomas J., Thomas J., Wilkins, Thomas)

Phillip W. Whitfield was born on March 8 , 1948 in Paris, Tennessee. He was the son of James Raymond Whitfield and Frances Daniel Whitfield. Phillip graduated from the University of Tennessee at Knoxville. He was employed as an engineer. He married first wife, Fonna Fay Warren, September 1969 . Divorced followed in April 1976 . No children of this marriage.
Phillip Whitfield married second , Mrs Victoria Daugherty Jacksen on July 31, 1976. In 1978 , Phillip Whitfield and family lived in eastern portion of Tennessee at Oliver Spring , Tennessee. Phillip and Victoria had one child, Kathy Renee Whitfield who was born on April 26 , 1978 . She has a step-brother,Victoria's child of her first marriage , named Shawn .

BRENDA GAIL WHITFIELD
  (James R., James D., Thomas J., Thomas J., Wilkins, Thomas)

Brenda Gail Whitfield was born April 7 , 1952 in Albany, Kentucky. She married Charles Dale Browning on February 17 - 1967 in Tennessee, and they had one child named Shelley Marie Browning who was born on July 6 , 1969.
After a divorce in 1970 , Brenda Whitfield Browning married Mickey Robinson on December 4 - 1971.   Brenda and Mickey in 1978 resided in Camden, Tennessee.
Brenda Whitfield's parents were Raymond and Frances Whitfield.

JANICE KAY WHITFIELD
  (James R., James D., Thomas J., Thomas J., Wilkins, Thomas)

Janice Whitfield was born in Paris, Tennessee on October 26 , 1949 . The daughter of James Raymond Whitfield and Frances Daniel Whitfield of Denver, Tennessee. She married first husband , Larry E. White at Waverly, Tennessee in Humphreys County,   July 19 , 1966. Larry White and Janice had two sons:
   1. James Ray White , born March 23, 1967 in Tennessee.
   2. John David White , born February 8 , 1969 in Tennessee.
After a divorce in 1970 , Janice White married second husband, Roy Trodglen , January of 1971. Janice and Roy Trodiglen lived at Tennessee Ridge , Tennessee in 1978 ; and share their home with White sons, and two Troglen sons , of a previous marriage.

SANDRA FAYE WHITFIELD
(James R., James D., Thomas J., Thomas J., Wilkins, Thomas)

Sandra Whitfield was born December 4, 1956 in Gallatin, Tenn - essee. The youngest child of James Raymond Whitfield and Frances Daniel Whitfield. She married Jerry Franklin Hurt in November 1973 , and resided in Waverly, Tennessee.

ELEVENTH GENERATION   G 11

KATHY RENE WHITFIELD , born April 1978 , eastern Tennessee . Daughter of Phillip Whitfield and Victoria Whitfield.

MARC WILSON WHITFIELD , born April 15, 1967 Tennessee, and living in Michigan . 1978 residing with mother and step-father.
MELLISA WHITFIELD , born April 15, 1967 , a twin to Marc Whitfield.
MICHAEL LEE WHITFIELD , born April 15 , 1968 in Tennessee.
Children of Jack Wilson and Linda Whitfield.

JEFFREY SCOTT WHITFIELD , born September 14 , 1972 .
NATHAN WHITFIELD
Sons of Richard Lewis Whitfield and Linda Whitfield of Tennessee.

EMILY WHITFIELD, born March 3, 1974.
TRACIE ROBYN WHITFIELD , born January 30 , 1977
Daughters of Ralph Wilson Whitfield and Vivien Gale Whitfield of Tennessee.

WHITFIELD IS FROM THE EARLY ANGLO-SAXON NAME OF WITEFIELD .

WHITEFIELD IS FROM THE LATER ANGLO-SAXON NAME OF WHYTFEILD.

The Genealogy is not the same.

In a few families the spelling of the name has occurred and Whitefield is Whitfield , and Whitfield is Whitefield ; but lineage are not definited.

PART III
PICTURE-PHOTOGRAPHS

JAMES DEE AND ODA
WHITFIELD 1926

Christa Whitfield

Joseph & Valley Fox
Wedding 1907

Robert & Vallie Jo Whitfield
Wedding 1943

Robert E. Whitfield
1921-

Ralph & Mildred Whitfield

James Dee Whitfield
1877-54

Oda & Rozella Whitfield

Vallie Jo Whitfield
1922-

Robert E. Whitfield
1948-

Rockdale Farm

Mary Hester Whitfield
1878-24

Raymond & Frances Whitfield

108

Lille May Whitfield-
Phillips 1871 - 19

Henry Edward Whitfield
1888 - 1972

John Regan Whitfield
1880 - 1901

Clara Whitfield
1894 - 1978

Sandra Whitfield
1956 -

Brenda Whitfield
1952 -

Janice Whitfield
1949 -

left to right
1954
Claude Chilton
Jack Meredith
Glen De Priest
Brodie Dreden
Thomas J. Whitfield
Don Manning

Whitfield House   1955   Waverly, Tennessee

Left Side of House
Whitfield

Whitfield Farm   1955

Henry Edward Whitfield
(left) 1888 - 1972
Thomas Cleveland Whitfield
(right) 1884 - 1965
Fish catch - Benton Co., Tenn.

Billie R. Daniel
Whitfield- Daniel
Farm

Rozelle
1916-
Billie R.
Daniel
1910 -

HUMPHREYS
COUNTY ,
TENNESSEE

Rita Ann Whitfield
1951-

Jason , Roger, Christa, Natasha
& Justin. Bundy Family 1976
Roger Lee Bundy 1941-
Christa Whitfield-Bundy 1945-

Joanne Vallie Whitfield
1955-

Whitfield Families   1946
Descendants & in-laws of
James Dee Whitfield .

Jeffrey, Linda G., Richard 1946 -
Whitfield 1975

James D., Delia , Cleveland,
Clara, Edward Whitfield 1940

Jack Wilson Whitfield
1938-

Martha Jane Nicks Whitfield
1855- 1930
Grandson, Robert Whitfield 1921-

Ruby Hensley Hopkins 1910-
Hicks Hopkins

Elizabeth Heiner Fox
1842- 1919

James David Whitfield 1953-

VIVIEN GALE AND RALPH WHITFIELD

Phillip Whitfield
Frances Whitfield

Elizabeth Schiefer Feldman

The McPhail Cliffe Office

East Main Street , Franklin , Tennessee

WHITFIELD LOG HOUSE 18 0
Franklin , Tennessee
Williamson County

John   W.   Whitfield

LIFE OF JOHN WILKINS WHITFIELD

John Wilkins Whitfield was born on March 11, 1818. Son of Wilkins Whitfield and Polly Mary Whitfield of Franklin, Tennessee of Williamson
County. The parents were born in Virginia of English descent.

Wilkins Whitfield and several Whitfield Families of his lineage moved
from Sussex County, Virginia to Williamson County, Tennessee in 1808,
and settled on a land grant.

1818-1825   John was educated on the plantation of his parents , and at the local school of Franklin , Tennessee.

1836 John joined the Hickory guard militia on Natchez Road.

1836-1845   He was a planter in Tennessee. He moved from William-son County to Hickman County in Tennessee . Settled at Centerville , Tennessee near Whitfield Town. Then the area was called Whitfield Postoffice. John was clerk at brother-in-law , Robert Charter mercan-tile store.

1839 , April 13 , John Whitfield   married Catharine Dansby . A historian Spence has written of Robert Charter as the father-in-law of John W. Whitfield but a study showed Catharine Charter to be very young for marriage.

1840   A daughter was born to John and Catharine Whitfield.

July 14 , 1845   Texas approved the resolution of annexation passed by Congress. The admission of Texas into United States was the cause of the Mexican War.

1846 Catharine Whitfield died at Centerville, Tennessee.
          John leaves daughter with relatives.

1846 John W. Whitfield answers the call of his country to save Texas. John Whitfield and his Hickory guards become Company **A** , First Tennessee Regiment , Volunteer Foot soldiers , of the Mexican War. The Regiment was commanded by Colonel William Bowen Campbell , who afterwards became governor of Tennessee. John Whitfield was Company Captain.

June 3, 1846 Company **A** , First Tennessee Regiment , of Mexican War organized at Nashville , Tennessee . On June 5th the Company journeyed by water to New Orleans and landed there June 15th.

June 17, 1846 Company **A**, First Tennessee Regiment with Captain John W. Whitfield embarked on three sailing vessels for Brazos Santiago , an island about nine miles from mouth of Rio Grande in Mexico. Two com-panies of the Regiment were on schooner Orleans and five companies on the ship Charleston , of Boston. John Whitfield and men placed on the third vessel with horses. They weathered out a storm of forty hours at anchor.

June 20 - July 20 , 1846   Camp at Point Isabel under Major Thomas ,

Captains Whitfield and Walton. The Company A is sick with 230 cases of dysentery. Captain John Whitfield and Captain Walton erected the hospital tents. Doctors Daniel Mc Phail and William C. Dorris. Dr. Daniel Mc Phail, the brother-in-law of John W. Whitfield died there. Every man was sick before reaching Monterrey. John W. Whitfield conducted a Bible Class for the Regiment.

July 8, 1846 Captain Whitfield, Colonel Campbell left Camp Brazos Santiago and marched to mouth of Rio Grande and up its waters, with the well soldiers. Tennessee Regiment a part of General Taylor's army.

July 23, 1846 The Regiment reached Camargo on the Rio Grande. It was here the sick of Whitfield's Company was discharged and sent home.

September 7, 1846 March on Monterrey in Mexican War. On the 21 day, Tennesseans made the best charge ever made by Americans against fortress and batteries, and placed the first flag from Tennessee on the walls of Monterrey.

Along with Tennesseans in this charge was the First Mississippi Rifles, commanded by Jefferson Davis. BLOODY FIRST BATTLE at Monterrey, Mexico. First Tennessee Regiment became known as the Bloody First. John Wilkins Whitfield fought in this battle.

October 25, 1846 Captain John W. Whitfield's Company had forty-eight men. Nine men had died and the remainder had been discharged for sickness.

In October and November 1846, John W. Whitfield was at Camp Allen in Mexico. Dr. Dorris wrote in his diary the complete list of Captain John Whitfield's Company in the Mexican War, and it was published in the book, "History of Hickman County, Tennessee" by Spences.

Winter 1847 The First Tennessee Regiment left General Taylor's Army and joined General Scott's Army and participated in the capture of Vera Cruz and in the engagements at Madeline Bridge and Cerro Gordo, which had an military affair on April 18, 1847. A few of the original Whitfield Company participated in these campaigns and Captain John was with his Company, old Hickory Guards.

List of men in this Mexican War in First Regiment of Tennessee in the book, "History of Hickman County, Tennessee," by W.J. Spence and David Spence.

The First Tennessee then went to Jalapa, from which place it was ordered to return to Vera Cruz. Here it embarked for New Orleans, where it was mustered out of service.

Summer 1847 Captain John W. Whitfield and the surviving Hickory Guards returned to Tennessee. The Mexican War with disciplined United States troops in Mexico continued.

1846 General Zachary Taylor led the First Tennessee Regiment. The town Reynosa holds an American grave yard; John Whitfield recovered from his sickness at Tampico. Expedition to capture New Mexico was assigned to the command of Colonel Stephen W. Kearney, an officer of regular army May 1846. He organized at Fort Leavenworth, Kansas 1,500 frontiersmen and advanced along Sante Fe Trail to California and later joined General Taylor.

General Winfield Scott engineered a plan to conquer Mexico City, by April 1847 there was ten thousand men in Vera Cruz.

The Doniphan expedition came from Westport, Missouri in 1847 to Mexican front. It was here that John Whitfield first link with Kansas men happened.

Fall 1847 At Pueblo, General Scott awaited reinforcements. When a second call was made for troops, Hickman County, Tennessee again furnished a Company, composed in part of discharged soldiers of Whitfield's first Company. It became Company K of the Third Tennessee Regiment, commanded by Colonel B.F. Cheatham. John Wilkins Whitfield, Captain enlisted at Nashville, Tennessee, October 8, 1847, Co. K, 3 Col. 13 F C. Tennessee Foot Volunteer. Elected Lieutenant, Regiment Colonel, Regiment three same day, transferred to field staff.

October 1847 Company K of the Third Tennessee Regiment was mustered into service. They went to New Orleans by boat, and from that point sailed to Vera Cruz. Although never engaged in battle, this Third Regiment was well drilled and saw much hard service in an unhealthy climate. The regiment did not reach the City of Mexico until after the fall of that City. At the close of the Mexican War it was mustered out of service at Memphis. After eighteen months of combat, it was the first successful offensive war, and one which United States paid 15 million dollars to Mexico for conquest. Texas now had a good place as a State in the union of United States.

July 24, 1848 John Whitfield was mustered out of service. President Polk was from Columbia, Tennessee and a neighbor to those citizens like John W. Whitfield at Centerville, Tennessee. It was President Polk that had ordered General Taylor to occupy the territory ; insure the annexation of Texas. This State was destined to be a part of the United States because the greatest warriors were from Tennessee, such as Houston, Travis, Crockett and thousands of others at the Alamo. John Whitfield and the others made the conquest a victory. Kansas men had allied with him and he was to form an alliance later with them , an alliance that made him one of their first leaders in the affairs of State.

1846-1847 William Gravett and John W. Whitfield and others borrowed money, chattel and used personal property to equip the Hickory guards Regiment. John Whitfield was summoned March 1847 by the Hickman County Court for a plea of Debt. William Gravett answered the Plea and a fifa was levied on one lot in the town of Vernon in August 1848. The Hickman County Court Minutes of 1847 and 1848 show the fiscal status of the family to be in debt. Much of the outfitting of the Hickory Guards was by the people of Hickman City , the County in Tennessee.

1848 in Tennessee an account had to be given of the regiment enlistees of the First and Third in the Mexican War. Willaim B. Campbell and John W. Whitfield talked with the County legislative Coun cil and came into open Court several times. The year 1848 John Whitfield was helping the judicary of the Hickman County and nearby Counties.

John Wilkins Whitfield appears as a juror in the following Hickman County Court Cases in 1848 : William L. Winners versus Nathan D. Frizzie ; State of Tennessee versus Lewis D. Adams ; State of Tennessee versus John Young ; Edward Arnold versus Robert J. Easley .

John Whitfield was a witness when L. B. Moore had issue against James H. Gill. In problems involving conduct of militia guards John Whitfield came into open Court and acknowledged with other officers as security for the fine fee and costs. John Whitfield was present when the State of Tennessee called Reuben D. Willey and Benjamin Arnold to judicary Court for hearings and indictment.

In 1848 the people of Tennessee honored John Whitfield and his Company of Hickory Guards that had helped to save Texas . They honored Campbell and others of the Regiments. Hickman County had been in the Sixth Congressional District with Hardin, Maury, Giles, Lawrence , and Wayne Counties before 1843 when it was one very large County . These Counties formed were now in 1848 with Mc Nairy, Perry , Decatur , Benton , Humphreys and Lewis Counties formed into the Seventh Congressional District. A legislative Act was passed establishing Taylor

County , which was to be composed of portions of Hardin and Wayne
Counties . The County seat was to be WHITFIELD , named in honor
of General John Wilkins Whitfield . This County was never organized.
The line between Hickman and Perry Counties was again changed.
Whitfield Town found some of the Whitfields living in Hickman County
and others living in Perry County.

Winter 1849 , John W. Whitfield was helping the County and State ,
and was in Court. 1849 the twenty-eighth General Assemby of the
State of Tennessee . John Wilkins Whitfield , of Hickman County ,
Tennessee , was in the Tennessee Senate , he being elected as a re -
ward for his services in the Mexican War. Samuel B. Moore was again
in the House of Representatives , and Landon C. Haynes . The Assembly
convened on October 1 , 1849.

1849-1850-1851 Senator John Wilkins Whitfield of Tennessee was busy
with the affairs of State , and those duties concerning the Seventh Congressional District.

In 1850 John Whitfield was thirty-one years old and living in Center-
ville , Tennessee, in the household was another young lawyer of twenty-
two years , E. P. P. Ny, his wife Margarite and child. A sister , Martha
Ann Whitfield Charter lived near John Whitfield , for her husband Robert
Charter had died in 1849 of March . James D. Easley and William G.
Clagett had taken over the mercantile business.

October 6, 1851 The Twenty -ninth General Assembly of Tennessee
met. This year John Whitfield was appointed major-general of the
Third Division of the State militia. In the House of Representative
was William Phillips, of Hickman County . The following were members
of this Assembly : Francis B. Fogg , Joseph C. Stark , J. D. C. Atkins,
David Campbell, Gustavus A. Henry , Stephen C. Pavatt, and John
Netherland.

In 1851 the Chancery Court at Centerville was the first Mondays in March
and September . John Whitfield was busy with legislative duties. The
Duck River Slack-water Naviagation Company planned a railroad through
Williamson and Maury Counties , or from Columbia to the Alabama
line or the Tennessee River . Hickman County stockholders were made
exempt.

1852 John Whitfield was Senator in the Twenty-ninth General Assembly.
There were duties as master and clerk of the new Hickman County
Chancery Court. The State Capitol building was being completed and
the Thirtieth General Assembly was to meet there on October 3, 1853

for the first time at the Capitol in Nashville , Tennessee , at the new building.

May 28 , 1853   John Wilkins Whitfield married Sarah B. Dibrell in Nashville, Tennessee. John was finishing his second term in the Tennessee Senate . Sarah was born December 11, 1827 in White County, Tennessee , and was the daughter of General George Dibrell of Tennessee.

February 1853 Term Tennessee Circuit Court :

The President and Directors of Bank of Tennessee versus John W. Whitfield , James D. Easley and A. C. Deshazo for Debt. The plaintiff appeared in Court but the defendants did not come and made default. The Court ordered them to pay two hundred dollars, further sum of fifteen dollars and ten cents at six per cent interest per annum , and the cost of Court.

1853 David Rice Atchison (1807-1886) in the Missouri State as a lawyer and politician of the proslavery Democrat party , and United State Senator from Missouri . The political party activities , and the developments of the west such as the consolidation of many small railroad lines into a transcontinental system of the west , and the labor problem of slaves and Indians in these important developments of the western territory found John W. Whitfield a trustee. Atchison was chairman of the Committee on Indian Affairs and was elected president pro tempore many times as a   proslavery Democrat.

John Whitfield had received the political influence of Tennessee men and Missouri men and accepted the job as United States agent in Indian affairs, but had to move from Tennessee to Missouri. John Whitfield had some friends and kinship that had moved to Missouri in 1849.

1853   John Wilkins Whitfield moved from Tennessee to Independence , Missouri to serve as an Indian agent to the Pottawatomies at Westport and Jackson , Missouri.

July 28 , 1853 Wyandot Indians organize Kansas-Nebraska into Provisional Territory of the United States , and elected delegate. Congress fails to recognize the act and delegate. Douglas Bill passed on May 30, 1854 . By this bill the Missouri Compromise was repealed and the territories of Kansas and Nebraska were organized with the right to

---

"History of Hickman County, Tennessee " by W. J. Spence and D. Spence. United States Census of Hickman County, Tennessee . Hickman Court Minutes of Hickman County, Tennessee 1844-1855 . Whitfield Family History.

determine the question of slavery for themselves.

June 1854 John W. Whitfield crosses Missouri border to Kansas.
The first territorial Governor , Andrew H. Reeder arrived in Kansas
October 1854. He called an election to chose a territorial delegate to
Congress . Reeder of Pennsylvania appointed Governor June 29 , in-
augurated.

November 29 , 1854 Pro-slavery party more interested than Free -
State Settlers in election and their delegate John Wilkins Whitfield is
elected to thirty-third Congress.

December 5, 1854 "On examing and collating the returns , John Wilkins
Whitfield is declared by the Governor to be duly elected Delegate " to
thirty-three Congress , the House of Representative of the United States."*

January 1855 John W. Whitfield lives at Doniphan, Kansas.
Andrew Reeder attends the land sales at Paoli and meets his "big border
ruffian friend Whitfield at Leavenworth ." **

March 30 , 1855   The election held for the Kansas Territorial legislature . Armed Missourians dominate election of so-called BogusLegis-
lature . Voting mostly by Missourians. The Kansas Free-State men
protested and a supplementary election held on May 22, 1855 . The
legislature favorable to slavery issue by more than two to one.

1855 Census is taken of Kansas. 8,501 people in Kansas exclusive of
Indians, 5,128 males, 3,373 females , 3,469 minors . There were only
2,905 voters in the territory. Missouri election districts were checked
by Congressional investigation.

1855 Massacre on the Potawattomie Indians while the Committee of
Congress were sitting in Leavenworth City meeting.

February 1855 John Brown and Sons settled at Osawatomie , Kansas.
He soon afterwards starts fanatical raids in Kansas in the name of
Freedom State.

---

* Transactions of the Kansas State Historical Society (Topeka, Kansas
Publishing House 1886 . F676.K33) Vol. 3 , pt. 2, p. 240 .

** "A Visit To Kansas in 1857 ," edited by William E. Connelley ,
which appears in the Mississippi Valley Historical Review , 1926-1927.
F351. M69 Vol. 13, p . 543 .

1855 General John W. Whitfield was in charge of the Upper Platte
agency   He served the Arkansas Indians as United States Agent. He
was busy with legislature beginning in Kansas.

June 5 - 25 , 1855 Free State Convention held at Lawrence , Kansas.
Convention with a threat of war talk and replied , "we are ready "
and adjourned.

July 2 . 1855 "Bogus Legislature" met at Pawnee, Kansas at the first
Capitol . Pro-slavery members in control. John W. Whitfield at Pawnee and moved to Shawnee Mission for more space to work , July 16 ,
1855 . Free State members expelled , and moved to Lawrence, Kansas.
1855 John W. Whitfield also rescued two Spanish boys from the Chey-
ennes and placed them in the Shawnee Mission school.

July 27 , 1855 Shawnee Mission Legislature asks President Pierce to
remove Governor Reeder because he does not approve of method
although member of slavery issue.

July 28 , 1855 United Court rules that Shawnee session is regular.
President Pierce removes Governor Andrew Reeder. Congressional
delegate, John W. Whitfield and Legislators elected takes full respon-
sibility of affairs of State.

August 8 , 1855 Le Compton, near Lawrence , Kansas is selected as
permanent seat of government. Wilson Shannon, Democrat is appointed
Governor.

August 14 , 1855 Free State Convention at Lawrence , Kansas calls
election of delegates to draw up a State Constitution . September 3,
1855 Free Stater , Big Springs , Kansas nominate Reeder as delegate
to Congress and organizes Free State political party.

October 3, 1855 Law and Order Society organized by pro-slavery
men at Leavenworth.

October 1855 election . Reeder versus Whitfield for seat in Congress.
In November Whitfield versus Wakefield and Flenneken the Free State
men, then candidate Reeder.

"Annals of Kansas" by Daniel W. Wilder . Pub. 1875, pages 69,104,109,110.
"Kansas" - A Guide to the Sun Flower State , by Federal Writers Project
Administration .
"The report for 1855 of the United States Commissioner of Indian Affairs."
United States Government Report.

October 30 , 1855 John Wilkins Whitfield receives his certificate as duly elected Delegate to the Thirty-fourth Congress.

October 23 - November 11, 1855 Free State Convention asks Kansas be admitted as Free State by Congress . Kansas favors slavery contest.

November 14, 1855 Pro-slavery convention at Leavenworth , Kansas repudiates Andrew Reeder and accepts John W. Whitfield.

November and December 1855 "Wakarusa War." General Whitfield in camp to protect the territory . John Brown raids Kansas places. Governor Shannon asks for United States troops and John W. Whitfield helps organize them . Finally the Pro-slavery group at Leavenworth destroys ballot-box of Free Staters and office of Free State newspaper.

John W. Whitfield when elected to 33rd Congress served as Democrat from December 20 , 1854 to March 3, 1855 ; presented credentials as a Delegate-elect to the thirty-fourth Congress and served from March 4, 1855 , to August 1, 1856 when the seat was declared vacant.

1856 was a hard political year for John W. Whitfield and Voters of territory , Kansas and Missouri.
January 15, 1856 . Territorial election held . President Pierce supports legality of Kansas Territorial election and denounces Free State Topeka Convention as insurrectionary.

February 4, 1856 John Wilkins Whitfield is sworn in as Territorial delegate to Congress. The first election of Robinson and Lane was not territorial legal and not supported by Congress of United States. Andrew Reeder contest election . Andrew Horatio Reeder (1807-1864) versus John W. Whitfield (1818-1879). February 16, 1856 , Marcy, United States Secretary of War places Federal Troops in Kansas at disposal of Governor Shannon.

February and March 1856 . Speech of Honorable John S. Phelps (1814-1886) , of Missouri, on the Kansas election . Delivered in the House of Representatives , February 19 , 1856.

Speech of Honorable Alex H. Stephens (1812-1883) of Georgia on the Kansas election . Delivered in the House of Representatives, February 19, 1856.

Speech of Honorable A.H. Stephens (1812-1883) of Georgia , delivered in the House of Representatives , March 11, 1856, on the resolution from the Committee of Elections asking for power to send for persons and papers in the Kansas election case.

Speech of Honorable Lemuel Todd (1817-1891) of Pennsylvania , on the resolution reported by the Committee of Elections in the contested - election case from Kansas Territory. Delivered in the House of Representatives of the United States , March 13, 1856.

Speech of Honorable John Letcher (1813-1884) of Virginia , on the resolution reported by the Committee of Elections in the contested-election case from Kansas Territory. Delivered in the House of Representatives, March 13, 1856.

Speech of Honorable Augustus Hall (1814-1861) of Iowa, on the resolution reported by the Committee of Elections in the contested-election case from Kansas Territory . Delivered in the House of Representatives, March 18 , 1856.

Speech of Honorable Alexander H. Stephens , (1812-1883) of Georgia , on the report of the Kansas Investigating Committee , in the case of Reeder against Whitfield. Delivered in the House ... July 31, 1856.

While the election contest is going on the Free State Constitution is presented to the United States Senate in March of 1856.

April 18, 1856 Congressional Committee arrives in Lawrence , Kansas to investigate Whitfield-Reeder election.

Northern emigration of people to Free State increase and land disputes arise . The pro-leaders laid an embargo on Missouri to stop the rifles sent by the Northern Emigrant Aid Society . John Brown's fanatical raids and ruffians deaths occurred in Kansas. The free - staters constantly ran into friction with the Indians.

1856 John W. Whitfield was the United States Agent for the Arkansas Indians in the Territory . He was still in charge of the Upper Platte Agency. John W. Whitfield had always lived near the Indians since the time of his birth . He knew their ways and shared their corn and talked their language . It was his duty to protect the treaties the United States had with the Indians and land holdings. Needless conflict of Kansas kept him in the army camp most of the time putting down crime and freeing prisoners and organiz ing relief for the troops . While speakers debated he earned the title Nimrod Whitfield for keeping order and protecting the frontier of Kansas for all who lived there.
Spring 1856 John Whitfield is General of Army in Kansas of troops.

He organized companies of men from Westport, Independence and Lexington in Missouri and used troops to keep order in Kansas. Pro-slavery men in troop close in on Lawrence town, Kansas and sack town for supplies.

John W. Whitfield 1856 in the Battle of Franklin. The objective was to relieve Captain Pate, and his fellow-captives, and to demolish "old Captain John Brown." They encamped on Bull Creek, twelve miles east of Palmyra. May 31, 1856 United States Marshal, Henry Pate arrests two of Brown's sons at Osawatomie town on charges.

June 2-5, 1856, Battle of Black Jack. John W. Whitfield was camped behind Palmyra with three hundred men to keep order. Confusion among people over Free-State or Slavery issue. Young boys behave as ruffians and call themselves "dragoons." Free-Staters under John Brown, capture sheriff and twenty-eight men. Governor Shannon orders use of United States troops to disperse all unauthorized armed bands. Colonel Sumner, with United States troops, overtake Brown party, with pro-slavery men. John Brown agrees to disband. Sumner joins John W. Whitfield at his camp.

June 1856 Whitfield promises to disperse bands. Bogus men call off law and order. The Topeka Free-State Constitution failed in the Senate. Colonel Sumner scouts area and General John Whitfield, and the other pro-slavery men pass word to disperse, and have no more trouble. Captain Ried, Captain Pate, Captain Bell, Captain Jenigen who came from Issouri started for Osawattomie town. John W. Whitfield and the remainder of his men started back for Westport, carrying several prisoners with them. Men frightened by the marching of Whitfield's army and Free-State men under tensions to resist. It was a three-cornered triangular fight with Free State men, pro-slavery men and the government forces of the Colonel Sumner pretending to keep order.

The Captains of Army who went to Osawattomie were now desperate for food and booty and they pillage the town of Osawattomie and caused destruction, moving then to Battiesville, an Indian Station with the cry the Abolitionists were coming after them to fight. Battle of Osawattomie town, Kansas.

July 2, 1856, Congressional Investigating Committee sustains charge that legislature of Kansas was illegal. The action of the House of Representative caused a vacancy in the Senate Congressional seat of the thirty-fourth Congress. Both John Whitfield and Andrew Reeder are refused as delegates to Congress.

August 2, 1856, Governor Shannon resigns, and John W. Geary is appointed.

August 7, 1856 James H. Lane enters Kansas with his "Army of the North" - 600 immigrants from New England. Missourians driven across border after Osawattomie War.
Governor prevails upon pro-slavery forces gathered in Lawrence, Kansas to disband, and John W. Whitfield helps cause of the Governor.

August 1856 The House of Representatives in Congress votes that John W. Whitfield is not entitled to a seat as the Delegate from Kansas, by 110 to 92. The vote to give A.H. Reeder a seat was 88 yeas to 113 noys. Whitfield had not been in the Congressional seat and Kansas did not have order. John Whitfield had held the seat up to this time by holding his credential, but the seat from August to December was officiallly vacant.

October 6, 1856 Pro-slavery election for Delegate to Congress, members of the Legislature, and on the question of calling a convention to form a State Constitution. The Free-State men do not vote. Of the 4,276 votes cast for Whitfield as Delegate by the people of Kansas, 1,458 were cast at Leavenworth, Kansas. The vote for a convention was 2,592; and against 1,454.

December 5, 1856 Congress seats John Wilkins Whitfield as Delegate from Kansas. He served from December 9, 1856 to March 3, 1857 actively in the House duties of the State of Kansas. The Governor gave him a certificate of election to the thirty-fourth Congress.

January 1857 Free State legislature ask Congress to admit Kansas as a State of the United States. Kansas is now settled with a large population of emigrants.

February 12, 1857 The House Committee on Elections (Washington, D.C.) reports that John W. Whitfield is not now entitled to a seat as Delegate of Kansas.

1857 Kansas is with Statehood. John W. Whitfield is given the duty to register land grants at the office in Doniphan, Kansas. He has registrar job in Doniphan where he resides with wife, Sarah Whitfield. A child named Anthony Whitfield was age 2. John Anthony Whitfield was born 1855 in Tennessee. John Wilkins was Registrar from 1857 to 1861.
October 1857 Pro-slavery men convene at Le Compton and frame Constitution for Kansas; a clause of which provides that the "rights of property is slaves now in the Territory shall in no manner be interferred with"; another clause forbinds any amendments in Constitution, if

ratified until 1864.
December 21, 1857 Le Compton Constitution before people who were to
vote merely "For the Constitution with slavery," or "for the Constitution without slavery." Vote'with slavery 6,143 " ;'without slavery 569. "

John W. Whitfield has many trusts of the people. He continues in his
hunting and scouting parties for order and perservation of law.
The Kansas State Historical Society has several references to his activities while land office Registrar.

1857 WHITFIELD POSTOFFICE established in Hickman County, Tennessee, and named in honor of John W. Whitfield. The most famous man
that ever lived in Hickman County, Tennessee.

1857 James Buchanan is President of the United States.
Lack of coordination with Kansas and Missouri voters.

1858 John W. Whitfield Registrar at land office in Doniphan, Kansas
where he resides. In 1853 he was in Independence, Missouri after
leaving Tennessee with relatives and friends, and 1854 in Westport,
Missouri but crossing the River soon afterwards.

1859 In December month, President Abraham Lincoln visits Kansas.
John W. Whitfield hears the President of the United States speak in
Kansas. Lincoln spoke at Elwood, Troy, Doniphan, Atchison, Leaven-
worth towns in Kansas.

1860 Whitfield Registrar at land office until middle of 1861.

1861 John W. Whitfield began his military career in the Confederate
Army. A Captain in Texas Cavalry of West Army.
Kansas under Wyandotte Constitution is admitted into the Union as the
34th State.

May 13, 1861 War Department of the United States ordered General
Ben Mc Culloch commanding the Indian territory to raise the first
Confederate Army. Mc Cullock had fought at Obispado in the Mexican
War.

Creek Indian Chief, Hopoetholoyahola battles November 19 and December 9 against alliance of Confederate men in Creek country. Cooper
retreats to Fort Gibson, but attacks again when Confederate forces
arrive from Van Buren, Arkansas. John W. Whitfield battalion rein-
forces him on the north side of Arkansas. Another Battle at Christenakla
won fought by the Confederate Indians.

December 1861 Trans-Mississippi armies of the west of the Confederacy had 16 regiments, three battalions under De Bray, 4th battalion
under John W. Whitfield, the 6th battalion; three Arkansas Companies.

February 1862 General Price Army in Missouri moved to Arkansas. He joins Whitfield and regiments group.

1862 Captain John W. Whitfield organized regiment of Indians under treaty and brought them into Confederate Army. He is promoted to Major rank. He was in Arkansas in the Spring of 1862. John W. Whitfield became Commander of twenty-seventh Regiment of Confederate Cavalry with 1,007 Confederate soldiers.
War Department placed Indians under command of Albert Pike and D.H. Cooper.

The first gun of the Confederate War was fired on Fort Sumter April 12, 1861. Tennessee was the last to secede from the Union June 8, 1861, and the first to join the Union again in 1865.

John Wilkins Whitfield was engaged in the Confederate Trans-Mississippi campaign in 1862. The District was placed under command of Earl Van Dorn. He tried to beat the enemy at Pea Ridge, Arkansas. March 6, 1862 John W. Whitfield was in the Battle of Elkhorn at Pea Ridge. General Van Dorn had the divisions of Price which included John W. Whitfield's regiment and Mc Culloch. The Confederate pressed forward and Federal forces retreated but the Confederate supplies were so low Van Dorn had to retreat, and after the defeat went to Corinth. Battle of Elkhorn, Confederates had less than 14,000 men, loss of 600 and 200 prisoners. The union force had 17,000 men, loss at 700 killed or wounded and 300 prisoners. At Corinth Van Dorn united with forces to attack Grant at Pittsburg Landing, Mississippi.

1862 General Earl Van Dorn and General Sterling Price with Whitfield division in command of the Confederate troops in Northern Mississippi. They settled to oppose General Grant and Rosecrans. The idea was to expel the Federals from Mississippi and Tennessee with the combined forces. They planned attack on Corinth but battle at Iuka.

September 19 and 20, 1862, Major John W. Whitfield was with General Sterling Price when they reached Iuka, Mississippi on September 13th and took possession. They were within thirty miles of Union General Grant and his forces. Rosecrans advanced by the Jacinto Road on Price. General Little's brigade moved and he was killed. Price and Whitfield were in the thick of the Iuka battle. Price feared General Grant joining Rosecrans and Ord. It was a severe fight for both armies.

"Biographical Directory of the American Congress 1774-1949."
"Confederate Cavalry West of the River" by Stephen B. Oates.

Iuka, Mississippi : <u>Union</u> , Stanley's and Hamilton's divisions in Army of the Mississippi under Major -General Rosecrans.
<u>Confederate</u> , General Sterling Price , Army of the West ; General Henry Little's Division, General Frank C. Armstrong's Cavalry. Losses for the Union , 144 killed, 598 wounded. Confederate , 263 killed , 692 wounded, 561 captured. John Whitfield was wounded and left near Iuka. He was given a military citation for "dashing boldness and steady courage ," and promoted to the rank of Colonel. He was cited by General Sterling Price. Major-General Van Dorn placed in command of General Price's army. General Price returned to Arkansas to fight for re-entry into Missouri.

Union General Sherman fights against Confederates. Battle at Corinth, Mississippi and Vicksburg gave the victory to the Union armies instead of the Army of the West. Fall season 1862 , John Whitfield recovering from Civil War wound. Under Van Dorn, John Whitfield moved to Tennessee, headquarters at Columbia, Tennessee. After the Battle of Murfressboro , Van Dorn with John Whitfield and men fought at Spring Hill in Tennessee.

March 4th and 5th , 1863 . Thompson's Station , also called SPRING HILL and Unionville, Tennessee. Civil War battle that John W. Whitfield participated in Cavalry army. <u>Union</u> , 33rd and 85th Ind. , 22nd Wis. , 19th Mich. , 124th Ohio , 18th Ohio Battery , 2nd Mich . Cav., 9th Pa. Cav., 4th Ky. Cav. <u>Confederate</u> Earl Van Dorn's Cavalry Coprs , Forrest's , Martin's and Jackson Division . Losses - <u>Union</u> 100 killed , 300 wounded , 1306 captured ; <u>Confed.</u>,150 killed , 450 wounded. Van Dorn and Whitfield met General Forrest at this battle . Forrest had Col. G.G. Dibrell , Whitfield's kin , in command of the 8th and 10th Tennessee Regiment.

May 9, 1863 , John Whitfield was made a Brigadier-General of the 27th Regiment in the Army of the West in charge of Texas Cavalry units.

April to August 1863 . John W. Whitfield of the Army of the West was engaged in Trans-Tennessee and Mississippi operations.

July 4 , 1863 . Vicksburg , Mississippi surrendered. General Grant

"The Civil War from a Southern Standpoint " by W.R. Garrett and R.A. Halley, pages 289,300,385.
"Photographic History of the Civil War", editor - Francis T. Miller . Pub. 1912 . Ten Volumes. Whitfield in Vol II, p. 324 and Vol. 10, page 313 where his picture appears.

and Sherman strip Mississippi. The Confederate Army left to pillage.

August 15, 1863. General Johnson had taken over the Army of Mississippi. On the summer day in August 1863 General Jackson sent General Whitfield and his Texas brigade in pursuit of a body of 800 or 900 Federal Cavalry that moved from Yazoo City, Mississippi toward Grenada, but learning that the Federals had united with a similar expedition from Grand Junction, Tennessee, General John W. Whitfield turned back and destroyed in his retreat the railroad and all the rolling stock that was found on it. The two Federal detachments moved north after leaving Grenada. The Confederate brigades joined General Bragg's army near Chattanooga, and assisted in the battle of Chickamauga.

Fall of 1863. Federal forces in entire control of Mississippi. General Kirby Smith placed in command of the Trans-Mississippi Department. General Joseph E. Johnston in command of Confederate forces in Mississippi. General John W. Whitfield in command of the Texas Cavalry units of broken detachments in the Army of Tennessee.

Winter 1864. General Whitfield and part of General Johnston's troops in Georgia near Tunnel Hill, the outpost of the Army of Tennessee station. General Johnston and men had expedition up the Yazoo River, Mississippi March 1864 but General Whitfield and Cavalry on the border of Tennessee and Georgia in winter of 1864.

The detachment of General Whitfield's Texas-Tennessee Confederate Cavalry lost the Civil War Battle, and May 26, 1865 General E. Kirby Smith of the Army of the Trans-Mississippi Department surrendered 17,686. General John Wilkins Whitfield was a survivor of the Civil War. He returned to his Hickman County, Tennessee homeland at Whitfield Town for a short visit but decided to move to Texas.

1865 John W. Whitfield, Sarah Whitfield, the wife, and the son, John Anthony Whitfield born in 1855 moved to Texas. John buys a farm. 1866 John Whitfield in public life in the State of Texas both in the military and in public administration until he settles on the farm. There are many accounts of John Whitfield in the State of Texas but it is too lengthy to print on Texas here.

April 14, 1866. A public meeting in Lawrence, Kansas strongly condemns the course of Senator Lane. The resolutions were reported by Major E. G. Ross, and a letter by John W. Whitfield written at Austin, Texas was read: "We got whipped, and there is no use to talk. I am the most loyal man now you ever saw."

1866-1867 John Whitfield in Austin, Texas. When it was apparent that
the northern idea was destined to rule , John Wilkins Whitfield settled
down to the life of a planter in Lavaca County, Texas , eschewing an
active participation in politics, though called to several important trusts
by the people of Texas. He was a member of the State Constitutional
Convention in 1866. He was a man of much force of character and much
esteemed.
John W. Whitfield went to Texas for several reasons. His brothers
George W. Whitfield and James Monroe Whitfield were living in Texas
in 1866 , and many of his relatives. Tennessee had not recovered from
the Civl War Reconstruction Period. The military left some of the members of the Army of the West at Texas . There were many new settlers
from Tennessee in Texas. The cattle trail from Kansas to Texas was
well established . Farming was a good way of life in the new State.

1867 - 1879 John W. Whitfield and family lived in Lavaca County, Texas
near the town of Hallettsville. He was a farmer. His son, John A. Whitfield born 1855 was married to Helena Briscoe and residing in Texas.
The son full name was John Anthony Whitfield (1855-1909 Texas).
John Anthony Whitfield and Helena Brisco Whitfield had four children :
1. George Dibrell Whitfield, born May 12, 1887 in Tennessee, and he
   lived 1965 in Devine, Texas. Married.
2. Miss Sadie Whitfield , lived 1965 in San Antonia, Texas . She worked
   at the Bank in San Antonia.   Unmarried.
3. Miss Ruth Whitfield , lived 1965 in San Antonia, Texas . She was a
   teacher in San Antonia school. Unmarried.
4. Mrs Mamie Whitfield Moore who was married to W. C. Moore ,
   a physician doctor who was deceased before 1965. They had children.
   Mamie Moore was living in 1965 at San Antonia, Texas.

Henry W. Whitfield was a descendant of Henry Whitfield of Tennessee.
He was living in 1965 in Austin County, Texas the son of Henry W. Whit-
field , the oldest son of Wilkins Whitfield and Martha Loftin Whitfield
of Tennessee. He was married to Susanna De Moss Oliphant in Maury
County, Tennessee on June 13, 1850. There are a number of Texas
relatives related to John Wilkins Whitfield , born 1818 at Williamson
County, Tennessee at Franklin , son of Wilkins Whitfield and Polly
Mary Whitfield who came from Sussex County, Virgnia. These relatives
are not of the lineal generation of John Wilkins Whitfield, of Tennessee,
Kansas , and Texas. They are the descendants of Thomas Whitfield
and Winifer Whitfield at Sussex County, Virginia who begin the known
lineage in Virginia.

In 1879 , John W. Whitfield was sick for some time , and died October
   27th day in 1879 in Lavaca County, Texas at his home. The newspapers
Lavaca Herald , Planter , and Galveston Daily News of Texas printed an
account of him this year.
>   "Once the event would have produced a national
>   sensation. IN THE OLD DAYS OF THE KANSAS
>   WAR JOHN WILKINS WHITFIELD WAS THE
>   RECOGNIZED LEADER OF THE SOUTHERN
>   PARTY ."

He is interning at Hallettsville Cemetery of Texas.

July 9th, 1890 , Sarah B. Dibrell Whitfield , widow of John W. Whit-
field filed for Pension , Mexican War. She was born December 11, 1827.
She was living in Medina County, Texas when husband Certificate
Number 7393 for her pension was issued. She died April 26, 1918 in
Texas.

A famous man but few historians know that John Wilkins Whitfield,
born in 1818 at Franklin in Williamson County, Tennessee , and died
on a 27th day of Oct . in 1879 near Hallettsville in Lavaca County ,
Texas was this man.

* A Soldier at Monterrey in Mexican War , and a Captain of the First
    Tennessee Regiment , 1846.
* A Senator of Hickman County, Tennessee , 1849 in the twenty-eight
    Tennessee General Assembly. 1852 in the twenty-ninth General
    Assembly.
* Clerk and Master of the Hickman County, Tennessee , 1852
    Chancery Court.
* United States Agent in Indians Affairs at Missouri and Kansas ,
    and Upper Platte Agency serving Arkansas Indians.
* Delegate of Kansas Territory , 1854 to the thirty-third Congress,
    House of Representatives of United States , and 1855 delegate to
    the thirty-fourth Congress.
* Leader of the Southern Party in the Kansas War 1855 and later,
    and a Soldier in Battles.
* Registrar of Kansas Land Office 1858.
* Captain 1861 and then General of the twenty-seventh Regiment
    Army of the West, Texas Cavalry in the Civil War.
* Soldier in Civil War Battles , Trans-Tennessee , Trans-Mississippi.
* 1866 State Constitutional Convention Member of the Republic of Texas.
* In 1879 the Farmer at Lavaca County, Texas.

P R O F I L E   O F   C O U R A G E
John Wilkins Whitfield (1818-1879)

PART IV
TENNESSEE RECORDS

TENNESSEE MARRIAGE RECORDS - Pages 138-144.
MARRIAGE RECORDS - Pages 212,

COUNTIES

Davidson 1788-1914	Rutherford 1804-1837
Hamilton 1854-1870	Shelby 1858-1863
Humphreys 1875-1945	Williamson 1800-1850
Montgomery 1790-1875	
Robertson 1842-1856	

DEATHS : Hamilton County and Shelby County.

TENNESSEE CENSUS RECORDS - Pages 145 - 149

COUNTIES

1870 Davidson	1850 , 1880 Humphreys
1820 Giles	1820 , 1830 Williamson
1830 Haywood	1820 Steward
1850 Henry	1810 , 1820 Rutherford
1830 , 1840 , 1850 Hickman	

RELATED   GENEALOGY - Pages 150 - 154
Bates , Claggett , Daniel , Whitfields

TENNESSEE WILLS AND INVENTORIES - Pages 154-157
1811-1818 ; 1825-1830

COUNTIES

Cheatham	Rutherford	Montgomery
Humphreys	Washington	
Lawrence	Williamson	
Henry	Sumner	

LAND GRANTS AND DEEDS - Pages 176-187

TENNESSEE COURT MINUTES - Pages 158-174

COUNTIES

Hickman 1844-	Davidson 1788-	Wilson 1816-
Maury 1823-	Montgomery 1788 -	Cheatham 1856-
Henry 1836-	Washington 1802-	Humphreys 1930 -
Sumner 1787-	Stewart 1811-	Rutherford 1804-
Knox 1798-	Shelby 1843-	

TAX RECORDS - Page 175

COUNTIES

Henry	Rutherford
Montgomery	Sumner

Contra Costa County, California .   "Kentucky Census 1800 of Taxpayers."

MARRIAGE RECORDS
WILLIAMSON COUNTY , TENNESSEE 1800 - 1850

Allen, Lewis married to Rebecca Whitfield , Oct. 11, 1823
by Levin Edney, M.G. Bondsman : Jeter Perkins.

Clagett, William G. to Theodosia Whitfield , July 21, 1835
by Wm. Roach. Bondsman : Elijah Walker.

Clow, John J. to Theodocid Whitfield, December 11, 1833
Bondsman : Thomas J. White.

Cliffe, Daniel to Virginia C. Whitfield , November 15, 1842
by Robert Davis, M.G. Bondsman : Jas. Hogan, Jr.

Charter, Robert married Martha Ann Whitfield, June 7, 1827 by John P.
Hicks . Bondsman : Basel B. Saterfield. L.D.M.E.P. Church.

Criddle, Smith married Lucy Whitfield , September 4, 1832 by Levin Edney
M.G., Smith Criddle by B.W. Drake, Blount W. Drake, to secure bond.

Mc Phail, Daniel married Sarah Whitfield, October 11, 1831
Bondsman : John Wheaton.

Owen, Robert C. married Eliza Whitfield, October 25, 1825
Bondsman : Sandy Owen.

Whitfield , Felix to Minerva Williamson, January 3, 1837
by Robert Davis, M.G., S.B. Mc Connico, Clerk Court.

Whitfield , George W. married Sarah Bond , March 5, 1849
by M.L. Andrews, M.G. Harrison Whitfield , Bondsman.

Whitfield , Harrison married Sophronia M. Conn, September 16, 1845
by M. L. Andrew, M. G. , James S. De Moss, Bondsman.

Whitfield , James M. married Rebecca A. Newson May 16, 1845
by J. L. Andrews, M. G., William Ewing , Bondsman.

Whitfield, Thomas Jefferson married Eliza Nolan , January 24, 1829
in Williamson County, Tennessee. Feb. 6, 1829 by G. Marshall J.P.
A. H. Evens, Bondsman. Thomas Jefferson Whitfield later married
Sallie L. Dillahunty , January 27, 1835 in Davidson County, Tennessee.

Whitfield , Wilkins to Elizabeth Ridley , September 3, 1846
by Robert Davis, M. G. Wm. H. Hill, Bondsman.

MARRIAGE RECORDS
ROBERTSON COUNTY, TENNESSEE

Whitfield, James H. married Sallie I. Boune. Solemnized December 10, 1856, at Nashville. Reside in Robertson County.

Fort, Joseph W. married Susan M. Whitfield, January 7, 1842. Solemnized R. B. Mitchell, J. P.

RUTHERFORD COUNTY, TENNESSEE 1804-1837

Whitfield, Benjamin married to Elizabeth Herrod, July 5, 1827. Bondsman, John Espey.

Whitfield, George W. married Wareena Spence, October 24, 1843 in Davidson County, Tennessee.

Whitfield, Matthew married Fanny R. Monahan, July 30, 1834 Bondsman, Eli Whitfield, by Martin Clark, E. M. E. C.

Whitfield, Thomas G. to Melinda Guiley, license issued December 31, 1825, and married January 4th, 1826 by B. B. Dickins, J.

Whitfield, Willis married Alemeada Rhodes married July 27, 1825 by B. B. Dickins, J. P.

Alfred Whitfield surety to William L. J. Bryant who married Elizabeth A. Thomas, September 3, 1833.

Benjamin Whitfield, surety to Caleb Gilley who married Ibby Bynum, issued February 27, 1827.

Thomas Y. Whitfield and B. B. Dickins, J. P. surety to Peterson Gilley who married Elizabeth Carnohan, Solmn. March 13, 1833.

Thomas Y. Whitfield, surety to Jesse M. Gilley who married Sarah Carnohan, issued November 6, 1835.

Eli Whitfield, surety and Martin Clark, E. M. E. C. to Matthew Whitfield who married Fanny R. Manahan, July 30, 1834.

DAVIDSON COUNTY, TENNESSEE

Whitfield, James H. married Sallie I. Boune, December 10, 1856 by F. C. Plaster, M. G.

Whitfield, William to Emeline Carington, date issued Feb. 19, 1847.

William Whitefield to Ellen Green, November 6, 1847 issued.

MARRIAGE RECORDS
DAVIDSON COUNTY, TENNESSEE 1789 to 1914

Davidson County records are whites and colored people licensed in County.   In Tennessee the negro man or woman with the name of Whitfield following the Civil War once lived in the household of a White family in North Carolina , Virginia, or Tennessee. The African origin family tree can be written by location of Whitfield families with slaves, plantation owners, and from records on the United States Census.

Negro Records , Colored

Whitfield , Martin married Mary E. Whitfield , license issued April 22, 1866 (negro).

Whitfield, Brigg to Fanny Hailton issued license April 18, 1866 (negro).

Whitfield, Watt to Annie Williams, Oct. 15, 1878 license issued (negro).

Whitfield, Stephen to Texas Barley issued December 23, 1886 (negro).

Whitfield, Math to Ellen Dezier license issued September 28, 1887 (negro).

Whitfield, Isaac to Louisa Canten Kennedy issued September 27, 1893(negro).

Whitfield, Sidney to Lula Cowan issued July 3, 1882 (negro).

White Records

Whitfield, Thomas W. to Sarah M. Berry , March 3, 1885.

Whitfield, Dr. Harry married Mary F. Baker issued Feb. 26, 1856.

Whitfield, John Wilkins married April 13, 1839 to   Catherine Dansby in Hickman County. Then John W. Whitfield married Sarah B. Dibrell, May 28 , 1853 . License issued April 27, 1853 Davidson County, Tenn.

Whitfield, Moses G. to Sallie Wells , issued December 25, 1870.

Whitfield, John W. married Susan Phipps issued March 8 , 1823.

Whitfield, Emil L. to Callie Phipps issued license May 7, 1887.

Whitfield, W. H. to Maggie Sloan issued license December 26, 1895.

Whitfield , Charles C. to Gracie Prewitt issued Feb. 20 , 1898.

Whitefield, Ben married Bessie Fitzgerald issued June 11, 1904.

Whitfield, R. W. married Ellen Nash issued August 20 , 1904.

Whitfield , Cliff to Iola May Vaughn issued license November 14, 1914.

Whitfield , Robert Edward married Vallie Jo Fox , March 26, 1943.
Solemnized by Thomas P. Duffy of Nashville, Tennessee.

Vallie Jo Fox Whitfield was working on these records for compilation November 22 , 1963 at the Courthouse in Nashville, Tennessee when her work was interrupted with a news message : "The President, Jack Kennedy has just been shot." She listened to the television broadcast at 12:30 noon to the tragic event concerning the President of the United States , John F. Kennedy, and did not complete the additional search for Davidson County marriage records on Whitfields after 1914 year. The Nashville Courthouse was closed one hour after the death of John Fitzerald Kennedy (May 29 , 1917- November 22, 1963), our thirty - fifth president , for the following days.
Mrs Whitfield travelled by airplane through Dallas, Texas the day following to her home in Contra Costa County, California.

Davidson County, Tennessee
Whitfield, George W. married Wareena Spence October 24, 1843.

John Fletcher married Esther Whitfield November 5, 1799.

Whitfield, Henry married Martha Ann Loftin Oct. 22, 1823.

Whitfield , William married Elizabeth Newson Dec. 4, 1832
by Levin Edney, M. G.

HUMPHREYS COUNTY, TENNESSEE

Daniel, Billie Randolph married Hester Rozelle Whitfield, December 8, 1934 at Waverly, Tennessee.

Whitfield, Ralph Wilson married Mildred Lucille Daniel October 6, 1942 in Dougherty County, at Albany, Georgia.

Whitfield, James Raymond married Martha Frances Daniel March 21, 1936 in Steele, Missouri.

Whitfield , John D. married Mollie Fowlkes December 18, 1878.

Whitfield , James Dee married Oda Daniel April 17, 1926.
And James Dee Whitfield married first wife, Mary Hester Mc Keel the daughter of William Hyman Mc Keel and Louisa D. Harder of Maury County, Tennessee on September 1, 1899 in Benton County.

Nolan, William Blessing and Nancy Delia Whitfield married 1917. Jewish rite of matrimony.

Whitfield, John Hedge married Arbie Hester Teas on Feb. 13, 1915.

Daniel, D. B. to Belle Whitfield married November 7, 1904.

Larkins, Wilson married Bessie Whitfield December 17, 1904.

Lytton, Bert C. to Fannie Mai Whitfield, July 14, 1906.

Whitfield, J. M. married Annie Porch on December 2, 1891.

Whitfield, J. L. to M. A. Christopher December 17, 1884.

Whitfield, S. D. married Eliza Richardson August 31, 1863.

Whitfield, Thomas Jefferson married Jane Nicks Cunningham, S. L. March 27, 1866.

Arleene Story was married to William R. Whitfield about 1949 in Tennessee. Son was Billy Joe Whitfield. Divorce decree 1952 in Humphreys County.

HAMILTON COUNTY, TENNESSEE 1865 - 1870

Whitfield, Scott married Louisa Whitfield, July 9, 1866 by J. D. Blackford, J. P. ; and Scott Whitfield to Louisa Williams, August 28, 1867 by J. D. Blackford, J. P.

SHELBY COUNTY, TENNESSEE 1858 - 1863

Curlin, T. H. married N. E. L. Whitfield, September 21, 1859, Charles Finley, security.

Farmer, L. married Sarah L. Whitfield, December 21, 1860 by G. J. Bibb, M. G.

Whitfield, L. H. married to L. E. Ruffin, April 14, 1854 by C. R. Hendrickson, Security, F. E. Whitfield.

DICKSON COUNTY and WILSON COUNTY

Whitefield, Ansel married to Fanny Tisdale, March 8, 1815 in Dickson County.

Whitefield, Ansel married to Janey Tisdale, March 8, 1815 in Wilson County.

TENNESSEE MARRIAGES from book : "Whitfield , Bryan , Smith and Related Families " by Emma Whitfield.

Whitfield, Needham Bryan married Hannah E. Wilcox in 1843.
MONTGOMERY COUNTY , TENNESSEE

Whitfield , Sarah married A. Dudley Bourne (1805-1878).
Whitfield , Eugenie Geraldine (1853-1872) married William M. Rallow.
Whitfield, Hervey married Ella Trigg , October 20 , 1875.
Whitfield , James Hervey (1834-1912) married 1856 to Sarah Jane Bourne.
Whitfield, Herbert Tera married January 22, 1902 to
   Leslie Hicks Johnston.
Whitfield , W. B. married Susan F. Samuels , issued January 22, 1852.
Bondsman, Thomas Trigg , performed January 29 , 1852 by R. W. Nixon.

Whitfield , William and Elizabeth Goodman-Whitfield's descendants marriage records for this County can be found in the book by Emma Whitfield.
   Marriages in North Carolina or Tennessee , and residing
      in Montgomery County, Tennessee then Christian County, Ky.
   William B. Whitfield married Mary E. Killebrew , Sept. 24, 1849.
Bryan Whitfield married Anne Neville about 1793 ; then
   Bryan Whitfield married Catherine Bailey about 1798.
Lewis Whitfield married Elizabeth Wimberly, and then Lewis Whitfield married Sarah Diggs. He resided in 1793 in Montgomery Co.

Thomas J. Whitfield (1826-1898) married Margaret M. Beck (1832-1867).

BENTON COUNTY , TENNESSEE

J. L. Whitfield married Lovellan _____ . Resided in 1903 in County.

James Dee Whitfield of Humphreys and Benton County , married Mary Hester Mc Keel on September 1, 1899 in Benton County.

KENTUCKY RECORDS

Catharine Whitfield married Thomas Ogilvie November 3, 1775.

Elizabeth Whitfield married Giles Cooper September 12, 1765.

Joseph Theodore Fox of Kentucky married Elizabeth Heiner , about 1860 on the Ohio River near Indiana , and moved to Simpson County, and they had a son named Joseph Edward Fox.

Joseph Edward Fox married Valley Schiefer February 7, 1907 in Campbell County , Kentucky . She was the daughter of Joseph Schiefer and Elizabeth Wilkins- Schiefer.

Joseph Schiefer married Francisa _____ 1876 ; and then in Kentucky
Joseph Schiefer married Elizabeth Wilkins July 10 , 1884.
He was the son of Joseph Schiefer and Elizabeth of Newport ,
Kentucky and his parents married in Austria.

DEATH RECORDS - Hamilton County

A. Whitefield , July 7, 1927 , Greenwood Cemetery. Hamilton County, Tennessee.
National Cemetery Interments - Josiah Whitfield , private , U.S.C. Inf. July 14, 1914 , Grave 13559-B , Section Q.

Shelby County, Tennessee

William Whitfield , boy two years, of William Whitfield of Shelby County, Tennessee. William Whitfield had negro worker named Thomas Whitfield , age 41 , Nov. 2 , 1855 , married , and his child Emma W. Whitfield, age 20 months, died Dec. 29 , 1854.

Tennessee

Daughter of American Revolution , Kentucky Toombstone Record .
Bryant Whitfield born 17th of February 1793 ; died 6th December 1863.
Wife, Seanea Whitfield , born 17th Nov. 1802 ; died 14th November 1884.
This is probably the son of William and Mary Whitfield of Wayne County,
North Carolina to Christian County , Kentucky and later in life to
Effingham County, Illinois in 1844 . The son , Bryant Whitfield was
33 years old in 1844.

Clara Estelle Whitfield born Oct. 23, 1929 died infancy. Daughter of James Dee Whitfield and Oda Whitfield of Waverly, Tennessee.

Mollie Blunt Whitfield died Jan 1 , 1931 at five months.

Ellen Louis Larkin died November 13, 1963 , Tennessee.

Catholics buried in GREENLAWN CEMETERY at Franklin in Simpson County, Kentucky , 20 miles south of Bowling Green , Warren Co. , Ky.
Joseph Theodore Fox, born April 2- 1832 Germany ; Died June 29 - 1883
in Nashville, Tennessee. Elizabeth Heiner Fox , born in Hawsville,
Kentucky of Hancock County on December 15 , 1842. Daughter of J. T.
and E. Fox , Fannie Fox , born April 13 , 1868 , d. June 28 , 1873.
Son of J. T. and E. Fox , Charley Fox , born April 13, 1870, died June
28, 1871. Son of J. T. and E. Fox, George W. Fox , born November 1,
1865 , and died February 23, 1942 at Nashville, Tennessee.
Joseph and Elizabeth had also children :Theodore J. Fox 1864-1920ca,
Nettie Fox, b. 1872, d. 1953, Albert J. Fox 1870ca, d. 1952, Eugene 1875-6,
Arthur 1869-d. 1926, Bernard Fox b. 1879, d. 1945, Joseph E. Fox, b. 1882,
d. 1942. Robert 1878 infant.

CENSUS RECORDS

1820 CENSUS,
Rutherford County,
 Tennessee
MATHEW WHITFIELD-over 45
His wife - over 45 years
1. Boy - under 10 years
2. Boy - 10 to 16 years
3. Boy - 18 to 26 years
4. Girl - 10 to 16 years
5. Girl - 16 to 25 years

WILLIS WHITFIELD
 - over 45 years
His Wife - over 45 years
1. Boy - under 10 years
2. Boy- 10 to 16 years
3. Boy- 18 to 26 years
4. Boy - 18 to 26 years
5. Girl - 10 to 16 years
6. Girl - 16 to 25 years

JOHN WHITFIELD
1. Boy - under 10 years
2. Boy - under 10 years
3. Boy - 10 to 16 years
4. Girl - under 10 years
5. Girl - under 10 years
6. Girl - 10 to 16 years
7. Girl - 10 to 16 years
His wife, over 45 years

1810 CENSUS
RUTHERFORD COUNTY,
TENNESSEE
Whitfield Family

1850 CENSUS
RUTHERFORD COUNTY,
TENNESSEE

1830 CENSUS   (page 265)
Hickman County, Tennessee
Thomas I. Whitfield
1. Boy - 20 to 30 years
2. Boy- 20 to 30 years
3. Boy - 20 to 30 years
4. Girl - 15 to 20 years
      Girl, slave - 10 to 24 years

1840 CENSUS
Hickman County, Tennessee
James M. Whitfield , born Tenn.
1. Boy- 15 to 20 years, born Tenn.

John Whitfield - 20 to 30 years
One male - 70 to 80 years
John's wife - 20 to 30 years
1. Boy - under 5 years
2. Boy- under 5 years
3. Girl - 10 to 15 years

Felix Whitfield - 20 to 30 years
His wife - 15 to 30 years
1. Boy - under 5 years
2. Boy- under 15 to 10 years
3. Boy - under 10 to 15 years
4. Girl - under 5 years

ROBERT CHARTER - under 40
His wife, Martha Ann Whitfield-
      30 to 40 years
1. Boy - 20 to 30 years
2. Boy - 20 to 30 years
3. Girl - under 5 years
4. Girl - under 5 years
5. Girl - 5 to 10 years
6. Girl - 10 to 15 years

Malvison Whitfield - Girl 15 years, born Tennessee
Willis Whitfield - 23 years , born Alabama. Farmer
Christina Whitfield - 23 Female, born Tennessee
Alfred Whitfield - 20 years , born Milfs. Farmer

1840 Census, Hickman County, Tennessee , 8,769 names appear on this Census.

1840 Census , Hickman County, Tennessee

JOHN W. WHITFIELD - 20 to 30 years . His wife , Catharine -
15 to 20 years .   (1) Girl - under 5 years

1850 CENSUS, HICKMAN COUNTY, TENNESSEE

September 28 , 1850 - Dwelling 542

JOHN WHITFIELD - 31 years , Male , Member of the Senate, born
in Tennessee.
E. P. P. Ny , 22 years , Male, lawyer , $ 30 . value , born Tennessee.
Maragritte " , 18 years. Female, born Tennessee.
Ellan   " , 6 months. Female , born Tennessee
Martha Charter , 38 years . Female.

1820 CENSUS - WILLIAMSON COUNTY, TENNESSEE

WILKINS WHITFIELD - 26 to 45 years . (He was 40 years , born Va.)
    (Polly Mary Sturdivant Whitfield . Born 1882 ca, Virginia)

1. Boy - under 10 years.	Names of Children:
2. Boy - under 10 years.	Henry Whitfield, b. 1802 ca. Virginia
3. Boy - under 10 years.	George Whitfield, b. March 12, 1806, Va.
4. Boy - 18 to 26 years.	William Whitfield
5. Girl - under 10 years	Harrison Whitfield , born Tenn.
6. Girl - under 10 years	Thomas Jefferson Whitfield, b. 1810.
7. Girl - under 10 years	Martha Ann Whitfield, b. 1812 Tenn.
8. Girl - 16 to 26 years	Theodosia Whitfield , b. 1816, Tenn.
Thirteen Slaves	Sarah Whitfield , b. 1817, Tenn.
	John W. Whitfield , b. 1818, Tenn.
	James Monroe Whitfield, b. 1819.
	Virginia C. Whitfield , b. 1821, Tenn.

HARRISON WHITFIELD - 26 to 45 years. (He was 37 years , born Va.)
    He was born 1783 ca in Virginia ; and died 1864 ca in Tennessee.
His wife, Polly Sledge Whitfield - 26 to 45 years

1. Boy - under 10 years	Names of Children:
2. Boy - under 10 years	Thomas Whitfield
3. Boy - under 10 years	Rebecca Whitfield
4. Girl - under 10 years	John Whitfield
5. Girl - under 10 years	Felix Whitfield
6. Girl - under 10 years	Harrison Whitfield
7. Girl - 10 to 16 years	Nancy Whitfield (Winstead), b. 1811 and
Five Slaves	d. 1885 , Tennessee

JOHN WHITFIELD - 18 to 26 years.
   Female (Mother) - over 45 years.

Williamson County, Tennessee in 1820 had a population 20, 640 males, 6,626 white females , 3,460 black slave males , 3,512 white slave females , 18 foreigners not naturalized, 4,810 persons engaged in agriculture, 310 persons engaged in manufacture , 23 persons en - gaged in commerce.

1830 CENSUS , WILLIAMSON COUNTY, TENNESSEE

WILLIAM WHITFIELD - years 50 to 60 (Born 1775 ca.)
His wife , 40 to 50 years   (Born 1785 ca)
1. Boy - 5 to 10 years
2. Boy - 5 to 10 years
3. Boy - under 5 years
4. Boy - 20 to 30 years
5. Girl - 5 to 10 years
6. Girl - 10 to 15 years
7. Girl - 15 to 20 years

HARRISON WHITFIELD - 40 to 50 years (b. 1783 ca -d. 1864)
His wife, Polly Sledge Whitfield - 50 to 60 years
Female - 60 to 70 years . His mother
1. Boy - 5 to 10 years
2. Boy - 5 to 10 years   (Harrison Whitfield's brothers
3. Boy - 10 to 15 years   were William Whitfield and
4. Boy - 10 to 15 years   Wilkins Whitfield and John
5. Girl - under 5 years   (Jack) Whitfield.
6. Girl - under 5 years
7. Girl - 10 to 15 years
8. Girl - 10 to 15 years

1820 CENSUS, MONTGOMERY COUNTY, TENNESSEE

NEEDHAM WHITFIELD - 26 to 45 years
His wife, 26 to 45 years
1. Boy - under 10 years
2. Boy - 18 to 26 years
3. Boy - 18 to 26 years
4. Boy - 18 to 26 years
5. Boy - 18 to 26 years
6. Girl - under 10 years
7. Girl - 10 to 16 years
8. Girl - 10 to 16 years

1830 CENSUS, HAYWOOD COUNTY, TENNESSEE

JAKE WHITFIELD   (page 441)
  His wife , 30 to 40 years
1. Boy - under 5 years
2. Boy - 20 to 30 years

1850 CENSUS , HENRY COUNTY

15 th Civil District		Birthplace :	(page 383)
John Whitfield	32 years	Farmer .	Tennessee
Elizabeth Whitfield	33 years		North Carolina
Mary Whitfield	10 years		Tennessee
William Whitfield	9 years		Tennessee
James Whitfield	8 years		Tennessee
Martha Whitfield	4 years		Tennessee
Needham Whitfield	2 years		Tennessee
Elizabeth Whitfield	6 months		Tennessee

| Cynthia Whitfield | 24 | | Tennessee |

Lewis Whitfield	33	Farmer	Tennessee (p. 385)
Rebecca Whitfield	32		Kentucky
Eliza Whitfield	13		Tennessee
James Whitfield	16		Tennessee

Needham Whitfield	29	Farmer	Tennessee (p. 376)
Araminta Whitfield	20		
William 22, Sarah 20 , Martha Ann 10			Tennessee

Whitfield does   not appear on 1870 Census of Henry Co., Tenn.

1820 CENSUS , GILES COUNTY , TENNESSEE

JOHN WHITFIELD   - 26 to 45 years
His wife - 26 to 45 years
1. Boy - under 10 years
2. Boy - 16 to 18 years
3. Boy - 10 to 26 years
4. Boy - 10 to 26 years
5. Girl - under 10 years
6. Girl - under 10 years
7. Girl - under 10 years

1850 CENSUS, HUMPHREYS COUNTY, TENNESSEE

D.A.R. Microfilm T 6 # 304 , 1 st part.

p. 127 , August 8, 1850		Real Est.	Birthplace
Thomas J. Whitfield	40 years	Value	Tennessee
Sarah Whitfield	32		Tennessee
Henry W. Whitfield	20	Physician $2000	Tennessee
Silas Whitfield	14		Tennessee
John Whitfield	11		Tennessee
George Whitfield	9		Tennessee
Thomas Whitfield	5		Tennessee
Sarah Whitfield	1		Tennessee

1820 CENSUS, STEWART COUNTY, TENNESSEE

WILLIAM WHITFIELD - over 45 years
  His wife, over 45 years

1. Boy - 10 to 16 years	4. Girl - 10 to 16 years
2. Boy - 10 to 16 years	5. Girl - 10 to 16 years
3. Girl - under 10 years	6. Girl - 10 to 16 years

1880 CENSUS, HUMPHREYS COUNTY, TENNESSEE

			Birthplace of	Father	Mother
FRANK WHITFIELD	41 years	Physician	Tenn.	Tenn.	Tenn.
Margaret Whitfield	30	Housewife	Tenn.	Tenn.	Tenn.
Bettie Whitfield	7		Tenn.	Tenn.	Tenn.
Beckie Whitfield	5		Tenn.	Tenn.	Tenn.

OBEDINK WHITFIELD	29	Farmer	No Carolina	No. C.	No. C
Emma Whitfield	24	Housewife	Tenn.	Tenn.	Tenn.
Sallie	6 months		Tenn.	Tenn.	Tenn.

THOR J. WHITFIELD	35 years	Dryland Merchant	Tenn.	Tenn.	Tenn.
Martha F. Whitfield	25 years	Housewife	Tenn.	Tenn.	Tenn.
Lafayette Whitfield	13		Tenn.	Tenn.	Tenn.
Nettie Whitfield			Tenn.	Tenn.	Tenn.
James D. Whitfield			Tenn.	Tenn.	Tenn.

Joseph Fox	22 years	Farmer labor	Tenn.	Tenn.	Tenn.

HENRY W. WHITFIELD	50 years	Physician	Tenn.	Va.	Tenn.
Nancy C. Whitfield	48	Housewife	Tenn.	Tenn.	Tenn.
Annie H. Whitfield	28		Tenn.	Tenn.	Tenn.
John Whitfield (negro)	8		Tenn.	Tenn.	Tenn.
John D. Whitfield	23	Farmer	Tenn.	Tenn.	Tenn.
Keary Whitfield (negro)	19	Housewife	Tenn.	Tenn.	Tenn.
			Tenn.	Tenn.	Tenn.
Shara L Whitfield	63 years		Tenn.	Tenn.	Tenn.

OTHERS : CENSUS OF TENNESSEE

The name Whitfield does not appear on the following Tennessee Census: 1870 Henry Co., 1870 Hickman Co., Hardin Co. in 1830, the 1830 Hardeman Co., 1830 Humphreys Co., 1820 Sumner Co., 1820 Warren Co., 1820 Wayne Co., 1820 White Co., 1820 Hickman Co., 1820 Humphreys Co., 1820 Jackson Co., and others although Whitfields lived in region.

1870 CENSUS, DAVIDSON COUNTY, TENNESSEE

Postoffice : Edgefield. Seventeenth District
Radg Whitfield (negro) 54 years. Male. Birthplace, Alabama, Real Property value 300.

1840 Census, Williamson Co ., Tennessee. Henry Whitfield and Family.

KENTUCKY CENSUS

The name Heiner , Fox , Fuchs does not appear on the 1840 , or 1860 Census of Simpson County, Kentucky but this family Fox lived there. These names on Kentucky are the maternal line of Vallie Jo Fox Whitfield, wife of Robert E. Whitfield , and the Whitfield family appears on the 1950 Census in Contra Costa County, California, and taken in 1951.

GENEALOGY - Bates and Clagett of Tennessee

LEWIS BATES , born 1825 and wife, Agnes E. Lancaster Bates was born 1828 in Hickman County, and had five children:

1. Jaseper A. Bates , born on Beaver Dam Creek near Whitfield in Hickman County, Tennessee , Jan. 15, 1848. He married May 3, 1876 Cordelia El Clagett and they had four children . In mercantile business in Centerville , Tenn. Jaseper A. Bates was the chairman of the county court and native of Hickman County, Tennessee.

2. John M. Bates , born August 22, 1853 . On Feb. 22, 1872 he married Anna Wright and they had seven children.

HORATIO CLAGETT (b. 1779-d. 1866). Rebecca Gantt (b. 1786- d. 1876) who married Horatio in Maryland. They both born in Prince George County, Maryland. They moved 1816 in a wagon from Maryland to Hickman County, Tennessee. They had eight children :

1. William George Clagett, b. Dec. 7 , 1813 in Maryland. He married Theodosia Whitfield who was born April 1, 1816 in Williamson County, Tennessee and died 1839 . He then married Elizabeth O. Hornbeak on Feb. 10 , 1842. She was born in Hickman County , Feb. 18 , 1818 , child of Eli B. and Sarah Hornbeak, and they had nine children. William G. Clagett was in mercantile business. Postmaster of Centerville, Tenn. Magistrate - Clerk of Circuit Court.

2. Horatio Clagett , b. Jan. 17, 1819 . At the age of sixteen years he went to Franklin , Tennessee , and for two years engaged as a clerk in the store of Robert Charter. He became president of the First National Bank 1885 . He married Elizabeth J. Montgomery of Hickman County, Tennessee, November 1, 1846 and they had children : Matilday Clagett, Mary J. Clagett , Laura E. Clagett , Anna S. Clagett , John H. Clagett, Robert M. Clagett and William G. Clagett.

Dr John Cafieald Ward, b. Smith County, Feb. 1828 and lived at Centerville, Tennessee . In 1846 he enlisted in Co. A , First Tenn. Regiment for Mexican War , under Capt. John W. Whitfield.

John Wilkins Whitfield was in twenty- eighth and twenty-ninth General Assembly of Tennessee from Congressional district of Tennessee.

Lucy Emiline Whitefield , daughter of Josiah and Dicey Perkins Whitefield of Dickson County, Tennessee was born June 2 , 1842 and died March 29 , 1921.

DANIEL GENEALOGY

In Perry County, Lobelsville town of Tennessee is a post-village on the west side of Buffalo River , about five miles below Beardstown lies the land of one William Andrew Daniel and his wife Nellie Daniel in 1941. They owned more than a thousand acres of land and all of Daniel Landing for boats. These Daniels had lived in Tennessee a long time. The Tennessee Valley Project changed the Daniel Landing and shore lands and Andrew Daniel moved with Billie R. and H. Rozelle Whitfield Daniel to Waverly, Tennessee on Trace Creek Road.

WILLIAM ANDREW DANIEL was born Feb. 16, 1869 and died on May 29 , 1965. In 1964 he was living at Waverly, Tennessee with his son Billie R. Daniel and wife. He married March 23 , 1887 Nellie J. Coble and the marriage was performed by squire Lancaster. NELLIE J. COBLE was born August 24 , 1870 and died Feb. 10 , 1941 at Lobelsville, Tenn. at the Daniel home.

William A. and Nellie J. Coble Daniel had ten children and all of them were born in Perry County, Tennessee.

1. Ida Daniel, born March 15, 1888, died young.
2. John Robert Daniel , born Oct. 16 , 1889 and died May 22, 1934.
3. Sallie May Daniel, born January 28 , 1893 . She married Clint Daniel and resided in 1964 at Nashville, Tennessee.
4. Annie Parlee Daniel , born April 11, 1894 and died young.
5. Charles William Daniel , born November 25, 1897. He married Oct. 20 , 1921 Myrtle Sweeney of the county and they resided 1964 in Lobelsville, Tennessee.
6. George Dewey Daniel , born March 20 , 1900 . He married Dec. 25 , 1924 Ruth Pace. They lived at Lobelsville and moved to Madison, Tennessee where they have a farm.
7. Porter L. Daniel , born Feb. 28 , 1903. He married Willie Burr Jan. 14, 1930. Porter Daniel was teacher and principal of a Waverly, Tennessee school where he taught for many years. Willie B. Daniel was a teacher in the Waverly School district.
8. Paul Daniel was born Feb. 28 , 1903.
9. Grace Bell Daniel was born January 20, 1908 . She married Andrew Broadway, March 23 , 1934 . They lived in Perry County, Tenn. and moved to Madison, Tennessee where they had a farm.
10. Billie Randolph Daniel was born September 11, 1910 . He married Hester Rozelle Whitfield at Waverly, Tennessee on Dec. 8th , 1934. They lived with William Andrew and Nellie Daniel in Perry County at Lobelsville, and moved to Rockdale Farm at Waverly, Tenn.

Willie Burr Daniel was a native of Tennessee and was born Jan. 10, 1907.

Ruth Pace Daniel was a native of Tennessee and she was born Oct. 18 , 1906.

Grandchildren of William A. and Nellie J. Daniel were the children of Sallie, Charles , George , Grace: (1) Hazel Daniel was born July 25 , 1922 (2) Homer Daniel was born Sept. 4, 1915 (3) Howard Daniel was born Dec. 9 , 1925. He married and resided at Madison, Tennessee in 1964 with his wife and children . 1. Nell Daniel

2. Audrey Daniel was born Oct. 30 , 1929 and teaching school in 1964 at Tennessee location.
3. Betty Daniel was born November 1930
4. Dannie Sue Broadway was born June 26 , 1940
5. John Daniel Broadway was born Sept. 24 , 1946.

TENNESSEANS in the book : Whitfield, Bryan, Smith and Related Families by Emma M. Whitfield. Pub. 1949 , by Times , Inc. New York.

William Whitfield 1764- 1825 , page 85.
Bryan Whitfield 1766 ca- 1825 , page 86.
Lewis Whitfield , page 87.
Joseph Buckner Killebrew 1831- 1906 , page 177.
Thomas Jefferson Whitfield , 1845 , page 179.
Hervey Whitfield , b. 1847 , and his son
Thomas B. Whitfield , page 187.
Eugenie Geraldine Whitfield 1853- 1872 , page 188.
Mary Clay Whitfield, b. 1875 , page 200
George William Whitfield 1829- 1871 , page 220
Richard Henry Whitfield , page 221.

NAMES   CALIFORNIA RESIDENTS

CALIFORNIANS - Whitfield names , non-related items.
Telephone Directory 1961 year   (Whites and Blacks)
San Francisco, California Residents.

Albert Whitfield	Lawrence Whitfield
Emma Whitfield	Melva Whitfield
George Whitfield	Peter Whitfield
Gertrude Whitfield	Philip J. Whitfield
Henrietta Whitfield	Preston M. Whitfield
	William Whitfield

Oakland, California Residents :

A.R. Whitfield	Claud W. Whitfield	Francis J. Whitfield
Ben Whitfield	Estella Whitfield	Inez Whitfield
Bennie Whitfield	Eura Lee Whitfield	Isabell Whitfield
Betty Whitfield	Robert Whitfield	Jack Whitfield

Whitfield names , non-related kinships.   <u>California</u>
Roy Whitfield , electronic teacher at Diablo Valley College in 1963 ,
Contra Costa County, California. He was born in Pennsylvania and
moved to California in 1950s. He is descendant of grandfather who
migrated from England to Penn. in 1900s. He married twice , two
children of first wife in California.
<u>Geneva Whitfield</u> , b. 1923- d. 1964. She was born in Oklahoma . She &
<u>Ofus Whitfield</u> and moved to California in 1959, resided 4177 Irene Dr.,
Martinez, California in Contra Costa County. Children : <u>Verlina Whit-</u>
<u>field</u> and <u>Ofus Whitfield</u> in California 1964. She was daughter of W. O.
Nance of Texas.
<u>Mary Whitfield</u> , d. 1963 , age 14 , Contra Costa County, California.
<u>Jane Whitfield</u> , daughter of <u>Harold Whitfield</u> , resided 1936 in Alameda
County, California.
<u>Peggie Whitfield</u> of Mission San Jose married Clyde Voorhees , Jr. of
Hayward, Calif. in 1938.
<u>Robert Whitfield</u>, Marine U.S. in 1955 at San Diego, California.
<u>Ronald Joe Whitfield</u> married Georgena Eskridge , daughter of George
M. Eskridge of Hayward, Calif., November 1959.
<u>Barbara Whitfield</u> , Orange County, Calif. in 1950s.
Grace married <u>Robert Allen Whitfield</u> , resided Oakland, Calif. in 1950s.
They married Jan. 1961 , San Leandro, California.
<u>Francis J. Whitfield</u> , Professor at the University of California.
1959- 1960s teacher of Slavic language, Berkeley Campus. He was an
author - languages.
<u>Herbert Whitfield</u> married first wife , Lillian Walker , 1936 in San
Francisco , California.
<u>Mabel and Hilton Whitfield</u> , annuled marriage Dec. 1929 in San
Francisco, California.
<u>Jerome Whitfield</u> , age 33 , Feb. 1958, Maintenance supervisor of
Irvington Elmentary School, Fremont, California. Lt. Colonel 1945 of
U.S. Army. <u>Joe M. Whitfield</u> , commanding officer of the Oakland
Army in California.
<u>W. G. Whitfield</u> , Federal Prohibition agent for the Fresno district of
California in 1937.
MAL WHITFIELD . In 1956 the Republican campaign organization.
Former Olympic running champion . Named vice-chairman of the Los
Angeles County, California United Republican Precinct Organization .
1954 and 1955 a goodwill ambassador on a world tour sponsored by the
U.S. State Department...800 meter track champion runner , holder
of the Sullivan Trophy Award 1955... Married Birget Johansson, Swe-
dish girl from Goteborg, Stackholm... U.S. Air force sergeant from
Columbus, Ohio.
RAOUL WHITFIELD , author . Resided New Mexico.
<u>Anson M. Whitfield</u> , U.S.N. copter pilot in 1962.

CONTRA COSTA COUNTY, CALIFORNIA

On Court Record . Rox M. Whitfield in 1959 ; Kenneth Glenn and
Francis Elaine Whitfield in 1960; Roy R. Whitfield in 1960 ; Edward F.
Whitfield , WILL , Sept .18, 1956 ; Gertrude E. Whitfield and Lloyd
T. Whitfield in 1951 ; H. H. Whitfield and W. G. Whitfield , WILL
#24239 ; Mary Whitfield in 1960.

JOSE WHITFIELD. Pioneer Family , Contra Costa County, California,
died 1888. Property in Clayton Valley 300 acres. Clerk title to land
ask by County Clerk S. C. Wells and Superior Judge, A. F. Bray on forty
-seven year estate of Jose Whitfield in 1935.

Kate   Whitfield , age 70 , died April 1958. Resided 126 Parish Avenue
Centerville of Fremont, California. She was born at Mission San Jose,
husband was MATT W. WHITFIELD , Sr. of U. S. Dept. of Agriculture,
representative of Castro Valley. Son, MATT WHITFIELD, Jr. general
manager of Alameda County Water district , daughter of Mrs.Clyde
Voorhees of Centerville.

ALAMEDA COUNTY, CALIFORNIA

Jimmy Eugene Whitfield , Albany, California in 1954.
Jim Whitfield , 1960 , student Bishop O'Dowd High School in Oakland .
Kathleen Sarah Whitfield, wife of school teacher of Oakland, California.
Charles Whitfield . Musician 1955 , Oakland, California.
Ernest J. Whitfield , 1943 policeman, 1003 Pine Street, Oakland, Calif.
Harry C. Whitfield , died February 1947 , Oakland , California.
Mona Glenn Whitfield , Oakland, Calif.
Robert Whitfield , 27 years , Sergeant 1945 , U. S. Army.   Prisoner of
Germany. Married Amelia Whitfield , 529 - 46 th Street , Oakland, Calif.
Robert H. Whitfield , 3438 Magnolia Street, Oakland, California in 1954.
Rubry E. Whitfield , son of Lena Campbell, Private in U. S. Army 1944,
Oakland, California.
Weyman W. Whitfield , corporal of Navy U. S. Died in War II , Son of
Mrs.Eulalie G. Porter , 675 Jean Street, Oakland, California.

State of Iowa

ALLEN WHITFIELD , age 51 in 1955 . Des Moines , Iowa. Attorney.
Republican. Nominated by President Eisenhower to five - member
Atomic Energy Commission, but Allen Whitfield withdrew. He is listed
in "Poor's Register" on business. Director and Attorney for corporations.

WILLS AND INVENTORIES

1811 - 1818 and 1825- 1830

WILLS AND INVENTORIES , WILLIAMSON COUNTY, TENNESSEE

" In Elizah Hunter account of sales which produced in open Court act.
session 1817." Wilkins Whitfield bought four briddles $ 3. 56 1/2.

Names from Telephone Directory. Court Records in Oakland and
Martinez , State of California. Prints appear in Oakland Tribune
Newspaper.

" In Samuel Mc Cutchen, Dec. d , account July session 1816 . Wilkins Whitfield one colt $ 5.12 1/2 , Jas. Shaw's note W. Whitfield $5.12 1/2, Jesse Porter one colt $ 10. 12 1/2 , note J. Porter Sec'y."

"In Samuel Smith dec'd settlement , Oct. session 1818 Wright Whitfield do $ 3.12 1/2".

Wilkin Whitfield , article, one cross out saw $ 3.56 1/4 part of the residue of the property belonging to estate of Joseph German Seur de - ceased in inventory and account of sales of the estate in open court . October 9, 1827.

WILL AND INVENTORIES - Tennessee

Washington County, Tennessee, then North Carolina.
Will of Walter Boyley, August session 1790 . " I give and bequeath to my wife, true and loving , one tract of land lying Suffix County in Virginia in care of Thomas Whitfield during her life afterwards equal property to my two daughters. June 10, 1790 , Washington County, North Carolina. (Suffix) of Isle of Wight. "

Montgomery County, Tennessee 1825. In Court session Will of Bryant Whitfield presented.   Bryan Whitfield left Will.
Humphreys County, Tennessee . The Will of Dr. H enry W. Whitfield of Bakerville, Tennessee is writing on the 1906 Humphreys County Courthouse book.

The Letters of Administration on James Dee Whitfield estate of Humphreys is on Henry County, Tennessee record. Will in the possession of Robert E. Whitfield of Contra Costa , California in Walnut Creek- Pleasant Hill town in 1955.

January 25, 1904 , Waverly, Tennessee.
Summary of Henry W. Whitfield's Will : Half of estate to daughter Ann Hedge Whitfield and half to children of dec. son, John Whitfield : Annie W., Fannie W. , Betsy W. , Dillie W. , Belle W. , John W. Doctor Henry W. Whitfield divided tract of land giving subdivision parcels to children heirs. Ann H. Whitfield , daughter received 350 acres in Bakerville town.

Cheatham County, Tennessee. Thomas W. Whitfield , administrator of John Berry , dec. 1856-71 Vol.

Davidson County, Tennessee. Will of Bernard J. Fox , and Will of his mother Elizabeth Heiner Fox at County Courthouse, B.J. Fox and Nettie Fox-Hager were administrators 1919 for Elizabeth Heiner Fox.

LAWRENCE COUNTY, TENNESSEE.
Inventory and Sale of property of the estate of William Whitfield,
dec. August 1, 1834.
James Whitfield do 1. 56 1/4 , 1 matox . 81 1/4 , 1 box of tools . 37 1/2,
1 hoe . 18 1/4 , do him 17. 50, one box of implements . 05 1/4, do him
candle box . 37 1/2, 1 lot of wear . 25 , 1 crewet . 12 1/2 , 1 bee of eleven
5. 00, four head of sheep 6. 00, four head of hogs 6. 00 , one grey colt
18. 00 , 1 pear geese 1. 75 , do him one box and knives for oats 4. 00 , one
check reel . 73, 1 washing tub. 25, 1 small trunk 2. 00 , 1 do wool . 50 ,
1 beef 1. 00.

And

John J. Whitfield , 1 lot of old tools . 75 1 iron wedge . 81 1/4 , 1 Bible
. 62 1/2 , 1 lot of table ware 2. 06 1/4 , 1 skillet and lid 1. 75 , 1 large oven
2. 00 , six chairs 3. 37 1/2 , 1 lot of leather . 30.

And

Sally Whitfield , 1 bed and furniture 10. 00 , 1 trunk . 50, 1 white face cow
6. 00 , six head of hogs 11. 00 , one grey mare 28. 00 , one pare of gear
1. 00 , 1 pot rack 1. 00 , 1 set of knives and forks . 50.

And

Fifty-five other articles and animals of the estate of William Whitfield
were sold to Webster Wolsey, William Johnston, William Hall, Jack
Belew , Mason Johnston, Willis Hammons, Jacob Belew , John Ezell,
A. B. Humphreys , Samuel Cole, William Hale , Amosia Smith , Mar -
shall Springer, John Horn who received one wagon at 67. 00, Aaron
Springer , James Belew , Ezelkiel Barnett, James M. Johnston , Cla-
born Palviore, John Barber , Joseph Dickson Hamilton , Dickson,
William Barber , A. B. Huphres, P. Winstead , Samuel Ellison , W. P.
Pettes, Thomas Hon, William Poteet.   The total estate value of articles
when sold was $ 222. 90 in 1834 of William Whitfield estate.   The men who
purchased the articles of his were pioneer settlers of Hickman Territory
of Chickasan Indian region . Lawrence County was then part of Hickman
County.

RUTHERFORD COUNTY, TENNESSEE.
1827-30 . Vol 7 , page 294. "In the name of God amen ... I, Mathew
Whitfield of the County of Rutherford and State of Tennessee being of
perfect sound mind and memory ... Blessed be God, do this sixth day
of September in the year of our Lord one thousand eight hundred and
twenty three make and publish this my last Will and Testament in manner following ... That is first .... I give and bequeath to my wife Levina
Whitficld the whole of my estate both real and personal of every description for her use entirely during her natural life or widowhood and at her
marriage or death , then my will and pleasure is that all my personal
estate be sold at public sale by my executors and the amount arising from
said sale to be equally divided between my children namely, Benjamin
Whitfield, Mary Whitfield , Mathew Whitfield and all, my real estate

or landed property at that time, I allow to my daughter Mary Whitfield and lastly I do hereby appoint and ordain my wife Levina Whitfield and my son William Whitfield, executors of this my last will and testaments by me made and establish this and no other to be my last will and testament. In testimony whereof I have hereunto set my hand and seal the day and year first above written. Signed and sealed in presence of, H. Robinson, Jurat: Jane Robinson; Levina Robinson, Jurat his mark X Mathew x Whitfield .. Seal"

DAVIDSON COUNTY OF TENNESSEE AT NASHVILLE.　　　　Will.
"I, Elizabeth (Heiner) Fox do this day Nov. 16, 1917, execute this my last Will and Testament, I devise that all my just debts be paid. My funeral expenses not to exceed two hundred and fifty dollars $ 250.00. I wish to be buried with Mass and taken to Franklin, Kentucky and buried by the side of my husband.

The house and lot on Spring Street and the house and lot on Joseph Avenue and the household furniture to be sold and the proceeds equally divided among my seven children, Nettie Fox Hager, Albert Fox, Arthur Fox, Ben Fox, Theodore Fox, George Fox, and Joe Fox.

To Nettie Fox Hager I give my clothes the silver goblet, silver butter dish and my picture in the oval frame and my mother's picture.

To Lottie Fox (Charlotte Sanders) Fox I give the china dishes, picture clinging to the Cross, and my sisters picture.

To Valley Fox I give my husbands picture in the small frame, the green and lavender comfort and the light weight feather bed.

To May Fox I give the life of Christ unbound, my picture in the gilt frame and the crazy quilt.

To little Marie my grand daughter I give the shell vase.

To Emma Fox I give my husbands picture in the large frame, the silk quilt and my brothers picture in the soldiers uniform.

My son George Fox I wish to have seventy-five dollars more than the rest, and my son Theodore I wish to have half as much as is the share of the others. If he tries to break the will he is to get nothing.
The quilts, blankets, sheets and comforts that are remaining are to be divided among my daughter, Nettie and my daughters in law.
　　　　　Signed : Mrs Elizabeth Fox
　　　Witnessed by Mrs Kak Hemberg
　　　　　　　　Mrs Florence Crawford
November 16, 1917, Nashville, Tennessee. "

This is the Will of the great grandmother of Robert Whitfield, Christa Whitfield, James David Whitfield, and Joanne Vallie Whitfield of Contra Costa County of California at Pleasant Hill town.

COURT MINUTES

John W. Walker and Edward   Versus   Thomas J. Whitfield , A.F.
Christian and George W. Whitfield.

A.C. Deshazo, an acting justice of the peace in and said County of Hickman returned into Court the papers in this cause which are in the words
and figures following , to : State of Tennessee, Hickman County, To
any lawful officer to execute and return summons Thomas I. Whitfield
and A. F. Christian, merchants trading under the style and firm of Whitfield and Christian , to appear before me or some other justice of the
peace for said County, to answer John W. Walker and I. Edwards, merchants trading under the style and firm of J. W. Walker and Edwards ,
on the plea of debt under one hundred dollars, this 17 th day of May , 1847.

W. Bird, JP

Nashville, Tennessee .   12 th February 1847.

One day after date we promise to pay John W. Walker and Edwards,
an order for fifty-two dollars for value received.   Witness our hands, etc.

Whitfield and Christian.

State of Tennessee, Hickman County.

To any lawful officer to execute and return you are hereby as heretofore
commanded that of the goods, chattles,   lands and Tenements of T. J.
Whitfield and A.F. Christian and George W. Whitfield , their security
as stay of judgment, it to be found in your County, you cause to be made
the sum of fifty-two dollars seventy-seven cents and cost of suit to satisfy a judgment that John W. Walker and Joseph Edwards, merchants trading under the firm and Style of John W. Walker and Edwards obtained
against them on the 19 th   of June , 1847 , before E. W. Hassel, Esq.

Seal 14 th day of August 1848 , A. C. Deshazo, JP

John W. Walker and Edwards   Versus George W. Whitfield.

W. G. Clagett an acting justice of the peace for said County of Hickman returned into Court the papers in this cause -Summons of George W.
Whitfield to appear before me or some other Justice of the peace for said
County, to answer John W. Walker and Joseph Edwards , merchants , trading under the title of John W. Walker and Edwards. Debt.

6 th of Dec.   1847 .   W. Bird . J.P.

I acknowledge the service of the within this 6 th day of Dec. 1847.

State of Tennessee, Hickman County.

To any lawful officer to execute and return cause on George W. Whitfield
and satisfy a judgment that John W. Walker and Joseph Edwards   were
issued against said Whitfield , Dec. 1847 , before W. Bird , Esq.; and
appears of record in my office when collected , pay owner as the law
directs. For want of Personal property levied this fifa on the tract of
land as the property of G.W. Whitfield , lying in the County of Hickman.
Beginning on L.B. Dodsons North-east corner running with the meanders

of Duck River to Dodsons North-west corner, thence with Dodsons line
to the Beginning, containing by estimation six-hundred acres, the land
whereon the said Whitfield now lives, this 25 th , May 1848,
P.W. Hornbeak, C.H.C.
Land condemned for the satisfaction of the judgment.

Hickman County Court Minutes 1844 - 1855.
G.W. Whitfield promised to pay two hundred dollars for value received
4 th day of Dec. 1847 to Thomas J. Whitfield and James Monroe Whitfield.

State of Tennessee Versus George W. Whitfield and James M. Whitfield.
To satisfy judgment that Thomas J. Whitfield obtained against them for
the use and benefit of Samuel St. William, before E. W. Hassell on the
4 th day of January 1847. Seal .   2nd day of May 1848 . J.P.
fees 50 ¢ , Warrant 50¢ . A.C. Deshazo , J.P. for Hickman County.

For want of personal property levied this fifa on a tract of land as the
property of George W. Whitfield supposed to contain six hundred acres
bounded on the East, north and west by Duck River and on the south by
the lands belonging to the heirs   of Elias Dodson and Claiborne B. Dodson, this 4 th day of May 1848,   J.W. Huddleston, Sheriff.

Whereupon on motion of the plaintiff, it is considered by the Court that the
land so levied upon as aforesaid be condemned for the satisfaction of the
said Judgment and execution of the plaintiff, and that he have his writ of
venditioni expenas and fifa, it is further considered by the court that the
plaintiff receive of the defendant his costs by him about his suit in this
behalf expended, and that he have his execution.

For want of Personal property levied this fifa on a Tract of land as the
property of George W. Whitfield supposed to be one hundred acres bounded
on the north and west by John Montgomery line, on the South of Duck River,
and on the East by Moors survey this 24 th August 1848.   Levy 50¢,
                    J.W.Huddleston, Sheriff.

On motion of the plaintiff, it is considered by the court that the land so
levied upon as aforesaid be condemned for the satisfaction of the said
judgment and execution of the plaintiff.

Moses Tidwell Vs T. I. Whitfield . Fifa.
Summons T. I. Whitfield and G. W. Whitfield to appear and answer
Moses Tidwell in a plea of debt. January 13th , 1848, W. Bird, J.P.
        On 25th of December next we or either of us promise to pay to
Moses Tidwell $ 53.00 for value received , date of 22 May 1847.
Seal, T.I. Whitfield .   Seal, W. G. Whitfield

HICKMAN COUNTY, TENNESSEE. COURT MINUTES 1844-1855.
Judgment for Moses Tidwell before W. Bird , Esq. on record Jan. 22,
1848. Fee 50 ¢ . W. G. Clagett, J. P.
A fifa was levied on tract of land of G. W. Whitfield, lying in the Hick-
man County on which said Whitfield was living , this 19th August 1848,
J. W. Huddleston, Sheriff.

H. Huddleston Vs G. W. Whitfield . Motion for Condemnation of land.
Summons of G. W. Whitfield to appear before some Justice for said
County to answer H. Huddleston in plea of debt, 15th , July 1848,
Jarrot Curl, J. P.
Judgment for plaintiff for $ 36. 27 ¢, July 29 , 1848, W. G. Clagett, J. P.
Note given by G. W. Whitfield for sum. W. G. Clagett 1848 issue judg-
ment against G. W. Whitfield for H. Huddleston.
Fifa levied on tract of land of G. W. Whitfield. August 1848 where said
Whitfield now lives.

George W. Whitfield paid these debts by levy on his land issued in Hickman Court. The people who sought judgment were kinship and friends.
The six hundred parcel of land was distributed in small pieces or a
parcel sold for repayment of debts. Whitfields were owners of much
of the land in northern Hickman County. Such division of land as that
of George W. Whitfield provided land for others to farm.

William L. Winners Vs Nathan D. Frizzie-Jurors included John W.
Whitfield.
L. B. Moore Vs James H. Gill - Witness : J. W. Whitfield.
State of Tennessee Vs Reuben D. Willey - Secured fine and cost,
John W. Whitfield and Josiah Jones.
State of Tennessee Vs Benjamin Arnold - John W. Whitfield , Allen C.
Deshazo , Thomas Arnold and Edward Arnold secured fine and cost.
State of Tennessee Vs Lewis D. Adams - Jurors included John W.
Whitfield.
State of Tennessee Vs John Young - Jurors included John Wilkins
Whitfield.
William Gravett and John W. Whitfield to answer S. H. Williams in a
plea of Debt.
Edward Arnold Vs Robert J. Easley - Jurors included John Wilkins
Whitfield.
Bank of Tennessee Vs John W. Whitfield and Others.
October 19, 1852.
State of Tennessee Versus Thomas J. Whitfield , Amos F. Christian,
James M. Whitfield , and George W. Whitfield : To satisfy a judgement
that Robert J. Easley recovered before E. W. Hassell, Esq. on the

6 th of July 1847 . Seal.   May 18, 1848.
Fees 12 1/2 ¢ . A. C. Deshazo, J. P.
This judgment resulted from the following case : Robert J. Easley
Versus Thomas J. Whitfield and others.   Motion to condemn land in a
plea of debt, seal.   June 27th , 1847.

State of Tennessee Versus George W. Whitfield and Pleasant M. Hornbeak. Debt $ 35.85 , to satisfy a judgment that James D. Easley and
William G. Clagett, administrators of the Estate of Robert Charter ,
deceased.   April 3, 1848 , Pleasant   Walker , J. P.

For want of personal levied on the following described tract of land as
the property of George W. Whitfield , beginning on C. B. Dotsons, north-
east-west corner, then with Dotsons line to the beginning containing by
estimation six hundred acres, the land whereon the said Whitfield now
lives in said County of Hickman , this   17 th of August 1848,   50 ¢.
P. M. Hornbeak, C. H. C.

Whereupon on motion of the plaintiff, it is ordered by the Court that the
land so levied upon as aforesaid be condemned for the satisfaction of the
said judgment and execution.

HICKMAN COUNTY, TENNESSEE 1847 - 1852, ADMINISTRATOR
SETTLEMENTS, AND COURT , AND GUARDIAN.
Settlement of the estate of William Redden March 1849. Credit by Whit-
field and Gravett , Account $ 16.58.

Settlement of Robert Charter estate March 1849.

I. W. Whitfield, Guardian. Test : T. E. Danslee.
Credit by Whitfield and Gravett proven account $ 20.90.
Credit by John W. Whitfield , Doctor bill, proven $ 2.50.

One receipt on I, W. Whitfield for collector of a note on I. C. Thorton.
Judgment, April 12, 1831 for $ 3.67.

One account on Mary Whitfield for seventy-five cents .

One account on F. I. Whitfield now for judgment in Court (circuit)
for $ 117.68.

In pursuance of an act of the assembly and an order of the County Court
of Hickman County, Tennessee made at the February term 1849 which order
was made agreeable to the provisions of an act of the Assembly , I, I. S.
Whitfield , have this day proceeded to settle with James D. Easley and

William G. Clagett, adm. of the estate of Robert Charter, Dec.

WHITFIELD TOWN of Tennessee merchant's store accounts explain some of the cause for settlements concerning estates.

Settlement of the estate of Stephen I. Easley, deceased, March 1850. Credit by note to Whitfield and Gravett $ 1.25.

Settlement with Alfred Forrestor, Deceased, December 1850. Credit by note to Whitfield and Christian for seventy-five cent.

Settlement of estate of Stephen I. Easley March 1850. Credit by note to Whitfield and Christian for $ 2.96.

Settlement of the estate of Richard Nall, sr. May 1849. Credit by T. I. to I. W. Whitfield account with interest $ 7.48.

Settlement of estate of James L. Reece, deceased, April 1849. Credit by William Whitfield, Guardian of minor heirs, two receipts for $ 45.31.

Settlement of the estate of Hugh Leeper, Deceased, December 1849. Credit to G. W. Whitfield the sum of $ 2.94.

Settlement of estate of Elias Dodson, Dec. Feb. 1850. Credit by note to G. W. Whitfield $ 138.56.

HICKMAN COUNTY, TENN.   , COURT MINUTE BOOK 1844-1855. James D. Easley and William G. Clagett, adm. versus George W. Whitfield and P. M. Hornbeak in settlement of the estate of Robert Charter, April 4, 1848.
        George W. Whitfield and P. M Hornbeak promised to pay Robert Charter $ 35. for the hire of a negro girl named Rachel on December 25th, witnessed January 4, 1847.

George Whitfield was summoned to appear before justice Allen C. Deshazo to answer Thomas J. Whitfield for the use of land involving S.H. Williams. January 4, 1847.

Wm. Phillips, sheriff of Hickman County, Tennessee collected fee from J. L. Craig and Thomas Jefferson Whitfield on the 4th day of January, 1845.
In Court 1847, John Kirkman Versus Thomas J. Whitfield and James Whitfield.
James M. Whitfield debt assumed by Thomas J. Whitfield in behalf of John Kirkman.

1848 James D. Easley and William G. Clagett Versus Thomas J. Whitfield , for the sum of $ 107. 68.
Thomas J. Whitfield for S. H. Williams Versus John Easley and James O. Lewis . Debt , 1849.

HICKMAN COUNTY, TENNESSEE, COURT MINUTES 1844-1855.
State of Tennessee Vs Aaron D. Cochran- Overseer of a Road. Cochran guilty and fined. John W. Whitfield acknowledged himself the defendants security for the fine and costs aforesaid.
February term Circuit Court 1853.
The President and Directors of Bank of Tennessee Vs John Wilkins Whitfield , James D. Easley , and A. C. Deshazo- Debt.

Harrison Whitfield , 1851 , February 27 one tract of land reported to the Clerk for double tax , but released by the court , lying in Civil district No. 2 , valued at $ 1, 200 , taxes $ 3 ... George H. Erwin one tract of land 600 acres lying in Civil district No. 4 , valued at $ 300 ., taxes 75¢. Daniel K. Mc Cord, collector of the public taxes of Hickman County.

Robert A. Hill executor of Wilkins Whitfield Vs William Spence.
"It is ordered by the court in this cause by the consent of the parties that each party have leave to take deposition generally upon giving to the adverse party the notice required by the rules in Chancery and that the plaintiff take depositions of Leroy G. W. Napier this day in the law office of Thomas Bateman in Centerville and that this order be notice to the defendant. "

Whitfield and Christian Vs William Gravette. Appeal.
"This day this cause was continued by consent. "
Whitfield and Christian Vs William Gravette. Appeal.
"This day came the parties by their attornies , and thereupon came a Jury of good and lawful men of the County of Hickman to wit : The issue in favor of the plaintiffs and judgment on Debt. "

"John Young gives up his land to be levied on and sold in preference to his personal property the place whereon he now lives bounded on the south by J. G. Tarkington on the east by the Whitfields and on the north by John Hassell said to contain 300 acres this 17 th day of Feb. 1852 . Levy 50 ¢ . J. W. Huddleston, Sheriff.
E. D. Morrison Vs John Young , J. F. Stanfiel and A. Nash. Motion to condemn land."

R. F. Bratton Vs J. A. R. Forgery and others - Debt. Land Property of John A. R. Forgery adjacent to Whitfield on the north . Oct. 5, 1852.

State of Tennessee Vs Wm. Gravett and James M. Whitfield .
The goods and chattles, lands and tenements of Wm. Gravett and James
M. Whitfield the cause to make the sum $ 114. 87 and costs of suit , to
satisfy a judgment that Samuel H. Williams obtained March 20 , 1848.
... Fifa levied on one lot in the town of Vernon near William Gravett.

HICKMAN COUNTY, TENNESSEE , COURT MINUTES 1847-1848.
"To any lawful officer to execute and summons William Gravett and J.W.
Whitfield to appear before some Justice for said County to answer S. H.
Williams in a plea of Debt.   March 1847.

Judgment in favor of the plaintiff for $ 114. 87 . March 1847 , $14. 87
one day after date I promise to pay T. B. and J. W. Whitfield $ 114. 97 ,
for value received this January 1, 1847.
        Seal .   Wm. Gravett
For value received I guarantee the payment of the within note to S. H.
Williams this 15th , March 1847.
        Seal.   J. W. Whitfield "

                MAURY COUNTY, TENNESSEE
                Chancery Court Minutes 1823-1829

        James Whitfield, justice of peace , James M. Dunn, J. P. and
Richard Moore, 67 years, in sixth circuit of Columbia , State of Tenn-
essee, 20 th day of May 1823 ...   This issue was before Putman County,
Georgia in town of Eatonton and then sixth circuit district at Columbia,
Tennessee. (From Wayne, North Carolina to Georgia to Tennessee).

                HENRY COUNTY, TENNESSEE
                Court Minutes 1836-1949 , Part I

May term session 1848. Adoption.
Lewis Whitfield - "On motion it is ordered by the court that Lewis
Whitfield be appointed guardian to Lucey , Sarah, Briant , and James
Whitfield deceased of deceased who thereupon appeared in open court
and entered into bond of six hundred dollars with William M. Williams
and John H. Williams as his security. "

In the 1836-1849 analytical index of minutes appear these names of
children : Briant Whitfield, Elizah Whitfield, Elizabeth Whitfield , Hannah
Whitfield , James Whitfield, John Whitfield . In part two of the book are
these names , Lewis Whitfield, Lucy Whitfield, Needham Whitfield , Sally
Whitfield , Sarah Whitfield , William Whitfield.
These could be children orphans in Lewis Whitfield and Needham Whitfield guardianship of the North Carolina line.

"On motion it is ordered by the Court that Lewis Whitfield be
appointed guardian in open Court and entered into bond of four hundred
dollars with Isaac Wimberly , John Whitfield, Needham Whitfield as
his security.
Monday, November 4, 1844.   John Walker guardian to Elizabeth
Whitfield , minor orphan of William Whitfield Court and tendered his
resignation which was received and ordered to be so certified.
Tuesday , May 6, 1845. Lewis Whitfield, guardian to the minor orphans
of William Whitfield, dec. "

SUMNER COUNTY , TENNESSEE
Court Minutes 1787-1805
Mero District of North Carolina.

Bryan Whitfield - Public tax D .80¢, County tax $ 1.20, publishing
in the Gazette $ 1.98 , total $ 4.23. Clerks fee for order and copy 25¢.
Bryan Whitfield 1,640 acres of land.
The Sumner County, Tennessee Court appoints for October term 1797 the
following Jurors, to wit: James Whitfield included in the names.
WILLIS WHITFIELD lived in Mero district of Bledsoe region in Tenn -
essee which was a part of North Carolina before 1796. He is probably
the Willis Whitfield on the Nash County, North Carolina Census of 1790.
"The Court appoints for January term 1797 the following Jurors to wit:
Willis Whitfield"included in the names.

"Deed of conveyance from John Boyd to Willis Whitfield for 67 acres
of land is proved by Richard Jones. "

Willis Whitfield is juror at July term of Court in 1797.
... "At a Court of pleas and quarter , sessions began and held for the
County ... Grand Jury empamuelled and sworn vize ; Willis Whitfield
included in the names. "
... "Ordered that Willis Whitfield be appointed overseer of the road
from the 20 mile tree to Mamskers Creek in place of Richard Jones. "
... The Court appoints for jurors to September term 1804 the following
jurors to wit ; Willis Whitfield name on juror list.

DAVIDSON COUNTY, TENNESSEE
Superior Court Minutes of North Carolina and Tennessee
1788 - 1803   Part I

Archibald Roane, Governor of the State of Tennessee , agent Nov.17,
1802, Pleas at Nashville.
George W. Neville , collector and William Ross, Sen.
James Adams, Needham Whitfield and Joseph B. Neville his securities.
Debt.   Judgment for $ 410.90 and costs.
"On the motion of Robert Search, Treasurer for the District of Mero ,
and it appearing to the satisfaction of the Court that George W. Neville,

collector of the County of Montgomery for the year one thousand eight hundred has failed to pay to the treasurer of said District , the sum of four hundred and ten dollars and ninety cents, part of the State taxes for the year aforesaid. It is therefore considered by the Court that Archibald Roane, Governor of the State of Tennessee recover against the said George W. Neville, collector, and William Ross. "

DAVIDSON COUNTY, TENNESSEE
Superior Court of Law and Equity , the Mero District
of Tennessee   1805-1807   Part I

Bryan Whitfield entered Plea at the Courthouse in Nashville at the term May 1807.
Benjamin John Vs Bryan Whitfield and William Sanders bail for James Berry. May 1805.
State of Tennessee. "To the Sheriff of Montgomery County Greeting. Execution of $ 224. 34 1/2 part of the damages and costs aforesaid still remain to be made, and whereas Bryan Whitfield and William Sanders undertook Jame Berry for charges. "
"November 1806 comes the said plaintiff by his attorney and the Sheriff of Montgomery County returns that he had made the same known to the said Bryan Whitfield and that the said William Sanders was not found in his County, therefore as before the Sheriff is commanded that he give notice to the said William Sanders , that he before the Judges of our said court, on the 2 nd Monday , May 1807 to show in form aforesaid. "

MONTGOMERY COUNTY , TENNESSEE
Court Minutes 1811 - 1813
John Johnson, administrator of Nancy Fowler estate , witnesses, William R. Gibson and Bryant Whitfield , J. P.

Lewis Whitfield Vs Walter Wyott
"This day came the plaintiff by his attorney and freely confesses here that he intends not further to prosecute his suit and that the said defend- ant came in proper person and assumes upon himself the payment of all costs herein insured. "
MONTGOMERY COUNTY, TENNESSEE , COURT MINUTES 1813-1815. Tuesday, July 20, 1813 . Bryant Whitfield. On petition of 274 acres of land from the State of North Carolina to Josiah Mc Dowel.
... Herbert Harwell Vs Mary Stewart . Wednesday, July 21, 1813.
    Bryant Whitfield a juror in the case.
... Bryant Whitfield, a justice in court Oct. 19, 1813.
... Bryant Whitfield present when given to Alexander Brown overseer
    of the Port Royal Road from the fork below John Edmondson. Oct. 19, 1813.
... Bryant Whitfield witness County marriage records ; and he was pre-
    sent at Court when the County courthouse tax set for year 1814.

Bryant Whitfield returns a list of taxable property for Capt. Allen's Company for the present year (1814).
Bryant Whitfield was present as a justice, April 19, 1814.
He was present when Court elected Coroner for Montgomery County, Tenn.

MONTGOMERY COUNTY , TENNESSEE , COURT MINUTES 1813 -
1815 ; 1817 to 1825.

Bryant Whitfield approved County Bonds and Securities with other justices.
Samuel Gattis and Bryant Whitfield commissioners of orphanage.

April 1814 . "On Motion it is ordered that the road leading from Clarks-ville to Russelville be attired so as to commence at a grove of Red Oak Timber about a half mile east of Sand White's house and intersect the old road of present road at plantation occupied at present by Thomas Travis, Senr. and that Jury of review to sit, " Bryant Whitfield, p resent.
Court Session 1825.
"This day was presented to the Court the last Will and testament of Bryant Whitfield , deceased, which was proven by the oaths of James H. Bryan, Reuben Ross and Edward S. Walter three of the subscribing witnesses thereto on motion ordered to be recorded. "

"On Motion ordered by the Court that Charles Minor and William B. Whitfield be furnished with Letters of Administration on the estate of Bryan Whitfield, deceased, with the Will annexed , and the said Charles Minor and William B. Whitfield came into Court and entered into Bond and Se - curity satisfactory to the Court and qualified agreeable to law. "

"On Motion ordered that William Killebrew be appointed overseer of that part of the Road leading from Russelville to Clarksville between William S. Whitfield and the lower end of Johnson's plantation. "
(Bryan (Bryan t) Whitfield , Lewis Whitfield, Needham Whitfield , and
William S. Whitfield appear in 1816-1817 Court Minutes of Montgomery County, Tennessee.)

WASHINGTON COUNTY, TENNESSEE   1802-1808
Court Minutes, pleas. Quarter session.
Henry Wilson and George Whitfield Vs William P. Chester.

William Chester owed H. Wilson and G. Whitfield one thousand dollars.
Sum of note reduced to $ 652. 84 , March 17, 1802. Judgment.

HUMPHREYS COUNTY, TENNESSEE, COURT MINUTES 1930-1945.
J. L. Whitfield was creditor of Mason Sanders the 13th day of Feb. 1911.
Arbie Whitfield Versus John T. Tate and all Nov. 8, 1928. Debt.

Court considered land acquisition. Land one and one-half miles southeast of Waverly, Tennessee on the waters of Blue Creek and on Bear Branch.

STEWART COUNTY, TENNESSEE , COURT MINUTES 1811-1812.
Briant Whitfield 640 acres North Waters of Tennessee River. Granted on
Warrant No. 377.

Ham Whitfield 100 acres Piney Fork of Red River.

August 1811 . Ordered that Needham Whitfield have leave to return 227 acres
of land for taxation in the County and be exonerated from paying Double T ax.

1811 Needham Whitfield 117 acres.
Bryant Whitfield 640 acres on Cub Creek. Warrant No. 1529.
 1815-1819 Court Minutes in Stewart County, Tennessee.
May 1816. Ordered by the Court that the Sheriff summon William
Whitfield, with others to appear at the next Circuit Court to serve as juror.

WILSON COUNTY, TENNESSEE, COURT MINUTES 1816-1819.

Court of pleas and quarter sessions of Wilson County in town of
Lebanon on Monday 16th day , December 1816 . Edmund Tisdell a paper
writing purposing to be a Will or ordered to be deposited with the Clerk
of said Court and Moore Stepherson and Anvil (Ansil) Whitfield have letters
of Administration pin dinte lite on the estate of said Ed (Edmund) Tisdale,
deceased. Record of Ed Tisdale.

"On Motion, ordered that James Gray , Benja Castleman, Wm. Robb,
Isham F. Davis and Deveraux Wynne or any three of them settle with
Ansel Whitefield and Thomas Rhodes administrators on the estate of
Edward Tisdale and report to next court. "

CHEATHAM COUNTY, TENNESSEE , COURT MINUTES 1856-1860

" It is ordered that Wilson N. Thompson oversee the road known as the
Hannah Ford road leading from Charlottle Tennessee pike to Nashville by
the way of Hannah Ford from where it leaves the said Tennessee pike road
near B.C. Andrews to the top of Hanican Hill and with the following hands, "
Witness - William Whitfield and Henry Whitfield . 1856.

Thomas W. Whitfield and wife , Sarah M. Whitfield was formerly Sarah M.
Berry of Davidson County, Tennessee . John Berry her father died 8 th
day Oct. 1856 , and her mother named Annie Berry of Cheatham County.
1858 note in book.

Cheatham County, Tennessee. 1858. "On Motion it is ordered by the Court that J. H. Baker overseer of the road known as the Hannah Ford road leading from the Charlotte Turn pike to Nashville by the way of Hannah Ford from where it leaves said turn pike road near B. C. Andrews to the top of Hurricane Hill and with the following named hands to wit, William Whitfield, John Whitfield, Henry Whitfield."

"On motion it was ordered by the Court that William Yates oversee the road leading from Houston Coopers to Hannah Ford road, at or near Harvey Thompsons and with the following hangs." Henry Whitfield was in the list of names.

HUMPHREYS COUNTY, TENNESSEE, COURT MINUTES 1930-1945

Chancery Court Minutes, Waverly, Tennessee. May 18, 1936. James Dee Whitfield, guardian indebted to his ward for sum of $ 750, and invested in two tracts of land with title in name of Oda Whitfield. And land had $ 1,500. mortgage lien in favor of Federal Commissioner with E. Rice as trustee. Land value $ 3,000, June 1, 1936. James Dee Whitfield and Oda Whitfield executed a deed to one-half un-divided interest to J. D. Whitfield, Oda Whitfield and Martha F. Daniel Whitfield and Raymond Whitfield and they to pay $ 550. of the mort-gage owed to Land Bank Commissioner and clear of present encumbranches. Martha F. D. Whitfield, the Ward, and husband, Raymond Whitfield want to accept said one-half undivided interest in the land in satisfaction of the $ 750. balance owing them, and to assume present payment of the $ 550. of the mortgage going to Land Bank Commissioner and that said arrange-ment was fair and to the interest of the Ward and her guardian. Land situated in the 2 nd Civil District of Humphreys County, Tennessee on Trace Creek, two miles west of Waverly town, and right near Highway No. one.

James Dee Whitfield appointed guardian June, 1936 by County Court of Perry County, Tennessee. She (Martha F. Daniel) ward of his with $ 750 and her mother Oda Daniel Whitfield.

Dr. Henry W. Whitfield, guardian for Robert Horner, Oct. 27, 1897.

16th of Feb. 1942. Waverly, Tennessee.
Bertha Powers Whitfield Vs John H. Whitfield. Decree of Divorce filed 1942.

Arleene Story Whitfield Vs William R. Whitfield, Decree of Divorce August 22, 1952.

RUTHERFORD COUNTY, TENNESSEE , COURT MINUTES 1804-1842

1811-1812 Minute Book E   and 1812-1813 Minute Book F .
"Ordered by the Court that William Carney be appointed overseer of the
road in the room and st ead of James Bowles and that the following hands
work under him as such to wit; Istham Medford, David Crocket , David
Elder , Samuel Bowles , William Carney , Willis Whitfield two hands ,
Charles Wills, James Jetton, Matthew Whitfield , James Gillis ; Elijah
Smith , John Ledgely, Herbert Hardy , Joseph Young , Abraham Pallet,
Alexander Duncan and William Ingram.   1811."

Rutherford County, Tennessee. 1817-1818 Minute Book L -
"Sam Carlisle Versus Ansel (Ansil) Whitfield . This day came the said
plaintiff in her proper person and saith that she intends no further to prosecute her action against the said defendant... Therefore it is considered
by the Court that the defendant go hence without day and recover against
the plaintiff his costs by him about his Defense in this behalf expended
and the plaintiff in mercy, etc. "

Genealogical Note: Ansil Whitfield of Rutherford County, Tennessee of
the family of Willis Whitfield and Rhody Whitfield of North Carolina and
Cannon County, Tennessee.
Ansel Whitfield , son, property in Rutherford County, Tennessee.
Ansel Whitfield , son, married in Wilson County, Tennessee.
Ansie Whitfield , son , soldier of 1812 War.
Ansel Whitfield , son , married in Dickson County, Tennessee
..... These are the early Whitfield names beginning with Ansel.

Rutherford County, Tennessee. Court Minutes 1817 - Book L.
John Leavid Versus William Whitfield and Ansel Whitfield 1817- Debt.
"This day came the said parties by their attornies and thereupon came also
a jury of good men to wit ; James Gibson , Joseph Kimbro , James Ford,
James Bell, John Weatherspoon , Benjamin Knox , William Thomas ,
Thomas Beavers , Nathan O. Osley , Pritchett Alexander, Daniel Park-
hurst, Samuel Burnett who being elected , tried and sworn well and truly
to try the issues joined between the parties , upon their oaths aforesaid do
say that the defendants hath not paid the debt of one hundred and eighty
dollars and sixty cents in the plaintiffs declaration mentioned and that
they assess the plaintiffs damages by reason of the detention of that debt
to thirty eight dollars and forty cents besides cost.
    It is therefore considered by the Court that the plaintiffs recover
against the debt the amount of the debt aforesaid together with the damages
aforesaid by the jury in form aforesaid assessed and all costs in this behalf
expended and the Debt in Mercy. "

Rutherford County, Tennessee. Court Minutes 1823-1824 Minute Book No. S.
John Whitfield Versus Joseph Sedgely . Trepass No. 32.

"This day came the said plaintiff in his proper person and saith he intends no further to prosecute his suit against the defendant, and thereupon the said defendant came into Court and assumed upon himself the payment of all the costs. It is therefore considered by the Court that the said plaintiff do recover against the said defendant all the costs in this behalf expended, etc. 1823."

Rutherford County, Tennessee. 1824-1825 Minute Book No. D.
"A Deed of Conveyance from Willis Whitfield to John Mc Creary for one hundred and seventy acres of land in Rutherford County was this day presented in Open Court and the execution thereof duly acknowledged by the said Willis Whitfield to be his act and deed for the purposes therein mentioned and ordered to be certified for registration."

Rutherford County, Tennessee. 1824-1825 Book D.
"Ansel (written Ansil) Whitfield for use of Milberry Whitfield versus Willis Whitfield - Debt. Number 10 app." "This day April 19, 1825 came the said plaintiff by his attorney, and saith he intends no further to prosecute his suit against the defendant.

It is therefore considered by the Court that the said defendant go hence without day and recover against the said plaintiff all the costs in this behalf expended."

KNOX COUNTY, TENNESSEE. Superior Court Minute Book, Vol C 1798-1803.

NEEDHAM WHITFIELD Versus NATHANIEL PETERS.
"Be it remembered that on the 31st day of March 1800 a Capias ad Respondendum was Issued Commanding the Sheriff of Knox County to take the Body of Nathaniel Peters to answer Needham Whitfield of a Plea that he render to him the sum of two hundred and fifty dollars which to him he owe and from him unjustly Detains & C to his Damage two hundred dollars. On which Writ, at September Term 1800 Robert Houston Sheriff of said County, by John Love, Specially Deputised returned "Executed." "
Whereupon Needham Whitfield by G. W. Campbell esquire his Attorney complains of Nathaniel Peters, in custody of the Sheriff & c of a plea that he render to him the sum of two hundred and fifty dollars, which to him he owes and from him unjustly Detains, for that whereas the said Nathaniel on the 13th day of October 1798, at, to wit, at Knoxville in the District of Hamilton, made his certain Bill Single Obligatory, his own proper hand being the reto Subscribed, and sealed with the seal of him the said Nathaniel, and to the Court now here shown, the date whereof is on the same day and year aforesaid, by which said Bill Single he the said Nathaniel, by the name of Nathaniel Peters did bind himself & promise on or before the twenty fifth day Decr. one thousand seven hundred and ninety nine, to pay or cause to be pay unto the said Needham Whitfield the full and Just Sum of two hundred and fifty dollars, value received of him. Yet the said Nathaniel Peters

(although often requested & c) has not yet paid the said sum of two hundred and fifty dollars mentioned in the said Bill Single obligatory or any part thereof , to the said Needham Whitfield ; but to pay the same to the said Needham, he, the said Nathaniel , hath hitherto wholly refused , and still does refuse to the Damage of the said Needham Whitfield two hundred dollars and therefore he brings his suit , and there are pledges to prosecute & c."

Plea again and issue, Whereupon let a Jury come at March term 1810 ... Judgment , $ 285.00 and costs.

Needham Whitfield Vs Nathaniel Peters - Debt . 30 th March 1800, Plea $ 100. Suit dismissed and plaintiff paid to Defendant. Book 66.

Needham Whitefield Vs Nathaniel Peters and William Peters. Debt. Monday , April 1806 . $ 1 30.90 in Court , July 1806. With Jury. Minute Book 5, 1805-1806.

KNOX COUNTY, TENNESSEE. Superior Court Record. Book B 1797-1804.

"Bryan Whitfield of Hamilton District.
Hamilton District in the Territory of the United States of America south of the River Ohio. In the Court of Equity.

The answer of Farguard Campbell and Elizabeth his wife surviving Executors of the last Will and Testament of Alexander Smith , deceased, to the Bill of Complaint of Samuel Smith, Adminstrator of the goods and chattles and coc. which were of the Estate of John Smith , Senr., deceased.. These Defendants now and at all times hereafter saving and reserving to themselves all legal benefit and advantage that may be had and taken to the many errors uncertainties and insufficiencies of the complaints said Bill of Complaint for answer to the same bill or to so much thereof as they are advised it is material and necessary for them to answer to ; they admit that John Smith , senr. in the Bill named did depart this life on or about the time stated in the Bill intestate; & that Complainant obtained Letters of Administration on his Estate as in the Bill set forth - they also admit that the said John Smith , Senr. deceased at the time of his death left a Daughter named Jane who had been married to Thomas Phelps & another Daughter named Pheruba the wife of John Hinton also a son Samuel Smith the Complainant living & that besides the said two Daughters & son who survived him he had a Daughter Anne who had married Needham Bryan, Elizabeth who married William Bryan, a son John and one named Alexander who died before him all of whom have left Issue. These Defendants also say the said Alexander son of said Intestate did previous to his Death make and publish in Due form of Law his last Will and Testament in writing & therein constituted David Smith, Bryan Whitfield & Elizabeth his wife then Executors.

Thats aid David Smith & Elizabeth Smith (now Elizabeth Campbell)
proved the said Will in due form of Law in the County Court of Cumberland County where the said Testator resided at the time of his Death and
took upon themselves the Execution of the said Will by qualifying them -
selves in due form of Law the said Bryan Whitfield never qualified as
Executor, nor hath acted as such but hath declined to do so. These Defendants further say that the intermarried with each other the 28th day
of March in the year 1782, whereby the said Farguard Campbell becomes
as he is advised Executor in right of his said wife — As to the Gifts
made by the late John Smith , Senr. for the advancement of his family the
said Farguard Campbell knows nothing but the said Elizabeth his wife
saith that her former husband Alexander Smith had sundry slaves ,
horses, cattle ,beds and furniture when she married him & she heard
from him and doth believe that he had a negro man about forty years of
age, a woman about thirteen years of age & a boy from the said late John
Smith, Senr., his father, the Boy however appeared to have been pur -
chased as there is among the papers of the said late Alexander a Bill
of Sale stating the consideration paid for him to be One hundred pounds,
she further states that the woman was given in the year 1758 and the
man about 1756 she admits of the Cattle, Horses, and Household furniture set forth in the Schedule in the Bill of Complaint — As to the negroes
or other property charged in the Bill to have been given to the children of
the said late Alexander by the said late John his father these Defendants
are advised that it does in no manner concern them being in no sort relative to the Estate of their Testator but they Humbly submit to the Court
whether the children of the said Alexander should not be made parties
and answer for themselves, all which these Defendants are ready to aver
& C. — Without that & these Defendants pray to be dismissed here with
the Costs & C   Ferguard Campbell
                                                  Elizabeth Campbell
Sworn to before us this 27th day of August 1796.
R. Draughon, J. P.   and Saml. Williams, J. P."

SHELBY   COUNTY, TENNESSEE
Court Minutes 1843-1848

Whitfield and Bateman Company issue.

DAVIDSON   COUNTY, TENNESSEE
Courthouse Index 8 , 1955-1960

Robert Flint Whitfield , N. C. M. Commitment. March 5, 1956, June 16,
1959, 1962 . Court issue $ 6, 419. 47 , disbursement $ 5, 988. 52 , balance $ 430. 95. Trustee National Bank of Nashville Account of Veterans
Administration. His mother, Mrs. Hardinure W. Swoopes of Nashville,
Tennessee.

Doris Edna Whitfield , Inq. Com. issue , August 10, 1955.

Flora Montgomery Whitefield, Deceased issue, Executor, Albert E. Whitfield , Sept . 30, 1958.

Albert C. Whitfield , deceased and administrator , David Thomas Whitfield , June 26, 1959.

Lowell Conrad Whitefield , minor, E. R. Dismarkes, guardian June 30,1959.

Ben Hasper Whitfield , Constr., Dec. 31, 1959.

Book 3 , 1936-1945 to 1955 inclusive.

Pear Whitfield , deceased. Hattie C. Whitfield , executor for Thomas Alfred Whitfield .

Wills of Vallie Jo Fox Whitfield's grandmother paternal and uncle are the following : Will, File 4899 , Jan. 31, 1919, Elizabeth Heiner Fox, deceased in Nashville , Tennessee records.

Will, File #26833 Bernard J. Fox, executor Charlotte Fox, Sept. 24, 1946.

ALAMEDA COUNTY, CALIFORNIA
Courthouse Records 1951 - 1956
Oakland, California Court Minutes.

Harry L. Whitfield   Bertha Whitfield

Jimmie Eugene Whitfield   John Whitfield

Matt Whitfield   Barton Whitfield

Contra Costa County, California 1951 to 1978 ,

Robert Edward Whitfield and Vallie Jo Fox Whitfield and children.

SUMNER COUNTY, TENNESSEE -
Court Minutes 1787 - 1805
Mero District of North Carolina.

Bryan Whitfield - Public tax D .80¢, County tax $ 1. 20, publishing in the Gazette $ 1. 98 , total $ 4. 23. Clerks fee for order and copy 25 ¢. Bryan Whitfield 1, 640 acres of land.

The Sumner County, Tennessee Court appoints for October term 1797 the following Jurors, to wit : James Whitfield included in the names.

WILLIS WHITFIELD lived in Mero district of Bledsoe region in Tenn - essee which was a part of North Carolina before 1796. He is probably the Willis Whitfield on the Nash County, North Carolina , Census of 1790. "The Court appoints for January term 1797 the following Jurors to wit: Willis Whitfield"included in the names.

"Deed of conveyance from John Boyd to Willis Whitfield for 67 acres of land is proved by Richard Jones. "

Willis Whitfield is juror at July term of Court in 1797.

"At a Court of pleas and quarter , sessions began and held for the County ... Grand Jury empamuelled and sworn vize ; Willis Whitfield"included in the names.

"Ordered that Willis Whitfield be appointed overseer of the road from the 20 mile tree to Mamskers Creek in place of Richard Jones. "

The Court appoints for jurors to September term 1804 the following jurors to wit ; Willis Whitfield name on juror list.

TAX RECORDS

Henry County, Tennessee- 1834. William Whitfield 80 acres of land and one free polls.

Rutherford County, Tennessee . Tax 1849. Willis E. Whitfield , One polls State tax . 30¢ in Civil District No. 23.

Ansel Whitfield , free polls one . 18 3'4 ¢. Property taxable 1812 year.

Stewart County, Tennessee . Tax. "Rec'd by order of Court , August term 1811 for ad. year. "Needham Whitfield 117 acres.

Montgomery County, Tennessee. Bryan Whitfield, Public tax D. inst. . 80 ¢, County tax $1. 20. Whitfield with 1, 640 acres of land.

On Sumner County record of Court Minutes 1787-1805 : Willis Whitfield polls one , land 100 acres, tax 1, 4.

John Whitfield polls - , land 740 acres, amount of tax - , 13, 3 1/4.

Montgomery County, Tennessee . Bryant Whitfield , witness when County Courthouse set tax for 1814 year ... Bryant Whitfield returns a list of taxable property for Capt. Allen's Company for 1814.

Sumner County, Tennessee . "Tax laid for the paying of the miles that employed in calling the road ascosting families from the own and of Clinch Mountain to the Cumberland Settlements. August 25, 1789. "

Contra Costa County, California - Robert Edward Whitfield and Vallie Jo Whitfield paid tax of 75. 04 for County , $ 181. 56 for school , and $ 64. 00 for district ; he paid a California State Tax and a Federal Income Tax in 1963 on Deed , Portion of Canada Del Hambre and Las Juntas tr adj. 4. 90 acres, and income.

Second Census of Kentucky 1800 is a list of "taxpayers appearing in the 79 manuscripts volumes extant of tax lists of the forty-two counties of Kentucky in existence in 1800."

Joseph Whitefield , tax , Washington County, Kentucky.

LAND GRANTS AND DEEDS

<u>Hawkins County, Tennessee.</u> Index to Deeds Vol. 1 - 1788-1861 list Needham Whitfield and Bryan Whitfield.

<u>Sumner County, Tennessee</u>. Bryan Whitfield 1,640 acres of land 1796-1802. "Deed of conveyance from John Boyd to Willis Whitfield for 67 acres of land ", 1797.

<u>Henry County, Tennessee</u>. Index to Deeds 1822-1883 book.

From 1822-25 years Grantors to Grantees :	Book	Page
Bynum Whitfield , D. to Howel Edmunds	C	103
Lewis Whitfield, Deed Instrument. Amt. 55 acres to Wm. Walker	M	372
Needham Whitfield , D. to A. J. and B. L. Walker	M	625
Bryant Whitfield , D. to James Walker	M	627
Lewis Whitfield , D. 80 acres , William Whitfield	N	108
Thomas W. Whitfield , D. D. L. to R. B. Foster	Q	251
Thomas Whitfield , D. , 100 acres to Calvin Lasiter	T	156
Sarah M. Whitfield , D. 231 , 160 acres to J. A. Craig	W	298

<u>Rutherford County, Tennessee.</u> Index to Deeds Book L , 1804-1842.

Grantors to Grantees	Instrument	Book	Page
B. Whitfield and others to T. Henderson	Deed	L	467
Willis Whitfield to John Mc Crary	Deed	Q	211 S 393
John Whitfield to James J. Whitfield	B Sale	W	529
Thomas Y. Whitfield to Peterson Gilly	Deed	Y	289
Bryant Whitfield	Grant		291-4
Bryant Whitfield	Grant		
___ Whitfield to William Doran		V	259

Grantor to Grantee			
Wood and Love , P. of Attorney to William Whitfield		X	623
Joseph Yourie , Deed to Thomas Y. Whitfield		Y	288

<u>Stewart County, Tennessee</u>. Court Minutes 1811- 1812.
Briant Whitfield , 640 acres, North Waters of Tennessee River granted on Warrant No. 377.
Ham Whitfield , 100 acres , Piney Fork of Red River.
Bryant Whitfield , 640 acres on Cub Water.

<u>Humphreys County, Tennessee.</u>
W. M. Byrn to Oda Whitfield . In 2 nd Civil District of Humphreys County. Mrs. Oda Whitfield , Deed to 246 acres in Book # 49 , page 32. Land about two and one-half miles west of Waverly town on the Memphis to Bristol Highway. Feb. 21, 1934 the Farmers and Merchants Bank of Waverly said land to her , her heirs and assigns ($ 2,622.) ; against lawful claims of all persons whomsoever.
Oda Whitfield and Frances Daniel gave Warranty Deed for $ 650. to Edward Mc Keel for 60 acres, 1935.

Chattel Mortgage - June 27, 1941. Book #5, page 26.
Record Book # 29 page 169 in County of Humphreys between Springfield
Production Credit Association, Waverly, Tennessee Vs James D.
Whitfield and James Raymond Whitfield for $ 1, 038. 50.

LAND DEEDS ON A SITE IN HUMPHREYS COUNTY, TENNESSEE

This land deed is a history of ROCKDALE FARM of the Whitfield
family who lived 1918 to 1978 and longer. It is the home that the book
ROCKDALE FARM tells about by Robert Edward Whitfield. It was the
part of a parcel of the Harris homestead filed 1858 which he secured land
from the part of the original State of Tennessee land grant in 1793. The
deed records of the early settlers were lost when the Humphreys County
Courthouse burned on June 10, 1891, but the history is in the early land
deeds of the owners. These deeds have been passed from owner of land
to new owner of land, and when the mortgage was paid in full by Billie
R. Daniel and Rozelle Whitfield Daniel, the title company gave the many
deeds to them. The collection of eighteen deeds tell a story :

Land grant began in 1793. The first release was to a militia man
for service in the Revolutionary War. January 3, 1815, deed, Jesse Williams, Jr. to Alfred Blackman of Caldwell, Kentucky. Then of Ruther -
ford County record. (Register, Book A, Pages 373-374, Sept. 11, 1816)
State of Tennessee to Benjamin Mitchel a Deed which sold 30 acres off of
the land on Dec. 26, 1818. Grantor Deed of Alfred Blackman to Thomas
Holland of Humphreys County, a parcel, January 22, 1817. This parcel
of Thomas Holland to J. B. Massey sold April 1820. Benjamin Mitchel
grantor sold his parcel to John B. Massey May 1839. A parcel of the land
of over a thousand acres was sold by grantor of Deed to Samuel Hemby on
November 3, 1853. Since a Rutherford County citizen sold to a settler in
Humphreys County this explains a westward movement of the Rutherford,
Hickman, Perry members of Whitfield families finally settling on the
land.

The Harris homestead was a 1,000 acres. D. A. Massey, grantor
of land to C. E. Harris on Deed filed September 25, 1858. There was
about thirteen Deeds on this original land grant before C. E. Harris took
over possession of the one thousand acres of land. The Deeds are on
small parcels of the original grant of the west. The Deeds do not tell why
parcels of land were sold but the State of Tennessee came into possession
of a few parcels. In those days citizens often paid debts or made exchanges
with land a trading thing.

The State of Tennessee grant to M. A. Brown, April 10, 1869. Date
of entry and survey November 25, 1859. This information recorded on

Feb. 21, 1884 on this transaction (Book I, page 319, Humphreys County, Tennessee). Several parcels of land developed into farms, and one farm was land January 28, 1900 from grantor Carnell to Nelson, then grantor Nelson to Horner. Some of the land had new houses placed upon it and the house and garden was sold as a farm, making smaller farms. The pre - sent Deeds are available after 1898 on the land in this region. The land of the Harris family was divided into sections.

When James Dee Whitfield purchased land he purchased the first farm and house from H. H. Harris, February 1918. James Dee Whit - fild, and wife Mary Hester Mc Keel Whitfield had the Federal Land Bank of Louisville to secure the former Harris land grant. The land is "situated in old sixth district and new second district of Civil District of Humphreys County, Tennessee, 260 acres, west three miles from the Waverly " town on Humphreys County Highway near Trace Creek. (Mortgage Book W., Page 203-4; Book 35, page 519 Humphreys County, Tennessee). The house was surrounded by acreage of flat land which graded off on the other side to flat land which was the edge of another valley. There was so many rocks along side of Trace Creek at the pro - perty line that the farmer thought of the hill, dale, and rocks as he plowed in the direction of the Creek. So the house, garden, and fields were in a dale and James Dee Whitfield named the place Rockdale Farm; later known as Billie Daniel's Farm. He soon found it was not enough flat land for farming for himself so he purchased the adjacent farm land that was clear and fertile land, and combined the two farms together.

The second farm he purchased from J. F. Shannon and wife on March 11, 1919. J. F. Shannon had purchased the land from J. A. Wright on Dec. 3, 1910. James Dee Whitfield paid $ 2,000.00 with lien note of $ 3,000.00 to complete the transaction on the $ 5,000.00 farm. The two par - cels when placed as one parcel of land from his two Deeds made a farm of 692 acres of land. "To have and to hold the said tract or parcel of land with the appurtenances, estate, title and interest thereto belonging to the said James Dee Whitfield, and his wife, Mary Hester Whitfield, theirs heirs and assigns forever."

Perhaps Grandfather Whitfield meant for the heirs of his to inherit this land assigned forever, for he must have taken this into consideration when he sold to his son-in-law and daughter, Billie and Rozelle Daniel in 1943. Rockdale Farm has continued to remain in the family and is a visiting place for the Whitfields and Daniels. The land is nurtured well by its present farmer and is a farm to be happy about. The young Whit - fields play there among the fertile fields and share the beauty of the hill. This hill has a public railroad track at its bottom. James D. Whitfield granted consideration to the railroad right of way for the Nashville and Chattanooga and St. Louis Railway, on March 23, 1917. Many, many people pass this farm and the children wave proudly to the passengers on the railway.

After the death of Mary Hester Whitfield, the mother , the land was held alone by James Dee Whitfield until he married Oda DePriest H. Daniel. She had a Deed to 246 acres in 2nd Civil District on Memphis to Bristol Highway , Feb. 21, 1934 but this was soon sold. This land was located near Rockdale Farm. After James and Oda Whitfield moved to Henry County, Tennessee in 1943 , and after the death of James Dee Whitfield , his wife returned to live out her golden years at Rockdale. Oda Whitfield and Andrew Daniel lived with the Daniels there.

Finances were ever changing on this land . Some of the records are found in note-form of this text , and tell about the family and their affairs.

Rockdale Farm is the golden land of Billie and Rozelle Daniel in 1978 and many years later, and the Whitfield Families now come to visit and bring their young to know this story on the Land site in the Humphreys County of Tennessee.

James W. and Sarah Van Dyke sold to J. D. and Oda Whitfield land in 4 th district of Henry County, Tennessee for $ 16, 000. 00 on October 20, 1943. In addition to this land C. B. Smith and Missie Smith, wife conveyed land to James Dee and Oda Whitfield in 6 th district , 114. 87 acres, located at Puryear town , on April 15 , 1948.

The ancestor of Mary Hester Mc Keel-Whitfield (1878-1924) was James Mc Keel, b. 1766 ca in Ireland , d. in North Carolina. James and his wife had sons James, Sham, Mayshach, Abedinago, and two daughters. ......
James Mc Keel , b. Aug. 15, 1802 No. C., d. Aug. 23, 1879 Tenn. He married (1) Darcas Walker, b. July 18, 1800 No. C., d. Oct. 23, 1846 Tenn. (2)wife, Edna C. Galloway , (3) wife, Mrs Jinkins . James and Darcas Mc Keel had children : Thomas W. (Jan. 10-1830 No. C-March 11-1857) ; James Lawrence (March 27-1831 No. C. -March 1870 Tenn.) ; William Hyman (1833-1880); John N. Mc Keel (May 5-1834 Tenn. -April 17-1910) ;Francis , b. May 28, 1838 ; Lewis C. (Jan. 21, 1842- 1917 at Arkansas): Martha J. (Nov. 2-1843-Nov. 15-1910 Tenn.). ..... James and Edna had children : Green H. (1847-1904); Lucrecia E. (1850-19--) ; Pleasant W. (1851-1910); George W. (1854-1925) ; Anderson Enoch (1856 died young) . James Mc Keel had a total of twelve children. He lived at Maury County, Tenn. when he died........
The son William Hyman Mc Keel, b. April 2-1833 Maury Co., Tenn- d. July July 23 - 1880 . William H. Mc Keel married Louisa D. Harder . She was born Nov. 18-1839 Tenn. and died Oct. 4 - 1900. They had children: Fannie , James J. (d. 1870), Sarah J., Robert Henry (b. Feb. 11-1866; d. 1955 Tenn.), Harrit L., William T., Dolly Mary, Laura A. (d. 1962) , and Mary Hester Mc Keel (Whitfield) , b. March 10-1878, D. May 15, 1924.

TENNESSEE LAND GRANTS TO PEOPLE OF NORTH CAROLINA.

Grant Records are the property of Tennessee Archives.

Eastern Tennessee

JESSE WHITFIELD (Jepe), Private   (1)
Grant No. 1657, acres 640, July 15, 1793.
Granted to Donelson. Slokley in Eastern District of Tennessee.

LEWIS WHITFIELD, July 29, 1793   (2)
Assignee - None, # 147 Warrant No. 600, Eastern District
on the north side of Tennessee River, Book B, p. 218.

NEEDHAM WHITFIELD, et al, Sept. 20, 1787.   (3)
Assignee - None, Grant Number 310, Warrant No. 513,
Green County - On the North side of Tennessee River, Book B,
p. 202-203.

NEEDHAM WHITFIELD, July 11, 1788.   (4)
Grant No. 675, acres 500 in Book 7, p. 419.
                              and
NEEDHAM WHITFIELD, July 13, 1788
Assignee - None. Grant No. 675, Warrant No. - None
Green County - Between Clinch Mountain and Clinch River.
Book 3, p. 604, 10 pounds per 100 acres.
                              and
NEEDHAM WHITFIELD, July 11, 1788
Assignee - None, Grant No. 675, Warrant No. 557,
Green County - On Flatt Creek and lying between Clinch Mountain,
Book B, p. 208.

NEEDHAM WHITFIELD, July 11, 1788   (5)
Assignee - None, Grant No. 676, Warrant No. - None,
Green County, (Tennessee) - Bull River, B. 3, p. 634,
10 pounds per 100 acres, also in Book 2, p. 387, and in
Book B, p. 273.
                              and
NEEDHAM WHITFIELD, July 11, 1788
Grant No. 676, Acres 400, Book 7, p. 463.
                              and
NEEDHAM WHITFIELD, July 11, 1788   (6)
Grant No. 676, acres 400, Book 7, p. 463.

NEEDHAM WHITFIELD, July 11, 1788   (7)
Assignee - None, Grant No. 677, Warrant No. - None,
Greene County - Both sides of the N fork of Bull Run,
Book 3, p. 602, and Book B, p. 237 and 238.

and

NEEDHAM WHITFIELD , July 11, 1788
Assignee - None , Grant No. 677 , Warrant No. - None
Greene County, Book 2 , p. 343 , Ten pounds per 100 acres.

and

NEEDHAM WHITFIELD , July 11, 1788   (7)
Grant No. 677 , acres 400.
Needham Whitfield was a Revolutionary War soldier , and the Grants
were # 310 in 1787 and # 675 , # 676 , # 677 in 1788. The locations were
on the north side of Tennessee River , and location lying between Clinch
Mountain.
The Knoxville Gazette newspaper had claims ready it was printed of
land for one Needham Whitfield and one William Whitfield in April 10, 1794.
Eastern Tennessee.
WILLIAM WHITFIELD , et al , Sept. 20, 1787   (8)
Assignee - None , Warrant No. 513 , Green County - On the
north side of Tennessee River, Book B , p. 202-203.

WILLIAM WHITFIELD and MARCUS and JOSEPH GREENE   (9)
Grant No. 310 , acres 500 , Book 7 , p. 185.

WILLIAM WHITFIELD , July 11, 1788 , Book 7 , p. 418   (10)
Grant No. 682 , acres 400 , Book 7 p. 418.

WILLIAM WHITFIELD , July 11, 1788   (11)
Assignee - None , Grant No. 683 , Warrant No. - None
Green County, both sides of the N fork of Bull Run : Book 3, p. 603.
The purcase 10 pounds per 100 acres , and in Book B , p 274.

WILLIAM WHITFIELD , July 11, 1788   (12)
Assignee - None , Grant No. 689 , Warrant No. - None
Green County , Book 2 , page 341 .   10 pounds per 100 acres
and also in Book 3 , p 599 , Book 7 , p. 414 , Book C, p. 74 & 75.

WILLIAM WHITFIELD , July 11, 1780 ? (1788)
Assignee - None , Grant No. 700 , Warrant No. - None
Green County - Both sides of the N fork of Bull Runer , Book 3, p. 600 ,
10 pounds per 100 acres, and Book B , p. 275 , and Book 7, p. 415.

WILLIAM WHITFIELD in 1787 shared Grant of land , Number 310 , Warrant
Number 513 with Needham Whitfield and all : Marcus and Joseph Greene
were included with others.   Location the north side of Tennessee River.
In the year 1788 grants # 682 (400 acres) , #683 (purchased) , # 689
(purchased) , # 700 (purchased) were obtained in the name of William
Whitfield. Location on both sides of N fork of Bull Run River.

LAND GRANTS

Hawkins County, Tennessee

In Eastern Tennessee it is Needham Whitfield, William Whitfield and Lewis Whitfield who received land grants. It is Needham Whitfield and Bryan Whitfield who are in Knox County Court Minutes, Book 1798-1803. George Whitfield in Washington County Court Minutes probably from Sufolk County in Virginia. Book 1802-1808.

WESTERN TENNESSEE

BRYAN WHITFIELD , May 20 , 1793   # 13 Grant
Assignee - John Johnston, Grant No. 1765 , Warrant No. 1529 .
Old Tennessee County - On north side Cumberland River . Book
No. E # 5 , page 179 .   Montgomery County region.

BRYANT WHITFIELD , May 20 , 1793   # 14
Assignee - Hughey Stephenson, Grant No. 1778 , Warrant No. 1530.
Davidson County - South side Stones River , Book E # 5 , p 185.

BRYANT WHITFIELD , May 20 , 1793   # 15
Assignee of William Frost , Grant Number 1879 , Warrant Number 3247 . Old Tennessee County - On head waters of Piny River , a branch of Duck River . Book E # 5 , p 235.

BRYANT WHITFIELD , May 20 , 1793.   # 16
Assignee of Totevine , Coleburn . Grant No. 1909 , Warrant No. 1096 , County - On Stones River . Book E # 5 , p 249.

BRYANT WHITFIELD , May 20 , 1793   # 17
Assignee - Eran Bass . Grant No. 1911 , Warrant No. 1531. Tennessee County - On east side of Stones River . Book E # 5 , p 250. The Davidson County region.

BRYANT WHITFIELD , May 20 , 1793   # 18
Assignee - Muesom, Aaron, Grant No. 2201 , Warrant No. 1502 Stones River , B 2 , p 51.

BRYANT WHITFIELD , May 20 , 1793   # 19
Assignee of John Smith   Grant No. 2202, Warrant No. 487 . Stones River B 2, p. 51. Region of Counties Rutherford and Davidson.

* This Bryant is Bryan t with a mark x. He was Bryan Whitfield , a North Carolina soldier. In 1793 he received the grants numbers #1879, 1919 , 1911 , 2201 , 2202 . These grants were for Bryant Whitfield and all. He is in Montgomery County Court Minutes but his Revolutionary War kinship inherited the land in Rutherford , Cannon, Williamson , and Wilson.

General grants of land :   #20 #21 #22 #23   Grants
BRYANT WHITFIELD number 13753 , 30 1/2 acres Montgomery County,
August 12, 1818. Book Q , p. 167 ; and No. 13754 , Bryant Whitfield
10 3/4 acres acres of land Montgomery County ; and No. 13755 grant ,
50 acres, Bryant Whitfield ; and Book Q , p .164 Bryant Whitfield ;
and Bryant Whitfield , August 12, 1819 , No. 13756 , B Q , p. 160
16 7/8 acres . Total 108 1/8 acres in Montgomery County.

NEEDHAM WHITFIELD , November 13, 1813 .   # 24 and # 25 Grants
Grant No. 5157 , 80 acres, Montgomery County, Tennessee , Book L ,
p. 54 ; and Needham Whitfield , No. 5158 of 94 acres, Book L , p. 53.
                              and
NEEDHAM WHITFIELD , Sept. 28 , 1815.   # 26
No. 7794 , 86 acres , Montgomery County, Book L, p. 110. No. 7794 ,
86 acres Montgomery County , Book L , p. 110.
                              and
NEEDHAM WHITFIELD , March 31, 1818   # 27
No. 11058 , 23 1/2 acres,Montgomery County, Book O, p. 457
                              and
NEEDHAM WHITFIELD , March 31, 1818   # 28 # 29
No. 11166 , 17 1/2 acres , Steward County . Book O , page 456 , and
No. 11395 , 100 acres and in Steward County , B Q , p. 458.
                              and
NEEDHAM WHITFIELD , June 14 , 1822   # 30
No. 17411 , 31 1/2 acres , Montgomery County , B T , p. 374 .
                              and
NEEDHAM WHITFIELD , Dec. 21 - 1822   # 31
No. 18541 , 50 acres , Book X , page 749 .
                              and
NEEDHAM WHITFIELD , Dec. 31, 1822 , No. 18550   #32
Montgomery County , 26 1/2 acres , Book W , p. 363.

NEEDHAM WHITFIELD , April 18, 1825   #33
No. 23682 , 50 acres , Montgomery County , Book Z , p 772.

NEEDHAM WHITFIELD , Sept. 14, 1832   # 34
General grant no. # 26208 , Montgomery County, Book EE, p. 99.

This is Needham Whitfield, Needham Whitfield , Needham Whitfield of
grants # 5157-7794-11058-11166-11395-17411-18541- 18550-23682- 26208 of
land in Montgomery and Steward.   Needham Whitfield received 117 1/2
acres in Steward County ; and Needham Whitfield and Needham Whitfield received 265 1/2 acres in Montgomery County, Tennessee. From
North Carolina to Tennessee. From 1813 to year 1832 , a total of 383
acres in region.

WESTERN TENNESSEE
HENRY W. WHITFIELD , February 18 , 1825   # 35
No. 23319 general grant , 72 1/2 acres in Madison County. Book Z,
page 665.
HENRY WHITFIELD , March 20 , 1827 . Grant No. 493 , 75 acres ,
Madison County, Tennessee . Book I , p 493.

     Original grants but from land of original grant to heirs :
WILLIAM WHITFIELD , June 24, 1823   #35 +
Grant No. 19356 , 10 acres, Rutherford County to a Whitfield, Book V., p. 765.

WILLIAM WHITFIELD , June 24 , 1823   #36
12 1/2 acres , Rutherford County in Book V , page 764.

WILLIAM WHITFIELD , November 7 , 1826   # 37
Grant No. 4353 , 50 acres, Rutherford County , Tennessee
in Book 5 , p. 809.

THOMAS YOUNG WHITFIELD , December 2, 1836   # 38
Grant No. 13872 , 50 acres , Rutherford County , in Book 16, p. 783.

HARRISON WHITFIELD , Jan. 30 , 1834   # 39
Grant No. 12406 , 50 acres , Davidson County , in Book 15 , p. 174.
HARRISON WHITFIELD , Grants numbers 12232 , March 5, 1834
and 13086 on June 1835 day.

LAVINA WHITFIELD , May 27 , 1846   #40
Grant No. 18244 , 168 acres , Rutherford County, Tennessee , in
Book 21, p. 256.
LEVINA WHITFIELD (wife of William Whitfield of Rutherford County,
Tennessee. Grant No 14429 . June 19, 1837 , 168 in Book 17, p. 407.

JOHN WHITFIELD , #42-43-44-45 Grants , to John Whitfield for family,
et al , Coffee County, Tennessee.
Grant No. 6840 , 5,000 acres , Coffee County, May 9 , 1839 in Book M, p 90.

JOHN WHITFIELD , May 8 , 1839 , Coffee County , Tennessee.
Grant No . 6847 , 5,000 acres in Book M , page 89.

JOHN WHITFIELD , May 9, 1839 , Coffee County, Tennessee.
Grant No. 6849 , 5,000 acres , Book M, page 91

JOHN WHITFIELD , May 9 , 1839 , Coffee County, Tennessee.
Grant No. 6850 , 5,000 acres in Book M, page 92.

WHITE COUNTY , TENNESSEE , LAND GRANTS

CARTER B. WHITFIELD , August 4, 1830   # 47
Grant No. 1821 , 300 acres , White County , Book C , page 523.

JOHN WHIT FIELD , July 1, 1829   # 48
Grant No. 1333 , 36 acres , White County , Book C , page 216.

THOMAS WHITFIELD , April 1829   # 49
Grant No. 1146 , 100 acres , White County , Book C , page 105.

JOHN WHITFIELD , September 26 , 1828   # 50
Grant No. 939 , 56 1/4 acres , White County , Book B. page 368 .

JACKSON COUNTY, TENNESSEE
WILLIAM WHITFIELD , August 25 , 1849   # 51
Grant No. 10181 , 37 acres , Jackson County , Book W., page 699.

HENRY COUNTY, TENNESSEE
WILLIAM WHITFIELD , Heirs of Grant No. 4777   # 52
150 acres , October 18, 1847 , Book 6 , page 675.

LEWIS WHITFIELD , October 18, 1847   # 53
Grant No. 4778 , 162 acres , Book 6, p. 676

WILLIAM WHITFIELD , November 10 , 1849   # 58
Grant No. 9981 , 60 acres

HUMPHREYS COUNTY, TENNESSEE
HENRY W. WHITFIELD , February 20 , 1874 ,
Grant No. 25941 , 72 acres , Humphreys County , Book 25474 , 26173 , p. 473.

OBION COUNTY, TENNESSEE
BRYANT WHITFIELD , April 27 , 1848   # 60
Grant No. 569 , 50 acres , Obion County , B 7 , p. 385

*   "These are purchased land grants , not given for Revolutionary service . Any person could purchase as many grants as he was financially able to , with certain restrictions as to number of acres in one grant, period of residence, and area . The word "grant" is used to indicate that this is the original owner. There were warrants given soldiers of the North Carolina Continental Line in lieu of pay, and many of these were sold in North Carolina by the soldiers or their heirs to those planning to settle in the western territory. There are no Whitfield grants based on Whitfield Revolutionary service in our files . There are no land grants in Tenn -

essee based on Revolutionary service performed in the Virginia Con -
tinental Line. "

The Revolutionary War service warrants and land grants were made
in North Carolina to soldiers before Tennessee became a State to a very
few who settled before 1796.

LAND DEEDS

Sumner County, Tennessee Deed Book # 1, 1793-1797 , p. 331.
File in Courthouse at Gallatin, Tennessee - John Boyd to William
Whitfield.

Needham Whitfield to Joseph Green . Registered May 20, 1797 .
(Transcribed from Liber E. P. 159) (page 200) Hawkins County, Tennessee . Deed Book # 1 , 1788 - 1800. State Library of Tennessee analytical index.

To all to whom these presents   shall come Greetings , — Know
ye that I Needham Whitfield of the County of Lenoir and state of North
Carolina for and in consideration of an exchange made in lands between
myself and Joseph Green of the County of Wayne and State of North Carolina have bargained sold and granted and do by these presents give grant
and make over unto him the said Joseph Green his heirs and assigns forever all my right title claim and demand to two certain messages tracts
or parcels of land lying and being in the State of Tennessee and County
of - - - - -

One survey containing five hundred acres lying between Clinch
Mountain and Clinch River and a few miles above the lower end of Clinch
Mountain on flat creek beginning at a large forked sycamore at a fork of
the   creek and runs north two hundred and eighty three poles to a stake
then south two hundred and eighty three poles to a stake then south two
hundred and eighty three poles to a white oak and then a straight line
to the beginning. The other survey containing four hundred acres lying
on both sides of the north fork of Bull Run that makes into Clinch River
beginning at a beech in a little island of the creek below a survey of said
Whitfields and runs east one hundred and sixty poles to a post oak then
north two hundred poles to a white oak then west three hundred and twenty
poles to a chestnut then south two hundred poles to a stake and then east
one hundred and sixty poles to the beginning containing in the whole nine
hundred acres as by the patent granted unto the said Needham Whitfield
the 11th day of July 1788 to have and to hold all my right title claim and
demand to the aforesaid land and premises with all the appertenances to
the same belonging or appertaining warranting and forever defending the
same against me and my heirs and assigns or any person or persons lay-
ing any claim to the same unto the said Joseph Green his heirs and assigns
forever.

In witness whereof I the said Needham Whitfield have hereunto set
my hand and seal this 12 th day of April 1796.   Seal - Needham Whitfield .
Signed   sealed and delivered in the presence of Bryan Whitfield and

Joseph Green , Jr.   -----------------
                            Maury County - Coffee County, Tennessee
      There was 25,000 acres of land in Tennessee given by North Caro-
lina Assembly to General Nathaniel Greene. They located it in what is
now Maury County. In February 1783, the land commissioners of Mero
District went from Nashville to Latitude Hill, in Giles County. After
they located the southern boundary of the western part of North Carolina,
they went fifty-fve miles to the north and ran parallel to this southern
boundary , a line known as the "Commissioners Line." This was boundary of land to be given to the Continental Soldiers before Tennessee
became a State. This line survey helped define the boundaries later of
Tennessee State. Through this did one John Whitfield get 20,000 acres
in the region ?   History of Hickman County by Spence .

      "A large number of the old settlers of the Williamson County took up
military claims of grants made by North Carolina to her Revolutionary
Soldiers. It was of this element that the country was largely peopled. "
(From book - History of Tennessee , by Goodspeed Publishing Company.)

      "Early explorers of what is now Hickman County came from the
Cumberland settlements."(p. 20 . History of Hickman County (Tenn-
essee) , by W. Jerome Spence and David Spence.)

      Thomas, George, John W. and James Monroe Whitfield had land at
Council Bend on Duck River in Hickman County, Tennessee and later
Whitfield Town.   Hickman County History , by W J. and D. Spence,
page 54-55.   -----------------
      Tennessee first settlement was North Holston (present County
of Sullivan,) the second settlement was Watauga settlement , the third
settlement was Carter's Valley west of the North Holston and at the same
time another third settlement was Nollichucky, Sevier , southwest of
Watauga in Tennessee . (A History of Rutherford County , by Carlton C.
Sims).   -----------------------

      The first Anglo-Saxon blood visiting Sumner County was in 1765 when
Henry Scaggs explored Cumberland Country and fixed camp at Mansker's
Lick. Men from Rockbridge County , and Valley of New River of Vir -
ginia came with him.

      "The Governor in 1792 turned attention to Civil government and on
the 11th of June 1792 , he issued an ordinance circumscribing the limits of
Greene , Hawkins Counties and created Knox and Jefferson Counties."
(History of Tennessee , by Goodspeed).

TENNESSEE, STEWART COUNTY. DEED Book 1804-1806, compiled
by W.P.A. Historical Records Survey , 1939.

Grantor	Granted
Daniel Whitfield	Jacob Chester
William Whitfield	S. Weatherford
Charles Whitfield and others	E. McKinney 1836
Jessie Whitfield	Samuel Wofford 1837

C. Whitfield , Ann, Mary and Willis Whitfield to Samuel Wofford.

CONNECTICUT   State of United States

Henry Whitfield (1597-1657) Clergyman, settler , was born near London,
the son of Thomas Whitfield of Martlake in Surrey, England who was a
lawyer and his wife Mildred Manning Whitfield . He became a minister
of Ockley in Surrey. B.D. in 1631-32 from University of Cambridge . Henry
Whitfield arrived 1639 in New Haven , Connecticut . He founded the town at
Guilford, Connecticut. In 1618 he married Dorothy Sheaffe and had ten children. He died September 17 , 1657. He was the author of several publications.

NEW YORK

Robert Parr Whitfield (1828-1910) Paleontologist of U.S. Department. Son
of William Fenton and Margaret (Parr) Whitfield. He was born New Hart-
ford, New York in Oneida County. Robert Whitfield married 1848 to Mary
Henry and they had a son , James Edward Whitfield, a chemist. Robert
was the state geologist of New York who is found in Who's Who in America ,
and published many geological papers.

In "Membership Roster and Soldiers." Tennessee Society of the D.A.R.
1894-1960 . Compiled by Edythe Rucker Whitley. On page 571. John Dilla-
hunty (John de la Hunte) was born Dec. 8, 1728 in Maryland, and died Jan. 5,
1816 in Davidson County, Tennessee. He married June 4, 1747 in Baltimore,
Hannah Neal , who was born in 1733 in Maryland and died 1816 in Tennessee.
John served as a Patriot and Minister when a resident of Newberry , South
Carolina , during the Revolution. (D.A.R. # 17151). Children of John and
Hannah (Neal) Dillahunty were John, born 1749 who married Rachel, Samuel,
Daniel , Thomas who was born Dec. 4 , 1765 and married Sarah Becton,
William , Rachel who married Colonel Joseph Johnson, Mary A. who was
born 1778 and married George West , Hannah who married   Snelling.

PENSION APPLICATION   AND   MILITARY SERVICE RECORDS
REVOLUTIONARY WAR PENSION APPLICATIONS

North Carolina. John Whitfield , Mildred. Reject 11396.

The North Carolina State Comptroller's Office certified that North
Carolina paid John Whitfield for service in the Revolution. He was of
Granville District.

The heirs of John and Milly Whitfield made claims for pensions
due their mother, Mildred. She had five children older than fifty-eight
years on Feb. 23, 1846.

John W. Whitfield age 56 years of Granville County, North Carolina on July 4, 1836 made a deposition, stating that he was a son of the late John Whitfield, the Revolutionary War soldier; that his father served three tours of duty in all nine months. John Whitfield believed that his father was married in 1774, to Molly Grimsley. They had nine children:

1. Polly Whitfield
2. Sally Whitfield
3. Mary Whitfield
4. Martha Whitfield
5. William Whitfield
6. Elizabeth Whitfield
7. Nancy Whitfield
8. John W. Whitfield
9. George Whitfield

John Whitfield, the father, died January 2, 1832, age 89 years. Milly Whitfield, the widow, died Nov. 15, 1839, and left five surviving children: Mary Whitfield who married John Vestal; Martha Whitfield who married James Hester; William Whitfield, Mary Whitfield who married Joseph Boothe; John W. Whitfield, the declarant.

This claim for a pension was rejected as evidence of service was not sufficient. R 11396. ─────────────

North Carolina. William Whitfield, wife - Mary   R 11395.
The data herein is from the Veterans Administration, Washington, D.C. by A. D. Hiller. "The data furnished was obtained from papers on file in Pension Claim R 11395, based upon the military service of William Whitfield, the only soldier by that name that is found in the Revolutionary War Records of this office.

On March 16, 1844, Mary Whitfield, a resident of Ewington, Effington, Co., Illinois. who was age 87 years, applied for pension as the widow of William Whitfield.

It was alleged that while living in Duplin County, North Carolina, William Whitfield enlisted in the spring of 1777 and served three months as private in Captain Quinsey's Company in Colonel Ben Sasser's North Carolina Regiment: that in the fall of 1777 he enlisted and served until after the surrender of Cornwallis as private in Capt. Ben Graham's or Grimes ' Company in the "Rockingham Regiment " and was in the Battles of Hichory Plains, Charleston, Ramsour's Hills, Broad River Cowpens, Eutaw Springs and Yorktown. "
" The claim for pension was not allowed as proof of the alleged service was never furnished. It was stated that William Whitfield was married September 9, 1775, in Duplin County, North Carolina, Mary Beck. William Whitfield died August 8, 1825, in Stewart County, Tennessee.

In 1844 the widow, Mary, stated that she had lived in Duplin Co., North Carolina, Christian County, Kentucky, Stewart Co., Tennessee; Fayette Co., Illinois, and Effingham County, Illinois.

William Whitfield and Mary Beck Whitfield had 13 children but only the four youngest were living in 1844. The oldest child was born about four months after William Whitfield went into the service, and the second child was born January 19, 1783.

The only names given were, Bryant Whitfield , who was the youngest and in 1844 was living in Effingham County, Illinois, age 33 years , and William who died in Kentucky several years prior to 1844.

In 1844 the widow's sister, Anna Slocumb, was about 85 years of age and was living in Wayne County, Illinois. "

This is all the data relative to the soldier and his family in Washington, D. C. Federal War pension files. However, the children of William and Mary Beck Whitfield were :

1. William Whitfield
2. Needham Whitfield
3. Joseph Whitfield
4. Lewis Whitfield
5. Hester Whitfield who married Charles Whitfield, son of
   William Whitfield III.
6. John Beck Whitfield
7. Harriet Whitfield
8. Mary Whitfield
9. Lucy Whitfield who died
   unmarried at the home of her brother Bryan Whitfield in
   Nauvoo, Illinois.
10. Bryan Whitfield

The father , William Whitfield was born 1764 in Wayne County, North Carolina. He married in Duplin County in 1785 to Mary Beck. So after the marriage he moved to Christian County, Kentucky and later to Steward County, Tennessee where he died August 8, 1825.

It appears that the war service claim data is confused with records of other generations. Bryan Whitfield , age 33 in Illinois with Mary Beck Whitfield was a son .

It is of significant historically and genealogically that these war service claim numbers are federal numbers Rejection 11 395, 11 396 , 11 397 . It was a custom in early years for brothers , cousins, kinfolks to enlist in the military together , and they usually filed claims about the same time. William Whitfield's # 11 395 widow was in Illinois and in early Cumberland Settlement of Tennessee , and lived at Steward County.

John Whitfield # 11 396 was from Granville County, North Carolina.

Willis Whitfield R # 11 397 was at Raleigh, North Carolina. Perhaps some early kinship line is found here.   This may even be a clue to the grandfathers of some of the backwood Regulators of North Carolina.

Willis Whitfield , wife, Nancy. North Carolina R 11397 Comptroller's Office, at Raleigh , North Carolina certified that the name of Willis Whitfield appears as having had a specie certificate issued in his favor for military service for 13 pounds, two shillings, etc.

and

Guilford County, North Carolina . The Clerk of the Court of Pleas and Quarter Sessions certified that no marriage bond for Willis Whitfield and Nancy Rayford could be found in the records of that County , Oct. 31, 1846.

Tennessee was in 1861 the last State to secede from a union and the first to be readmitted in the south after the Civil War.

REVOLUTIONARY WAR PENSION APPLICATION

State of Virginia .   William Whitefield   S. 38, 466

William Whitefield was born in January 1751. Place and parent's names not given. He enlisted in Goochland County, Virginia , Feb. 16, 1778. He marched in Capt. Norris's Virginia Company to Valley Forge ; then served in Capt. Custis Kendall's Company , in Colonel Richard Parker's Virginia Regiment , and was discharged Feb. 16,1779 in Middlebrook, New Jersey. He was allowed a pension on his application executed Nov. 25 , 1829 , when living in Saint Clare County, Alabama. In 1829 , he stated that he had reared twelve children, all married but one who had lately died . No reference to his wife , nor names of children. He received a pension of $ 8. 00 per month.

State of Virginia   Solomon Whitfield   S. 18281

Solomon Whitfield was born in Nansemond County, Virginia , date not given. He enlisted in Nansemond County, in 1780 and during that year he served three tours of six weeks each as a private in Capt. Demsey Sumner's Company, Colonel Lemuel Reddick's Virginia Regiment. He enlisted again in 1781 and served two tours of six weeks each in that year under Captains Robert Reddick and James Mc Clenny in the Virginia Troops. He was allowed a pension on his application dated May 13, 1832, when he was seventy years old and a resident of Nansemond County, Virginia , where he had always lived. He died September 10, 1836 . No information regarding his family is given.

State of North Carolina   Willis Whitfield , wife Rhoda   W 1013

Declaration of Rhody Whitfield , January 10 , 1840 , Cannon County, Tennessee. She was a resident of said County , aged 72 . She declared that she was the widow of Willis Whitfield , who was a pensioner of the United States and drew his pension in Nashville, Tennessee, for Revolutionary War service. They were married Nov. 1, 1788 . Willis Whitfield died September 3 , 1836. Rhody Allen (Whitfield) was the daughter of Arthur Allen and Elizabeth his wife , and was born Dec. 1, 1767. They had twelve children , half of them born in North Carolina and half born in Tennessee. The children:

1. Ansil Whitfield , born Aug. 25, 1789.
2. Wright Whitfield , born March 20 , 1791.
3. Christian Whitfield , born Nov. 1, 1793.
4. Sally Whitfield , born May 5 , 1795.
5. Temperance Whitfield , born Feb. 26, 1797.
6. Rhody Whitfield , born Dec. 27 , 1798.
7. Thomas Yough Whitfield , born Feb. 5, 1801.
8. Arthur Allen Whitfield , born Jan. 30 , 1803.
9. Willis Whitfield , born Jan. 30 , 1805.
10. Eli Whitfield , born July 2, 1807.
11. Eliz. Eason Whitfield , born Feb. 26 , 1810.
12. Alfred Whitfield , born Jan. 19, 1812.

The father , Willis Whitfield was living in 1832 and made this declaration- August 23 , 1832 , Rutherford County, Tennessee.

He, Willis Whitfield declared that he was a resident of this County , aged 71 or 72 ; that in Nash County , North Carolina, he was drafted under Capt. Carter and served two or more tours of duty in the Revolution as a private . He was under General Greene, and was stationed near Charleston , South Carolina.

He was born in Nash County, North Carolina , but does not know in what year. He was living in Nash County when called into the service, and since then lived in North Carolina and Tennessee.

Rhoda Whitfield received a pension of $ 58. 33 per annum under the Act of Congress of July 7 , 1828 . Rhoda Whitfield , widow of Willis Whitfield who was a pensioner of the United States, died Sept . 3, 1826 , Cannon County, Tennessee. He was a private in the Company of Captain Carter , in the Regiment Commanded by Colonel Source in the North Carolina Line for seventeen months.

MEXICAN WAR PENSION
Act of Congress , January 29 , 1887

Sarah B. Whitfield , widow of John W. Whitfield, Lt. Col. Third Tennessee Volunteers. Certficate No. 7393.

Declaration of Sarah Whitfield , widow for a Pension, Medina County, Texas , July 9 , 1890.

Sarah B. Whitfield , aged 62 , widow of John Wilkins Whitfield, Captain of Company A, commanded by John Wilkins Whitfield in the first Regiment Tennessee Volunteers commanded by Colonel W. B. Campbell, and afterwards served as Lt. Col. commanding the Third Regiment Tennessee Volunteers.

Her husband enlisted at Nashville , Tennessee in May 1846. She was married under the name of Sarah B. Dibrell, on May 28 , 1853, in Nashville, Tennessee, by the Rev. Berry M. Stevens. John Wilkins Whitfield died Oct. 27 , 1879 in Lavaco County, Texas. Sarah Dibrell was born December 11, 1827 in White County, Tennessee. She died April 26 , 1918. She died in Medina County, Texas.

Lucinda Dibrell Herd declared that she knew Sarah B. Whitfield since birth , being her older sister.

John Wilkins Whitfield and Sarah Dibrell Whitfield had a son John Anthony Whitfield born 1855 in Tenn . John Anthony Whitfield married Helena Briscoe of Augusta, Arkansas . John and Helena met while she was visiting relatives near Hallettsville, Lavoca County, Texas. John Anthony Whitfield died on April 19 , 1909 at the age of fifty-four years at Devine, Medina County, Texas.

<u>Austin County, Texas.</u> Statement before a Notary Public of H. W. Whitfield , Sr. who declared that Catharine Whitfield , former wife of John W. Whitfield died at Centerville, Hickman County, Tennessee in the month of July 1846.   Signed Henry W. Whitfield   Feb. 18, 1891.
Henry W. Whitfield was the son of Henry Whitfield of Williamson County, Tennessee living in Texas , and grandson of Wilkins Whitfield and wife of Williamson County, Tennessee.

War Department , Record and Pension Division
John Wilkins Whitfield , Co. A, First Tennessee Volunteers of Mexican War. Enrolled May 31, 1846, and mustered out with this Company, May 23, 1847. Also enrolled Oct. 8, 1847 , as Lt. Colonel, Third Tennessee Volunteers and mustered out with Field Staff , July 24, 1848.
From enrollment in 1846 to mustering out, in 1848, he held the rank of Captain and Lt. Colonel.   ---------------

WAR SERVICE RECORDS

Captain Luke Whitfield , born 1719 in North Carolina, died in South Carolina. He married _____ Powell who was born in South Carolina. He served as a Captain in the Regiment of Col. G. G. Powell , in the Revolution.   Recorded in the "Journal of the Council of Safety," Feb. 21, 1776. A child of Luke was Benjamin Whitfield who married Anne Station.

Benjamin Whitefield (Mary, wife) , private in Co. E, 4th Tennessee Volunteers. Widow applied for pension July 20 , 1907 under Act of January 29 , 1887. Residence in Tennessee.

Army accounts of the North Carolina Line , settled at Warrenton, 1786. Jesse Whitfield .   Claim receipted by Jesse Whitfield , and received by B. Mc Culloch (p 567).
Willis Whitfield , private, Raifor's Company. Enlisted in 1782. Served eighteen months. (p 176).
Willis Whitfield . On Pierce's Register of North Carolina Soldiers of the Revolution. (p23)

THE REVOLUTIONARY ARMY ACCOUNTS gives the names of Whitfields in the Revolution War as official soldiers. Vol. Page   Folio of Books.

Ben	Whitfield	J.	Whitfield	Needham	Whitfield
Bryan	Whitfield	Jacob	Whitfield	Reuben	Whitfield
Bryan	Whitfield	James	Whitfield	W.	Whitfield
Bryan	Whitfield	James	Whitfield	W.	Whitfield
Bryan	Whitfield	Jesse	Whitfield	Jesse	Whitfield
C.	Whitfield	John	Whitfield	Wilson	Whitfield
C.	Whitfield	John	Whitfield	Benjamin	Whitfield
Const.	Whitfield	N.	Whitfield	Copeland	Whitfield
Hartwell	Whitfield	Needham	Whitfield	Needham	Whitfield
Israel	Whitfield	Needham	Whitfield	Constantine	Whitfield

Revolution War Accounts:
Thirty-one men or boys with the name of WILLIAM WHITFIELD in the
American Revolution War.

Needham	Whitfield	Capt.	Whitfield
William	Whitfield	William	Whitfield
William	Whitfield, Jr.	William	Whitfield, Jr.
Capt. William Whitfield		Capt. William Whitfield	
Bryan	Whitfield		

REVOLUTIONARY SOLDIERS OF VIRGINIA - Ninth Annual Report 1911-12
Virginia State Library :
These men received Military Land Warrants , Continental Line of Virginia.

Edward Whitfield	John Whitfield
William Whitfield	William Whitfield ,
Haynes Whitfield	heir of Jesse Whitfield

WAR OF 1812

Ansil Whitfield , private , Nov. 21, 1812 of Rutherford County, Tennessee.
Tours Col. Benton , Capt James Mc Ferrin? Vol. Inf. Dec. 10 , 1812
and tour Feb. 10 , 1813 . Col. Pallon, Capt. James Mc Ferrin tour
Sept. 26 , 1813.

Killebrew Whitfield , private , Sept. 24, 1813 of Montgomery County,
Tennessee. Capt. David Smith , North Carolina Volunteer. Wulisin?
(probably Willis or Wilson) Whitfield , private Oct 1, 1813 . Col. Wyome,
Capt. Barless Prince , in Tennessee Infantry.

MEXICAN WAR

John Wilkins Whitfield - Capt. Co. A. First Tennessee Volunteers
and Third Regiment Tenn. 1846 , 1847 Hickman Co., Tenn.

Aaron Whitfield , private enlisted Sept 24, 1847 , Nashville, Tenn.
Co. D, Capt. Daniel Trigg . Third Regiment , Tennessee Volunteer,
Col. B.J. Cheatham. Aaron Whitfield died Mexico City, Mexico ,
January 14 , 1848.

Tennessee Pension Roll - Revolution Account -
First Session 23rd Congress. Historical Records project # 465-44 ,
3 - 115 . Statement and account of Rutherford County, Tennessee . Willis
Whitfield , private of infantry annual allowance 58.33 . Sum received
174.99 , description of service - Do
When placed on the pension roll - Nov. 15, 1832
Commencement of pension - Do
Aged - 72

CIVIL WAR RECORDS

Captain S. D. H. Whitfield , Company Captain of Co. I, 10th Tennessee Cavalry. In the summer of 1862. Alonzo Napier of Humphreys County raised the Company during the Civil War. As Co. G. it became a part of 10th Co., with men from Humphreys and Perry Counties of Tennessee.

Thomas J. Whitfield (1810-1873) and Thomas J. Whitfield (1845-1908) Captain Thomas Jefferson Whitfield of Company D , later Company H, 42th Tennessee. The 42th had men from the County of Humphreys as members.

In 1845 , Thomas Jefferson Whitfield was in Davidson County Militia as Brigadier - General of the seventeenth Brigade. In 1862 he felt grievances because peace was not a permanent thing. When slavery became an issue in Tennessee and war seemed evident he considered going to England but friends and relatives put him in jail so he could not leave according to a family legend. He was a brave soldier in the Tennessee Infantry and was wounded. They started to bury him but happened to see one of his eyelids move and saw he was alive, and did not bury him but came near burying him alive. In some way he came in possession of thousands of acres of land in Texas but sold it for small sum of money, for in those days land was looked upon as blame nothing. Some of the famous cities of Texas now stands on that ground once owned by Thomas Jefferson Whitfield. *

He was known as General Jeff Whitfield to the family. He appears with this name in the public records of middle Tennessee. It was his brother , John Wilkins Whitfield who was the first Volunteer guards that was organized in 1846 to the Mexican War of Hickman County where they then lived. The land warrant account was probably through him.

Thomas Whitfield did not go to Mexico , but he fought actively on Tennessee land in the Civil War. His sons, Silas S. Whitfield , George Monroe Whitfield , and Jack H. Whitfield fought in the Civil War.

The son, Thomas Jefferson Whitfield (1845-1908) and the other soldiers in the family helped to swim the horses across the Tennessee River at Pavatts Landing and close by. They swam six or eight horses to each canoe , one man paddled canoe and another man held the bridle reins of the horses. He made several trips in swimming horses across from Humphreys County across to Benton County. He was in the Cavalry under General Nathan Bedforest . They had a battle at Johnsonville , Tennessee. A boat sunk and one went down at Pavatts Landing. It was pitiful for the people to have to live the days of war. Thomas Jefferson Whitfield came near drowning in the transaction of getting many horses across the Tennessee River.

_____

* Account from grandsons and sons: Contributors were Thomas C. Whitfield, Henry Edward Whitfield , and daughter , Clara Whitfield.

There were many Whitfields and relatives in the Civil War. General Forrest Division has a park close to Camden, Tennessee named in his honor, and his company division of War has a historic momument.

Thomas Jefferson Whitfield (1810-1873) was a Davidson County Brigadier General of the 17th Brigade. Assisted in organization of service for Mexican War; and soldier in Civil War. His son, Thomas Jefferson Whitfield (1845-1908) was soldier in Civl War and in a Tennessee Company.

George Monroe Whitfield 1841-1863. Civil War Confederate soldier. Died in 1863.

Jack H. Whitfield, soldier and Captain. Civil War.

Hervey Whitfield - Confederate Soldier, Company A. 2 nd Kentucky Regiment. Commanded by Colonel Malone, General N. B. Forest Cavalry, General Lyons Brigade.

Hervey Whitfield enlisted August 1864. Company sent to Pan's Tennessee and then to Mississippi. After enlistment in the three months the Company went into battle at Corinth, Mississippi : "After this battle we turned north being organized under General Lyon. He was assigned to enter Kentucky to cut off supplies from General Thomas at Hopkinsville. We were in battle against General Mc Cook and small fight on to Elizabeth town, Kentucky where we turned south and discharged at Selmen, Alabama."
(Account of War by Hervey Whitfield. Tennessee Archives State files on Civil War soldiers.)

Smith Whitfield.   From Pensions from War Department. The
           Adjutant General's Office, Sept. 26, 1927.

The records show that Smith Whitfield (not borne as S. C. Whitfield) private, Company B, 24 th Tennessee Infantry, C. S. A. enlisted Sept. 14, 1862 at Glasgow, and on muster roll for Sept. 1 to Dec. 31, 1862 is shown "sick at hospital."

Union prisoner of War records show him captured Feb. 13, 1863, at Triune, sent to Louisville, Kentucky, forwarded to Camp Chase, O. transferred to Fort Mc Henry Baltimore, Maryland, May 10, 1863, paroled at that place and sent to City Point, Virginia, May 14, 1863 for exchange.   Signed by Luty Wabl.

A citizen of Franklin, Tennessee of Williamson County, Company of 24th, Tennessee Regiment. Col. Bratton, Battle at Perryville and Mumfordsville.

John Wilkins Whitfield of Mexican War from Hickman County, Tennessee and of Civil War in the State of Kansas. He was Captain of Whitfield's Battalion in Confederate Cavalry Unit raised in 1861. He brought Indians into the Confederate Army. Battle at Fort Gibson, he reinforced Douglas

Hancock Cooper when fighting the Union Indian Hopoetholoyqholq. He becomes Colonel of Texas Twenthieth-seven Regiment, and later General in Command of the Texas regiment of the Army of the Confederate WEST. He engaged in the Battles of Pea Ridge and Iuka in 1862 in Kansas. He was cited by General Price for "dashing boldness and steady courage," engaged in the Cavalry battle near Spring Hill in 1863; and commissioned Brigadier -General May 9 , 1863. He was one of the best and bravest soldiers that ever lived.

CIVIL WAR

Thomas Harrison Whitfield (1838-1921) Williamson County and Hickman County, Tennessee.

In May 1861 when the Civil War broke over the South , he volunteered, enlisted Company E, 20th Tennessee, June 8 , 1861 , afterwards trans - ferred to Company H. First battle at Fishing Creek , then to Shiloh battlefield , during the battle the enemy retreated to their gun boat. Discharged and sent home after the battle. Was compelled to take the oath, and enlisted again and joined my old command 20th Tennesseans, and went into fights at Murfressboro ; Hoover Gap ; Chickamaugo ; and at Missionary Ridge at Chicamaugo he was captured in the battle , Nov - ember 1863 , with his earlier discharge in his pocket. "The Yankees offered to release him at Nashville if I sooner take the oath " but he re - fused and was sent to Rock Island prison , where he was held until the hostilities were over.

The twentieth Tennessee regiment which included boys from Will- iamson County , commanded by Colonel Will Shy , who fell near there . Comrades included Nathan Morris , Joe Carl, William Roberson, John Miller, Isaac Wright of Lynnhurst , Tennessee , Joseph Smith, Jesse Short and others.

He was released March 26, 1865 . He had a sick friend released with him. He came home anyway he could get convey, and besides walking was the usual hardship at that time . He was released under oath at Rock Island Barracks, Illinois.

WORLD WAR I

Josiah Whitfield , private , Company K , 16th U.S.C. Infantry killed July 7, 14 , 1914 of Hamilton County, Tennessee.

Floyd E. Whitfield, private 11th infantry, killed in war . On the State of Tennessee list at Historical Museum Building Shrine in Nashville, Tennessee.

John Boyd came to Granville County, North Carolina and lived near Bullocks and Hawkins family. His father was born in Ireland and came to Maryland port then to Virginia and North Carolina. Their home was earlier within bounds of Cumberland Parish. This Vestry at its first meeting appointed Lewis Deloney, William Howard, and John Boyd in 1749 to "fix on some convenient place near the fork of the Roanoke to erect a Chapel and make report to the next vestry."

On the records of Lunenburg County, dated Oct. 15, 1749 is the Will of Mary Lawson in which she mentions the name of eight children among them being John Boyd's wife Margaret.

May 18, 1764 at the Inferior Court of Pleas and Quarter session : James Boyd versus John Walker of Granville County.
(Book: "Colonial Granville County, North Carolina") by W. Ray.

A John Boyd married Milly Wright Sept. 28, 1785 in Virginia, but in Lunenburg County, North Carolina there were several other members of this Boyd family, including Alexander, Richard and Robert Boyd. The Hawkins family lived there also, as well as in Nutbush, North Carolina. The daughter of John Boyd of Granville was the wife of Governor William Hawkins, and Nancy Hawkins married William Hawkins in Mecklenburg County, Virginia, Dec. 24, 1803. (Cumberland Parish Register, p. 316)

In Duplin County, North Carolina lived several Whitfield families at this time. Joseph Whitfield died in Duplin County in 1765. In his Will he named his wife, Mary Whitfield and children : John, Joseph, William Bryan, Henry, Timothy (sons), Elizabeth Outlaw, Hester Grady, Sally Whitfield, Charity Loften, Rachael Whitfield (daughters). (Will Book I, p. 64)

Revolution War in North Carolina - Battles at Alamance, Camden, Cowpens, Guilford Courthouse, Eutaw Springs, Charleston and King's Mountains in which many of the pioneers of Tennessee gained imperish - able renown. These Tennesseans list of names include several Whitfields, frontiermen of the backwoods of Virginia, North Carolina and South Carolina.

The first battle of the Revolution which gave independence to the Colonies, and the first blood shed in that cause was on the sixteenth of May 1771, when the forces of Governor Tryon, numbering 1,100 men, met about 200 of the "Regulators" at Alamance, in Orange County, North Carolina.

Later under Major General Nathanael Greene in South Carolina some new 2,400 fought Cornwallis. Greene received large militia reinforcements in the vicinity of Guilford courthouse. Whitfields among those at Cowpens, March 15, 1781, then another battle under Greene at Eutaw Springs.

After the war Greene was appointed by the North Carolina to distribute the land warrants, and he did not forget the men of the frontier who fought with him. Some of the Whitfield's land grants to middle Tennessee was won and purchased through this cause and they moved to the new land.

PART V

HISTORICAL NOTES
by Vallie Jo Fox Whitfield

"Dr. John Cafieald Ward, born in Smith County Feb. 1828 and lived at Centerville, Tennessee. In 1846 he enlisted under John W. Whitfield, Capt. of Company A , First Tennessee Regiment . They fought in the battle "Bloody First " of the Mexican War , commanded by Colonel William B. Campbell."

"The soldiers of the First Tennessee Regiment of Hickman and Tennessee State in the Mexican War were mustered out of service at New Orleans; and the soldiers of the Third Tennessee Regiment , at Memphis ."
" On May 29 , 1846 , John L. Temple enlisted in Whitfield's Company of the First Tennessee of Mexican War ... In 1847 Patrick Sims Smith , born 1823 , enlisted under J. W. Whitfield. "

In the twenty-eighth General Assembly, John Wilkins Whitfield of Hickman County, Whitfield Town west of Centerville, was in the Senate . He was elected as a reward for his service in the Mexican War by the people of the County. Samuel B. Moore was again in the House of Representatives, of which Landon C. Haynes was speaker. In this Assembly , which convened on Oct. 1, 1849, Sumner County was represented by William B. Bate.

John Wilkins Whitfield was a Confederate soldier in Texas Calvary of Civil War, commander of 27th Regiment Army of the West.

The post office, WHITFIELD , was established in 1857 , and was named in honor of John W. Whitfield , who was perhaps the most famous man who ever lived in Hickman County. He was State Senator of Tennessee Seventh Congressional District twice. He was in twenty-eighth assembly in 1849 and re-elected to the twenty-ninth assembly 1851. He had served in the Mexican War 1846 , 1847 and commanded the Hickman County Company in Campbell's "Bloody First ." He was Clerk and Master of Hickman Chancery Court in 1852. He was a United States agent in the Indian Bureau, Department of the Northwest , 1853 and served the Pottawatomies at Westport, Missouri ; and the Arkansas Indians in 1855 and 1856 . He lived at Independence, Missouri and upon admission of the territory of Kansas was elected Democrat to the thirty-third Congress, and to the thirty-fourth Congress. In 1857 to 1861 Registra at the land office at Doniphon, Kansas. He was Captain of Texas Cavalry, Whitfield's battalion 1861, promoted to Major 1862 and engaged in Battle of Pea Ridge and Iuka. He was cited by General Price for "dashing boldness and steady courage." Engaged in battle near Spring Hill in 1863 and cited again. He became Brigadier-General of 27th Regiment of Texas Cavalry , the Trans-Mississippi Army of the West.

John was married to first wife, Catharine about 1838 and she died in Tennessee in 1846. He married Sarah B. Dibrell May 28 , 1853 of White County, in Nashville, Tennessee. John W. Whitfield died October 27 , 1879 in Texas and buried at Hallettsville, Texas. 1.

J. A. Cunningham was deputy sheriff of Hickman County, and his father John Cunningham , husband of Grace Cunningham , was the census taker for Hickman County.

John W. Walker & Company commenced the mercantile business at Whitfield Town in 1852 , and continued until 1860. They were succeeded by others Walkers, the business was one mile southwest of Whitfield , Flowers and Cable.

William George Clagett married July 21, 1835 Miss Theodosia C. Whitfield who was born in Williamson County, Tennessee April 1, 1816, daughter of Wilkins and Mary Whitfield who were Virginians. She died Oct. 1, 1839 and he married Elizabeth O. Hornbeak Feb. 10, 1842 . He was a brother-in-law of John Wilkins Whitfield.

John M. Winstead was born March 9 , 1807 in Williamson County, Tennessee, and he married Nancy A. Whitfield on March 8th, 1827. She was the daughter of Harrison Whitfield and Mary Whitfield. She was born August 5, 1811 in Williamson County, Tennessee. John and Nancy Whitfield Winstead had ten children . She died Feb. 7, 1885.

Thomas W. Whitfield was born Feb. 1827 in Williamson County, Tennessee. He married Sarah Berry 1855. He became a physician and served at Davidson County and fifteen years in Henry County ; then he returned to Williamson County and died there July 13, 1879.

John Boyd sells property to John Whitfield of Granville, North Carolina before Revolution War ; and afterwards a John Boyd sells to Whitfield, land in Cumberland settlement in Tennessee.

" My father 's name was Bryan Whitfield Killebrew . His father was Buckner Killebrew , born Edgecombe County, North Carolina on April 11, 1753. After his marriage he settled in Duplin County from which place he removed to Tennessee in 1795 to 1796 , and settled on Spring Creek in Montgomery County, " and he died July 15, 1824.

" My father's mother was Mary Whitfield, the daughter of William

1. History of Hickman County, Tennessee by W. and D. Spence.
2. Recollection of My Life by J. B. Killebrew . Vol. I , 1896.
   Autobiography. Montgomery County, Tennessee.

Whitfield , the third , and the grand-daughter of a Revolutionary Captain whose name was also William Whitfield.

"William Whitfield III lived on Nuese river fifty five miles above New Bern. He was father of 28 children , and was married four times. " My paternal grandmother was born June 4th , 1765. She was a daughter by the first wife. Her father gave to each one of his children property valued at $ 10, 000 to the children. " 2.

Mrs.Mary Catherine Killebrew wrote her "Recollection" in 1902. The Whitfields and Killebrews inter-married with each other.

In 1884 Mattie Whitfield visited Mary C. Killebrew.

In 1885 Louisa Wimberly Whitfield came from North Carolina to visit Mary C. Killebrew.

Catherine Bailey married Bryan Whitfield and later AMW Bryan. She had Whitfield children : Anna Marie W., Catherine W., Margaret W., Duncan W., William Whitfield, J ames W., and Mary G. Whitfield. Bryan Whitfield died 1823.

Senate Document I Session 23 , C ongress 1833-4 , Tennessee , has pension legislature on earlier wars for filing applications. William Whitfield and John Whitfield do not appear on the Tennessee list.

"Tennessee Cousins" by Worth S. Ray is a history on Tennessee people. He wrote the book ,"The Lost Tribes of North Carolina. " Worth Ray list John Whitfield 1561 as the pedigree English ancestry of Tennesseans.

"Another list of land patents are advertised in the Knoxville Gazette , on April 10 , 1794, as ready for the claimants to' come and get em. ' The names of the grantees is a rather notable group, as follows:

David Campbell	Robert Mc Teer
Andrew Lewis	William Huges
John Hannah	William Tate
John Walker	Sam Montgomery
Abe Swaggerty	Isaac Taylor
William Whitfield	Hugh Beard
Needham Whitfield	John Stone

Knoxville, Tennessee , April 4, 1794.   Newspaper ."

"William Whitfield , Sr. was born in England 1688 ; died 1770. He came from England in his own ship , "The Providence ", in early part of the 18th century and settled at Nansemonie , Virginia. Later in Lenoir County, North Carolina . He married Elizabeth Goodman (1697-1773) of Gates County, North Carolina in 1713. "
(Vertical file at Tennessee State Library & Archives .)
                    And
This statement is repeated in Magna Carta , part III, page 590.

Index to Biographical sketches in the HISTORY OF TENNESSEE by Goodspeed Publishing Company, 1896, list a sketch of Dr. Henry Whitfield of Humphreys County, page 1284. Hervey Whitfield of Montgomery County, Tennessee, page 1116. Joseph W. Whitfield of Montgomery County, page 1115. T. H. Whitfield of Montgomery County, page 1117. Dr. Thomas W. Whitfield of Williamson County, page 1017.

In the book, HISTORY OF TENNESSEE by Goodspeed Publishing Co. 1886-1896 are the sketches on Whitfields of Hickman County, page 911.

"William Clagett married July 21, 1835, to Theodosia C. Whitfield who was born in Williamson County, April 1, 1816, the daughter of Wilkins and Polly Mary Whitfield who were Virginians. She died Oct. 1, 1839 and he married Elizabeth O Hornbeak, February 10, 1842."

JOHN M. WINSTEAD was born March 9, 1807 in Williamson County. He died in 1896 in Tennessee. On March 8, 1827 he married Nancy A. Whitfield, daughter of Harrison Whitfield and Polly Mary Sledge - Whitfield, who was born August 5, 1811 in Williamson County, Tennessee. They had twelve Children:

1. James M. Winstead
2. Harrison Winstead
3. John M. Winstead
4. Walker W. Winstead
5. William E. Winstead
6. Robert O. Winstead
7. Meredith P. G. Winstead
8. Thomas E. Winstead
9. Mary E. Winstead
10. Winfield S. Winstead
11. Lucy T. Winstead
12. Ida Winstead (born 1837-1911)

The mother, Nancy A. Whitfield - Winstead died Feb. 7, 1885.

Joseph W. Whitfield came from a line of ancestors who came from North Carolina to Tennessee in 1793. He lived after time of George Whitfield, the preacher, and is consequently of Welsh-English descent. They were hardy, industrious and law-abiding, and were ever ready to protect the weak in those times of lawlessness and savage war. His father, Louis, and his uncles, Needham and Bryan Whitfield, were of a family of twenty-eight children, and their descendants are found in nearly all the Southern States. The three brothers settled in Montgomery County, Tennessee. Louis Whitfield on land now owned by Watton Barker and C. N. Meriwether, which land (now worth $500,000) he traded for a negro woman, and eight children. His eldest son, Joseph Whitfield, our subject was born August 23, 1806, and was married in 1833 to his cousin, Mariam Whitfield- Fort, daughter of Needham Whitfield and widow of J. D. Fort. To their union were born these children: 1. Joseph N. Whitfield

2. Constantine Whitfield
3. Needham Whitfield
4. Robert C. Whitfield
5. Sallie C. Whitfield
6. Mary L. Whitfield
7. James W. Whitfield
8. Henry C. Whitfield
9. Joseph N. Whitfield

Joseph N. Whitfield graduated from the medical department of the Louisville University at Kentucky in 1854 , and practiced his profession in Clarksville, Tennessee until his death in 1859.

Constantine Whitfield received a common school education , and was married to Laura Waller in 1860 , and became the father of five children: Martha Whitfield , Mary Whitfield, Constantine Whitfield, Joseph Whitfield , and Jennie Whitfield .

Needham L. Whitfield at the age of eight years was placed under the tutelage of Professor Q. M. Tyler and acquired the rudiments of a good classical and English education . He then attended the Oakland Institute and was there fitted for college . He entered the Bethel College at Russellville, Kentucky in 1855 , graduating in 1858 , and received the degree of A. M. in 1860 . He was twice married . His first wife , Anna E. Mart , lived four years and bore him two children , both of whom died in infancy. His present wife, Lou E. Bourne , has borne him three children : Herbert Whitfield , Nannie Whitfield and Edward Whitfield.

Before entering college Needham Whitfield had selected civil engineering as his avocation , but owing to ill health was compelled to abandon his cherished project . He then began teaching , and in 1873 was elected superintendent of schools in Montgomery County . At the end of four years he began teaching at New Providence , continuing two years , and after a term of fifteen months at Ringgold was tendered the presidency of the graded school at St. Bethlehem , where he is at present teaching.

Robert C. Whitfield was educated at Bethel College , Kentucky in 1858 , and then graducated in the law department of the Cumberland University , at Nashville , and was admitted to the bar in 1861. He was among the first to enlist in the regular service in 1861 , and was in the First Tennessee Regiment and transferred to the Fourteenth Tennessee. He was a gallant soldier, but unfortunately was killed at the battle of Fredericksburg , Virginia , December 13, 1862. He was much beloved by all who knew him, and his death was greatly lamented. He was a member of the F. and A. M.

Sarah C. Whitfield was married to N. C. Lovelace in 1869 and has four children . Mr.Lovelace is a farmer.

Mary L. Whitfield was married to George R. Taylor in 1870. He was a one time local editor of the Liverpool , England paper Mercury, and is now a prominent minister of the Primitive Baptist Church . He came to America in 1862. He and wife had five children.

James W. Whitfield was educated at Russellville, Kentucky , and graduated in 1872. He wedded Margaret M. Carney in 1873. She bore him two children. He was afterward divorced and resided at the old homestead with his mother.

Joseph W. Whitfield and family were the organizers of the old Baptist Spring Creek Church. They, in conjunction with the Killebrews, Johnson, Forts, Metcalfs, Redfords, and other branches of the family, hold a family reunion each year. Marion Whitfield, the mother, has a fine recollection. All the family are Democrats.

Henry Whitfield, Montgomery County, Tennessee.
From the Tennessee Historical Committee Questionnaire to Civil War Veterans. On the latter application sheet he says: My father "Needham Bryan was born near Gawettsburg in County of Christian County, Kentucky. He lived in district two on Spring Creek, seven miles from Clarksville, Tennessee. After he was 21 years old was chairman of County Court, and died aged 37. My mother's maiden name was Hannah Eglantine Wilcox. She was the daughter of Samuel E. and Elizabeth Wilcox who lived in Montgomery County, four miles off Port Royal." ... " My paternal grand parents were Needham Whitfield and Miriam Neville, whose parents came from England to North Carolina both of whom did service in the Revolutionary War. My grand-parents came to this section in early life from North Carolina. My maternal grandparents of English decent came from Spartanburg vise South Carolina and settled on a land grant at Port Royal. My paternal grandmother's father on the same grant for service to miles west .... My father died and left my mother 800 acres of land, thirty slaves, and stock, tools, etc. Value about $ 4,000. The original house was log weather boarded " to which was added additional rooms.

In " History of Tennessee " by Goodspeed Company we found that Hervey Whitfield was a native of Tennessee who was born July 3, 1847. He was the second of nine children to Needham and Hannah. The father died in 1858 and the mother still resides on the farm she and her husband settled on coming to this County. Hervey Whitfield was educated in the County schools of his native County, and when only sixteen years of age enlisted in the Fourteenth Kentucky Cavalry, a portion of General Forrest's command, in which he served one year, and then until the close of the war.

After reaching his majority he took charge of his mother's farm for eight years, and in October 1875, was married to Ella Trigg, daughter of Thomas S. and Elizabeth Trigg, and to them were born these children:
"History of Tennessee ", published by Goodspeed 1886- 1896. pages 1115 and 1116. Montgomery County, Tennessee.

Arthur G. Whitfield , born in 1876 ; Roy Whitfield , born in 1878 ; and Thomas B. Whitfield . born in 1882. After his marriage Hervey Whitfield moved to Arkansas, where he remained until 1882, when he returned and purchased the farm where he now lives. In 1900 he lost a eighteen year old son and his wife . He went to Clarksville edited Tennessee Paper . Then with the Times and in 1905 with the Leaf Chronicle . In 1912 was President of Tennessee Press Association , and in 1917 he was Secretary of Middle Tennessee. He was private secretary to Governor Rye and in 1909 he served in the Legislature . He was a leader on the Prohibition Law.

HISTORY OF TENNESSEE - Humphreys County.

" DR. HENRY WHITFIELD , a successful practicing physician of Bakerville in Humphreys County , was born July 3 , 1830, in Hickman County, Tennessee , and is the son of Thomas Jefferson and Eliza Nolan - Whitfield , natives of Williamson County. The father , a well - known farmer, was elected colonel of the militia of Davidson County , and afterward elected brigadier- general. At the time of his death , which occurred in 1873 , he was living in Perry County, Tennessee. Our subject was reared on a farm and received the rudiments of his education in the common schools, but in 1848 he entered the Memphis Medical College , but being in adverse circumstances was compelled to walk the entire distance from this County to Memphis.

In 1849 he returned to Humphreys County and practiced medicine until 1856 , then attended one term in the Nashville Medical University, where he graduated and received his diploma in March 1857 . After this he returned home and followed his profession in the vicinity of Bakerville , of Humphreys County, and has at present a large and increasing practice. He has a fine farm of 100 acres and is surrounded by all the comforts of life . In 1851 he wedded Miss Nancy C. Porch , and to this union were born two children : Annie Whitfield , and John D. Whitfield . Henry Whitfield is a Democrat in politics and he and family are members of the Christian Church. "

" JOHN D. WHITFIELD , a farmer of the Twelfth District of Humphreys County, Tennessee. He was born December 29 , 1857 in this County and is the son of Henry and Nancy Porch- Whitfield . He was reared on the farm and secured a fair education in the County schools. After reaching the age of twenty-one years he started to make a livelihood for himself on life's rough journey. At first he undertook clerking in his father's store but soon gave that up and went to farming on a portion of his father's land, and has been quite successful , having control of 250 acres of well improved land in the Twelfth District. On December 18 , 1878 , he married Miss Mollie B. Fowlkes, and the fruits of this union were an interesting family of three children , named Annie Whitfield , Fannie M. Whitfield , and Belle C. Whitfield . John D. Whitfield is a stanch Democrat and a moral upright man. He and his wife are consistent members of the Christian Church and have the esteem of all who know them."

DR. THOMAS W. WHITFIELD was born February 1827 in Williamson County, Tennessee. In 1853 he lectured at Nashville Medical College . Thomas Whitfield married Sarah Berry in 1855 , and they had eight children . He resided in Davidson County , then moved to Henry County for fifteen years, and returned to Williamson County, Tennessee where he died on July 13 , 1879.

JOHN HEDGE WHITFIELD was the son of John Hedge Whitfield and Arbie Teas - Whitfield of Waverly , Tennessee , and was born on October 17, 1916 at Waverly, Tennessee of Humphreys County. He is the grandson of the late John Dee Whitfield , and the great grandson of the late Henry W. Whitfield.

The father, John Hedge Whitfield died when his son was only six years of age. He and his only sister , Mary Anne Whitfield , were reared by their mother and maternal grandfather , Dr. J.J. Teas , physician of Waverly, Tennessee.

John Hedge Whitfield attended the public schools of Waverly, Tenn -essee , graduating from Waverly High School in 1934. While in High School he was very interested in history, being named the Historian of his class. He played on both the basketball and football teams 1932-1934. He attended Fall's Business College in Nashville , Tennessee from September 1934 to October 1935. His first full time employment was as clerk in Waverly Post Office from 1936-1939 , at which time he accepted a job as bookkeeper at Citizens Bank of Waverly.

John Whitfield married Bertha Powers , daughter of a minister ; and divorce decree February 16 , 1942.

In August 1942 , John Hedge Whitfield was inducted into the Armed Forces of the United States. He was attached with the 566th Sqdn. , 389th Bomb Group , 8 th Air Force , and stationed for two years in Norwich , England . He was discharged from service in September 1945.

John Hedge Whitfield returned to his job at the Citizens Bank in Waverly, Tennessee , and was cashier of the bank, the position he held in 1979, and continued to be employed by the Citizens Bank .

John Hedge Whitfield married Margaret Louise Rice, the daughter of Alfred Walker and Amanda Johnson Rice of Humphreys County on April 28 , 1946 in Corinth, Mississippi.

The children of John and Margaret Rice- Whitfield are the following:
1. James Alfred Whitfield , 1951 , died in infancy.
2. Donna Elaine Whitfield , born October 16, 1952 in Davidson County, Tennessee.

3. Margaret Anne Whitfield , born August 17, 1954 in Davidson , Tennessee .
4. John Hedge Whitfield, Jr., born December 12, 1959 in Humphreys County, Tennessee.

John Hedge Whitfield has been twice elected Commander of the American Legion Post 34 . He has been a member of the Humphreys County Library Board and was instrumental in getting the " Great Books Discussion Group " started at Waverly. He has been a member of Waverly Housing Authority ; Past President of Humphreys County Methodist Men's Club ; a President of the Exchange Club of Humphreys County , Tennessee; and a President of the Humphreys County Historical Society. John Hedge is a member of the Methodist Church , where he has taught the Adult Sunday School Class for a number of years. His wife, Margaret Rice Whitfield teaches a class for small children at the Church of Christ.

HUMPHREYS COUNTY RECORDS

A note lien created by the deed of trust of James D. Whitfield and Mrs. Whitfield to Mason Sanders , trustee , for the use and benefit of Henry C. Whitfield and Thomas C. Whitfield securities on a note for money. Book Y page 10 , May 1921 , Humphrey County, Tennessee.

James Dee Whitfield visiting in Sunshine, Tennessee , and April 2, 1898 he wrote Miss Anne Rosenian of Waco, Texas ... James Dee Whitfield visiting Indian Hill near St Francis River , Missouri , June 26, 1898 and wrote Miss Mattie Whitfield , Miss Hester Mc Keel , W. R. Dreaden , Dave Daniel and Jefferson Lafayette Whitfield , all of Tenn -essee.

Annie Carr (Baker) , at Tennessee Orphan Home at Columbia, Tenn -essee , and later James Dee and Hester Whitfield take her in their home.

Justices of the County Court of Humphreys County, State of Tenn-essee appointed James Dee Whitfield notary public in and for said County, April term 1933. 12th day of May 1933. Governor Hill Mc Alister set his hand and great seal of State .

James Dee Whitfield with public notice after the marriage gives up guardianship of Martha Frances Whitfield when she married to Raymond Whitfield .

James Raymond Whitfield and Martha Frances Daniel Whitfield sold land to Johnie Rushton and note with Federal Land Bank of Louis-ville . Dec. 31, 1943.

A book , " A History of Humphreys County, Tennessee " by Jill Knight Garrett , 1963 . Jill K. Garrett resided at 610 Terrace Drive, Columbia, Tennessee. The following is recorded from this book :

1920 , Lytton - Whitfield and Company, Tire dealers , page 146.

"Captain S. D. H. Whitfield , Company Captain for Co. I, 10 th
Tennessee Cavalry. In the summer of 1862 of Civil War, Alonzo Napier
of Humphreys County raised the Company which as Company G became
a part of 10th Company, with men from Humphreys and Perry Counties."

" Captain Thomas Jefferson Whitfield 's Company D, later Co. H,
42 Tennessee had men from the County as members - Civil War. "

" Margaret Whitfield (Mrs. John H. Whitfield) , vice-president
of Ladies Auxiliary of Hickman , Patherson Unit 34 , 1963 term ,
American Legion Post 34 of Waverly, Tennessee."

"John D. Whitfield ran a store on old Fowler's Landing on the
Tennessee River in 1879 . The last business here was run by John E.
Porch , Sr., who was later City Recorder at Waverly, Tennessee."

Wealth in Humphreys County, 1870 , real estate , William H.
McKeel 3, 000 ; Hulda J. McKeel 6, 000 ; Henry Whitfield 6, 000 :
Thomas Jefferson Whitfield 3, 000.

G. M. Whitfield and John H. Whitfield of American Legion Post.

The 17 th Tennessee, Confederate Regiment , T. W. Newman , Colonel
was mustered in May 5 , 1861 Civil War . Disciplined at Camp Trousdale , transferred to Virginia and returned to east Tennessee. It joined
Zollicoffer's Kentucky Campaign Feb. 1862 , transferred to Mississippi,
then turned to Chattanooga and moved into Kentucky , fighting at Perryville and lost many men .

Rutherford and Williamson Counties, Tennessee.

General Griffith Rutherford (1721- 1805) . He was son of John R.
Rutherford of Ireland , a farmer who went to live with family in New
Jersey for his parents had died at sea. The son, Griffith moved to North
Carolina. On the records of Rowan County of North Carolina he was the
King's surveyor , and in sympathy with the revolutionists. He went to
Tennessee to survey land and died there.

One of the first lawyers to be admitted to practice in the Rutherford
County Court was Thomas Benton who later represented Missouri in the
United States Senate.

Tennessee Census . The First Census taken by Governor Blount in
1795 that leaves a record : "Of a total State population of 77, 262
only 11, 924 were living in the three middle Tennessee Counties of Davidson , Sumner and Old Tennessee. By 1800 the seven Counties Robertson,
Smith , Wilson and Williamson boasted a population in excess of thirty -
two thousand. " In 1800 the population was 105, 602 and most of the
increase took place in middle Tennessee. This note appears in the
book , " A History of Rutherford County " by Carlton C. Sims, 1947.

At the time of the admission of the Tennessee State into the Union, 1796 , there were only three Counties in Middle Tennessee. Davidson established in 1783 , Sumner in 1786 , and adjacent lands Old Tennessee in 1788.

In 1799 Williamson County was taken from Davidson . Previous to this date settlers began coming to what is now Williamson County . David Mc Ewin with several families arrived in Nashville in 1796 , but as there were still fears of Indian disturbances in remote settlements, they remain -ed in that village until 1798. The pioneers located at Roper's Knob and College Grove. It was here at this location or near there that Wilkins Whitfield (1780-1851) had his plantation .

Sam Houston , born Valley of Virginia 1793 , and moved to frontier of Blount County, Tennessee. Elected to Congress from the Nashville district in 1823. Under Andrew Jackson, earlier he had fought in the Creek War with the Indians 1813. He learned the saddler's trade . In 1811 elected State Senator from Williamson County, Tennessee.

Andrew Jackson, seventh President of the United States . He was born in Mecklenburg County, North Carolina on March 15, 1767 . When he left North Carolina he took the trail and the Regulators , and Whitfield frontiersmen took the same trail into Nashville , Tennessee later .

Hickman County, Tennessee is bounded on the north by Dickson County, east by Williamson and Maury, south by Lewis , and west by Perry and Humphreys , and has an area of 559 square miles. The total area of Hickman County is 390, 400 acres, of which 76 , 215 acres are improved. The population is 12,100 in 1885.

Centerville town was founded in 1823 , and incorporated in 1825 . A merchant from 1840 to 1850 was Thomas J. Whitfield , and WHITFIELD AND BLISS. In 1871 Whitfield, Tennessee , a town nearby had a post-office. Whitfield, Tennessee was a name change to Centerville, Tenn.

Of the schools in 1885 , Whitfield Academy was in the Ninth District of Hickman County.

The Chancery Court held its first session in Centerville , Tennessee on the 6 th of September 1852 , with Chancellor John S. Brien presiding, and John Wilkins Whitfield as Clerk and Master.

For the War with Mexico , in 1846 , Hickman County furnished her full quota . Under the Call of the State for volunteers a Company was organized in the County and sent out under the Command of Captain John W. Whitfield in May 1846.

This John W. Whitfield was born in Williamson County, Tennessee, and moved to Hickman County, Tennessee . He later moved to Missouri, then Kansas , and then to Texas where he settled and died.

The Kentucky - Tennessee line via Cumberland Gap , Tazewell and Morristown.
United States 25 E today follows old Wilderness Road between Cumberland Gap to Bean Station. This was a trail across the mountains blazed by Daniel Boone in 1775 for benefit of immigrants. This route became the main artery for settlement of much of the territory south of Ohio River . U. S. 25 E road crosses into Tennessee again. Cumberland Gap, named for the pass in the mountain is in that corner of Tennessee that first was explored by white man.

-- --------------

During the slavery time they put negroes up on a punching pole before they got into the river for making foot paths. A " foot log" was tree lumber log for making a bridge and was called "punching pole. "

WILLIAM ANDREW DANIEL (1869- 1965) was a farmer of Perry County. Residing at Lobelville, Tennessee he practically owned Crooked Creek in 1925 for he had 1, 000 acres of land on the river town . Cuba Landing was on Blue Creek running into Tennessee River. The Show Boat came every week down the river causing much excitement among the citizens in the community. You could hear calliope musical tunes playing from the river and everyone anxiously waited until quitting time to go to night show, for they had electric lights on the boat by steam and battery operation. ------------

The Whitfield Bible Family Record was owned by Clara May Whitfield of Mc Kenize , Tennessee and has been before officials of the County several times for proof of births . All of the Whitfields living in the territory were not on Census or public record. Court has accepted this Bible record as an authentic source.

"Dictionary of American Family Names," by Elsdon C. Smith , published by Harper & Bros., 1950. This book list the name WHITFIELD as an English name. One who came from Whitfield meaning white field , the name of several places in England and United States.

Whitfield , Alabama	Towns
Whitfield , Florida	Whitfield (County) , Georgia
Whitfield , Texas	Whitfield , Mississippi
Whitfield , Tennessee now Centerville, Tennessee.	

The Tennessee legislature met in 1822 of July month and nominated Andrew Jackson for the office of President of the United States . This was the first time that a State in the west had placed a candidate   in nomination , it set a new precedent for history.

Montgomery County, Tennessee.

Up to 1826 there were only forty families unaccounted for in Montgomery County, or two hundred and fifty whites in Clarksville. Earlier it was the land of the Cherokee Indians. Granville Bank was chartered 1818 there and several other banks established. It was the location for the first Court in west Tennessee. Many Whitfields lived among the populous of the County.

Emma Morehead Whitfield wrote from her home, 1800 Grove Avenue, Richmond, Virginia on November 11, 1929 to Mrs. John Trotwood Moore, librarian at the Tennessee State Library that " in 1793, a branch of the Whitfield family left Virginia and settled in Tennessee. The Tennessee Whitfields are known to us only through tradition. "

Mississippi State Mental Hospital at Whitfield, Mississippi, 1962.

MEN OF SCIENCE. In the book "The American Men of Science ", S-Z, 10th edition are the top men in science in 1960 of United States.
Dr. George Buckmaster Whitfield, born Dec. 4, 1923.
Professor George Danley Whitfield, born Dec. 12, 1930.
Harold Barnard Whitfield, born Dec. 24, 1927.
Robert Edward Whitfield, born August 11, 1921 in Waverly, Tennessee.
Dr. Robert Day Whitfield, born Oct. 26, 1910.

1768 Farmers of Orange, Anson and Rowan in North Carolina struggled against local government which seemed inefficient. They organized in 1768 as the "Regulators", pledged to regulate the evils of local government. They rioted in Hillsboro and battle at Alamance Creek on May 16, 1771 over local revolution but Governor gave pardon proclamation. Later hundreds migrated to the Tennessee Country.

General John W. Whitfield was a friend and associate of Governor William Bowen Campbell who was born near Nashville, February 1, 1807. He studied law under his uncle, Governor David Campbell of Virginia. In 1829 he was elected attorney-general, and in 1835 a member of the Legislature. In 1836 a Captain in Trousdale's Regiment. 1837 to 1843 member of Congress. In 1847 he led the First Tennesseans in Mexican War. 1851 elected by Whigs as Governor of Tennessee. In 1857 served as circuit judge till death in 1867 on August 19 th.

General John Wilkins Whitfield was a friend and associate of Senator David Rice Atchison who was in the Missouri Senate and led some of the raids into Kansas. He served in the Senate 1843 and re-elected in 1849. John W. Whitfield was Chairman of the Committee on Indian Affairs, and a pro - slavery Democrat. He was instrumental in having the Kansas- Nebraska Bill passed. It was under the strong political influence of these two men that John W. Whitfield served. Atchison was born 1807 and died 1886.

VIRGINIA

VIRGINIA HISTORICAL INDEX by E. G. Swem lists these Whitfields in the
Volume 2 L-Z. Virginians and their references in VIRGINIA MAGAZINE
OF HISTORY AND BIOGRAPHY.

Anne Whitfield , 15 V319, 320; 36 V 40; 3 W(1) 274.

Anne Jeffries Whitfield, 9 W (1) 50.

Charles Whitfield , student at William and Mary
   College , 30 V 238.

Elizabeth Kinley Whitfield , 8 W (2) 175.

G. Whitfield , 6 C 225 ; 8 W (2) 175.

Gilbert Whitfield , 30 V 262 ; 31 V 210.

Harrison Whitfield , 7 W (1) 274 ; Lieutenant
    Harrison Whitfield 11 V 84 ; 7 W (1) 273.

Henry Whitfield , 2 T 199.

Jane Allen Whitfield , 3 T 206.

Jemima Whitfield , 8 T 268.

John Whitfield , 3 T 206 ; 9 V 209 ; 1 0 W (2) 257.

Louisa Whitfield , 2 N 46.

Margaret Williams Whitfield 2 T 199.

Mary Whitfield , 23 V 48 ; 3 W (1) 274.

Mary A. Whitfield , 9 W (1) 50.

Miriam Whitfield , 6 W (1) 65.

Robert Whitfield , 7 W (1) 146.

Roger Whitfield , 26 V 97, 102.

Ruth Whitfield , 27 W (1) 43.

Sallie Warren Whitfield , 2 T 199.

Sarah Whitfield , 15 V 320 ; 3 W (1) 274.

Sarah Juxon Whitfield , 15 V 319 ; 17 W (1) 229.

Thomas Whitfield , 29 V 259 , 260.

Tobias Whitfield , 15 V 277

Walter Whitfield , 15 V 319 , 320 ; 3 W (1) 27;
   17 W (1) 229.

               and   some Virginians who moved to
     North Carolina in this list.

Wesley Whitfield , 2 T 199.

William Whitfield 5 C 566 ; 8 C 228 ; 2 N 46 ; 5 V,
    341 ; 15 V 193.

Willis Whitfield 5 C 632.

Whitfield Family 10 W (2) 101.

These Virginians in the Swem's Historical Index was found
and studied by Vallie Jo Fox Whitfield , and printed in the
book, VIRGINIA HISTORY AND WHITFIELD BIOGRAPHIES,
PUBLISHED BY WHITFIELD BOOKS in 1976.

The "Virginia Magazine of History and Biography"may
carry in print later names of Whitfields not in the list.

CHRONOLOGY OF VALLIE JO FOX WHITFIELD

1922	Birth of Vallie Jo Fox on March 18 at Nashville, Tennessee. Daughter of Joseph Edward Fox and Valley Schiefer Fox.
1928-1931	Boarding in girls school, St Cecilia Academy.
1931-1935	Primary School Student at Holy Name School, St Joseph School, and Cathedral School.
1935-1939	Student at Cathedral High School. Graduated in 1939.
1939-1940	Preparatory College Program, St Bernard Academy.
1940-1941	A Freshman Student at Ward-Belmont College, Nashville.
1941-1943	A Sopohomore and Junior Student, University of Tenneesse Knoxville, Tennessee.
1943	On March 26 married Robert Edward Whitfield of Waverly, Tennessee at Nashville; and moved to Berkeley, California
1943-1945	Chemical Laboratory Technician with Shell Development Company. Analytical analysis and colloid research.
1945 1946	Birth of daughter, Christa Marie Whitfield, December 30. August month moved to Cambridge, Massachusetts.
1946-1948	Domestic Social Service through the Harvard University Student Co-op Program. House and child care. Chestnut Hill and Cambridge.
1948	Birth of son, Robert Edward Whitfield on November 21.
1949	Resided at Brighton, Massachusetts and moved to New Brunswick, New Jersey in June.
1949-1951	Attended Rutgers University.
1951	Moved to California.
1952	Purchased house and ranch in Walnut Creek- Pleasant Hill, California in Contra Costa County.
1952-1962	Operated Whitfield Farm.

1952	Began Community Service Work. Programs and Projects. Member of Committees, Boards, Commissions.
1953	Birth of son, James David Whitfield, February 21.
1955	Birth of daughter, Joanne Vallie Whitfield, March 14.
1959-1963	Attended Diablo Valley College, University of California, and College of Holy Names.
1964	First book published. Began 1960 writing, compilation, and publishing.
1965	Real Estate Subdivision on Whitfield Farm.
1966	Member of Organizations. Girl Scout Leader.
1968	Attended Anthony Business School, Walnut Creek. Licensed Real Estate Associate, June 21, 1968.
1971-1976	Student in Bible Study Fellowship.
1974	Licensed Real Estate Broker, February 1, 1974.
1978	Author and Publisher.
1978	Realtor.

* SCIENCE ASSISTANT

* WIFE AND MOTHER OF FAMILY

* TRUSTEE WHITFIELD FARM

* COMMUNITY SERVANT

* WHITFIELD REALTY PROPRIETOR

* WHITFIELD BOOKS PROPRIETOR

VALLIE   JO   FOX   WHITFIELD

HISTORICAL NOTES

HENRY LEWIS WHITFIELD ... Governor of Mississippi 1925.
He was born on a farm, four miles east of Brandon, Mississippi on the June 20, 1868, son of Robert Allen and Mary (Fitzhugh) Whitfield.
On August 25, 1879 he was married at Florence, Mississippi to Miss Mary Dampeer White, daughter of Dr. William White and Mary Ellen White (Dr. White for many years was a member of the State Board of Health, and Physician). Children : 1. Robert Allen Whitfield 2. Knox White Whitfield 3. Henry Lewis Whitfield 4. William White Whitfield.

Governor Whitfield was a representative of two of the largest and most widely dispersed families in the South, the Whitfields originating in North Carolina and the Fitzhughs in Virginia. As a result of the Civil War his father found his slaves free and with an increasing family he had to turn to the schoolroom for a living.

The Children Henry L. and brother Robert had to till father's farm of 80 acres. Henry earned his teaching license degree from Mississ - ippi College in 1895. Principal of the high school at Westville Mississ - ippi and Steen's Creek in Florence, Miss. Appointed State Superinten - dent of Education September 17, 1898. Elected President of Mississ - ippi State College for Women. Then Superintendent of B.B. Jones Farm School near Columbus, Mississippi until Feb. 1, 1923.

In Governor Race in the State of Mississippi won over opponent by 16 or 17 thousand votes. Governor in 1925. Issue when he told Legis - lature he would not approve appropriations in excess of the revenues provided. ---------------

HISTORY OF TENNESSEE . Montgomery County, Tennessee .

Thomas H. Whitfield was born December 17, 1839 and is the son of M. Whitfield and Agnes Boan - Whitfield . The father of our subject was born in the year of 1811, and his mother in the early part of the present century. They are both natives of the State of Tennessee . Thomas H. Whitfield is a miller by profession, and has followed this trade from early boyhood. In 1866 he began milling at the Ringgold Mills, of this County, and has been regularly employed there ever since. He is an extra fine miller, and to him the people of Montgomery County are indebted for the extra quality of flour they receive from that mill.

Immigrant came over from England led by a Catholic Priest named Father Lindle. Joseph Whitfill (or Whitfield) born in Kentucky between 1765 and 1784, probably at Grayson County. He had a son, Marten Whit- fill, born 1801 in Kentucky.

Marten Whitfill married Rebecca Shaw, and they both of Big Clifty, Kentucky. Rebecca was born 1815. They had a son, William Whitfill born August 26, 1833 at Big Clifty, Kentucky. William Whitfill married Margaret Durbin . They had a daughter Rebecca Whitfill, born Feb. 11, 1870 at Big Clifty, Kentucky.

William and Margaret Whitfill moved from Big Clifty, Kentucky in
1877 to Texas, and settled in Johnson County which is now part of Ellis
County, Texas where the descendants live in 1977.

Rebecca Whitfill born 1870 married and had a daughter , Mrs.
Bertha Newman Tayman living 1977 at Falls Church, Virginia.

NORTH CAROLINA FIRST CENSUS 1790
Heads of Families with the name Whitfield.

Alexander Whitfield	148 Halifax District , No. C.
Benjamin Whitfield	72 Nash County , No. C.
Benjamin Whitfield	
Bryan Whitfield	137 Newbern District , Dobbs Co.
Constance Whitfield	132 Newbern District , Craven Co.
James Whitfield	137 Dibbs Co.
John Whitfield	67 Halifax District , Martin Co.
John Whitfield	72 Nash County , No. C.
John Whitfield	137 Dobbs County
Joseph Whitfield	190 Wilmington District , in Duplin County, No. C.
Lewis Whitfield	151 Newbern District , Wayne Co.
Luke Whitfield	137 Dobbs County
Matthew Whitfield	72 Nash County
Nancy Whitfield	72 Nash County
Needham Whitfield	149 Newbern District , Wayne Co.
Ruben Whitfield	72 Nash County
Sol. Whitfield	72 Nash County
Thomas Whitfield	72 Patriot of Nash County, No. C.

He was born 1721 in Virginia , and died
1781 in Nash County, North Carolina.

William Whitfield	53 Fayette District , Sampson Co.
William Whitfield	61 Halifax District , Halifax Co.
William Whitfield	67 Martin County, No. C.
William Whitfield	72 Nash County
William Whitfield	147 Newbern District , Pitt Co.
William Whitfield	184 Salisburg District , Surry Co.
William Whitfield , Jr.	149 Wayne County, No. C.
William Whitfield, Sr.	149 Wayne County, No. C.
Willis Whitfield	72 Nash County

From the 1790 Census Books recording the North Carolina
enumeration of the inhabitants of the United States.

CENSUS 1850 , WILLIAMSON COUNTY, TENNESSEE

The 1850 Census appears published in a book 1970 at Franklin , Tennessee
and Whitfield is on pages 6 - 7 - 72 - 121 - 129.

#20   (Farmer)

Harrison	Whitfield	24 M Tenn.
Mary	Whitfield	60 F Va.
Sophronia	Whitfield	22 F Tenn.
Agatha	Whitfield	2 F Tenn.

----

201   (Farmer)

John	Whitfield	33 M Tenn.
Martha	Whitfield	32 F Tenn.
Henry	Whitfield	13 M Tenn.
John	Whitfield	11 M Tenn.
Mary	Whitfield	9 F Tenn.
Eliza	Whitfield	7 F Tenn.
Lucy	Whitfield	4 F Tenn.
Thomas	Whitfield	2 M Tenn.

----

86 (Physician)

Daniel B.	Cliffe	27 M Ohio
Virginia C.	Cliffe	26 F Tenn.
Daniel M.	Cliffe	6 M Tenn.
John B.	Cliffe	5 M Tenn.
James B.	Cliffe	3 M Tenn.
Margaret J.	Cliffe	1 F Tenn.

----

87 (Physician)

James M.	Whitfield	27 M Tenn.
Rebecca A.	Whitfield	22 F Tenn.
Sally M.	Whitfield	3 F Tenn.

----

759 (Farmer)

Felix G.	Whitfield	34 M Tenn.
Minerva G.	Whitfield	34 F Tenn.
Mary E.	Whitfield	12 F Tenn.
Thomas H.	Whitfield	10 M Tenn.
Martha S.	Whitfield	8 F Tenn.
James H.	Whitfield	6 M Tenn.
Smith C.	Whitfield	3 M Tenn.
Felix G.	Whitfield	1 M Tenn.

----

760 (Farmer)

Wilkins	Whitfield	24 M Tenn.
Elizabeth	Whitfield	22 F Tenn.
Mary E.	Whitfield	3 F Tenn.
Martha	Whitfield	8/12 F Tenn.

----

874 (Farmer)

James M.	Winstead	43 M Tenn.
Nancy	Winstead	39 F Tenn.
Harrison W.	Winstead	19 M Tenn.
John	Winstead	17 M Tenn.
Walker	Winstead	15 M Tenn.
William E.	Winstead	13 M Tenn.
Robert	Winstead	11 M Tenn.
M. G.	Winstead	9 M Tenn.
Thomas	Winstead	7 M Tenn.
Mary E.	Winstead	5 F Tenn.
Lucy	Winstead	5/12 F Tenn.
Harrison	Whitfield(None) 65 M Va.

1830 CENSUS , RUTHERFORD CO., TENNESSEE.   ----

Thomas Y.	Whitfield	
William	Whitfield	Jn. Whitefield
Willis	Whitfield	
Cincy	Whitfield	

The 1850 Census of Williamson County, Tennessee shows the descendants of Thomas Whitfield and Winifer Whitfield of Sussex County, Virginia living in Williamson County, Tennessee, Franklin area. Harrison Whitfield his son, and his daughter Nancy Whitfield- Winstead and the Winstead family. His son, Harrison Whitfield who in 1870 moved to Lincoln County, Texas.

The Census 1850 gives the family of Virginia C. Whitfield- Cliffe, the youngest daughter of Wilkins Whitfield and Polly Mary Whitfield at Franklin , Tennessee ; and the granddaughter of Thomas Whitfield , and Winifer Whitfield of Sussex County, Virginia . Winifer Whitfield in 1808 moved from Virginia to Williamson County, Tennessee with her sons and their families.

We have the family group for Felix G. Whitfield and his family . The family group for John Whitfield and Martha Whitfield. These are the grandchildren of the mother Winifer Whitfield of Franklin. The families of Wilkins Whitfield and Polly Mary Whitfield of Franklin are known ; and the families of Harrison Whitfield and Polly Sledge-Whitfield are partly known. The brothers of Wilkins Whitfield were also William Whitfield and Jack (John) Whitfield of Franklin, Tennessee.

----- WILLS AND INVENTORIES ----

"Williamson County, Tennessee . Wills and Inventories. Book 2, 1812-1818 " , gives Accounts and Wilkins Whitfield was a purchaser along with the other neighbors of the location.

Accounts of Sales : Samuel Mc Cutchen, Deceased , July session 1816.
Thomas L. Atkins , Deceased , January session 1817.
Elijah Hunter , Deceased , October session 1817.
Thomas S. Adkins , Deceased , October session 1818.

James Whitfield of Maury County, Tennessee died in Texas . His wife was Mary Whitfield . An Account appears on Inventory; between 1880 and 1910 . The family names in the Account .

Account		Purchaser	Item	Price
James Whitfield		Bessie	1 Spool Thread	.05
"	"	Mary		
"	"	Mat		
"	"	Sarah	8 # Sugar	.50
"	"	Stella	1 Box Snuff	.05
"	"	Wife	5 # Honey	.50
Mary			1 Yard Veiling	.20

MISSOURI RECORDS

In 1853 John Wilkins Whitfield moved from Hickman County, Tennessee to Independence, Missouri , and he took kinship Whitfields with him.

Elizabeth Morgan married (1) Frederick Stolting and then married (2) Thomas R. Whitfield in Carrollton town of Missouri. They lived there in 1865 and moved later. Thomas Whitfield was of Tennessee.

Jefferson Lafayette Whitfield moved from Benton County, Tennessee to Steele, Missouri in 1916 .

Virginia and North Carolina

The THOMAS Family of Virginia and North Carolina. Just one of the
Tribes whose members and descendants settled along the Chowanoke, the
Meherrin , Moratuck, Neuse and Pamticough in Old Albemarle before and
after the end of the Seventeenth Century. There were other names Bryans,
Hills , Hardys , Blounts, Whitfield.

In the contingent that arrived in Virginia in 1610 with Sir Thomas Gates
and Sir George Somers "Admiral of the Fleet" came, among others Sergeant Samuel Sharpe , a member of the first Legislative Assembly , with
Samuel Jordan , of Jordan's Journey , in 1619. After Sharpe's death his
widow married Thomas Parker. Elizabeth Sharpe-Parker took out a patent
to lands "between Curles and Varina ," in July 1636. After the death of the
wife Elizabeth , he married Cicelie , the widow of Samuel Jordan , and of
Peter Montague, the patentee of lands in Nansmond, Virginia , adjoining
Thomas Jordan , John Thomas , and Humphrey Scowen. Later they become the friends of Whitfield in Nansemond County.

The Lawrence families own land 1680 on the Western Branch of Nansemond. In 1704 Robert Lawrence , a brother of Priscilla Lawrence-Whit
-field owned land plantation on the line of Isle of Wight and Nansemond,
400 acres being in one County and 400 in the other County. A sister of
Priscilla Whitfield married John Thomas , and she was second wife.

In the book , "Old Albemarle And Its Absentee Landlords " by Worth S.
Ray , published in 1947 , reprinted in 1976 on listing of Whitfield on pages
607, 614 , 656 , 657, 658 , 682. The book has many records of the Seventeenth Century of associated families to Whitfield in the Virginia and North
Carolina boundary region. It gives light on the lost tribes , and the print
in the book , "Virginia History and Whitfield Biographies " by Vallie Jo
Whitfield, published in 1976.

The prolific and prominent Whitfield Families with several immigrant
first fathers joined the tide of migrants from Virginia and settled in Old
Albemarle region of North Carolina. This is the land region districts
about the River Albemarle Sound and not the Albemarle district that is
a parish district in Sussex County, Virginia where we find a settler who
has moved north into Virginia , and not southward into North Carolina.
The descendants of both of these families later   move to Tennessee.

The book , VIRGINIA HISTORY AND WHITFIELD   BIOGRAPHIES
by Vallie Jo Fox Whitfield was published by Whitfield Books in 1976. The
Colonial Historic Records of Virginia from 1610- 1800, and dealing with
Whitfield sources , and all the colonial Virginia records and family history.
415 pages, off set print , 8 x 11 size book, index in hard and soft bindery
covers. A book that has the beginning of the final family history of period.
Whitfield Books , 1841 Pleasant Hill Road, Pleasant Hill, California 94523.

WHITFIELD LAND DEEDS IN BENTON, HUMPHREYS
AND HENRY COUNTIES.

The land lineal Whitfields are from Virginia and North Carolina.
The land grants are mostly to those Whitfields from North Carolina.
The Virginia Whitfield families first settled at Williamson County ,
Tennessee , and descendants settled at Hickman County, Tennessee and
at Whitfield Town which was changed to Centerville town.
   BENTON COUNTY, TENN. Land Deed. August 16, 1901. Jones Hooper
and Company a mercantile firm sold tract of land for $ 3, 360. 00 to Jeffer-
son Lafayette Whitfield in first Civil District of Benton County, Tennessee,
to wit ; "Beginning on the west bank of the Tennessee River , at Pavatt's
Landing, at the water's edge at low water mark, then 145 poles west, then
north 108 poles, then west 36 pole, then north 52 poles to a stake in line of
Skelton's land, then east 204 pole to Tennessee River , then up said River
160 1/2 poles to beginning , containing 156 3/4 acres, in the State of Tennessee , Benton County. 'I. L. E. Goodwin, of County registered Deed in
Book KK , page 552 in notebook C page 131.

   Thomas Jefferson Whitfield 's descendants settled in Bakerville,
Tennessee , and moved to Benton and Henry Counties, and some moved
to Missouri. A descendant , James Dee Whitfield and Mary Hester Whitfield in 1918 had two tracts of land containing 108 , and 44 acres respec-
tively in Benton County before moving to Rockdale Farm in Humphreys
County, Tennessee . In 1943 James D. Whitfield with Oda Whitfield purchased land in Henry County. Some of the land owned by other Whitfields
of kinship in this family had land taken over by the State of Tennessee in
1940 for the Tennessee Valley Authority Project, and a small part of this
land was covered over with water.

HENRY COUNTY, TENNESSEE.
Jame W. and Sarah Van Dyke grantor to James Dee Whitfield , Oct. 20th,
1943... C. B. Smith and Missie Smith conveyed land to James Dee Whit-
field on April 15, 1948... James Dee Whitfield and Oda Whitfield grantor
conveyed land unto Ira Scates in 4 th Civil District of Henry County...
James Dee Whitfield conveyed land to Clyde Hathaway on August 7, 1948...
J. D. and Oda Whitfield convey to Jackson Production credit on acres
located at Puryear town in 6 th Civil District of Henry County . Sum of
$ 173. 90 ... Chattel mortgage in Dec. 1948 and held title through the
Federal Land Bank of Louisville, Kentucky on Bostick Farm that J. D.
Whitfield purchased , and the grantor of that Deed was Lemoine Bostick
which had been in the Bostick family possession since 1879. Tract near
Tyson Rifle Range , May 22, 1948.

BIRTH RECORDS

John David White born on February 8 , 1969 , the son of Janice Whitfield -White of New Johnsonville , Tennessee.

James Ray White born on March 23, 1967 , the son of Janice Whitfield- White and Larry White , in Tennessee.

Ruby and Hicks Hopkins married June 10 1929.
Ruby Hensley - Hopkins was born June 13, 1910 at Lobelville, Tennessee, the wife of Hicks Hopkins . They lived in Nashville, Tennessee ; and later in Florida . Two daughters : 1. Judy Hopkins born in Nashville, Tenn- essee married Billy Joe Anderson of Tennessee . Judy and Billy Anderson had three children : 1. Donny Anderson   2. Ricky Anderson 3 . Brad Anderson . Three sons of Tennessee.

Joan Hopkins married David Kilpatrick and they had two daughters: 1. Vickie Kilpatrick 2. _____ Kilpatrick.

Felix Whitfield was born 1783 , and died 1864 in Tennessee.

Felix Whitfield was born about 1815 on Lick Creek, Hickman County , Tennessee and died there . He married and had three sons and daughters.

Felix Whitfield on Lick Creek in Hickman County had a son named Felix.

On the 1840 Cenus of Hickman County, Tennessee , Felix Whitfield is between 10 to 15 years of age. He was born between 1825 to 1830.

Felix G. Whitfield of Williamson County, Tennessee at Franklin is thirty four years of age on the 1850 Census , and he is married to Minerva G. Whitfield ; and they have a son named Felix G. that is one year old in 1850. Felix Whitfield at Williamson County in Franklin is the descendant of the grandfather Thomas Whitfield and Winifer Whitfield of Sussex County, Virginia.

Bureau of Vital Statistics , State of Tennessee.
County of Humphreys , Civil District 6th , Waverly, Tennessee.
Certificate of Birth File No. 269 , Registered no. 45.
Name of Child - ROBERT EDWARD WHITFIELD .
Sex- Male .   Legitimate - yes .   Date- August 11, 1921

Father	Mother
Name- James D. Whitfield	Mary Hester Mc Keel
Residence- Waverly, Tennessee	Waverly, Tennessee
Color - White , age at birthdate 44.	White , age 43
Birthplace - Humphreys County, Tenn.	Humphreys County, Tenn.
Occupation - Farmer .	Housewife

I hereby certify that I attended the birth of this child, who was born alive at 12:30 p. m.   Signature - J. J. Teas , August 15, 1921

Birth Records : State of Tennessee , Bureau of Vital Statistics.
County of Davidson , Civil District Inglewood 1 , Nashville .
Certificate of Birth , File no. 121 . Registered no. 683.
Name of child - VALLEY JOE FOX   (name change to Vallie Jo Fox)
Sex of child - female . Legitimate - yes . Date- March 18 - 1922.

Father	Mother
Name- Joseph Edward Fox	Maiden name- Valley Johanna
102 Stratford Avenue	Schiefer
Nashville, Tennessee	102 Stratford Avenue
color- white , age at birthday 39 .	Color- white , age 30 years.
Birthplace - Tennessee	Birthplace - Kentucky
Occupation- Railroad foreman	Occupation - Housewife

Number of children born to this mother including present birth -
three.   Born at full term - yes. Number of children of this mother
now living - one. Certificate of attending physician or midwife.
I hereby certify that I attended the birth of this child, who was born
alive at 10:30 p. m.   Signature - Bate Dozier , M. D.
                    802 Monroe Street , Nashville, Tennessee
Filed March 28, 1922.   Register , Nora Hollister.

Vallie Jo Fox Whitfield gave birth to four children : Christa Marie Whitfield born in Berkeley, California of Alameda County on Dec. 30 , 1945 ;
Robert Edward Whitfield born in Boston, Massachusetts of Suffolk County,
November 21 , 1948 ; James David Whitfield born in Berkeley, California
of Alameda County on February 21, 1953 ; Joanne Vallie Whitfield , born
in Berkeley , California of Alameda County on March 14, 1955.
The father was Robert Edward Whitfield of Tennessee and California. *

STATE OF MISSOURI .   James Lafayette Whitfield (born 1912 Tenn.)
married Estelle Hamilton on January 25, 1934 in Missouri.

Sandra Lynne Whitfield (born 1936 Missouri) married Jimmy Jones of
Missouri.

Thomas C. Rye Whitfield (born 1915 Tenn.) married Kathlene Fisk,
September 1935 of Steele , Missouri.

Wilson Durwood Whitfield (born 1923 Missouri) married Betty Ruth
Fromes on August 7 , 1943 in Missouri.

----

* The vital statistical Birth Records were printed in the book:
   WHITFIELD , MC KEEL , FOX , SCHIEFER FAMILIES by
   Vallie Whitfield, published 1965 , pages 244 to 247.
   Tennessee and California records.

NORTH CAROLINA
MARRIAGE RECORDS

WILLIS WHITFIELD , born Nash County, North Carolina , and later moved to Tennessee. He married Rhoda Whitfield . She died September 3, 1826 in Cannon County, Tennessee. Willis Whitfield was in Rutherford County, Tennessee in 1832. Children four boys and two girls.

WILLIS WHITFIELD , born in Virginia or North Carolina ; and died Sept. 3 , 1836 in Sumner County or Rutherford County. Willis Whitfield was married to Rhody Allen on November 1 , 1788 . She was born Dec. 1 , 1767. They moved to Sumner County in 1792. Rhody Allen Whitfield when a widow was living in Cannon County, Tennessee in January 1840. They had twelve children. She was the daughter of Arthur and Elizabeth Allen.

WILLIS WHITFIELD married Nancy Rayford on October 31, 1846 in Guilford, North Carolina.

WILLIAM WHITFIELD (born 1688 ca) married Elizabeth Goodman in 1715 in North Carolina.

VIRGINIA RECORDS
Marriage of Southampton County, Virginia .
Elijah Whitfield and Martha Whitfield , April 15, 1784.
Solomon Whitfield and Sally Howell , July 25, 1782.
Davis Whitfield and Polly Francis , Oct. 25, 1789.

MARRIAGES OF SUSSEX COUNTY, VIRGINIA

Augustine Whitfield married Lucy Knight , December 26 , 1789.
Sec. -Elizabeth Knight Molhie .

Elizabeth Betsy Whitfield married Benjamin Sturdivant , January 20 , 1793.
Bond - January 3, 1793. Daughter of Thomas Whitfield and Winifer Whitfield . Sur- James Knight . Minister- Henry Moss. (Betty Whitfield).

Elizabeth Whitfield married Benjamin Sturdivant January 20 , 1783.
Daughter of Thomas Whitfield and Winifer Whitfield .
Sur- James Knight . Minister - Henry Moss.

Harrison Whitfield married Polly Sledge , August 29 , 1804. Ward of Mary Sledge. Sur.- Benjamin Sturdivant . Minister- Rev. James Rogers .

Martha Patty Whitfield married William Hobbs , December 24 , 1789.
Consent of Thomas Whitfield . Sur.- William Whitfield . Minister - Henry Moss .

MARRIAGES OF SUSSEX COUNTY, VIRGINIA :

Mary Whitfield married Laburn Hobbs , May 21 , 1778.
Sur. - Thomas Whitfield , his daughter .

Sally Whitfield married Edmund Moss , December 19, 1801.Date of Bond.
Sur. - Ephraim Knight .

Wilkins Whitfield married Polly Sturdivant , Bond was December 23,
1801 . Sur. - Harrison Whitfield .

William Whitfield married Elizabeth Tomlinson . July 26, 1782 Bond.
Minister- Jessee Lee. Sur. and parent - Alexander Tomlinson .

Nancy Whitfield married William Knight , December 18 , 1799.
Sur. - Ephraim Knight. Minister- Stith Parham.

Thomas Whitfield married Rebecca Nibitt , August 7 , 1819.
Sec. Nath'l Tomlinson .

Susanna E. Whitfield married Thomas Birdson , August 5, 1841.
Bondsman - Miles Birdsong.

On these marriage records of Sussex County, Virginia , the father
was Thomas Whitfield and the mother was Winifer Whitfield to the
children : Elizabeth Betsy called Betty Whitfield , Elizabeth Whitfield,
Harrison Whitfield , Martha Patty Whitfield , Mary Whitfield , Nancy
Whitfield , Wilkins Whitfield , William Whitfield . Eight of these
children have marriage records of Sussex County, Virginia. This family
moved to Williamson County, Tennessee in 1808 and settled at Franklin.
There is no marriage record for Francis Whitfield . Jack "John" Whitfield married.

In Tennessee , Willis Whitfield married Alemeada Rhodes , and he had
the son , Thomas Y. Whitfield of Rutherford County, Tennessee.

Ralph Wilson Whitfield (b. 1918 Humphreys County, Tennessee , and
died 1964 at Paris , Tennessee) married Mildred Lucile Daniel in
Dougherty County, Albany.

Richard Lewis Whitfield , born 1946 at Paris, Tennessee. Richard Whitfield married Linda Gale Pendergrass on December 23 , 1967 , a daughter
of Ben Frank Pendergrass by adoption .

Ralph Wilson Whitfield , born September 16, 1943 in Albany , Georgia
married Vivien Gale Brewer on June 11, 1966 at Crossville , Tennessee.
The daughter of Elmo Mitchell Brewer.

HICKMAN COUNTY, TENNESSEE
MARRIAGE RECORDS

HENRY W. WHITFIELD married Nancy C. Porch in 1851 in Hickman County, Tennessee.

MARTHA ELIZA WHITFIELD married J. D. Murray who was born May 2 , 1829 - Hickman County, Tennessee.

SARAH VIRGINIA WHITFIELD , born Feb. 26, 1849 in Hickman County, Tennessee married James H. Mullinicks.

MARY DELILAH WHITFIELD , born Feb. 24 , 1851 in Tennessee married Robert Horner.

JOSEPHINE WHITFIELD , born March 20 , 1854 in territory of Hickman County which changed boundary to Perry County, Tennessee where she died 1919 . She married John D. Mullinicks before 1873 .

THOMAS HARRISON WHITFIELD (father ____ , Felix) was born 1838 and died 1921 in Tennessee. He married 1865 Nancy Ann Stephens in Tennessee.

BENTON COUNTY, TENNESSEE . MARRIAGE RECORDS

Thomas Jefferson Whitfield married (1) Jane Nicks Cunningham, March 27 , 1866 in Humphreys County, Tennessee. Then second wife (2) Martha Jane Nicks, April 1875 of Benton County, Tennessee.

Delie Ann Whitfield, born 1891 in Decatur County, Tennessee , and living 1979 in Mc Kenize, Tennessee of Benton County . Delie Whitfield married Jim Sikes before 1917 in Tennessee.

Thomas Wesley Whitfield, born 1889 in Tennessee , and died 1942 in Missouri . He married Leza Belle Hatley on December 1, 1907 in Benton County, Tennessee.

Jefferson Lafayette Whitfield , born 1867 in Tennessee, and died 1937 in Missouri. He married first wife , and then married second wife , Lou Ellen Natlock in 1888 at Benton County, Tennessee.

Thomas Cleveland Whitfield , born 1884 in Tennessee , married Bessie Lee Primm on December 17 , 1905 in Benton County, Tennessee.

Thomas Jefferson Whitfield , born 1910 in Benton County, Tennessee , and married Earlene Dobson in 1928 in Benton County.

Benton County, Tennessee

Gladys Irene Whitfield , born 1908 in Benton County, Tennessee, and lived in Steele, Missouri, and later moved to Holladay, Tennessee in Benton County, Tennessee. Gladys Whitfield married William Leslie Hatley in Tennessee on August 6, 1937.

Dauthitt Glendall Whitfield , born 1928 in Missouri , married Laura Moore June 1947 . They moved to Camden, Tennessee in Benton County.

TENNESSEE COUNTIES , MARRIAGE RECORDS

William G. Clagett married (1) Theodosia Whitfield on July 21, 1835. After her death he married Elizabeth O. Hornbeak on Feb. 10, 1842 in Williamson County, Tennessee.

Nancy A. Whitfield married on March 8 , 1827 John M. Winstead in Williamson County, Tennessee.

George W. Whitfield married (1) Miss Louisa King 1836 in Williamson County, Tennessee. Then (2) married Miss Sarah Bond on March 5 , 1849 in Williamson County, Tennessee.

George W. Whitfield married Warreena Spence on October 24, 1843 in Davidson County, Tennessee.

John Whitfield married (1) Catherine C. Dansby in Maury County, Tennessee on April 13, 1839 ; and married (2) Sarah B. Dibrell on May 28 , 1853 in Davidson County, Tennessee.

Thomas Jefferson Whitfield married Eliza Nolan on January 24, 1829 in Willi amson County , Tennessee , and then married second wife Sallie L. Dillahunty on January 27 , 1835 in Davidson County, Tenn.

Thomas W. Whitfield (b. 1827-d.1879) married Sarah M. Berry on March 4, 1855 . She was daughter of John and Annie Berry of Cheatham County, Tennessee.

N. Chrestine Whitfield, born 1910 in Tennessee, and married Emmette Eugene Yates of Repley, Mississippi in January 1931 in Tennessee. They resided in 1962 at Memphis, Tennessee.

Andrew Alford Whitfield (1829-1859) married Emeline Eleanor Lyon (1834- 1920) on August 31 , 1851 . They resided in Rutherford County, Tennessee.

THOMAS JEFFERSON WHITFIELD 1845-1908 AND
JAMES DEE WHITFIELD 1877- 1954 . Locations in Tennessee.

Thomas Jefferson Whitfield moved 1886 to Rockport of Benton County
when son, James Dee Whitfield was age nine . James went to Pegram
school. James Dee Whitfield was born in Bakerville, Tennessee .After
about three years he moved to Davidson Landing and from there to Vernon
in Hickman County for three months and back to Davidson Landing. From
there to Forks of River in Tennessee . From there to Bakerville at Denton
Bone place and then north of Bakerville . From there to Rockport in December 1886. From there to Camden. From Camden town to Pavatts landing in summer of July 1890. He moved January 1891 to Parkers Landing
in Decatur County of Tennessee. January 1893 he moved to Pavatts community close to school. January 1894 he moved back to Parkers Landing
in Decatur County. January 1895 he moved back to Pavatts where Thomas
Cleveland Whitfield lives.

In 1895 on December 20th, James Dee Whitfield moved on a ferry
boat up to Dixie below Cuba Landing where he was married in 1899 .Janu-
ary 1900 Thomas J. Whitfield moved back to Rockport , and James Dee
Whitfield moved across the Tennessee River to ROCKPORT. November
15 , 1900 , James Dee Whitfield moved down on Eagle Creek at Matlock
place. January 1902 he bought two shares of Matlocks. 1903 he moved to
Pavatts at Thomas Cleveland Whitfield place.

Thomas Jefferson Whitfield moved to Pavatts in January 1902 to
their home place. James Dee Whitfield moved to Waverly , Tennessee
January 12 , 1912 and then he moved back to Pavatts Landing , January
1, 1916 on a ferry boat leaving out at cold branch at Duck River . July
1916 he moved back to Waverly to his house and lot and bid the Tennessee
River goodbye. He moved to the Farm he called Rockdale Farm on
April 1, 1919. In January 1944 he was at Mc Kenzie, Tennessee , and
in April 1944 went to Detroit, Michigan because his son, Raymond Whitfield was living there for a short time. He went back to Henry County,
Tennessee January 2, 1945, and lived at Oakdale Farm in Henry County.
James Dee Whitfield had along with him his wife, Oda Whitfield in these
later moves. James D. Whitfield died 1954 , and is buried at Mc Keel
Cemetery in Humphreys County, Tennessee.

A Thomas J. Whitfield burial yard is at Bakerville, Tennessee
on the farm of Dave Anderson who was the father of John Anderson who
was captain and pilot of the submarine ship NAUTILUS that sailed in the
North Atlantic depth of the Ocean. Pavatt Landing was Whitfield place
on Eagle Creek in Benton County, Tennessee.

Always near the Tennessee River they tended to live.

Newspaper print on Whitfield

The Knoxville News - Sentinel Newspaper , Knoxville, Tennessee
on February 28 , 1943 .

-HERE AND THERE - BEGINNINGS OF ENGAGEMENTS TOLD IN
STORIES OF SCHOOL-DAY ROMANCES.

........" It was the first day of registration at University of Tennessee
more than a year ago , and Robert E. Whitfield thought he was talking
to another "bewildered" freshman when he began a conversation with
Vallie Jo Fox , standing before him in the registration line.

Later they were formally introduced by the brother-in-law of
the pretty Nashville girl and Robert learned that she was transferring to
University of Tennessee from Ward- Belmont and was really a sophomore.
Today they are announcing the engagement with promise of wedding date
in March."

-    -   -   -

The engagement to marriage was announced in the THE KNOXVILLE NEWS
Newspaper in March 1943.

-    -   -   -

THE TENNESSEAN Newspaper , March 1943.

" Mrs. Joseph Edward Fox of Nashville announces the engagement
of her daughter , Vallie Jo to Robert E. Whitfield, son of James D. Whit-
field of Waverly . Miss Fox attended St. Bernard Academy and Ward-
Belmont College , where she was a member of the Eccowaisin Club. She
is a junior at the University of Tennessee. She was a member of the
Girls Industrial Club of Nashville and is an active member of the Newman
Club. Mr. Whitfield will receive his Bachelor of Science Degree at the
University of Tennessee in March . He is a member of Phi Kappa Phi
honorary fraternity . Following graduation he will accept a position at
Berkeley, California . The wedding will take place the latter part of
March ."

-    -   -   -

THE TENNESSEAN Newspaper And THE NASHVILLE BANNER News-
paper , March 1943 both had print in the newspapers on the Wedding .
Article headline reads : "Miss Fox Is Wed To Mr.Whitfield This Morning."
.... "Whitfield - Fox Vows Are Said."

"Taking place Friday morning, March 26, 1943 , at nine o'clock was
the marriage of Miss Vallie Jo Fox , daughter of Mrs. Joseph E. Fox ,
and the late Mr. Fox to Robert Edward Whitfield of Knoxville , son of
James Dee Whitfield of Waverly and the late Mrs. Mary Hester Whitfield.

The Reverend Thomas P. Duffy officiated in the presence of a limited
guest company at St. Mary's Church.

The altar vases were filled with white flowers , and ivory tapers
burning in branched candelabra illuminated the wedding scene.

The bride, who was given in marriage by Lt. C. L. Stevens, of the
United States Army, stationed at Camp Rucker , Alabama, wore a gown
of white satin simply styled and self-trimmed.   Her veil of illusion

was caught to a Juliet cap of the lace , and she carried a cascade bouquet of gardenias and lilies of the valley.

Mrs. C. L. Stevens , of Ozark, Arkansas who attended her sister as matron of honor , was attired in a pale blue taffeta and lace gown. She carried an arm bouquet of pastel shaded spring flowers.

Beecher R. Spees of La Belle, Missouri , served as best man.

Immediately following the ceremony, a breakfast was given at the Hermitage Hotel for the bridal party and the two families . Mrs. Fox , the bride's mother, wore a navy blue crepe model, and her hat and accessories were in a matching shade.

Later in the day , Mr. and Mrs. Whitfield left for Chicago , Illinois, where they will spend several days enroute to San Francisco, California where they will make their home. For traveling, the bride chose a salute blue wool suit and a navy blue hat and accessories .

The bride attended Ward-Belmont and the University of Tennessee in Knoxville, Tennessee.

Mr. Whitfield was graduated from the University of Tennessee."

- - - - - -

And the news went out for a girl named Vallie Fox and a boy named Robert Whitfield and both of them from the University of Tennessee.

The formal announcement of Wedding :

Mrs. Joseph E. Fox

requests the honor of your presence at the marriage of her daughter

VALLIE JO

To

MR. ROBERT E. WHITFIELD

Friday, March twenty - sixth , Nineteen hundred and forty-three

Nine o'clock A. M.   St. Mary's Church

Nashville, Tennessee

And they held their land deed in Pleasant Hill-Walnut Creek, California and made their home where they resided for all of their days.

" Grant to Robert Edward Whitfield and Vallie Jo Whitfield, his wife , as joint tenants , in joint tenancy, the real property situated in County of Contra Costa, State of California, described as follows:

A portion of the Rancho Las Juntas, and a portion of the Rancho Canada Del Hambre, Southern Part, Contra Costa County, California, being a portion of the property described in the deed dated November 21, 1932, executed by Mary Counsil Davidson, to Charles W. Moore, et ux, recorded December 2, 1932 in book 333 of Official Records, page 76, records of Contra Costa County, California, described as follows:

Commencing at the northeast corner of the 10.00 acre parcel described in deed herein before referred to ; thence, along the easterly line of said property, South 2°45' East , 275.00 feet; thence leaving said line, South 89° 50' West to the westerly line of the 2.49 acre parcel described in said deed; thence along the westerly line of said 2.49 acre parcel. North to the

northwesterly corner of said 10.00 acre parcel, North 89° 50' East, "
792.00 feet to the point of commencement.   Dated, January 14, 1953."

TEXAS   RECORDS

John Wilkins Whitfield in 1861 enlisted a Company near Petersburg and became Captain of the 27th Texas Cavalry of the Confederate Army. He later commanded the force known as WHITFIELD'S LEGION. After the Civil War, he settled on the Navidod River in Lavaca County, Texas. He was a delegate to the Constitutional Convention of 1866 and again to the Constitutional Convention of 1875 in which he was chairman of the Committee on Education, which advocated direct taxes for school purposes and the establishment of a University of Texas with a branch for negro students. John Wilkins Whitfield died near Hallettsville, Texas on October 27, 1879.

WHITFIELD LEGION originated with a Confederate Cavalry Company organized in Lavac County early in 1861 and marched to Missouri to join Ben Mc Culloch. In Missouri the Lavaca County Company was combined with a Hunt County Company from Arkansas. John H. Broochs Company from San Augustine County, and a Jasper County Company under B. H. Norsworth to form a battalion with John Wilkins Whitfield as major. In January 1862 E. R. Hawkins returned to Texas and recruited eight other companies which were combined with the original five to form the legion in April 1862. The Arkansas Company was transferred to another command, and the legion remained at twelve companies with Whitfield as Colonel, Hawkins as Lieutenant Colonel, and Broocks as major.

While organized as a battalion, the unit had already participated in the battle of Elkhorn Tavern in Arkansas. Soon after organization of the legion, it was dismounted and sent with other units of Earl Van Dorn's Army to reinforce P.G.T. Beauregard at Corinth, Mississippi. After various Mississippi engagements, the legion was mounted in the fall of 1862, and became the 27th Texas Cavalry Regiment. Whitfield was promoted to brigadier general and the 3rd, 6th, and 9th Texas Cavalry Regiments were added to his command to form a brigade. When Whitfield retired because of ill health, L.S. Ross assumed command on December 16, 1863 and the unit became known as Ross Brigade.

John W. Whitfield had a son, John Anthony Whitfield, and his son was George Dibrell, born at Devine, Texas on May 12, 1887. The parent John A. was born in Tennessee, and his mother Helena Briscoe Whitfield was born in Arkansas. John Anthony Whitfield came to Texas in 1859, settling in Lavaca County at that time; and in 1886 came to Devine, attended schools and after leaving school employed locally, and later entered drug business with D.M. Howard where he remained six years and enlisted in the Army, serving in the Cavalry and Artillery at Fort Sam Houston, Camp Bowie and Fort Sill, Oklahoma, discharged Feb. 1919. He became the owner of Devine Motor Company.

TEXAS RECORDS

Harrison Whitfield moved from Williamson County, Tennessee in 1870 to Lincoln County, Texas, then to Cook County, Texas. He was the son of Harrison Whitfield of Williamson County, Tennessee, and the grandson of Thomas Whitfield and Winifer Whitfield of Sussex County, Virginia. He had brothers named John Whitfield and Felix Whitfield, and sisters named Rebecca Whitfield and Nancy Whitfield. The Harrison Whitfield that was born 1783 and died after 1864 was the father of this son named Harrison Whitfield of Texas. Harrison Whitfield married Sophronia Conn about 1845 in Williamson County, Tennessee, and later they moved to Texas and had children.

Lavaca County, Texas. John Wilkins Whitfield (1818-1879). He married first wife, Catherine Dansby in Maury County, Tennessee on April 13, 1839. They had two children, probably both girls. Then he married second wife, Sarah B. Dibrell in 1853. The license issued April 27, 1853. Marriage on May 28, 1853.

WHITFIELD names appear in several sources in Texas. History of Lavaca County, Texas; and Dallas County, Texas Records.

George W. Whitfield who is called George Washington Whitfield was born Feb. 12 - 1806 in Sussex County, Virginia, and died after 1891 at Garland town, in Dallas County, Texas. He has biographical sketches in "Memorial and Biographical History of Dallas County, Texas." Pages 615, 616, a book published in 1892. In the Marriage Records - "Williamson County, Tennessee Marriages" by Bejach Wilena Roberts, Pages 5, 48, 53, 63, 193, 203, 280. In the book, "Old Cemeteries of Dallas County" by Willie Flowers Carlisle, page 147. In the book, "History of Dallas County, Texas," page 615.
Ancestry of this family appears in"Albermarle Parish Register 1739-1778", Virginia of Sussex County --- Richards, pages 98, 221, 243, 295.

Texas Record : James Whitfield was married January 3 - 1845 in Maury County, Tennessee to Mary Dansby Oliphant, daughter of Tabitha and Samuel Oliphant. They had eight children : three of the children were born in Tennessee and brought to Texas as small children. He had kinship Frances B. Starr (Mrs.William T. Starr), Dallas 18, Texas, who was living there in 1965. ---------------
Austin County, Texas : Henry W. Whitfield was living in 1965 in Austin County, Texas and was the son of Henry W. Whitfield, the oldest son of Wilkins Whitfield and Martha Loftin Whitfield of Tennessee. He was married to Susanna De Moss Oliphant in Maury County, Tennessee on June 13, 1850. ---------------
From Virginia to Tennessee to Texas and at Cook County, Lincoln County, Dallas County, Lavaca County, and cities of San Antonia and Devine, and others.

DESCENDANTS

Descendants of Samuel Whitfield (1714-1758) and Elizabeth Whitfield of Isle of Wight County, Virginia . Page 43

Descendants of Thomas Whitfield (d. 1694) and Ann Whitfield of Virginia . Page 44 . .... And the grandson , Thomas Whitfield (1721 Va. -1781 N .C.) and Mary Whitfield , of Nash County , North Carolina . Page 45 ·

Descendants of William Whitfield I (1688-1770) and Elizabeth Goodman Whitfield (1697-1773 N .C.) , of Bertie County, North Carolina. Pages 48 - 236-237. .... And their son, William Whitfield II (1715 N .C. -1795 N .C.) and Rachel Bryan Whitfield of Lenoir County , North Carolina .... And their son, William Whitfield III (1743 N . C. -1817 N . C.) and first wife, Hester Williams Whitfield, of Wayne County, North Carolina.... And their sons in Tennessee named William Whitfield (1764-1825) and wife , Mary Beck ; Needham Whitfield (1766-1858) and wife , Miriam Neville ; Bryan Whitfield (1766-1825) and wives , Ann and Catherine ; Lewis Whitfield and wife , Elizabeth Wimberly.

Descendants of Thomas Whitfield (1735- 1794 Va.) and Winifer Whitfield (1740 ca Va. - 1838 Tenn.). Pages 240 and to 248. Sussex County, Virginia and Williamson County, Tennessee.

Descendants of Willis Whitfield (1761 N . C. -1826 Tenn.) and wife , Rhoda Whitfield (1768 ca. - living 1844) , of Rutherford County , Tennessee. Page 191 .

Descendants of John Whitfield (1779-) and Lucy Whitfield (1781 Va. -1858) of Giles County , Tennessee. Pages 238 and 239.

Descendants of Thomas Rush Whitfield and Elizabeth Morgan S. Whitfield (1845 ca. -) of Missouri . Pages 253 - 254.

Descendants of William Whitfield (1831 Tenn. - 1915 California) and Sarah Ann Prigmore Whitfield (1833 Missouri - 1917 California) of Dallas County, Texas and California. Pages 255 - 256

Descendants of other Whitfield Immigrants to Tennessee in this book ; but have only records here and not genealogy on the families.

Descendants of Joseph Schiefer (1808 Hungary- 1876 Kentucky) and wife , Mary Schiefer (1820 Czechoslavakia - 1884 Kentucky) , of Newport , Kentucky of Campbell County. Page 258

Descendants of Joseph Theodore Fox (1832 Germany - 1883 Tenn.) and Elizabeth Heiner Fox (1842 Kentucky - 1919 Tennessee) , of Franklin Kentucky of Simpson County ; and Nashville , Tennessee of Davidson County. Page 259

KINSHIPS

William Whitfield and Mary Beck Whitfield, who moved from North Carolina to Tennessee territory early had kinship in 1805 living in Steward County, Tennessee.

Genealogy Family Group :

Mathew Whitfield, born Virginia or North Carolina about 1772 , and died 1827 in Rutherford County, Tennessee . He was married to Levina Whitfield. They had children Mathew , Benjamin, William Whitfield between 10 and 26 years of age in 1820 , Mary , a girl . Descendants were in Rutherford County, Tennessee.

Whitfield of White County, Tennessee had some kinship in 1965 in San Antonia , Texas.

Genealogy Family Group :

William Whitfield died 1834 in Lawrence County of Tennessee, then the territory of Hickman County, Tennessee before the County boundary was formed. He had children James , John L., Sally.

Bryan Whitfield , born about 1766 in North Carolina ; and died 1825 at Montgomery County, Tennessee was married first to Anne Neville 1797 ca, and after her death to Catherine Bailey , 1798 ca. They have children and the descendants in Tennessee and Mississippi . Some dates worthy of note. James Whitfield, born March 22, 1804 in Tennessee, and died Dec. 21 , 1834. Bryan Whitfield, born Feb. 23, 1808 in Tennessee and died July 30 , 1831. Duncan Whitfield , born March 31 , 1818 in Tennessee , and died April 7 , 1860 in Mississippi.

Genealogy Family Group : Alfred Whitfield and descendants of Tennessee. #37 Alfred Whitfield . # 150 Andrew Alford Whitfield and he had children: #151 Andrew Willis Whitfield , Elizabeth Whitfield , # 152 Nathan James Thomas Whitfield , # 153 Alfred Johnson Whitfield , # 154 Jesse Blackburn Whitfield was a grandson.

In Steward County in 1805 lived Daniel Whitfield , William Whitfield , Charles Whitfield , Jessie Whitfield , C. Whitfield , Willis Whitfield .

In White County, Tennessee in 1829 lived Carter B. Whitfield , John Whitfield , John Whitfield, Thomas Whitfield .

Thomas I. Whitfield lived in Hickman County, Tennessee in 1830, and his wife was over forty-five years of age. They had three boys and one girl.

Thomas J. Whitfield wife was Marthy , and their children were Lafayette, Millie , James D. of Hickman County, Tenn.

John Whitfield lived in Rutherford County, Tennessee in 1820 , and in the family were three boys and four girls.

William Whitfield moved to Sumner County, Tennessee in 1792 , and migrated from Eastern district of Tennessee , and from North Carolina. Also John Whitfield moved to Sumner County, Tennessee. Willis Whitfield (1761-1836) went from Nash County, North Carolina to Sumner County, Tennessee in 1792 , and later moved to Rutherford County, Tenn.

<u>Genealogy Family Group</u> : Willis Whitfield was born 1761 in Nash County, North Carolina. He served in the Revolution under Captain Carter . In North Carolina Willis Whitfield married Rhoda Allen on November 1, 1788. The daughter of Arthur Allen and Elizabeth Allen. In 1792 the family moved to Sumner County, Tennessee , and they later moved to Rutherford County, Tennessee. Willis Whitfield died September 3, 1836 in Rutherford County, Tennessee. Rhoda (Rhody) Allen Whitfield was born December 1, 1767 , and was a widow living 1840 in Cannon County, Tennessee.

They had twelve children , seven boys and five girls :

<u>Boys</u>	<u>Girls</u>
Wright Whitfield , b. 1791	Ansil Whitfield , b. 1789
Christian , b. 1793	Sally Whitfield , b. 1795
Thomas Y. Whitfield , b. 1801	Temperance Whitfield, b. 1797
Arthur Allen Whitfield , b. 1803	Rhody Whitfield , b. 1798
Willis Whitfield , b. 1805	Elizabeth Eason , b. 1810
Alfred Whitfield , b. 1812	
Eli Whitfield , b. 1807	--------------

Lewis Allen married Rebecca Whitfield on October 11, 1823 in Williamson County, Tennessee . She was born in Virginia . She is a descendant of Thomas Whitfield and Winifer Whitfield. On the 1850 Census of Williamson County, Tennessee is the family of Allen :

Lewis C. Allen	49	Va.	L. C.
Rebecca (Whitfield) Allen	44	Va.	R.
Seletha Allen	24	Tenn.	S. E.
Searcy D. Allen	20	Tenn.	S. D.
Felix Allen	18	Tenn.	F. G.
Wilkins Allen	16	Tenn.	H. W.
Harrison Allen	15	Tenn.	J. W.
John W. Allen	13	Tenn.	M.
Mary U. Allen	9	Tenn.	A. E.
Ewing Allen	5	Tenn.	G. W.
Joe Allen	1	Tenn.	

On the 1860 East Subdivision , Franklin Post Office Census of Williamson County, Tennessee appear the initials for Allen Family.

In the WESTERN WEEKLY REVIEW , dated March 11, 1836 appears: " L. C. Allen had a thorough bred dapple grey stallion - will stand the

present season at my farm one half mile from the Courthouse on the turn
pike road, leading from Franklin to Nashville."
Dated March 17, 1837 L.C. Allen advertised the service of his horse
John Randolph at his stable near Franklin.
Dated March 20 , 1838 , L.C. Allen advertised the service of "John Randolph Bertram at my stable at Degraphens _____ Plantation , one half
mile from Franklin on the Charlotte Road."

There are so many with the name of John Whitfield that it is difficult
to take a record and know the family group for which John Whitfield has
blood kinship lineage. There are several with the name on Census records.
John Whitfield on 1820 Census Rutherford County, Tennessee had three
sons , and three girls , and one of the children was named John. The
ancestor probably from North Carolina. Another John Whitfield on the
1850 Census of Henry County, Tennessee , and his wife was Elizabeth
Whitfield.

There is the son Jack "John" Whitfield of Thomas Whitfield and Winifer
Whitfield of Sussex County, Tennessee , and he has a son John Whitfield
at Williamson County , Tennessee ; and there is a line of Johns for lineage .

The brother,William Whitfield of Sussex County, Virginia in 1808 moved
to Williamson County, Tennessee at Franklin probably has a line of blood
kinships with the name of William Whitfield. He had four sons and three
girls when his wife of age forty-five years. William Whitfield was born
1780 ca in Sussex County, Virginia. The family and descendants lived at
Williamson County, Tennessee.

DESCENDANTS OF WILLIS WHITFIELD (1761 N .C. - 1826 Tenn.), and wife,
RHODY WHITFIELD (b. about 1768-living 1844) are in family group on page
191 in book. They had twelve children , and one half born in North Carolina,
and one half born in Tennessee. They began at Nash County, North Carolina.
Then lived in Bledsoe Region and from North Carolina, then moved 1792 to
Sumner County, Tennessee , and then later to Rutherford County, Tennessee. Their descendants are in this location in Tennessee.

Also WILLIAM WHITFIELD settled in 1792 in Sumner County, Tennessee,
along with JESSE WHITFIELD who settled in 1792 in Sumner County, Tenn.,
and along with John Whitfield in 1792.

The son , Willis Whitfield of Rutherford County, Tennessee has records on
pages in book 64- 66- 79 - 190- 223.

For ancestry go back to Willis Whitfields at Nansemond County, Virginia,
and Norfolk , and then to John Whitfield.

WHITFIELD S FROM NORTH CAROLINA TO TENNESSEE
****
GENEALOGY - Blood Kinships .

From Wayne County , North Carolina region to Christian County ,
Kentucky and Montgomery County, Tennessee ,   and to Steward
County, Tennessee.   And grandchildren at Henry County, Tennessee
were orphans of Whitfields.

Four brothers from North Carolina to Tennessee. Descendants of Will-
iam Whitfield (1688-1770) and Elizabeth Goodman Whitfield (1697-1773).
Sons of William Whitfield III (b. June 1 - 1743) and his first wife , Hester
Williams of North Carolina.

WILLIAM WHITFIELD , born 1764 , Wayne County, North Carolina , and
    died August 8 , 1825 at Steward County, Tennessee. He married 1785
    Mary Beck. Thirteen children. Sons William, Needham, Joseph,
    Lewis and their families at Christian County, Kentucky and Steward
    County, Tennessee.

BRYAN WHITFIELD , born 1766 in North Carolina and died 1825 in Montgom -
    ery County , Tennessee. He married (1) Anne Neville about 1797
    and (2) Catherine Bailey about 1798. Eight children . Sons, William
    Whitfield , James Whitfield, Bryan Whitfield and their families were
    born and died in the region of Montgomery County, Tennessee. The
    son, Duncan was born there but moved to Mississippi and died there,
    and his children lived in the Mississippi location.

NEEDHAM WHITFIELD , born 1776 in North Carolina and died 1858 in
    North Carolina. He married Miriam Neville (1776-1852), sister of the
    wife of his brother Bryan Whitfield , and resided at Montgomery County,
    Tennessee. They married in 1798. Fifteen children but only four that
    reached maturity.   George Neville Whitfield married Mary Anne
    Killebrew , and lived in Montgomery County, Tennessee. Needham
    Bryan Whitfield, born 1821 and died at Montgomery County, Tenn.
    In 1843 he married Hannah Eglentine Wilcox. Nine children. Four
    sons, Hervey Whitfield , b. July 3-1847 in Montgomery County, Tenn-
    essee and lived at Clarksville, Tennessee. He married (1) Ella Trigg
    (1875-1900) and (2) Mrs.Jennie (Vaughan) Price. Hervey and Ella Whit-
    field had sons : 1. Arthur G. Whitfield of Tennessee. 2. Roy Whitfield,
    (b. June 8 - 1878) and married in 1907.   3. Thomas B. Whitfield, born
    Dec. 8 , 1882 - d. Dec. 23, 1899.

      After the death of Arthur G. Whitfield (b. July 30-1876 Tenn. -
    d. August 1920 Tenn.), his widow , Mrs.Lula Hayden Whitfield(who he
    married Dec. 29-1910 of Frankfort, Kentucky) moved to Texas , and
    became matron at Buckner's Orphanage, at Dallas, Texas. Two child-
    ren moved from Tennessee to Texas : Ella E. Whitfield, b. Jan. 11-1911
    and Hervey Whitfield, b. Feb. 22- 1913.

      Needham Whitfield's (1776-1858) two daughters were Sarah Collier
    Whitfield who married Richard Nixon, a Baptist minister ; and Miriam
    Richardson Whitfield (b. 1808 Tenn. - d. 1888) . In 1827 she married

(1) John D. Fort (1804-1829) (Two Fort children) , and
(2) Joseph Whitfield, in 1833, her cousin, the son of Lewis
Whitfield (b. in North Carolina and died in Tennessee). They
had eight children.

LEWIS WHITFIELD, born in North Carolina and died in Tennessee. He
moved to Tennessee about 1793. He married (1) Elizabeth Wimberly,
daughter of Joseph or John Wimberly and Sarah Diggs (2) Sarah Wall,
a widow. Ten children, four girls , Sarah, Elizabeth, Susan, Catherine.
Six sons. Needham Whitfield married Sallie Bourne.
Lewis Whitfield married Ann Williams, a cousin.
Robert Whitfield .   Bryan Whitfield.
George Whitfield .
Joseph W. Whitfield , born August 23, 1806 married Mrs. Miriam
Richardson Whitfield Fort, his cousin, in 1833. She had two Fort
children , and eight Whitfield children. Three daughters, Constantine,
Sarah Cornelia, Mary L. Five sons. Joseph Whitfield, b. 1833 ca.
Tennessee and died 1859 Clarksville, Tennessee. A physician.
Needham Lewis Whitfield , born about 1837 He married (1) Anna Mart,
of Russellville, Kentucky and they had sons Herbert Tera Whitfield , b.
June 22, 1864 who married in 1902 Leslie Hicks Johnson of Clarksville,
Tennessee and they had three daughters , Justine, b. 1902 and moved
to New York. Alice L. Whitfield. Helen Tera Whitfield who married
1930 Dr. John Maxwell of Alabama, and moved to Temple, Texas.
Another son, Edward Whitfield who married Arista at Mississippi
and the family lived in Mississippi. Daughter unmarried, Nannie.
Robert Christian Whitfield, b. 1839 ca , Tennessee, and killed Dec. 13,
1862 in Virginia.
James W. Whitfield , b. 1848 ca. Tennessee , and married 1873 to
Margaret M. Carney.
Henry C. Whitfield, b. Tennessee.

Kinship Whitfield orphans at Henry County, Tennessee.

In the Henry County, Tennessee Court Minutes for 1836 to 1849 is a
list of the Whitfield children that were orphans.
Elizah Whitfield   .   Hannah Whitfield
Elizabeth Whitfield (Father, William Whitfield , died 1842) Her guardian
was John Walker of Henry County, Tennessee.
James Whitfield .   John Whitfield .   Lewis Whitfield.
Needham Whitfield. Sally Whitfield .   William Whitfield.

After James Whitfield, died before 1848 and left children Bryan, Lucy,
Sarah. The Court of Henry County, Tennessee appointed Lewis Whitfield
of the same County guardian for the children in 1848, Isaac Wimberly,
John Whitfield, and Needham Whitfield secured the Bond.

GENEALOGY   Blood Kinships

DESCENDANTS OF JOHN WHITFIELD of Paris , Tennessee in Henry
County . 1960 Chiropractor Physician.

JOHN WHITFIELD was born September 5, 1779 Suffulk, Wilderwhite   G 5
County, Virginia. In 1779 this was a name for Isle of Wight County,
then Suffolk County of Wilderwhite in Virginia.   John Whitfield moved
to Giles County, Tennessee in a covered wagon with nine children .
He married Lucy ___ who was born December 9 , 1781 in Virginia ,
and died May 9 , 1858 in Giles County, Tennessee.

G 6

ALFRED WHITFIELD was one of the nine children of John Whitfield
and Lucy Whitfield whose children were born in eastern Virginia and
North Carolina, but mostly in Tennessee the children were born.
Alfred Whitfield was born January 28 , 1823 , and died December 5,
1882. He married Elizabeth Jane ____ who was born March 8 , 1824 ,
and died August 27 , 1914 in Tennessee. They had six children , all
of Tennessee.   G 7

1. Alice Whitfield . She married a Gilbert.
2. Mattie E. Whitfield . She married a Chambers.
3. Mary F. Whitfield . She married a Scott , born June 24, 1850 ;
     and died August 1907.
4. John R. Whitfield (Bob) , born 1848 ; and died 1934.
5. Willie T. Whitfield , born 1866 ; and died 1899.
6. James Thomas Whitfield , born Dec. 5, 1852 ; and died Nov. 10 , 1899.
                                                                     G 8

JAMES THOMAS WHITFIELD (1852- 1899) had three children :
 1. George Gray Whitfield , born November 3, 1881 in Giles Co., Tenn.
 2. _____ Whitfield married 1902 in Giles County, Tennessee .
     Georgia Hughey , born Nov. 23, 1881 . Had six children.
 3. _____ Whitfield .
                                                                     G 9

JAMES THOMAS WHITFIELD was born 1904 in Tennessee .
Descendant of Grandfather James Thomas Whitfield (1852-1899).
James Thomas Whitfield married Mabel Gatt and they had two children.
They moved from Tennessee to Baytown , Texas where they reside in
1964.   Children : 1. George Carl Whitfield.
                 2. Joy Whitfield married Joe Cernoch and
                     had four children .

ANNIE LOUISE WHITFIELD was born 1910 in Tennessee.
She married Joe Di Misa and had three children . Annie Louise Whitfield
- Di Misa moved to Falls Church , Virginia , and resided there where her
children were born.
1. Joann Louise Di Misa married Pactrick Seine, and resided in Indiana.
2. Janet Lucile Di Misa.
3. Joyce Linda Di Misa.

JOHN HUGHEY WHITFIELD was born 1912 in Paris , Tennessee.
He married Regina Presnell and they had one child .
1. John Hughey Whitfield , Jr. He resides in North Carolina.

GEORGE CARL WHITFIELD born 1914 ; and died 1936 . He was born
twin to Georgia Cathron Whitfield.

GEORGIA CATHRON WHITFIELD was born 1914 . She was born twin
 to George Carl Whitfield . Georgia Whitfield married Thomas Lawton
Gregory , and they had three children born in Tennessee. Georgia and
Thomas Gregory reside in Oak Ridge, Tennessee in 1964. Children :
1. Mary Louise Gregory . Married.
2. Thomas Lawton Gregory , Jr. Married.
3. George Coleman.

ROBERT GRAY WHITFIELD was born 1906 . In 1964 he resides in Paris,
Tennessee. Robert Gray Whitfield married Dec. 22, 1934 Carrie Bell
Wilson Drake who was born 1912 in Big Cove of Huntsville , Alabama.
She was the daughter of William Pickens Drake . He and his wife had
twelve children .
Robert Gray Whitfield and Carrie Whitfield have two children of Tennessee in 1964 . Children:
1. George Robert Whitfield . He was born Dec. 24, 1935 , Elkton . He
resides in Paris , Tennessee of Henry County.
2. John Beasley Whitfield was born Feb. 12, 1961 , in Paris , Tennessee
of Henry County.

Nita Elizabeth Whitfield was born May 2, 1939 in Camden, Tennessee.

---

* The Gile County Tennessee records were submitted by George R.
Whitfield , 206 Greenacres Drive , Paris, Tennessee in 1964.
Lieutenant in the U. S. Military in Tennessee, 1964.

J.S. Beasley family in Blountville, Tennessee.

Virginia Records :
Oct. 3, 1758. John Gawith, Mariner, Master of the ship JOHNSON belonging
to Liverpool in Great Britain, power of attorney to Robert Jackson of Fredsbg.,
Virginia. Mercht. Witness, John Whitfield , Dec. 5, 1758.

July 11, 1763. Dickey Swan Edwards of Northumberland County, Virginia
to Robert Jackson of Fredsbg., Virginia . Mercht. Jr 25 curr. Lot 54 in
town of Fredksbg.   John Whitfield , Oct. 3, 1763

DESCENDANT OF JOHN DE WHITFIELD . ENGLAND.

DESCENDANTS OF _____ WHITFIELD FROM ENGLAND TO VIRGINIA.

DESCENDANTS OF THOMAS WHITFIELD 1735-1794 AND
   WINIFER WHITFIELD 1740ca- 1838.   FROM VIRGINIA TO TENN.

The Study on Whitfields for the ancestors for those Whitfield Families at Williamson County, Tennessee , Franklin, 1808 , was made by Vallie Jo Fox Whitfield in 1976 , and the results were published in the book , VIRGINIA HISTORY AND WHITFIELD BIOGRAPHIES , 1976.

The beginning is a sketch based on this material. Ancestors very early to Virginia Colony would have been William Whitfield and John Whitfield. Then later to Thomas Whitfield, Mathew Whitfield , and others. The location is the Elizabeth City Island of Virginia, across the James River to Nansemond or Isle of Wight Counties. The beginning starts in these locations.

Charts were made on genealogy. Ages were also charted with the men likely to be an ancestor. The migration and moving on the land was studied and recorded. Women were studied closely for clues. Names of Mary, Elizabeth, and Ann at Virginia were studied. Then the record on Anne Whitfield in Sussex County, Virginia led the author to find a mate for the ancestor. Thus William Whitfield was selected. Although it could possibly have been a John Whitfield , Thomas Whitfield , or another.

ANNE WHITFIELD lived in Albemarle Parish, Sussex County, Virginia in 1751. She was a sister or the mother of Thomas Whitfield who died in 1794. Albemarle Parish, the south side of the Blackwater River in Sussex County, Virginia.

Thomas Whitfield was born about 1735, and died 1794 in Sussex Co., Virginia . Thomas Whitfield married Winifer before 1760. She was called Winney. Winifer Whitfield gave birth to ten children in Sussex County, Virginia . She was a church member and wife to a farmer. This family was on a planting farm . They had three black workers with this house.

Thomas Whitfield took an Oath of allegiance to the Revolution before George Rives, one of the justices , Sussex County, Virginia, August 9 , 1777 . In the Will of his in 1794 he leaves lands to his children. The names of the children :
1. MARY WHITFIELD, b. September 21, 1760 in Virginia. She married
   Laburn Hobbs in 1778 .

2. WILLIAM WHITFIELD , b. August 6, 1762. He married Elizabeth
   Tomlinson, July 19 , 1782. He had children.

   A son, William Whitfield on the 1830 Census of Williamson County,
Tennessee was 50 to 60 years of age. Wife was 40 to 50 years. The children : Boy-5 to 10 yrs ; Boy-5 to 10 yrs ; Boy- under 5 yrs ; Boy- 20 to 30
yrs.; Girl- 5 to 10 yrs ; Girl- 10 to 15 yrs. ; Girl - 15 to 20 years.
3. ELIZABETH WHITFIELD- STURDIVANT. Elizabeth married Benjamin
Sturdivant.
4. FRANCIS WHITFIELD who was called "Franky." She was born Feb.
14 , 1765. In 1794, she carried the name of Francis Whitfield in the Will
of her father , and he left cash to her. Unmarried.
5. MARTHA PATTY WHITFIELD, b. March 16, 1767 . She married William
Hobbs in 1789.
6. WILKINS WHITFIELD , b. 1770. Wilkins Whitfield married POLLY
MARY STURDIVANT in 1801 . They had seven boys and four girls.
   1. Henry (b. 1802 Va- died before 1850 , Tenn.). Married and had
      son, Henry Whitfield.
   2. George W. (b. 1806 Va. - died 1894 Texas). He married wives.
      Children at Dallas County, Tennessee.
   3. William Whitfield.
   4. Harrison (b. Tenn. -)
   5. Thomas Jefferson (1810 Tenn- 1873 Tenn.). Records of this book
      from pages 75 to 103 are of this lineage.
   6. John Wilkins (1818 Tenn- 1879 Texas). He married Catherine
      and then Sarah .
   7. James Monroe (1819 Tenn - d.   Texas). He married , and
      moved to Texas with his family.
   8. Martha Ann (b. 1812-d. 1847 Tenn.). She married Robert Charter.
   9. Theodosia (b. 1816 - d. 1839 Tenn.) She married William G.
      Clagett.
   10. Virginia C. (b. 1821 ca- Tenn.). She married Dr.Daniel Cliffe.
   11. Sarah, b. 1817. She married Daniel Mc Phail and James Nichols.
7. BETTY WHITFIELD called Betsy. She was born 1774. She married
   Benjamin Sturdivant in 1793.
8. NANCY WHITFIELD , b. 1774, the youngest daughter. She married
   William Knight in 1799.
9. HARRISON WHITFIELD , b. 1778 ca. but Tennessee Record has the
   birth in 1783 , and died 1864 .
10. JACK ("JOHN") WHITFIELD , born 1780 , the youngest child.

   All of the births and marriages in Sussex County, Virginia , but the
family migrated to Williamson County, Tennessee in 1808 , and the death
records are in Williamson County, Tennessee and near there. The children and descendants are of Tennessee except for the few that moved to
Texas , or Missouri and Kansas. Whitfield Families at Hickman County,
Tennessee and other Counties , and many still live at Tennessee in 1979.

Thomas Whitfield probably had a brother named Robert Whitfield who was ten years older than himself and living near him in Sussex County, Virginia at the Albemarle Parish.

Ancestors relatives are believed buried at the old Lawne's Creek church ground. The ancestors believed to be of Isle of Wight and Nansemond Counties.

In 1770 the Whitfield Family in Sussex County, Virginia of the Albemarle Parish were associated with Anne Whitfield, Donald Mc Innish, Sarah Mc Innish, Mary Lessenberry, Elizabeth Gilbert, Amy Sledge, John Shands, John Mason. The Sturdivant families. The Hobbs families. The Tomlinson families.

Thomas Whitfield was a planter and farmer. He died and left a will in 1794. Winifer Whitfield and the children of hers with their own families were established in Williamson County, Tennessee at Franklin. They had left for new land in the west at Tennessee in 1808. The land is the grants of Harrison Whitfield, grant no. 12406, 50 acres, Davidson County, Tennessee; and a grant of land # 12232, March 5, 1834; and a grant of land # 13086, June 1835. William Whitfield probably also had a grant of land of this family.

The descendants of these Whitfield family had land in Virginia of Thomas Whitfield, and new lands for Whitfield families were opened at State of Tennessee, State of Texas, State of Missouri, and State of California.

The wife and mother, Winifer Whitfield lived in Tennessee with her sons Harrison Whitfield and Wilkins Whitfield. She lived to be very old. A death notice appeared in the WESTERN WEEKLY REVIEW of Franklin, Tennessee dated July 13, 1838: "On Monday 9th at the residence of Wilkins Whitfield, Esq. Mrs. Whitfield, a upwards of 100 years. She lived long, respected, loved and esteemed by all who knew her, and died in good old age, mourned, regretted by a large circle of relatives and friends." Thus she died on July 9 - 1838 in Franklin, Tennessee.

WHO WAS THE FATHER AND GRANDFATHER OF
THIS THOMAS WHITFIELD MARRIED TO WINIFER
AND LIVING IN SUSSEX COUNTY, VIRGINIA ?

WHO WERE THE ANCESTORS ? WHAT WERE THE NAMES
OF THEIR GRANDCHILDREN AT WILLIAMSON COUNTY,
TENNESSEE ?

Any person in the United States or another country have more information on this family lineage ? Send it to the author, Vallie Whitfield, 1841 Pleasant Hill Road, Pleasant Hill, California 94523.

WILL OF THOMAS WHITFIELD , 1794 , Sussex County, Virginia.

"In the name of God. Amen. I, Thomas Whitfield of the County of Sussex and parish of Albemarle being weak of body but sound of mind and disposition and in memory and calling to mind the uncertainty of this human life do make and ordain this my last Will and Testament in manner and form following that today.

First, I recommend my soul to God who gave it me and my body I desire may decently intered at the discretion of my Executors hereafter mentioned and as for what worldly goods it hath pleased God to bestow on me my will and desire it they shall be disposed of in manner and form as following. Inprimis I lend to my loving wife WINIFER WHITFIELD during her natural life or widowhood all the lands I now possess also my following negroes mainly Savei, Sylva and Hampshere also all my household furniture of every kind except such as I shall hereafter mention.

Item. I give to loving daughter FRANCIS WHITFIELD one feather bed and furniture one pine chest and ten pounds in cash to be raised out of my estate to her and her heirs and assigns forever.

Item. I give to my loving daughter MARTHA HOBBS one feather bed and furniture and pine chest one iron pot one table and one cow, and heifer which she hath now in possession to her and her heirs forever.

Item. I give to my daughter BETSY STURDIVANT one negro girl named Grease she and her increase to her and her heirs and assigns forever.

Item. I give my loving NANCY WHITFIELD one negro girl named Dinah she and her increase also one feather bed and furniture also one cow and calf, one pine chest to her and her heirs forever.

Item. I give to my loving son HARRISON WHITFIELD one sorrel filley to him and his heirs forever.

Item. I give to my three sons WILKINS WHITFIELD, HARRISON WHITFIELD and JACK WHITFIELD all my lands at my wifes death or marriage.

Item. My will and desires that all that part of my estate I here before lent to my loving wife WINIFER WHITFIELD should be at her death or marriage exposed for public auction by my executor on twelve months credit and the money arising from the sale there of be equally divided between my three sons WILKINS WHITFIELD, HARRISON WHITFIELD, and JACK WHITFIELD to be equally divided between them to them and their heirs forever.

Item. I will and desire that the money due to me from different people may be collected by my executors or execute and applied to this payment of my lawful debts and if any be left my will and desires is the remaining parts should be put to the use of raising my three youngest children Viz Nancy Whitfield , Harrison Whitfield , and Jack Whitfield.

Item. My Will and desire is that my Estate be not appraised. I do constitute and appoint my loving wife Winifer Whitfield and my worthy friend Benjamin Mason my lawful executors of this my last Will and Testament hoping they may all have every part of the same executed agreeable to the same.

Item. Lastly I do hereby revoke all former Wills and bequest heretofore made by me and do declare this and no other to be my last Will and Testament.

Signed. Sealed and publish and declare this to be my last Will and Deeds.

Signed sealed and delivered in presents of Fedk. Sillev, William Whitfield . THOS. WHITFIELD "

"At Court held for Sussex County the 4 th day of December 1794.

The last Will and Testament of THOMAS WHITFIELD . Deeds was presented into Court by WINIFERD WHITFIELD. The executrix therein named the same was proved by the Oaths of WILLIAM WHITFIELD and Frederic Sillv the witnesses thereto and ordered to be recorded and motion of the said Executrix who made Oath and gave bonds and security according to Save Certificate is granted her for obtaining aprotake thereof in due form. Examined. Testa. Michael Bailey, csc "
Probate Court 1794 . Albemarle Parish . Sussex County, Virginia. "

REFERENCES:(1) The Albemarle Parish Register, Sussex County, Virginia. (2) Marriage Bonds and Ministers Returns of Sussex County, Virginia 1754 - 1810 . (3) Oath of Allegiance to Revolution. Copy at D.A.R. File # 523756. (4) U.S. Census of Virginia, 1790. The 1782 Census enumeration. (5) "Whitfield History and Genealogy of Tennessee," first edition published 1964. (6) "Virginia History and Whitfield Biographies" by Vallie Whitfield, pub. 1976 , Whitfield Books publishing. Pages 33-66-68-73-75-101-103-108-118-124-147-158-159-180- 222-223-224 pages this sketch appears - 228 - 244- 245- 251-252- 266- 267- 271 - 281 - 297 - 301 - 302- 305 -312 -313- 316- 347.

Reprint of the Albermarle Parish Register 1717-1778 of Sussex County, Virginia and records in the book , "Births , Deaths and Sponsors from the Albemarle Parish 1717-1778 Register of Surry and Sussex Counties, Virginia " , by John Bennett Boddie , pub. 1958.

WHITFIELD
15th to 20th Century
GENEALOGY
England
Virginia
Tennessee
California

JOHN WHITFIELD 1561 of England . Generations in   England.

Immigrant to North America Colony. 16th Century. Generations 1-2-3 .

WT4   WHITFIELD = ANNE WHITFIELD # 8 , Virginia.

WT5 #265 THOMAS WHITFIELD=1759ca WINIFER WHITFIELD #297
Sussex County, Virginia   Ten children.

WT6 # 272 WILKINS WHITFIELD = 1801 POLLY STURDIVANT #214 (11c)
(b.1781ca Sussex Co., Va-d.1841)
Wilkins and Polly Mary had eleven children. Williamson Co., Tennessee

WT 7 THOMAS JEFFERSON WHITFIELD =1829 ELIZA NOLAN (2c)
(b.1810 Williamson Co. -d.1873 Hickman = 2nd wife, SALLIE L. DILLAHUNTY1835
of Perry Co., Tennessee)   Nine children.   (7c)

WT 8 THOMAS JEFFERSON WHITFIELD = 1866 M.L. Cunmingham (3c)
Hickman Co., Tennessee.   = 2nd wife, April 1875 , Martha Jane Nicks (6c)
(1845-1908)   Nine children.
WT 9 JAMES DEE WHITFIELD = 1899 MARY HESTER MC KEEL (4c)
(1877-1954) Humphreys Co., Tennessee . Waverly town.
= 1926 2nd wife, Oda DePriest-Hensley-Daniel (Perry Co., Tenn.)
Four children:Raymond, Ralph, Robert, Rozelle; 2 children Ruby Hensley & Frances D.

WT 10 ROBERT EDWARD WHITFIELD = 1943 VALLIE JO FOX (4c)
(b.1921-living 1979) Lived Humphreys & Davidson Counties, Tennessee and Pleasant Hill town,
Contra Costa County, California . (She b. 1922-living 1979)
Four children: Christa , Robert (1948-1971), James David , Joanne . -California
Grandchildren : Jason Bundy, b. 1970, Natasha Bundy, b.1973 -California, Alameda Co.
Justin Bundy, b. 1975 .

WT 11 JAMES DAVID WHITFIELD. b. Feb. 21,1953 .   Contra Costa County, California

England to Virginia of United States , and to Tennessee.
GENEALOGY OF WHITFIELD.

1165 ROBERT WHITFIELD, Chaplain of Countess Ada. England. Generations.

1561 JOHN DE WHITFIELD . England

1590 _____ WHITFIELD . England

1635 John Whitfield = Mrs. Whitfield 1638 . Or another named.
1636 William Whitfield = Anne Whitfield 1640.

1660 _____ WHITFIELD = Mrs.Whitfield - Virginia.

1700 _____ WHITFIELD = ANNE WHITFIELD . Virginia.

1735 THOMAS WHITFIELD = WINIFER WHITFIELD , Sussex County,
      Virginia.   (1735ca-1794 Va.)   (1740 ca. - 1838 Tennessee)

1770 WILKINS WHITFIELD = POLLY MARY STURDIVANT WHITFIELD
      (1770 ca. Virginia- 1851 Tennessee)   (1780 ca. - 1850 living Tenn.)
      Sussex County, Virginia to Williamson County, Tennessee.

1810 THOMAS JEFFERSON WHITFIELD = SALLIE DILLAHUNTY .
      (1810 Tenn. - 1873 Tenn.)   (1817 Tenn. - 1885 Tenn.)

1845 THOMAS JEFFERSON WHITFIELD = MARTHA JANE NICKS
      (1845 Tenn. - 1908 Tenn.)   (1817 Tenn. -1885 Tenn.)

1877 JAMES DEE WHITFIELD = MARY HESTER MC KEEL
      (1877 Tenn.- 1954 Tenn.)   (1878 Tenn. - 1924 Tenn.)

1921 ROBERT EDWARD WHITFIELD = VALLIE JO FOX
      (1921 Tenn. - living 1979 California) (1922 Tenn. - living 1979
                                              California)
1953 JAMES DAVID WHITFIELD
      (1953 California - living 1979 California)
      Sister, JOANNE VALLIE WHITFIELD (195 5 California -)
      Brother . ROBERT EDWARD WHITFIELD 1948 Massachusetts- died
        1971 Africa at Ghana.
      Sister , CHRISTA MARIE WHITFIELD BUNDY (1945 California-
      living 1979 California.) She had children :
1970 JASON EDWARD BUNDY (1970 California -).
1972 NATASHA MARIE BUNDY (1972 California -).
1975 JUSTIN ALEXANDER BUNDY (1975 California -).

THOMAS WHITFIELD (1735-1794 Va.) AND WINIFER WHITFIELD (1740ca-1838)
had ten children , four boys and six girls. They moved from Sussex County,
Virginia to Franklin, Tennessee of Williamson County in 1808.
The daughters were Mary Hobbs , Elizabeth Sturdivant, Martha Patty Hobbs,
Betsy Sturdivant, Nancy Knight , Francis Whitfield. The sons were the following

WILLIAM WHITFIELD 1762-18--	WILKINS WHITFIELD 1770-1851	HARRISON WHITFIELD 1783-1864	JACK "JOHN" WHITFIELD b. 1780 Va.
wife, Elizabeth Tomlinson	wife, Polly Mary Sturdivant	wife, Polly Sledge	wife
They had children.	They had eleven children :	They had ten children:	They had children
Grand- Son, William Whitfield	William Whitfield Henry Whitfield George W. Whitfield Thomas Jefferson W	Five boys, Five girls. Thomas Whitfield Harrison Whitfield	Son, John Whitfield
wife and seven children in 1830 : Four boys ages between 1- 20 to 30 years 2-5 to 10 years 3- 5 to 10 years 4- under 5 years Three girls ages between 1- 15 to 20 years 2- 10 to 15 years 3- 5 to 10 years	John Wilkins W James Monroe W. Harrison Whitfield Martha Ann W. Theodosia Whitfield Sarah Whitfield Virginia Whitfield	Boy- died young Boy- Boy- Rebecca Whitfield Nancy Whitfield Girl Girl Girl	Some names: Felix John Henry William Wilkins James

++++++++++++++++++++

Thomas Jefferson
Whitfield had nine
children : 5 boys
Henry   &4girls
Martha
Silas
Jack
George
Thomas Jefferson
Sarah
Mary
Josephine

+++++++++++++++++

Thomas Jefferson
Whitfield had nine
children : Jefferson,
Salle, Lillie, Henry,
James Regan,
Thomas Cleveland,
James Dee
Clara , Delie

+++

James Dee Whitfield
had four children :
James Raymond
Ralph Wilson
Robert Edward
Hester Rozelle

Robert Edward Whitfield
had four children :
Christa Marie
Robert Edward
James David
Joanne Vallie

Christa M. Whitfield Bundy
had three children :
Jason Edward Bundy
Natasha Bundy
Justin A. Bundy

THOMAS
WHITFIELD
1735-1794
& Winifer
Whitfield
Had ten
children:
WILKINS ——→
WILLIAM
HARRISON
JACK "John"
Mary
Elizabeth
Martha Patty
Betsy
Nancy
Francis

Wilkins Whitfield # 51
& Polly Mary
Had eleven
children:
William
Henry
George W.
Thomas J.
John Wilkins
James M.
Harrison
Martha Ann
Theodosia
Sarah
Virginia

THOMAS JEFFERSON # 53
WHITFIELD had
nine children:
Thomas J. ——→
Martha
Silas
Jack
George
Henry
Sarah
Mary
Josephine

Thomas Jefferson # 85
Whitfield had
nine children:
Jefferson
Salle
Lillie
Henry
James Regan
Thomas C.
James Dee ——→
Delie
Clara

James Dee # 101
Whitfield
had four
children:
James Raymond
Ralph Wilson
Robert Edward ——→
Hester Rozelle

Robert # 131
Edward
Whitfield
had four
children:
Christa Marie Bundy #143
Robert Edward
James David
Joanne Vallie

Jason Bundy
Natasha Bundy
Justin Bundy

DANIEL MC PHAIL (1799-1846) and SARAH WHITFIELD MC PHAIL
NICHOLS (1817-   ).

Dr Daniel Mc Phail ,born in Inverness, Scotland in 1799. The
Mc Phail family settled in Williamson County, Tennessee. On October ll,
1831 , Dr Daniel Mc Phail married Sarah Whitfield . Her parents , Wilkins
Whitfield and Polly Mary Sturdivant Whitfield lived at Franklin . Dr Mc
Phail office was the brick building located on East Main Street in Franklin,
Tennessee , and thought to have been built in early 1813. It is said, the
first anesthetic successfully used in Middle Tennessee was administered
by Dr Mc Phail about 1831 when he treated a man for gunshot wounds in
this building . In 1846 Daniel Mc Phail died while serving as a   surgeon
in the United States Army in the Mexican War. A monument in old City
Cemetery in Franklin , Tennessee marks his final resting place.

At Dr Mc Phail's death , Dr Daniel Cliffe (1823-1913) inherited a
part of his uncle's estate under a partnership agreement. In 1849 Sarah
Whitfield Mc Phail , the widow , married James Nichols and moved to
Hickman County, Tennessee where two of her sisters , Martha Ann (Mrs.
Robert) and Theodosia (Mrs.William G. Claggett), had previously moved.
Their seven brothers , Henry (b. 1802 Ca- died before 1870) , George
(1806 Va. - 1894 Texas) , William , Harrison , Thomas Jefferson (1810
Tenn. - 1873 Tenn.), John Wilkins (1818 Tenn. - 1879 Texas) , James Monroe
(1819 Tenn- 18-- Texas) were prominent residents in Williamson County,
Tennessee for several years.

The youngest sister, Virginia C. Whitfield married Dr Mc Phail's
nephew , Dr Daniel B. Cliffe on November 15 , 1842. Daniel Bonapart
Cliffe (1823-1913) came from Ohio as a boy of thirteen to live with his
uncle in Franklin . He began the study of medicine under Dr. Mc Phail's
guidance. Daniel Cliffe was the son of Joseph Stephen Cliffe who was
born in London, England in 1799 and Isabella Mc Phail Cliffe born in
Scotland that same year of 1799. They were married in Wooster , Ohio
in 1822. Isabella after his death married R.W. Smith of Vermont , and
they had a daughter , Julia A. Smith , born in Ohio in 1828. Isabella lived
at Franklin and died in 1891.

Dr Cliffe used Dr Mc Phail's office to see his patients , and later
the yard and house adjoining became his residence. When the Civil War
broke out in 1861 , Dr Cliffe served in the Twentieth Tennessee Regiment
as General Felix Zollicoffer's Brigade Surgeon. After a while , Dr Cliffe
disenchanted with the Confederacy, espoused the cause of the Federal
forces, and used his influence wherever possible to intervene between the
Union Army and the townspeople.

The name of Dr Daniel B. Cliffe has always been synonymous with
the highest medical knowledge in Franklin , Tennessee. The medical

excellence was carried on by his grandson , also with the name of Dr Daniel Cliffe.

In later years, the Mc Phail-Cliffe medical office building was used many years as the Henerson law offices, and in 1960 both the office and Cliffe home were still preserved in Franklin.

JOHN MATTHEWS WINSTEAD (1807 - 18   ) AND NANCY WHITFIELD WINSTEAD (1811 - 1885)

When the Winstead family members first came to Williamson Co. , Tennessee they came from Northumberland County, Virginia, and settled on Mill Creek between Brentwood and Nolensville in 1799. They first lived in a log cabin. It continued their home until a majestic brick house , tree embowered and white-columned, was constructed on higher ground to the north between 1855-58. Colonel John M. Winstead and his family moved into the brick house in the spring of 1858. It was and continues to be one of the County's most beautiful and elegant ante-bellum homes with its long shady ell and stately pillars. It was built to face south toward the old Nolensville-Franklin Road, the bed of which is still visable , and that pike was abandoned and the entrance to the place was changed to Concord Road. Colonel John Winstead has a colorful family and Civil War history, and he died in 1896. The house is on Pleasant Hill and is called B. Pleasant Hill, home of Colonel John Matthews Winstead (-d. 1896).

The son, John Matthews Winstead was born in the old log cabin to the parents on March 9 , 1807. When he was twenty years old he married Nancy A. Whitfield (1811-1885) of that location , the daughter of Harrison Whitfield (1783 V a. -d. 1864 Tenn.). To this union were born three daughters Mary E. , Lucy T. , Ida , and nine sons. James M. , Harrison , John M. , Walker , William , Robert O. , Meredith , Thomas E. and Winfield S. Five of these sons were soldiers in the Confederate Army. Harrison Whitfield lived with the Winstead Family in his old age. The family cemetery is near the house where parents , grandparents , other relatives, and their best loved servants   rest .

William E. Winstead (1837-1911) was the fifth son of John Matthew Winstead and Nancy Whitfield Winstead whose home , Pleasant Hill, was near Brentwood. He held an office in the courthouse in Williamson Co. This beautiful house, Winstead Place ,passed out of the family hands when the house and eight and eight-tenths acres were bought from the last heir relative in November 1956.

_____

"Historic Williamson County " of Tennessee by Virginia Bowman.

GEORGE W. WHITFIELD   (Wilkins , Thomas ,   )
     George Washington Whitfield was the second born son   of
Wilkins Whitfield and Polly Mary Sturdivant Whitfield from Virginia.
He was born February 12, 1806 in Sussex County, Virginia. In 1808 the
family moved to Williamson County, Tennessee. The father. Wilkins
Whitfield spent the residue of his days , dying at the age of sixty. His
mother lived to be eighty years old.   The names of their eleven children
are as follows : Henry , George W. , William, Harrison, John Wilkins ,
Thomas Jefferson , James Monroe , Martha Ann - wife of Robert Charter,
Sarah - wife of Dr.Daniel Mc Phail , and after his death the wife of James
Nichols, Theodosia - wife of William Clagett , and Virginia - wife of
Daniel B. Cliffe .

     George W. Whitfield has been twice married. In 1836 , he wedded
Miss Louisa King , by whom he had three children :
     1. Daniel Whitfield   2. Virginia Whitfield - wife of Rev. Oliver
     Parker   3. Sarah Whitfield , deceased .
The wife, Louisa King Whitfield departed this life in 1848 in Tennessee,
at the age of twenty-five years. George W. Whitfield purchased land at
Council Bend on Duck River , Whitfield Town in Hickman County where
his brother , Thomas Jefferson Whitfield lived. George Whitfield left
several Tennessee Court records .

     On March 5th , 1849 George Whitfield married Sarah Bond in William-
son County, Tennessee . At Franklin town of this County is where George
grew up to be a man. Miss Sarah Bond was born in Tennessee, April 1 ,
1822 , daughter of John Bond and Sarah (Hunter) Bond . Her mother died
in 1822 , at the age of thirty-one years, and her father passed away in
1848, aged seventy- two. After the death of her mother her father married
again. By his first wife he had seven children , Mrs. Whitfield being the
youngest. The names of her brothers and sisters are Lucy , wife of George
Holland ; Joseph ; Mary, wife of Nusum Barham ; Nancy , wife of James
Southall ; John P. ; Catharine, wife of William Trimble. Mr Bond's second
wife was before her marriage Mary Anderson . She bore him eight children:
William ; Angeline, wife of John Sandefer ; Elizabeth , wife of Samuel Thompson ; Susan , wife of William Crutcher ; Myra , wife of Mr. Bingham ;
Martha , wife of Thomas White ; Henry and George.

     George W. Whitfield was a gentleman farmer in a changing society.
He had slaves , for farming , he paid for one female slave in Hickman
County records. He had one hundred acres of land on the south side of
Duck River bound on the north and west by John Montgomery , August 1849.

     George and Louisa Whitfield lived in Whitfield Town , Tennessee . He
lived on six hundred acres bounded on east, north and west by Duck River ,
and on the south bound by lands of Elias and C. B. Dodson . He was living
there in 1847.   The minutes of Hickman County Court involve debts. He

purchased often   from the town's mercantile stores. He assisted his brothers Thomas Jefferson and John Wilkins in their military activities.

George W. Whitfield and Sarah came in December 1849 to Texas making the journey by water by way of Shreveport. He first located in Harrison County , where he lived four years. Then, after a year spent in Limestone County , he came to Dallas County, Texas and purchased 160 acres of land , located a mile northwest of where Garland now stands. He afterward made money enough to increase his landed estate to 900 acres. This land he later divided among his children , with the exception of 240 acres reserved for himself and wife. In 1891 he was eighty-five years of age, and to all appearances held a lease on life for some time to come. His wife, Sarah Bond Whitfield was sixty-nine and full of life and vigor.

When George Whitfield and family settled in Dallas County , Texas the country was sparsely inhabited. All their goods had to be hauled from Houston with ox teams. The Indian and the buffalo had left the country the year previous to his arrival in Dallas County. Game of all kinds was plenty. Their meal they ground in a steel mill something on the style of the old - fashioned wall coffee-mill. George and Sarah Whitfield lived to see all their children married except one son. The children by his last marriage are as follows : 1. John Whitfield 2. Thomas Whitfield 3. Dundenah Whitfield , wife of Charles Kennon 4.   Belle   Whitfield , wife of William Prigmore 5. Eugenia Whitfield , wife of L. P. Cabaniss 6. Walter C. Whitfield , twin brother of Mrs. Cabaniss 7. Davis Whitfield , wife of John Clemenson who was deceased .

In all George W. Whitfield was the father of four sons and six girls. The sons were Daniel , John , Thomas, Walter C. The girls were Virginia, Sarah , Dundenah , Anna Belle , Eugenia , Davis .

George Washington Whitfield had brothers to move from middle Tennessee to the State of Texas and they were John Wilkins Whitfield , James Monroe Whitfield , Harrison Whitfield ; and the nephews that moved to Texas were Henry Whitfield , John Anthony Whitfield , and probably William Whitfield.

The Mexican War had won the western land for the United States . Whitfield had been given land holdings   which was sold for little of nothing. General John Wilkins Whitfield had a part in the development of Texas. Thus George Whitfield lived there and died at Garland Town , Texas.

"Memorial and Biographical History of Dallas County, Texas ." 1892 pub. by Lewis Publishing Co., Chicago, Ill. , Whitfield on pages 615, 616.

Genealogy.   THOMAS RUSH WHITFIELD AND ELIZABETH
MORGAN STOLTING WHITFIELD.

Elizabeth Morgan of Missouri , first married Frederick Stolting in Missouri. Elizabeth was the daughter of James Morgan. Elizabeth Stolting then married second husband Thomas Rush Whitfield in Carrollton town of Missouri. Elizabeth was born in Carroll County, Missouri. In the first marriage, Frederick and Elizabeth Stolting had one child , Mattie Stolting .

The parents of Thomas Rush Whitfield were residents of Tennessee where he was born . Thomas R. Whitfield left Tennessee in 1849 , and moved to Pike County in Missouri. One of the first Whitfield members of a middle Tennessee family. He enlisted in the Civil War in Pike County and was discharged in 1865.   # 90 Thomas R. Whitfield and Elizabeth Whitfield had three children born at Carrollton town, Missouri :

    # 91   1. Charles Rush Whitfield
            2. John William Whitfield . Unmarried.
                He was a Spanish American War Soldier.
            3. Ada Whitfield , died in 1920s.

91 .   CHARLES RUSH WHITFIELD (1865-   ).
        Charles Whitfield was married and to this union were born three children : 1. Grover Whitfield   2. Ada Whitfield   3. Nellie Whitfield who married Walter Mahaffey . They lived in Tulsa, Oklahoma in 1964. They had one child, Ada Pearl Mahaffey.
        Charles Rush Whitfield was married the second time to Ellen Jane Rinkenberger Robbins. Her first husband was Samuel Robbins. The children of Charles Whitfield and Ellen Jane Whitfield :
1. Ralph Henry Whitfield, born October 19 , 1899. He married Lida
    Simpson of New Jersey, where they reside in Nortonville, New
    Jersey in 1964.
2. Gladys Whitfield , born September 25 , 1901. Gladys married Philip
    Blake , who was deceased in 1964. Their children are Donna Lorraine
    Blake Eaton, wife of Max Eaton , Waterloo, Iowa.
    Barbara Jean, married , and living in Racine, Wisconsin in 1964.
    Ellen Betty Dimmitt, wife of Robert Philip , and they lived in 1964
    in California.
    Darryl Blake also lived in California in 1964.
3. Charles Rush Whitfield , born July 2, 1903.
4. Bessie Eveline Whitfield.
                    (Charles R., Thomas R.)
CHARLES RUSH WHITFIELD was born July 2, 1903 in Carrollton, Missouri. He married Lauris Ida Spencer. They had children :
1. Alice Clements Whitfield who married Zerrel T. Walker. Their child-
    ren are Thomas, Terry , Timothy , and Todd Whitfield Walker. They
    live in Amarillo, Texas. Alice C. Whitfield , their mother was born
    October 11, 1934.

2. Roberta Lauris Whitfield was born on December 31, 1936.
   Roberta Whitfield married Byron Lindsay Brown and they had a daugh-
   ter Lauris Lynn Brown. They reside in Dallas , Texas.
Charles and Lauris Whitfield reside in 1964 in Fort Collins, Colorado.
He travels over the ten great states in connection with the College at Fort
Collins and for the government.

BESSIE EVELINE WHITFIELD was born January 29 , 19___ , Missouri.
Bessie Whitfield married Errol Lynne Gailey and had children :
1. Mary Whitfield Gailey , born September 1931. She married Edward
   Williams. They had children : Sarah Ann Williams, Michael Edward
   Williams , Patrick Alan Williams. In 1964 the family lived in Fort
   Dodge , Iowa.
2. John Whitfield Gailey , born August 12, 1934 . John Gailey married
   Sheilah Sue Smith and had children : Mary Beth Gailey , John Wesley
   Gailey , Patricia Susan Gailey.
   John Whitfield Gailey is an attorney in Fort Dodge, Iowa where they
   reside in 1964.
3. Margaret Whitfield Gailey was born September 2, 1935. Margaret
   married Franklin Mick. Their children are Mary Eveline , Margaret
   Regina Lynne called Lindsay, Sidney Ellen, Kelly Elizabeth , Caroline
   Annette and Sheryl Sue. They live in Bismarck, North Dakota in 1964.
4. James Whitfield Gailey, born February 7 , 1937. James married
   Evelyn Frances Whelan , October 24, 1964 , and resided in Newell,
   Iowa near Storm Lake where he is an Attorney.

TENNESSEE

Tennesseans can credit the building of the Tennessee frontiers
to WILLIAM WHITFIELD (1743- 1817) , Wayne County, North Carolina ;
WILLIAM WHITFIELD (1764-1825) ; NEEDHAM WHITFIELD (1758-1812);
NEEDHAM WHITFIELD (1776- 1858) ; BRYAN WHITFIELD (1766- 1825);
LEWIS WHITFIELD ; AND WHITFIELDS ; JOSEPH GREEN and
FAMILIES : WILLIAM KILLEBREW and FAMILIES from North Carolina .
And from Bledsoe Region , North Carolina to Tennessee these men :
WILLIAM WHITFIELD 1792 ; JOHN WHITFIELD 1792 ; WILLIS WHITFIELD
(1761 N . C - 1826 Tenn.) ; JESSE WHITFIELD .

GENEALOGY OF WILLIAM WHITFIELD and SARAH ANN PRIGMORE
WHITFIELD of Texas and California.

William Whitfield was born in Tennessee, Feb. 18, 1831. This Whitfield family moved to Arkansas in 1841. In 1849 William Whitfield went to Dallas County, Texas. On October 28 , 1852 William Whitfield married Sarah Ann Prigmore , the daughter of Joseph Prigmore. She was born June 16, 1833 in Missouri. The Prigmore family moved to California in 1849 , then returned to Texas , and entered California again in 1854.

The Prigmore and Whitfield families went to California via the Utah route. First they settled at Scott's Valley where they engaged in mining. Later they moved to Danville, California in Contra Costa County. About 1860 , they returned to Texas for the livestock business. The Civil War found him in the Confederate Army and William Whitfield served for three years , and discharged in 1862, and after malaria and a bullet wound.

In 1870 the Whitfield family made their second trip to California by covered wagon. They settled at Cucamonga, California . William Whitfield and Sarah Whitfield had nine children :

1. Mary Jane Whitfield , b. July 7 , 1854 along the Green River , Utah , and died December 18 , 1928. On May 24, 1876 at Rivera , California Mary Whitfield married James Robert Pallett , b. July 27 , 1850 in Tennessee and died January 1, 1891 at Rivera. They had three sons.
2. Sarah Elizabeth Whitfield , born October 22, 1856 near Danville, California , and died February 12, 1916 at Rivera. She married on January 20 , 1873 to William Armstrong Pallett who was born Oct. 16, 1851 in Tennessee , son of George W. Pallett. He died November 22, 1931 in Santa Ana , California.
3. Joseph Benjamin Whitfield , born September 26 , 1859 and died October 31, 1862.
4. Mohala Lucinda Whitfield , born January 16, 1862 in Texas , and died June 12, 1932 in California.
5. William Crockett Whitfield , born March 14 , 1866 in Texas , and died December 30 , 1940 in Esticata, Oregon. William C. Whitfield married November 15, 1892 to Annie Myers who was born at Rochester, Pennsylvania , January 25, 1869 , and died Oct. 6, 1949 .
6. Lee Jettie Whitfield , born November 2, 1870 at Winslow, Arizona, and died January 30 , 1942 at Martinez, California, and buried at Bakersfield, California.
7. James Whitfield , born November 16, 1872 , and died Feb. 5, 1874.
8. Henery Alvan Whitfield , born March 4, 1876 , and died January 18, 1880.
9. Anna Belle Whitfield , born January 16, 1879 and died Nov. 21 , 1957. Anna Whitfield married January 17 , 1900 to Harry Wagner Milner, who was born Feb. 19, 1876 at Springfield, Missouri.

William Whitfield and Sarah Ann Prigmore Whitfield were among the first to come to California named Whitfield in 1854. A travel from Tennessee to Arkansas , and then to Texas , and westward to California.

About 1910 , William Whitfield and Sarah Whitfield moved to Pico-Rivera in California to be near their daughters, Mary Jane Whitfield Pallett, and Sarah Elizabeth Whitfield Pallett. Around the time of 1914 they moved to San Bernardino to live with their daughter , Mohala Lucinda Whitfield Montgomery. William Whitfield born in 1831 in Tennessee then died October 30 , 1915.

The widow , Sarah Ann Prigmore Whitfield lived with her youngest daughter Belle Milner . Sarah Whitfield died November 13 , 1917. William Whitfield and Sarah Whitfield are buried in Mountain View Cemetery , San Bernardino, California. *

These records have three with the name of Whitfield who had a stay at Arkansas , and several others who moved to Texas from 1849 to 1865.

Standing, from left: Sarah Elizabeth Whitfield Pallett; Anna Belle Whitfield Milner; Lee Jettie Whitfield Haag; Mohala Lucinda Whitfield Montgomery. Seated, from left: William Crockett Whitfield; Sarah Ann Prigmore Whitfield; William Whitfield; Mary Jane Whitfield Pallett.

* "History of Pomona Valley California " , pub by Historic Record Co, Los Angeles, California , 1920.

GENEALOGY CHART - WHITFIELD - MC KEEL - SCHIEFER - FOX

From England to Colony of Virginia , then to Tennessee in 1808.

Whitfield   Whitfield   Whitfield   Whitfield

THOMAS WHITFIELD = WINIFER
(1735 Va. - 1794 Va.)   (1758 - 1838 Tenn.)

WILKINS WHITFIELD = POLLY MARY STURDIVANT
(1781 Va. -1841 ca Tenn.)   (1780 ca. Va. - after 1850 Tenn.)

THOMAS JEFFERSON WHITFIELD = SALLIE DILLAHUNTA
(1810 Tenn. - 1873 Tenn.)   (1817 Tenn. - 1885 Tenn.)

THOMAS JEFFERSON WHITFIELD = MARTHA JANE NICKS
(1845 Tenn. - 1908 Tenn.)   (1817 - 1930 Tenn.)

JAMES DEE WHITFIELD = MARY HESTER MC KEEL
(1877 Tenn. - 1954 Tenn.)   (1878 Tenn. 1924 Tenn.)

ROBERT EDWARD WHITFIELD = VALLIE JO FOX
(1921 Tenn. - living 1979 Calif.)   (1922 Tenn. - living 1979 Calif.)

CHRISTA MARIE WHITFIELD   ,   ROBERT E. WHITFIELD
JAMES DAVID WHITFIELD   .   JOANNE VALLIE WHITFIELD

JOSEPH EDWARD FOX   = VALLEY SCHIEFER
(1882 Tenn. - 1942 Tenn.)   (1892 Ky - 1968 Washington, D.C.)

JOSEPH T.(Fuch) FOX   = ELIZABETH HEINER
(1832 Germany- 1883 Ky.)   (1842 Ky. - 1919 Tennessee)

JAMES MC KEEL 1766 b. Ireland; d. North Carolina
JAMES MC KEEL (1802 No. C. -1879 No. C.) = DARCAS WALKER(1800-1846)
WILLIAM HYMAN MC KEEL (1833 Tenn. -1880 Tenn.) = LOUISA HARDER
                                    (1839 - 1900 Tenn.)

MARY HESTER MC KEEL WHITFIELD (1878-1924 Tenn.)

JOSEPH SCHIEFER   = MARY
(1808 Hungary-1876 Ky.)   (1820ca Bohemia, Czechoslovakia- 1884 Ky.)

JOSEPH SCHIEFER =   ELIZABETH WILKINS
(1841 Austria - 1904 Ky.)   (1863 Germany - 1925 Newport, Ky.)

VALLEY SCHIEFER = JOSEPH EDWARD FOX (1882-1942 Tenn.)

VALLIE JO FOX = ROBERT EDWARD WHITFIELD

Christa Whitfield . Robert E. Whitfield . James David Whitfield
Joanne Vallie Whitfield .

SCHIEFER

The maternal lineage of Vallie Jo Fox Whitfield is Schiefer -Wilkins of Europe. The Schiefer name originated in the Germanic part of the Holy Roman Empire . The Seventeenth Century saw the addition of Bohemia and Hungary to the holding of land. In this location the Schiefer family history began.

JOSEPH SCHIEFER (1808-1876) resided in Hungary and Vienna, Austria and moved to Newport of Campbell County, Kentucky with his family. He married Mary about 1838 in Austria. Mary Schiefer was born 1820 in Bohemia of Czechoslovakia, and later died October 1884 in Newport , Ky.

The 1860 Census of Campbell County, Kentucky list Schiefer family : Joseph Schiefer , age 52, a vinegar merchant, born in Hungary and re - sided in Austria before coming to Kentucky.
The wife, Mary Schiefer , age 40 . The children : Four born in Austria, and they died in State of Kentucky. 1. Frank S. Schiefer , born 1839.
2. Joseph Schiefer , born 1841 .   3. Charles Schiefer , born 1845 in Aus - tria. 4. Rudolph Schiefer , born 1847 in Austria . 5 . Andrew , born 1854 in Kentucky.

JOSEPH SCHIEFER , a son , born 1841 in Vienna, Austria , and died 1904 in Newport , Kentucky of Campbell County. He married first wife, Francisca (1835-1883) . Joseph Schiefer married sec ond wife , Elizabeth Wilkins on July 10 , 1884 in Newport , Kentucky. She was born October 19, 1863 in Berlin , Germany , and came to Kentucky in 1877. She gave birth to three children . After the death of Joseph in 1904 she later married on May 3, 1913 Charles Feldman in Newport, Kentucky.

Joseph Schiefer and Elizabeth Wilkins Schiefer lived on Isabella Street in Newport town wher e Schiefer Inn was a saloon and restaurant. Three children were born of this marriage :
1. Charles Schiefer , born 1888 at Newport, Kentucky ; and died 1952 in Illinois. He married twice . A daughter, Margaret Schiefer , and two sons.
2. Valley Johana Schiefer , born March 13, 1890 ; and died March 6, 1968. in Washington, D. C. She married February 7 , 1907 JOSEPH EDWARD FOX , and they had five children all born at Nashville. Tennessee.
1. Daisey Elizabeth Fox , b. 1914, d. 1914.
2. Florence Elizabeth Fox , b. 1918 and died March 18, 1921.
3. Vallie Jo Fox , born 1922 ; and living 1979 in Pleasant Hill, Calif. She married Robert Edward Whitfield on March 26, 1943.
4. Charlotte Fanning Rita Fox, b. 1923 ; living 1979 in Washington,D. C.
5. Joseph Edward Fox , b. 1925 ; and living 1979 in Madison , Tenn.
3. Daughter, Austina Flora Marie Schiefer , born 1894 in Newport, Ky. and living in 1979 at Cincinnati, Ohio. She married , and had one son, Frederick Miller.

"Whitfield , Mc Keel , Fox , Schiefer Families " , published 1965. by Vallie Jo Whitfield.

F O X - HEINER

The lineage of Vallie Jo Fox Whitfield is of (Fuch) Fox and Heiner, and Schiefer. Mr. Heiner came from Germany about 1820 to Kentucky. He married Elizabeth about 1822. Mr. Heiner and Elizabeth Heiner had about 8 children, and more girls than boys. A son fought in the Civil War. They lived in Kentucky, and for a while along the Ohio river at Indiana , and then back to Kentucky. The Heiner family lived in 1842 at Hawesville in Hancock County, Kentucky. There the daughter , Elizabeth E. was born on December 15, 1842. About 1861 Elizabeth Heiner married Joseph T. Fox , a German immigrant about 1840 to Kentucky.

JOSEPH THEODORE FOX was born April 2, 1832 in the republic of Bohem of Bavaria, Germany ; and he later died June 29, 1883 at Nashville, Tennessee. In 1850 the Fuchs were settled in Kentucky in Simpson County and laid to rest in Greenlawn Cemetery at Franklin, Kentucky in Simpson County. Joseph T. Fox served as a soldier in the Confederate Civil War. He was a baker and candy-maker in Franklin, Kentucky and Nashville , Tennessee. From 1879 to 1946 the family lived at Nashville, Tennessee. Joseph Fox was the son of Joseph Fuch and Elizabeth Fuch. Name was translated language.

JOSEPH T. FOX , 1832 Germany ; and died 1883 Tennessee , and his wife , ELIZABETH E. HEINER FOX , b. 1842 Kentucky ; and died 1919 Tenn. They had eleven children. Two girls and nine boys. Nine of these children were born in Franklin, Kentucky , and half of them died there.

1. Theodore Joseph Fox , b. 1864 Ky ; died after 1919.
2. George Washington Fox , b. November 1, 1865 Ky ; d. Feb. 23, 1942 Tenn.
3. Fannie Fox, b. 1868 Ky ; d. 1873 Ky.
4. Charley Fox, b. 1870 Ky ; d. 1874 Ky.
5. Nettie Fox, b. 1872 Ky. She married Andrew Hager. She died 1953 Ky.
6. Albert J. Fox, b. 187- Ky ; d. 1952 Bridgeport, Connecticut.
7. Eugene Fox , b. 1875 Ky ; d. 1876 Ky.
8. Arthur Fox, b. 1869 Ky ; d. 1926 Cincinnati, Ohio.
9. Robert W. Fox, b. 1878 Ky ; d. 1878 Ky.
10. Bernard Fox, b. 1879 Tennessee ; d. 1946 Nashville, Tennessee.
11. Joseph Edward Fox, b. 1882 Tennessee ; d. 1942 Nashville, Tennessee.

Joseph E. Fox married Valley Johanna Schiefer on Feb. 7, 1907 at Newport, Kentucky , and moved to Nashville. They had five children : Daisey, Florence, Vallie, Charlotte, and Joseph. The daughter Vallie Jo Fox married Robert Edward Whitfield. They were the Fox family at Nashville, Tennessee.

Albert Fox married Mae Elizabeth Hoyt in 1912 and had William Fox, Marie Fox, and Dorothy Fox. They were the Fox family at Bridgeport, Connecticut.

Arthur Fox married 1912 Emma Hirschmiller and had a son, Arthur Fox at Cincinnati, Ohio.

Bernard Fox married Charlotte Sanders and their son was Richard Fox of Madison , Tennessee.

On January 7, 1919 Elizabeth Heiner Fox died at Nashville, Tennessee of Davidson County. While Elizabeth Fox had eleven children she had only nine grandchildren.

LIFE OF ROBERT EDARD WHITFIELD

CHEMICAL   SCIENTIS T

On August 11 , 1921 , Robert Edward Whitfield was born in Waverly, Tennessee of Humphreys County . Son of James Dee Whitfield (1877-1954) and Mary Hester Mc Keel Whitfield (1878 -1924). Grandson of Thomas Jefferson Whitfield (1845-1908) and Martha Jane Nicks Whitfield (1855-1930). The ancestors were residents of Tennessee , Virginia , and England .

1921 - 1927   Robert E. Whitfield was a youngest on the farm in the community of Waverly, Tennessee which had about two hundred families. Mother, Mary Hester Whitfield died May 15, 1924. Father married Mrs. Oda Daniel, April 17, 1926 in Humphreys County, Tennessee.

1927-1934   Primary education at Spann School of Waverly, Tennessee, a one room school house. Good scholastic record during elementary training.

1934   He entered Central High School , Waverly, Tennessee.
1935-1936   Sopohomore in High School . January 1936 , father , James Dee Whitfield was sick in hospital.
1937   Robert E. Whitfield became a farmer.
Father required son to remain out of school to assist him in farming , and to help meet the financial debts of the family.
November 1937 he was selected as a member of the National Honorary Beta Club for his previous scholastic work.
1938   Robert Whitfield chose to return to school. Entered the Junior class . Elected President of the Junior Class of Central High School.
1939   Senior year of High school. Robert E. Whitfield was President of the High School Science Club. He was a member of the Future Farmer of America Club , and President of that Club one year in school. Robert was Valedictorian of the Central High School at Senior graduation . He received his High School diploma , May 1939.

High School Studies :
English, Algebra , History, Civics,
            Physics, Chemistry, Economics, Agriculture.
Teachers:
        Dr. H. A. Gray taught science and mathematics.
        Miss Garrett - History and homeroom work.
        Mr. Behrens - Algebra.
        Miss Betty Lee Daniel - English
        Mr. Mc Clary and   Mr Young - Agiculture.
        Mr. Sabin - Chemistry and Geometry. He was
                a coach in Physical Education.
        Mr. Burrum , Principal of High School - Civics and
                Engli sh classes.
        Mr. Duncan - Physics. He was a coach in
                Physical Education.

Robert E. Whitfield walked eight miles a day in the junior and senior year to school and home. He was a member of the basketball team in High School and elected a term as Captain of the team. Central High School basketball team won 1939 in the district tournament,which was held at Cumberland University in Lebanon, Tennessee. The basketball team won two trophies but lost in final Regional Tournament to Perry County School in Tennessee.

Summer of 1939 The young life of Robert E. Whitfield was spent in Humphreys County, Tennessee on the farm and at school. In the teen-age years he went on a trip to East Tennessee to visit his parent's friends ; to Steele , Missouri to visit relatives ; to Louisville , Kentucky with his father on business ; and took a trip into Arkansas.

He decided to go on to school to learn more about the things he had studied in high school. Robert wrote many colleges and universities for information regarding their tuition , expenses of other nature , scholarships, and student jobs.

Harding College , Lynchburg College and David Lipscomb College awarded him scholarships.

Robert Whitfield wanted to go to a University of great rank. He applied at Louisiana State University , Alabama Polytechnic Institute , and the University of Tennessee. The University of Tennessee offered a National Youth Association job for the 1939-1940 year.

Robert E. Whitfield chose the University of Tennessee.
He planned to study electrical or chemical engineering , and was eager

to get in on four or five years of hard study and work. Beneath the transitory and fleeting affection for ROCKDALE was the impulse to get away from a set way of life into a new one. He wanted to see the world and learn more about life. The family financial status was uncertain at times and many failures wrecked his ambitions to remain on the farm, although he loved the broad fields of Rockdale Farm. In the summer months he had plowed and hoed in the fields and earned two hundred and seventy-five dollars for a tomato crop his parents had given him. Robert planned to enter the University of Tennessee on this and accept the National Youth Association job offer of twenty-five cents an hour. He could meet all the expenses the first year and then enter the cooperative engineering plan. This plan consisted of spending one quarter in school followed by a quarter of work in some job. The student would alternate in three months periods between school and work. The system of school and work required one year longer for completion than the four years.

September 1939   Robert E. Whitfield left the farm. His father said, "be a man , my boy." He entered the University of Tennessee, September 23 , 1939 and was a freshman student in chemical engineering . The National Youth Association job was an offer to do maintenance work in the chemical engineering building. The University also gave him a part-time job in the athletic association.

The winter quarter of school he decided to change to the College of Agriculture and had a view of going in Agronomy or Agriculture Engineering. He stayed in Agriculture for two terms.

Summer 1939   He was on the farm . At the end of the first year of college , he said , "I began to realize that life was difficult at most , there were no short cuts to success."

Fall 1940   Sopohomore student at the University of Tennessee. Robert E. Whitfield chose to be a chemistry student and settled in his college program. This was the beginning of the career in Chemistry.

Robert entered the second year of college with ten dollars only, and resumed the part-time job with the athletic association which consisted of waiting on the tables where the football team ate meals. In return for the work he was given his own meals.

He obtained a job with the Tennessee Valley Authority in the chemistry laboratory paying fifty cents a hour for three hours a week. He had the athletic job and one hundred dollars per quarter he borrowed from the Student Loan Fund of the University of Tennessee . The note was signed by James Dee Whitfield and Parker White. And with some money that Ralph Whitfield sent from home he got along through the Sopohomore year.

Summer 1940   The last summer at home on the farm in the college years. It was the summer that preparation were made for competitive examination for an appointment to the United States Military Academy or the United States Naval Academy. Europe was at war and a shadow of restlessness was cast over the American people. R.O.T.C. drill was required of boys at the University of Tennessee for discipline and country.

October 1940   Robert E. Whitfield took the competitive examination at Fort Knox , Kentucky for a military appointment to West Point Academy.

December 10 , 1940 Wirt Courtney, M. C., Sixth district of Tennessee, the House of Representatives of the Congress of the United States recommended Robert Edward Whitfield "to the War Department as Alternate for the Military Academy at West Point."

February 3, 1941 . In Addition to naming Robert Edward Whitfield alternate to the Military Academy at West Point, Wirt Courtney named him as Alternate to his appointment to the Naval Academy at Annapolis.

January 27 , 1942 . Wirt Courtney nominated Robert E. Whitfield as the First Alternate to the Naval Academy at Annapolis.

It was in the vigorous physical examination and educational testing of the examinations for the Academy that Robert E. Whitfield was told for the first time that someday he would wear glasses for his vision.

Winter 1941   Robert was settled in the College of Liberal Arts studying Chemistry. He continued on the R.O.T.C. program taking military science, and considered the recommendation to the Academy. He held jobs of fifteen to twenty hours a week in addition to his studies, and was a laboratory assistant with the Tennessee Valley Authority as employer. He worked in the analytical laboratory affiliated with the Chemical Engineering Research Group located at the University of Tennessee, and was a student in charge of this laboratory in the senior year.

Tennessee Valley Authority (1940-1943)
Part-time job. Research analysis of fertilizers , alloys and minerals, and analytical research work.

Summer 1941   Junior student at the University of Tennessee.

Fall 1941   Robert E. Whitfield and Miss Vallie Jo Fox registered for a chemistry class the same hour during the registration days. Misses Vallie Fox and Charlotte Rita Fox were sisters transferring to the University. In October Vallie Jo Fox was formally introduced to Robert E. Whitfield by his friend C. L. Stevens with whom he worked with at the Athletic Association. Carlyle Lewis Stevens had a class with her sister. Robert Whitfield and Vallie Jo Fox became friends.

July 1942 . Robert visits Nashville, and attends funeral of his friend's father, Joseph Edward Fox .

Fall 1942   Robert is a senior student at the University of Tennessee. Elected to Phi Kappa Phi November 19, 1942 , the University honorary society.
Robert invites Vallie Jo to visit the Chemistry Engineering laboratory, and courtship days are followed by an engagement in December 1942.

Winter 1943   Completed college in the winter of 1943 . Bachelor of Science degree in Chemistry , University of Tennessee.
Honorary Student.

College Studies :
Chemistry , engineering, english, mathematics, physics, botany, economics, agriculture, military science , physical education , german , french, geology . Many classes in chemistry , mathematics, physics.
Chemistry job offers were made in Tennessee, Texas , California through the University of Tennessee office.

Robert chose the job offer in California.

March 26 , 1943   Robert Edward Whitfield and Vallie Jo Fox married in Nashville, Tennessee. Wedding at St Marys Church, and afterwards they left Nashville on the Nashville and Louisville Railroad train. Transferred at Chicago, Illinois to the Union Pacific Railroad taking the Challenger Pullman car for three and one half days on the Overland route to California arriving April 1, 1943 in Oakland, California.

April 2, 1943   Residence in Berkeley, California .
Robert started work with Shell Development Company near Oakland.

April 1943 - July 1946   Shell Development Company . Employer
                          Emeryville, California .
                          Position - Chemist .
A member of a research chemistry science team which studied alkylations,

isomerizations, chlorinations, hydrogenations and oridation reactions of hydrogenations and oxidation reactions of hydrocarbons and related compounds. The group developed a successful commercial procedure for the catalytic hydrogenations of nitroxylenes to the corresponding amines. It also developed a successful process for the oxidation of propylene to acrolein.

1944 - 1946   Robert began the hobby of creative writing which served as the beginning for his scientific writings. In these years he wrote his autobiography , ROCKDALE FARM , a ninety thousand word book . A book on RELIGION ASPECTS . A book of PROSE AND POEMS.

April 1944. Received first I A World War II draft card, but granted military service deferment for classification in essential industry.

May 1943- July 1945 . Wife , Vallie Jo Fox Whitfield was employed with Shell Development Company . Position of Laboratory Technician.

December 30 , 1945   Daughter , Christa Marie Whitfield was born in Berkeley, California.

Winter 1946   When the World War II was announced as being at an end, Robert knew that he had only scratched the surface of the kingdom of knowledge and prepared to return to the University.

February 1946 . Ohio State University offered graduate assistantship in the Department of Chemistry . Letter to Robert E. Whitfield from Henry E. Wirth.

April 1946 . Recommended for appointment to a graduate assistantship in the Department of Chemistry for the year 1946-1947 by A. W. Laubengayer of Cornell University , Ithaca, New York.

June 1946 . Half-time student assistantship for private work offered by Paul D. Bartlett of Harvard University .

Summer 1946   They moved from California to Massachusetts. Travelled four thousand miles by railroad on the far Southern Pacific route to Tennessee to visit at Rockdale Farm of the Whitfield Family , then to Massachusetts.

September 1946   Robert E. Whitfield entered Harvard University , Cambridge , Massachusetts . Examinations. Full- time graduate student , all classes in chemistry. Studied under Professor

Paul D. Bartlett, Organic chemistry.

October 1946 . Accepted cooperative housing and work via the Univ-sity office. The wife, Vallie Jo held full-time job in domestic social service under the house and work program . Job activities of house-keeping and child care.
1946-1947 Resided at home of Mr. and Mrs. Charles Hovey (attorney) in Chestnut Hill, Massachusetts.
1947-1948 Resided at home of Mr. and Mrs. S. Everett Gleason (author and teacher) in Cambridge , Massachusetts.
1948-1949 Apartment in Brighton, Massachusetts.

November 21, 1948 . Son , Robert E. Whitfield , Jr. was born in Boston, Massachusetts.

Private Research Assistant. Professor Paul D. Bartlett, Harvard University (1946-1947).
General duties . Included library research on special assignments. Laboratory synthesis of very highly strained molecules. Initial studies on sulfur chemistry as related to vulcanization , and related work.

Harvard University , Department of Chemistry , Cambridge , Massachusetts . September 1947-1948 .

Graduate student in chemistry . Job position - Teaching Fellow. Quiz sessions and supplementary lecture sessions in general chemistry and qualitative analysis. Laboratory section leader , fifteen hours per week.

June 10 , 1948 Master of Arts degree. Harvard University . Announced by letter to him in 1947.
" Sir, I beg to inform you that at a meeting of
the President and Fellows of Harvard College
held May 20 , 1947 , you were appointed
Teaching Fellow in Chemistry
to serve for one year from July 1, 1947.
Your obedient servant ,
David W. Bailey, Secretary
To Robert Edward Whitfield.

1948- 1949 . Harvard University Graduate student in Chemistry. Scholarship plus tuition . $ 1, 100. 00 Grant from ALLIED CHEMICAL AND DYE COMPANY.

June 1949   Graduation . Harvard University .
              Doctor of Philosophy Degree (Ph. D.)

Chemistry thesis : Mechanisms of Reactions of Elementary
                   Sulfur in Solution.

Many applications to colleges and industries for a job . Job offer in
teaching at University of Georgia, at Athens , Georgia by Alfred W.
Scott ; and Fordham University , New York, New York .
Three job offers in industry.

July 1949-July 1951   Employed by American Cyanamide Company.
                        Bound Brook , New Jersey.

One year was devoted to the study of color lake and pigment formation;
study of molecular complexes and adronplan complexes. The second
year was concerned with development of correlations between structure
and electronic spectra of organic molecules, the objective being that
of prediction color correlations for providing better use of electronic
spectra in the general research programs in the laboratory for new
dyes, pigments, and related work.

In 1949 rented first house for family , resided New Brunswick , New
Jersey. Wife, Vallie Jo Whitfield attended Rutgers University.

July 1951. Left Company to return to California to live . Summer 1951,
resided in Oakland, California . January 1952 moved to Walnut Creek,
California.
January 1952   Purchased first home in Walnut Creek town . A house
and farm of five acres.

1952-1961   Whitfield Farm in Contra Costa County, California.
Happy years on the California chicken ranch. It was a house and farm
of five acres of land with a walnut and almond orchard beside a hill
top. A large chicken barn stood on the property. A parcel of original
land of the Mexicana Rancho Las Juntas . A parcel in Contra Costa
County, California.

The land in 1900 was on the division line of Las Juntas and Canada Del
Hambre original ranchos. In the mid - century it was a point on the
County map and boundary lines for towns of Lafayette , Walnut Creek
and Pleasant Hill.   The Smith family in 1916 acquired the land which
was the original Geary land parcel , and Mrs Smith was one of the
girls of the Rogers family on the north side of land parcel. The house
was built that year.

From 1916 to 1948 the land was twenty-five acres and owned by Smith ,
Mc Vicker , John Ward, and Charley Moore who divided the acreages
into two parts that were purchased by Bullock and then King. The owners of the north portion became King, Olney, Clarabell Bell and Robert
Whitfield. Robert and Vallie Jo Whitfield subdivided the land of three
acres into city lots. He kept the hill top of the Whitfield Farm and
purchased two lots of 3. 6 acres in Brookwood Acres from Lottie Frances
Withers. The Withers family was a ranch owner in Lafayette town and
held these lots since 1913. The farm became a subdivision and Whitfield
hilltop.

Thousands of people moved into the Diablo Valley of Contra Costa County
when it was still farm land with the new subdivisions , and finally all the
farm land was rezoned into quarter acre lots. In 1961 houses were built
around Whitfield Farm and the land was rezoned when plans were laid
for nine home sites. The residence address on Pleasant Hill Road ,
Walnut Creek , California was changed to Whitfield Court , Pleasant
Hill, California. The street was named Whitfield Court at the inter-
section of the road of Pleasant Hill Road . 1961 Pleasant Hill town was
incorporated.

The Whitfield hilltop remained in the family and passed to new owners
who built houses on the land . Eight acres of land developed . Robert
and Vallie Jo kept three-fourth of acre and the original house in
their possession for over thirty years.

<u>July 1951 - July 1958</u>   Employed by Dow Chemical Company
Pittsburg, California
Position - Senior Research Chemist.

Engaged in a variety of problems related to the synthesis and character-
ization of chelate resins , ion exchange resins and memberances , water
soluble polymers. Structural mechanism of polymerization active part
in the discovery and development of <u>Separan 2610</u> , a new flocculating
agent , and general utility water soluble polymer, additional problems
related to the synthesis of monomers were included as time permitted.

1958 Job terminated as part of a general layoff due to recession.

1951-1958 Robert E. Whitfield had been a member of the American
Chemical Society since 1944 , but he also became a member about 1953
in The Chemical Society of London , and a member in the American
Physical Society.

He was busy most of the time with his work at Dow Chemical Company ,

but, he worked the farm with the cooperation of his wife , Vallie Jo
Whitfield . Her parents, Jack , step- father and mother , Valley
Fox Westkamper visited the farm often on the weekends. In the evening
hours he studied and abstracted in Chemistry and contributed to the
Chemical Abstracts Journal over one hundred reviews of articles that
were published.
The Whitfields participated in the Great Books Program from 1951 to
1958. Robert returned to be a book leader of the discussions on the
Great Ideas of the Program in 1962-1963-1964 at the County Library.

February 21 , 1953 . Son, James David Whitfield was born in Berkeley,
California of Alameda County.

March 14, 1955 . Daughter , Joanne Vallie Whitfield was born in
Berkeley, California of Alameda County.

1958-1960 Robert completed at Diablo Valley College , Concord -
Pleasant Hill, California , eight college classes in business , manage-
ment, law , and real estate.

1960 California State Board on Real Estate examination passed. Robert
E. Whitfield granted real estate license and the privelege to operate
therein.

1963 Robert is a Boy Scout of American, Cub Master , Pack 230 ,
John Muir District , Northern California.

October 1958 - 1979 and continued .
 Employed by Western Regional Research Laboratory,
 United States Department of Agriculture ,
 Albany, California
 Positon - Principal Research Chemist .
United States Government application in twelfth Civil Service Regions ,
San Francisco , California. 03975 Civil Service form.
Name - Dr. Robert Edward Whitfield , Organic Chemist.

Research to increase the utilization of wool and mohair . This includes
basic research on the proteins of wool, chemical modifications of the
wool fiber , and investigations related to the causes of wool deterior-
ation and damage during processing , storage , or use. It also in -
volves applied research directed towards "easy care" wool products -
machine washability , permanent creasing, non-iron effects , improved
appearance in wear ; and improved "comfort" in wool products , stretch
yarns and fabrics , better drying behavior and the like . The so- called
 WURLAN process involving interfacial polymerization , for making

shrink-resistant wool was co-discovered in this work. Extensive study
of polymers , as substances for modification of wool , is included in the
research . Patent Application , Washington, D. C.

Writings and Publications of Robert Whitfield are numerous.
He has written mostly journal articles for publications and over a
hundred published articles. Chemical and Science Journals. These
titles are listed in the first edition , 1964 volume of this publication
title "Whitfield History and Genealogy of Tennessee."

Robert Whitfield did over one hundred Reviews of Articles , 1955-1960
for Chemical Abstract Journal , published by American Chemical Society.

Confidential Company Research Reports where written for Shell Development Company , 1943 to 1946. American Cyanamide Company , 1941 to
1958. Dow Chemical Company , 1951 to 1958 . United States Department of Agriculture, 1959 to 1979 and continued.

United States Department of Agriculture publications have had a national
and international response. Whitfield's articles appear in Textile
Research Journal , The Vortex , American Dyestuff Reporter ,
Journal Applied Polymer Science , Science , Bull. Centre de Re-
cherches de la Bonneteric (France) , Journal Organic Chemistry .

Robert Whitfield has written four books.

Robert has other print in small editions at Conferences and meetings.

.... 1961 - 1964 . Robert E. Whitfield gave fourteen scientific presenta-
tions of papers at Technical Conferences and Meetings in the United
States. These lectures were given in State of California , New Hampshire , Massachusetts , Louisiana , New York , Pennsylvania.

TRAVELOGUE . R. E. Whitfield and V. J. Whitfield travelled by rail-
road 9,000 miles : business , family visits , vacations (1943-1951) .
R. E. Whitfield and V. J. travelled by automobile 13, 500 miles ,
business trips (1953-1957).
R. E. Whitfield travelled by airplane 65, 000 air miles , United
States Government business and scientific meetings (1961-1975).

REFERENCES

Vallie Jo Fox Whitfield visited the Tennessee State Library and Archives in Tennessee , and searched thirty Counties of Tennessee in the indexed analytical records of the library that was sponsored by Mrs.John Trotwood Moore. It was in November 1963 that she located the Whitfields in the following Counties of Tennessee 1788 - 1875.

Montgomery County	Steward County
Sumner County	Rutherford County
Hawkins County	Hickman County
Washington County	Lawrence County
Knox County	Henry County
Robertson County	White County
Davidson County	Humphreys County
Williamson County	Coffee County
	Shelby County

- Sumner County, Tennessee . Deed Book # 1, 1793-1797 , p. 33.
-Hawkins County, Tennessee. Deed Book #1 , 1788-1800.
    W. P. A. Historical Records Survey.
-Stewart County , Deed Book 1804-1806.
-Civl War Service Records , Tennessee State Library and Archives.
-Tennessee Land Grants , Tennessee State Library and Archives ,
    Nashville, Tennessee.
- Notes in vertical file at Tennessee Archives and State Library.
- C E N S U S :
1810 Rutherford County, Tennessee , and 1820 .
1830 Census of Hickman County, Tennessee, and 1840 and 1850.
1830 Census of Haywood County, Tennessee.
1820 and 1830 Census of Williamson County, Tennessee.
1820 Census of Montgomery County, Tennessee.
1820 Census of Stewart County, Tennessee.
1850 Census of Henry County, Tennessee.
1820 Census of Giles County, Tennessee.
1850 Census of Humphreys County, Tennessee, and 1880 census.
1870 Census of Davidson County, Tennessee.
... 1790 Census of North Carolina ; and 1790 Census of Virginia.

-Tennessee Newspaper , KNOXVILLE GAZETTE , April 10, 1794.
- Histories : HISTORY OF TENNESSEE . Published by Goodspeed
    Company 1886 .
- Williamson County, Tennessee. WILLS AND INVENTORIES ,
    Vol B 1811-1818 , p.348 ; 1825-1830.
- Hickman County, Tennessee . COURT MINUTES 1844-1855.

REFERENCES

Analytical Index Public County Records of Tennessee , by Mrs.
John Trotwood Moore and friends, Tennessee State Library and
Archives , Nashville, Tennessee ....

- Williamson County, Tennessee . RECORDS OF WILLS 1825-1830.
    Part II, p. 282.
- Rutherford County, Tennessee. WILLS, SETTLEMENTS ,
    INVENTORIES . Vol. 7 , 1827-1830 , p 294 .
-Henry County, Tennessee. COURT MINUTES 1836-1849.
-TENNESSEE WILLS AND INVENTORIES : Washington County ; Hum-
    phreys County 1900-1950 ; Davidson County 1788- ; Cheatham County
    1856-1871 Volume ; Montgomery County 1793- ; Lawrence County
    1834 ; Rutherford 1827- 1830, Vol. 7 , p 294.

- Marriage Records : Compiled from State Library and Archives
    Analytical source by Vallie Jo Whitfield of Tennessee and California
    on the Whitfields of Tennessee :   Robertson County, Davidson
    County 1780-1914 ; Montgomery County 1793 - ; Humphreys 1850-;
    Hamilton County 1865-1870.

- Hickman County , Tennessee. COURT MINUTES 1844- 1855.
- Hickman County, Tennessee . COURT , GUARDIAN AND ADMIN-
    ISTRATOR SETTLEMENTS , 1847 - 1852.
- Maury County, Tennessee. COURT MINUTES 1836-1849 , Part I.
- Henry County, Tennessee. COURT MINUTES 1836-1849 , Part I.
-Sumner County, Tennessee. COURT MINUTES 1787 - 1805.
- Davidson County, Tennessee . SUPERIOR COURT MINUTES OF
    NORTH CAROLINA AND TENNESSEE 1788-1803 , Part I , and
    1805-1807 , Part I , and Courthouse Index Book 8, 1955-1960.
- Montgomery County, Tennessee. COURT MINUTES 1811-1813 ;
    1813-1815; 1817-1825.
- Washington County, Tennessee . COURT MINUTES 1802-1808.
-Humphreys County, Tennessee . COURT MINUTES 1930-1945.
- Stewart County, Tennessee (Steward) . COURT MINUTES 1811-1812 ;
    1815-1819.
- Wilson County , Tennessee . COURT MINUTES 1816-1819.
- Cheatham County, Tennessee. COURT MINUTES 1856-1860.
- Rutherford County, Tennessee . COURT MINUTES 1804-1842 ;
    1811-1812 Book E ; 1817-1818 Book L ; 1823-1824 Book S ; 1824-1825
    Book D.

- J. B. Killebrew , RECOLLECTION OF MY LIFE , Vol I , 1896.
- TRADITION by Whitfield Families living 1962 in the State of Tenn-
    essee, and their personal histories of Humphreys, Benton and
    Hickman Counties.

REFERENCES

- Letters of Clara May Whitfield, Mc Kenize, Tennessee 1961-2-3.
- Bible Record of the Whitfield Family in the possession of Clara May
    Whitfield
- Letters of Gladys Irene Whitfield Hatley, Holiday, Tennessee, 1962.
  (Jefferson Lafayette Whitfield and Descendants.)
- Manuscript of Margaret Rice Whitfield , Waverly, Tennessee, 1961.
  (Henry W. Whitfield and Descendants .)
- Manuscripts of Kate F. Maver , genealogist , Washington, D.C.
    Two papers 1963 , Daughters of American Revolution Library Search.
- Letter of Mrs. Oscar Beach , Clarksville, Tennessee, 1962.
- Letter of Ralph Wilson Whitfield , Paris, Tennessee , 1963.
- Letters of James Dee Whitfield and Oda Whitfield . Collection 1940-1960.
- Letters from Tennessee State Library and Archives Staff : Gertrude
    M. Parsley, Hermione D. Embry, Mrs. Cleo A. Hughes.
- General letters to Vallie Jo Whitfield 1960-1964 concerning her search
    on kinship families . Collection is records, papers, letters, pictures,
    and titled , WHITFIELD FAMILIES OF TENNESSEE.
- Letter by A. D. Hiller, Veterans Administration , Washington, D.C.
- Copy of Emma M. Whitfield's letter to Tennessee State Library, 1929.
- KENTUCKY RECORDS , Daughters of American Revolution books,
    Colonial Abstracts.
- SECOND CENSUS OF KENTUCKY 1800 . Taxpayers list. Kentucky
    State Library.
- Daughters Of American Revolution Lineage Books. Volumes.
- Library of Congress , and D.A.R. Library sources on Whitfields .
    Washington , D.C.
- D. A. R. French Lick Chapter Records , Davidson County, Tennessee.
    Copied by Sarah Tucker Blair. Indexed by Pauline Palmer.
- University of California Library, Berkeley, California.
- Mississippi Genealogical Records Committee, N.S. of D.A.R., 1950.
- INDEX TO PENSIONS , War Records , D.A.R. Library, Washington, D.C.
- Membership Roster And Soldiers Tennessee , Society of the D.A.R.
    1894-1960. Compiled by Edythe Rucker Whitley, 1961.
- WHO'S WHO IN AMERICA .
- Oakland Tribune Newspapers , 1950-1963.
- Telephone Directories , 1961, San Francisco , California , and
    Oakland, California.
- Williamson County, Tennessee . Censuses.
- "Maury County , Tennesseans Who Died in Texas." Vol XVIII, page 78.
- S. J. Clarke Publishing Company, TENNESSEE THE VOLUNTEER STATE,
    1769-1923.
- WHITFIELD FAMILIES OF TENNESSEE is the Collection of Records,
    and these are compiled into this book as WHITFIELD HISTORY AND
    GENEALOGY OF TENNESSEE.

REFERENCES

- BURGAMY AND ALLIED FAMILIES . Lineage of Miss Alma Gibson
  Burgamy , Birmingham, Alabama , pp 107-112.
- MEMBERSHIP ROSTER OF SOLDIERS. The Tennessee Society of the
  D. A. R. 1894-1960.
- A HISTORY OF RUTHERFORD COUNTY,   TENNESSEE , by C. C. Sims.
- KANSAS RECORDS and Public Library Sources , and Historical Sources
  on John Wilkins Whitfield.
- Schools , and Chemical Business Companies records , and the United
   States Department of Agriculture Records on Robert Edward Whitfield.
- Letters of Vallie Jo Fox Whitfield.
- Western Weekly Review Newspaper 1838.
- History of Tennessee, published 1886.
- Tennessee The Volunteer State 1769-1923.
- "Tennessee Cousin " by Worth S. Ray.
- "Old Albemarle And Its Absentee Landlords" by Worth S. Ray.
- Tennessee Genealogical Records, edited by Edythe Rucker Whitley,
   Vols. 1 to 10 , 1779- 1850 years.
- "Whitfield, Mc Keel, Fox, Schiefer Families ", published 1965, by
   Vallie Jo Whitfield , Whitfield Books publishing house.
- Manuscript of Bessie E. Whitfield Gailey of Storm Lake, Iowa, 1964.
- State of Tennessee, Vital Statistics Records. Humphreys and Davidson
   Counties.
- "The Knoxville News- Sentinel "Newspaper , Knoxville, Tennessee on
   February 28 , 1943 .
- "The Tennessean" Newspaper ,Nashville, Tennessee , 1943.
- " The Nashville Banner " Newspaper , Nashville, Tennessee , 1943.

STATE OF NORTH CAROLINA REFERENCES

Abbreviations found for North Carolina - N. C. and No. C.
- ABSTRACTS OF NORTH CAROLINA WILLS , 1768-1800.
- NORTH CAROLINA WILLS , 1680-1760 , by J. Bryan Grimes.
- PICTURESQUE CLARKSVLLE, TENNESSEE , 1887, by W. P. Titus.
- ROSTER OF NORTH CAROLINA SOLDIERS IN THE REVOLUTION.
   Published by North Carolina Press . D. A. R. 1932.
- THE LOYALISTS IN NORTH CAROLINA DURING THE REVOLUTION ,
   by Robert O. De Mond . University Press, 1940.
- North Carolina Military Land Warrants, Continental Line . Washington, D. C.
- Index and Digest to HATHAWAYS'S NORTH CAROLINA HISTORICAL AND
   GENEALOGICAL REGISTER , compiled by Worth S. Ray.
- NORTH CAROLINA LAND GRANTS IN TENNESSEE 1778-1791. Compiled
   by Betty Goff Cook Cartwright and Lillian Johnson Gardiner, 1958.
- Marriage and Death Notices in Raleigh Register and North Carolina.
   Gazette Newspaper 1826-1845 . Compiled by Carrie Broughton (12).

REFERENCES

In this book on pages with numbers ( ) are the sources and reference to source , a collection of Vallie Jo Whitfield.

- Gazette Newspaper 1826-1845 , compiled by Carrie Broughton (12) .
- Death Records (12).
- Wills of North Carolina 1690-1760 (12).
- Abstracts of North Carolina Wills by Fred Old 1768-1800 (13).
- "North Carolina Marriage Records by William M. Clemens (13).
- 1790 Census, North Carolina (13).
- North Carolina Deed Book L (15).
-    WHITFIELD, BRYAN, SMITH AND RELATED FAMILIES , 1949 ,
       by Emma M. Whitfield (pages 26 to 29 - 48- 53- 54 to 58 - 59 -
       69 - 72 - 73 - 74 - 85 - 86- 87).
- NORTH CAROLINA HISTORICAL AND GENEALOGICAL REGISTER ,
    Volume 1 - 1900.

COLONY AND STATE OF VIRGINIA REFERENCES

- Calendar of Virginia State Papers , 1776   (6).
- "The Lower Norfolk County, Virginia Antiquary" by Edward James (6).
- "Virginia Magazine of History and Biography"Vol. 5, 15, 29 (6).
- "Virginia Magazine of History and Biography " , Vol. 29, 1921 ;
       Vol. 15 , p. 193 ; Vol. 5 , 1897-8 , (6) .
- "Virginia Magazine of History and Genealogy " , Vol. 29 , pp 259-260.
- "Early Virginia Immigrants 1623 - 1666," (6).
- "Lists of Emigrants to America 1600- 1700 " , by John C. Hotten (6) .
- "The Edward Pleasants Valentine Papers "(7).
- "Wills of Williamsburg , Virginia." (8).
- "Darden Family History " by Newton J. Darden (8).
- "Spotsylvania County, Virginia 1721 - 1800 , Deed Book F, 1761-1766"(8).
- "Seventeenth Century , Isle of Wight County, Virginia " by John
       Bennett Boddie (8)(42)(43).
- "Deed Book 1704-1715 , Nansemond County, Virginia"(8) .
- "Will and Deed Book I , 1662-1682 , Isle of Wight County, Virginia"(9).
- "Wills and Administrations of Elizabeth City County , Virginia
       1610-1800 "(10).
- " Cumberland Parish , Lunenburg County , Virginia 1746-1816 "(10).
- "York County , Virginia 1648-1739 " (10).
- "Lancaster County, Virginia, Record Book No. 2, 1654 "(11).
- "Nansemond County, Virginia 1743- 1793 , Vestry Book of
       Upper Parish"(11).
- "Virginia Tax Payers 1782 - 1787 "(13).
- "William Byrd of Virginia " by Wright and Tinling (25).
- "Newport Vestry Book"(26) .

REFERENCES

- "Colonial Virginia , Vol. 1 . The Tidewater Period 1607-1710'(22).
- "Albemarle Parish Register 1739-1778 "(41) .
- "Virginia History and Whitfield Biographies , " by Vallie Whitfield (83).
- "Virginia Historical Index ," by E. G. Swem , Vol. 2 , L - S.
- "Virginia Cousins , " by G. Brown Goode (6) .
- Williamsburg County, Virginia - Records of Wills.
- "Isle of Wight County, Virginia . DEED BOOK 1704-1715 ."
- "Isle of Wight County, Virginia . WILL AND DEED BOOK I , 1662-1682."
- VIRGINIA COLONIAL ABSTRACTS. Several Colonial Counties Public Records and Vestry Book Records.   And "Virginia Colonial Abstracts 1648-1739."
- REVOLUTIONARY WAR PENSION APPLICATIONS . War Department and Pension Division . Washington ,   D. C.
- "Revolutionary Soldiers of Virginia - Ninth Annual Report 191-12. " Virginia State Library.
-"Revolutionary War Records of Virginia , " by Gaius M. Brumbaugh.
- "Virginia Military Bounty Land Warrants , " U.S. Land Office Records.
- MARRIAGE OF SOUTHAMPTON COUNTY, VIRGINIA 1750-1800.
- MARRIAGE OF SUSSEX COUNTY, VIRGINIA 1778 -1810.
- MARRIAGE AND MINISTERS RETURNS , Prince Edward County, Virginia 1754- 1810.
- Marriage Bonds and Ministers Returns of Sussex County,Virginia 1754- 1810.
- MARRIAGES OF SUSSEX COUNTY, VIRGINIA.

Letter and sketch by George R. Whitfield , 206 Greenacres Drive , Paris, Tennessee.

"Historic Williamson County Homes " of Tennessee , by Virginia Bowman.

"Dictionary of American Family Names " by Elsdon C. Smith.

"The American Men of Science " , S-Z 10th edition for biography of Robert Edward Whitfield.

"History of Pomona Valley California " published by Historic Record Company , Los Angeles , California , 1920.

REFERENCES TO LIFE OF JOHN WILKINS WHITFIELD ,
by Vallie Jo Whitfield . Pages 118 to 136.

-WHITFIELD FAMILIES OF TENNESSEE (RECORDS) by V. J. Whitfield.
-THE HISTORY OF HICKMAN COUNTY, TENNESSEE by W. Jerone
    Spence and David Spence. Pages 54-55-74-283- 333-334- 454 to 463.
-HICKMAN COUNTY, TENNESSEE MINUTE BOOK 1844-1855.
    Pages 97-103-112-129-138-139-157-167-172-174-493-497-523.
-HICKMAN COUNTY, TENNESSEE : Guardian and Administrator
    Settlements . Vol. D 1847-1852 . Pages 97-108-192-231.
-HICKMAN COUNTY, TENNESSEE MINUTE BOOK 1844-1855.
    Pages 24 -266-278-437-438-439-506.
- UNITED STATES CENSUS, HICKMAN COUNTY, TENNESSEE 1840& 1850.
-WHITFIELD, BRYAN, SMITH AND RELATED FAMILIES by Emma
    Whitfield.
-THE CONQUEST OF KANSAS BY MISSOURI AND HER ALLIES , by
    William Phillips of the New York Tribune for Kansas , 1856.
    Published Boton, Phillips , Sampson and Company.
-A HISTORY OF KANSAS by Anna E. Arnold. Published 1915.
- Publications of THE KANSAS HISTORICAL SOCIETY . Vol II. Pub. 1920.
- KANSAS - A Guide to the Sunflower State. Compiled by Federal
    Writers Project. The Viking Press , N. Y. 1939.
-GROWTH OF THE NATION FROM 1837-1860 , by Enoch W. Sikes
    and W. M. Keener.
- TRANSACTION OF THE KANSAS STATE HISTORICAL SOCIETY,
    (Library of Congress F 676. K33 Topeka, Kansas. Pub. House 1886)
    Vol 3, pt 2, pages 240 and 290.
- 1855 REPORT , United States Commissioner of Indian Affairs.
-A VISIT TO KANSAS IN 1857 , edited by William E. Connelley, which
    appears in the Mississippi Valley Historical Review. (Library of
    Congress F 351. M69 V. 13, page 543.)
-THE METHODIST MISSIONS AMONG THE INDIAN TRIBES IN KANSAS,
    by J.J. Lutz . Page 189.
-CONFEDERATE CAVALRY WEST OF THE RIVER , by Stephen B.
    Oates , University of Texas Press , Pub. 1961, pages 31-32-33-36.
-MISSOURI , by Edwin C. Mc Reynolds : A History of the Crossroads State.
-BIOGRAPHICAL DIRECTORY OF THE AMERICAN CONGRESS .
    A sketch on John Wilkins Whitfield . Published U. S. Govt. printing
    office 1950. Directory 1774-1949.
-THE CIVIL WAR FROM A SOUTHERN STANDPOINT , by William R.
    Garrett and Robert A. Halley . Pages 291, 300 , 385.
-PHOTOGRAPHIC HISTORY OF THE CIVIL WAR , editor, Francis T.
    Miller. N. Y. The Reviews of Reviews Co. Pub. 1912. Vol II ,
    P. 324 , and John W. Whitfield's picture in Volume 10, page 313.
-NEWSPAPERS : Missouri and Kansas Papers 1854 to 1860 .

Kansas Newspapers :
Liberty City - THE DEMOCRATIC and PLATFORM ; Platte City -
THE ARGUS ; and Atchison , Kansas - the SQUATTER SOVEREIGN.
- Texas Newspapers - GALVESTON DAILY NEWS , the LAVACA
    HERALD , and the PLANTER 1879 newspapers.
- 1860 U.S. Census of Kansas, town Doniphan.
- 1870 U.S. Census of Texas , Lavaca County.
- 1866 - 1870 Transactions in Austin , Texas.
- Congressional Speeches at the Library of Congress, Washington, D. C.

------------------ ANNALS OF KANSAS ------------------------
John Wilkins Whitfield 1818 - 1879 .   Kansas Collection , compiled by
Mrs.James W. Smith, 311 E. Comanche, Dodge City, Kansas , 1964.
KANSAS HISTORICAL COLLECTIONS
Vol. IX print 1905-1906 , John W. Whitfield , page 189.
Vol. X print 1907 - 1908 , John W. Whitfield , pages 128 - 324 .
Vol. XI print 1909 - 1910 , John W. Whitfield , page 348.
Vol. XII , John W. Whitfield , pages 353- 354 - 355 - 410 - 425- 427.
Vol. XIV print 1915-1918 , John W. Whitfield , pages 499 - 500- 501 -
    511 - 550.
Vol. XV print 1919-1922 , John W. Whitfield , pages 348 - 410 - 412.
Vol. XVI print 1923-1924 , John W. Whitfield , pages 583 - 659 - 720-
    731 - 732.
Vol. XI print 1942 , John W. Whitfield , page 139.
Vol XVII print 1949 , John W. Whitfield , pages 32 - 33 - 137 .
Vol XX print 1952 - 1953 , John W. Whitfield , page 472.
Vol XXI print 1954 - 1955 , John W. Whitfield , page 92.
Vol XXII print 1956 , John W. Whitfield , pages 148 - 151.
Vol XXII , John W. Whitfield , page 239.
Vol XXV , John W. Whitfield , page 50 .

Book Sources : " The Needless Conflict " by Allan Nevins. 4th series
    on times of trial In America Statecraft . American Heritage booklet.
-"Publications of the Kansas Historical Society ". Vol II , 1920. Chapter 4.
    " Border Ruffian Turbulence ."
- "Conquest of Kansas by Missouri and Her Allies " by William Phillips,
    chapters 2 and 3.
- " Whitfield , McKeel , Fox , Schiefer Families " by Vallie Jo Whitfield,
    1965 , published Whitfield Books , pages 254 to 262 , and 269 - 270.
.... Texas Collection ....
- " A History of Lavaca County " Texas by Paul C. Boethel, 1959.
- " The Handbook of Texas ". Volume II , 1952. Editor , Walter Prescott
    Webb , Austin, Texas : The Texas State Historical Association.
- " Nueces Headwater County " Texas (Edwards County) by
    Allan A. Stovall.

STATE OF TENNESSEE

United States

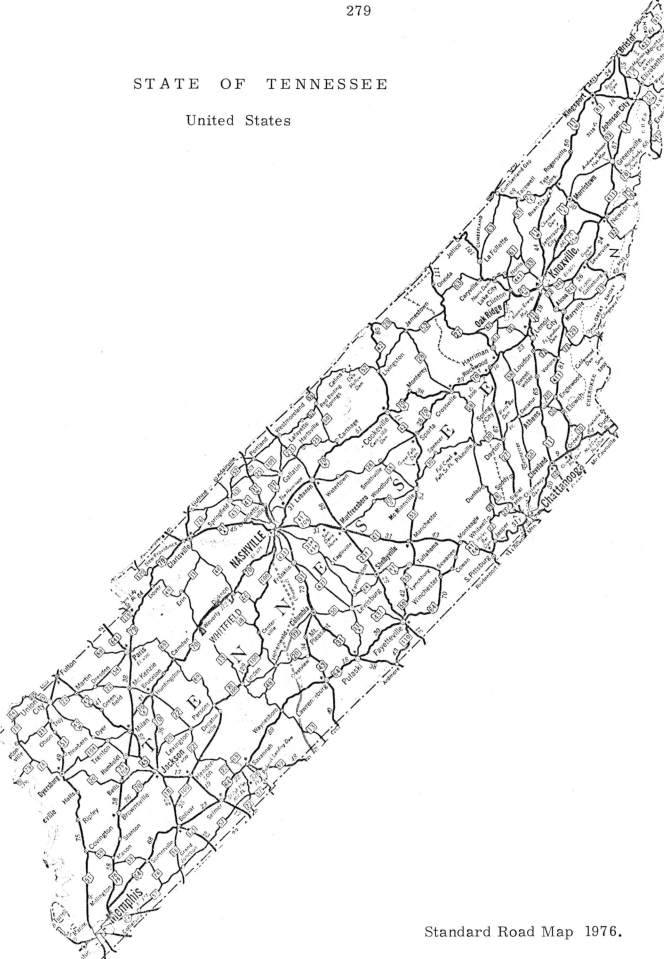

Standard Road Map 1976.

INDEX

A

E

F

G

N

S

Copeland 9-27-28
Copeland 43
Cynthia 79
Cynthia 148

- D -
Daisy 14 - 81
Daniel 69- 251- 252
Daniel 64- 188
Daniel 88- 89-94-141-177-233
David ... See James David
David Thomas 174
Dauthitt Glendall 91-97-226
Davie Kay(Whitfield) Carey 91
Davis (Clemenson) 69- 223-252
Delia 82
Delie Ann Sikes 76-83-225-247
    -248
Dinah (negro) 54
Donna Elaine 101 - 206
Doris Edna 174
Douglas 97
Duncan 33- 52-53-54-233-236
Dundenah (Kenon) 69-252
Dwane 97

- E -
Earlene (Dobson) 90-225
Edward 153
Edward Mark 97
Edward 203-237
Edwin Bates 13- 81
Eine 11
Eli 33- 56- 66-139-191
Elijah 223
Elisah 12-56
Elisah 29
Elisha 45
Elisha 46
Eliz 10-42
Eliz J. 81
Eliz (Whitfield) Smith 8
Eliza 12
Eliza 79
Eliza 217

Eliza (Nolan) 71-74-226-245
Eliza (Whitfield) Owen 33-59
Eliza(Richardson) 75-143
Elizabeth 10
Elizabeth 10-45
Elizabeth 12
Elizabeth 32
Elizabeth 33
Elizabeth 44
Elizabeth 45
Elizabeth 46
Elizabeth 48
Elizabeth 48
Elizabeth 22-25-27
Elizabeth 49
Elizabeth 50
Elizabeth 43- 232
Elizabeth 57
Elizabeth 82
Elizabeth 79-80-81-89
Elizabeth 68- 165- 237
Elizabeth 78-79-233
Elizabeth 217
Elizabeth 237
Elizabeth (Eason)33-56-191-234
Elizabeth (Goodman) 17-24-141-
    223-236-232
Elizabeth Betsy (Betty) 76-61-80-
    223-224-241-243-248-247
Elizabeth (Hatch) 51
Elizabeth (Herrod) 64-139
Elizabeth Jane 238
Elizabeth (Kinley)212
Elizabeth Morgan 232 - 253
Elizabeth (Newson) 144
Elizabeth (Ridley) 63
Elizabeth (Whitfield) Cary 48-212
Elizabeth (Whitfield) (Smith)
    Campbell 13-32-49-173
Elizabeth (Whitfield) Cooper 57-143
Elizabeth (Whitfield) Fort 12
Elizabeth (Wimberly) (Whitfield)
    Fort 56
Elizabeth (Whitfield)(Metcalf)
    Trigg 58

WHITFIELD

WHITFIELD

George Carl 238
George Gray 238
George Monroe 71- 75-196-247
    -248
George N. 33 - 56
George Neville 236
George Robert 239
George W. 69 - 139-226
George Washington 34- 37 -39
    -62- 66- 69 - 135-139- 158-
    159- 160-161-162-226-231-
    241-247-248-249 -251
Georgena E. 153
Georgia Cathron (Gregory) 238
Georgia Hughey 2388

Gertrude 152
Gertrude E. 153
Gilbert 7-20-212
Gladys Irene (Whitfield) Hatley
    91- 96- 226
Grace 90
Grace 153
Grace (negro) 54
Gracie (Prewitt) 141
Grover 253
Gus 82
Gwen 97

- H -
H.H. 153
Ham 78- 168
Hanah (negro) 54
Hannah 68- 164- 237
Hannah 10- 42
Hannah 42
Hannah E. (Wilcox) 143-204-236
Hardy 13-27-28-29-45
Hardy 46
Harley 90
Harold 153
Harold Barnard 211
Harriet 33 -52
Harrison   62- 63- 247-248-249

Harrison 68- 83- 138- 163- 217-
    231-240-247-248-252
Harrison 33-34-59-60-61-73-80-
    146-147-184-202-217-218-224-
    231-241-242-243-248-250-251
Harrison 8-9-27-212
Harry 140
Harry C. 152
Harry L. 174
Hattie C. 174
Hattie (Campbell) 14
Haynes 9 - 43
Helen Tera 237
Helena (Briscoe) 70-135-192-230
Henery Alvan 255
Henrietta 152
Henry 44- 135
Henry 144
Henry 79-168-169
Henry 81- 135-193
Henry 62-80-193-231-241-247-248-
    249-251-252
Henry 188
Henry 198
Henry 63-212
Henry 8- 42-44
Henry 216
Henry C. 202-203-207
Henry E. 44
Henry Edward 76-86-210-247-248
Henry Lewis 215
Henry W. 74
Henry W. 65- 184
Henry W. 80- 252
Henry W. 80- 135 - 193
Henry W. 71- 76-84-149-155-185-
    205-210-225-247-248
Herbert 203
Herbert 153
Herbert 11
Herbert Tera 143- 237
Hervey 236
Hervey 143-196-204-236
Hester 24- 43

WHITFIELD

Robert 237
Robert Edward 77 - 95- 96- 98- 99- 107-149-157-213-222-245- 246- 247- 248-266
Robert E. H. 81
Robert Flint 173
Robert Gray 239
Robert H. 152
Robert Henry 8 - 42-44
Robert P. 44
Robert Parr 188
Robert S. 14
Roberta (Brown) 254
Roger 212
Roger 7 - 21 - 42
Ronald Joe 153
Rose 14 - 81
Rozelle ... See Hester Rozelle
Roy 153
Roy 205- 236
Roy R. 153
Ruben 13 - 216
Rubry E. 152
Rushie 90
Ruth 212
Ruth 70-135-193
Ruth 21

- S -

S.J. 90
Sadie 70- 135- 193
Salle 76- 85- 247-248
Sallie I. (Boune) 139
Sallie (Wells) 140
Sallie (Bourne) 58- 191- 192-237
Sallie L. (Dillahunty) 71- 76- 144- 226-245-246-247-248
Sallie Warren 212
Sally 33 - 56- 191
Sally 33- 66- 156-233-234
Sally 48
Sally 198
Sally 68 - 164- 237

WHITFIELD

WHITFIELD

Sally (Howell) 223
Sally (Whitfield) Moss 212
Sally M. 217
Samuel 43
Samuel 44
Samuel 91
Samuel 7 - 26-43-232
Samuel 9- 27- 28- 43
Samuel 44
Samuel G. 44
Sandra Faye 94
Sandra Lynne (Whitfield) Jones 97 - 222
Sandra 101 - 103
Sarah 21-22
Sarah 218
Sarah 10 - 24
Sarah 11 - 24-72
Sarah 32
Sarah 33
Sarah 33 - 58
Sarah 44
Sarah 48
Sarah 45
Sarah 251
Sarah 68 -237
Sarah 69
Sarah 237
Sarah 252
Sarah Ann (Prigmore) 232 - 255
Sarah (Berry) 79
Sarah (Bond) 69 - 138- 226- 251-252
Sarah Bryan (Hatch) 50
Sarah C. (Lovelace) 203
Sarah (Collier) (Nixon) 236
Sarah (Collier) George 50 - 236
Sarah Cornelia 237
Sarah (Dibrell) 70- 81- 124- 130- 134- 136- 140-192-199- 226-231
Sarah (Diggs) 57
Sarah Elizabeth (Pallett) 255
Sarah (Green) 32 - 49- 59

INDEX TO COUNTIES, TENNESSEE

WHITFIELD

Errata (And Correction)

1. allegiance not alleg ance on page 7.

2. James D. Whitfield was born Feb. 21, 1953 not March 14, 1955 on page 95.

3. Page 116 , Log House 1840.

4. Missouri not Issouri on page 129.